In Other Words

Artists Talk about Life and Work

Anthony DeCurtis

In Other Words

Artists Talk about Life and Work

Anthony
DeCurtis

HAL•LEONARD®

Published by Hal Leonard Corporation
7777 West Bluemound Road
P.O. Box 13819
Milwaukee, WI 53213, USA

Trade Book Division Editorial Offices:
151 West 46th Street, 8th Floor
New York, NY 10036

Library of Congress Cataloging-in-Publication Data

DeCurtis, Anthony.
In other words : artists talk about life and work / by Anthony DeCurtis.— 1st ed.
p. cm.
Includes bibliographical references (p.) and index.
ISBN 0-634-06655-2
1. Rock musicians—Interviews. 2. Country musicians—Interviews. 3. Motion picture producers and directors—Interviews. I. Title.
ML394.D43 2005
781.64'092'2—dc22

2005002298

Printed in the United States of America
First Edition

10 9 8 7 6 5 4 3 2 1

Visit Hal Leonard online at:
www.halleonard.com

This one goes out to the ladies:

Gracie the St. Bernard, my daily sweet companion;

Sue Erikson Bloland, for her essential
insight and encouragement;

And, as always, in all things, my wife and soul mate, Alex.

Contents

Acknowledgments

A project of this sort, which collects work done over a period of nearly 25 years, necessarily entails a wide array of acknowledgments. The brevity of these citations reflects neither the quality of those contributions nor the depth of my gratefulness.

I must begin by thanking my late parents, Rose Marie and Renato DeCurtis; my brother, Dominic; and my sister, Carmela, for their encouragement when it mattered the most. Professionally, I am ever in debt to Dave McGee, who hired me at *Record* magazine (which folded in 1985); Jim Henke, who hired and edited me at *Rolling Stone*; and Jann Wenner, the founder, owner, and editor of both those magazines, and a man who continues to provide me with welcome opportunities. Those three men are responsible for a great deal of whatever is worthwhile about this book.

Other editors at *Rolling Stone* who worked with me on these interviews and to whom I owe sincere thanks are: Jason Fine, David Fricke, Holly George-Warren, Joe Levy, Barbara O'Dair, Peter Travers, Bob Wallace, and David Wild. At *Entertainment Weekly*, my dear friend John McAlley gave me the assignment that led to my interviewing Nile Rodgers. My lawyer, Josh Grier, helped arrange for me to write the Uncle Tupelo liner notes that led to the interview included here with Jeff Tweedy. Tony Margherita, who managed Uncle Tupelo and manages Wilco, and John Jackson at Columbia/Legacy played important roles as well.

Fletcher Roberts was the kind, focused editor of the pieces that originally appeared in *The New York Times*. Brad Tolinski edited the interview with Trey Anastasio that originally appeared in *Guitar World*. The interviews with Martin Scorsese and Don DeLillo, which both originally ran at shorter length in *Rolling Stone*, were later given a home at greater length in *South Atlantic Quarterly*, where my editor was Frank Lentricchia. Paul Raushenbush and Paul O'Donnell helped with the interviews with Bono and Marilyn Manson that originally ran on Beliefnet.com. Sting's manager, Kathy Schenker, arranged for my interview with him, and David Konjoyan helped prepare it for publication in *Grammy Magazine*.

Sandy Smallens hired me to work at GetMusic.com, and my friend Joe Rosenthal was an excellent colleague and the executive producer of my show on that site, "The A List with Anthony DeCurtis," for which I interviewed Iggy Pop. My buddy Richard Skanse assigned and edited my interview with Lucinda Williams for *Texas Music*. Mitchell Schneider recommended me when *L'Uomo Vogue* was looking for a writer to interview David Bowie.

My agent, Sarah Lazin, represented me on this project with her characteristic graciousness, tenacity, and skill. Ben Schafer first expressed interest in my putting together this collection for Hal Leonard, and John Cerullo followed up on that interest and helped transform our idea into a reality. Belinda Yong worked closely and carefully with me on taming an unwieldy manuscript. Robert Burke Warren, Dan Brillman, and Catherine Wise transcribed many of the original tapes for these interviews so that I could expand them for the book. My appreciation, of course, goes to all the artists who sat for hours of all this good talk.

Finally, Gracie, Sue, and Alex more than deserve – and deserve more than – a nod here, as well as their more prominent recognition on the dedication page.

My thanks and gratitude to all.

Introduction: The Art of Talk

"Great questions!"

That's the sort of compliment you tend to get when someone's read an interview you've done and liked it. It's well intentioned, of course, and it's churlish to overthink anyone's kind words. But I still find myself cringing whenever anyone says that to me. It somehow suggests that, as with many television interviews, anyone armed with a list of "great questions," even if they didn't write them, could have done the interview just as well. If you've never done one, you'd have no way of knowing that good questions are barely the first step to a successful interview.

I learned that myself nearly 30 years ago the first time I attempted to do an interview. I was in graduate school at Indiana University, and Patti Smith was coming to Bloomington to perform. Her first album, *Horses*, had just come out, and I'd been enraptured by it. I'd read just about everything that had been written about her, and I managed to convince an editor at the IU daily student newspaper, who had never heard of her, to assign me an interview. I'd never done one, but I'd read a million of them. It was just talking, right? And knowing enough to ask "great questions." How hard could it be?

I learned how hard when Smith showed up barely able to stand and incapable of keeping her eyes focused. My dutifully prepared questions went out the window as she drifted off on whatever cloud of thought floated through her head. Finally, her manager led her out of the room, and Lenny Kaye, her guitar player, stepped in and we had a friendly chat for 15 minutes or so. Unfortunately, I was so flustered by that time that I didn't really manage to get enough information to craft into a readable story. I was disappointed, but that was only the first lesson in my still ongoing discovery that even the most careful preparation might not equip you for what you discover when you first encounter your subject.

Being able to read the person in front of you is one of the intangible skills of the interview. True, it's the rare interviewee who shows up too incoherent to speak. The problems you more typically find are the stuff of everyday annoyance: surliness, shyness, anger, defensiveness, glibness, brusqueness, exhaustion, or someone who simply isn't in the mood to talk. (For the best dramatization in this book of the more irritating of those problems, I refer you to my Van Morrison interview.) While you soon learn that if someone genuinely doesn't want to speak to you – or to answer a particular question – there's no way you can make them, every interviewer develops an arsenal of techniques to encourage cooperation.

One of my favorite strategies came by way of U2's the Edge. I first met him in Dublin in 1987 when I was working on a U2 cover story for *Rolling Stone* to coincide with the release of *The Joshua Tree*. The evening I arrived, I went out for a getting-to-know-you dinner with the Edge and Adam Clayton. We weren't really working, just getting a sense of each other and what the next few days might bring. The Edge mentioned a journalist we both know, and told a funny story about him. "He'll ask you a question, and you'll answer it," he said. "Then he won't say anything. I'll think, 'Maybe I didn't give a good enough answer,' so I'll just start talking again. It's really unnerving."

That was a trick that had never occurred to me: say nothing. Before that I suffered from the A-student syndrome. I'd typically look for opportunities to demonstrate to subjects how much thought I'd given their work, and that usually involved a lot of talking. My yakking could sometimes trigger smart discussions, but they also occasionally led to stupefied, one-word replies, or befuddled responses like, "What was the question again?" In a piece I once wrote called "The Naked Transcript," I described burying Peter Gabriel in such an inarticulate avalanche of words that he could barely muster a response. I'd always subscribed to Fran Liebowitz's axiom that the opposite of speaking isn't listening, the opposite of speaking is waiting.

But being quiet forces the subject to deal with his own emotions. It's easy when interviewing famous people to assume that they have no insecurities, but I've found that what the Edge said is often true. If someone answers a question but doesn't really deliver the goods, sitting in silence when they finish is a deft way of sending the message that you'd like them to continue and actually say something this time. It works about half the time. It's also the kind of thing that doesn't get represented when you read an interview in black-and-white on the page.

My overall approach to doing interviews primarily derives from reading the long interviews that Jann Wenner did in the early days of *Rolling Stone* with the likes of Pete Townshend, John Lennon, and Phil Spector. Jann's questions were always direct and clear; they boiled issues down to an unavoidable essence. Sometimes they weren't even questions – "You were angry with Paul," he would say to Lennon, characterizing something the former Beatle had said and leaving him little choice but to deny, refine, or expand on the statement. He would also lead his subject, the way an attorney might in a cross-examination. His tone is sympathetic, but no nonsense. He's tenacious, much moreso than I am. Jann would rephrase the same question over and over again in his determination to get an answer that satisfied him. He would not be denied. I'll typically go back to something and try again, but if a line of questioning isn't working I'll head somewhere more promising.

But the primary message I got from Jann's interviews was, "Don't get too fancy." Often when you ask an elaborate question, you're providing the answer yourself and not leaving room for your subject to say whatever it is he wants to say. The point is to get your subject thinking and remembering, exploring himself, and you can best do that by asking questions that are suggestive and provocative, but not essays in themselves.

I've found that it's also good to start slow. In news interviews, you can get right to the point, but in the types of interviews I tend to do, I try to allow for some degree of build up. I normally start with as simple a question as I can think of. If someone is about to release an album, for example, I might ask something as basic as, "What were you setting out to do this time around?" Such open-ended questions enable me to get a sense of what sort of mood the subject is in and what the conversation is going to be like.

If the person honestly and openly responds, it can take a while to answer a question like that, which allows me to get my bearings, take some notes about what the person looks like and is wearing so that I don't have to remember to do it later, and judge the quality of what he has to say. If he answers honestly and energetically you can tell that he wants the interview to go well, and you can start thinking about ways to push the boundaries of what he might be willing to discuss. On the other hand, if a question like that elicits a testy response, you know you've got a hard slog ahead.

These types of comparisons are dodgy, needless to say, but interviews really are like seductions – or at least like dates. They go best when you take the time to build some trust and when you're true to who you are and respectful of and attentive to the person you're with. If you aren't funny, don't try to be a jokester. If you tend to be shy, don't overcompensate by being too assertive. And, most important of all, listen.

Which brings us back to the "great questions." I approach interviews with only a few prepared questions – another problem with the "great questions" compliment. Instead, I have a list of ideas I want to talk about. I view the most significant of those as landmarks that we eventually need to get to, however indirectly. But the vast majority of the interview takes place in the spaces between those markers. You can – and should – prepare as thoroughly as possible for an interview, but ultimately you're meeting a person, not a media creation and not the imagined product of your research.

That's sometimes hard to keep in mind when you're speaking to a subject who has been so much and so long in the public eye that you feel as if you know him already. But if you don't allow for the possibility that the people you're meeting are different from what you've been led to believe, you'll never really find out anything about them and the quality of your interview will suffer. You need to prepare as extensively as you can and then walk into the room and be willing to set all your preparation aside if more interesting possibilities present themselves.

The goal in one sense is to make your subject forget that he is being interviewed. That's less a matter of hiding your tape recorder – and I always tape – than of getting to a place where the conversation takes on a life of its own. That's obviously difficult to sustain over a long period of time – typically, you move in and out of self-consciousness, with particular topics taking on emotional momentum until the spell breaks and reality intrudes again.

With certain wary subjects it may be impossible to ever escape awareness of the interview situation. I've interviewed Mick Jagger a number of times and he's one of my favorite subjects. He's smart, charming, entertaining, and complex – a fascinating person to write about. But he's not a great interview. His sense of self-possession is so complete that the idea of revealing himself to a journalist seems absurd to him. "I'll just look like a cunt," is how he memorably described the risk of going on the record about a project he was working on that might not work out. He needs to be interpreted – that is to say, observed, profiled, written about, quoted in context – and the question-and-answer format necessitates that the subject be willing to open himself up

So what are the advantages of the Q&A format? Its most obvious virtue is that if you're interested in an artist, hearing him speak at length in his own voice is a riveting experience – and one that is becoming harder and harder to find. Stories of all kinds are getting shorter just about everywhere, and fewer magazines run long interviews. The interviews in *Rolling Stone* that I read while growing up made an enormous impact on me, and it's one of the most satisfying aspects of my professional life that I've gotten to do so many of them. As I was working on the Keith Richards interview included here, for example, I could scarcely get over my delight that it was exactly the sort of interview that I would have loved to read. Afterwards, I went out for a celebratory champagne dinner – though already drunk from knocking back cognac for three hours while Keith sipped his bourbon and ginger ale concoction – and then for the first and only time in my life I went home and immediately listened to the entire interview straight through just to make sure it was as strong as I thought it was.

Some rock writers regard doing interviews or even writing profiles as somehow less pure than criticism or reviews, as if associating with artists were somehow inherently sullying. Given the contents of this book – and the 25 years of experience it documents – it should surprise no one to learn that I strongly disagree with that view. Unless you talk with artists in depth, it's difficult to gain a three-dimensional understanding of the work they do. There is no substitute for spending time in a recording studio or traveling with a band if you want to comprehend what it's like to make a record or to be out on the road. Those experiences are not only valuable in themselves – they sharpen your critical acumen.

That personal understanding is especially important for the kinds of exploratory interviews I like to do. I've never been interested in doing "gotcha" interviews. Some charged issues come up in this book – the Rufus Wainwright interview comes immediately to mind – but in every case, I determined beforehand that the subject would be willing to talk about them. While I don't accept unreasonable preconditions for interviews, I also don't enjoy pressuring people to speak about things they'd rather not discuss. If it's going to be a fight, I'd rather pass. If a subject isn't willing to open up, it's not worth the effort as far as I'm concerned.

Similarly, if I felt I was so much smarter or otherwise superior to my subject – not to mention my audience – that I couldn't do a straight interview, I wouldn't bother doing the interview at all. I don't ask trick questions, and I hate "cute" interviews. I remember reading an interview in which a reporter asked Madonna what Sean Penn smelled like. Cute, but not my beat. A friend once remarked, while bemoaning the demise of the long Q&A, that "Every interview you read these days is 800 words and exclusively about sex." I like reading about sex, too, but I also like reading 5,000-word interviews with artists who don't mind speaking in depth about their work and motivations. That, finally, is what this book is about.

I first thought about assembling a book like this about 10 years ago when I started pulling together *Rocking My Life Away: Writing About Music and Other Matters* (Duke University Press, 1998), a collection of my essays, reviews, and profiles. I thought of that book and this one as companion pieces: the first a collection of prose, the second of interviews. It didn't quite work out that cleanly, of course. I couldn't resist cajoling Peter Buck of R.E.M. to do a lengthy Q&A with me about rock criticism in *Rocking My Life Away*, and that turned out to be one of that book's most popular pieces. And while this book does consist entirely of interviews, it also includes a good deal of discursive prose to provide background and some sense of perspective and personal history.

A couple of pieces in here also served as specific inspirations for doing the book in the first place. The short version of my interview with Bryan Ferry, which originally ran in *Rolling Stone*, failed to convey what had been a surprising and powerfully moving experience for me. In 800 words, you have to keep the exchanges so short that quips work far better than anything more substantive. The longer version here is much more satisfying. Similarly an assignment to interview Nile

Rodgers of Chic for *Entertainment Weekly* in order to get a quote about the Sugarhill Gang's "Rapper's Delight" – which is driven by a sample from Chic's "Good Times" – turned into a fascinating half-hour conversation about disco. *EW* got its quote, but I was left with a great story and nowhere to go with it – until now.

The Q&A format also provides readers with more direct access to the artist they're interested in reading about – another not terribly flattering reason that some critics resent it. When they're done well, you can hear a clear representation of the artist's voice and get a real feel for how his thought processes run. In order to provide that access to the reader, the interviewer has to create an environment of emotional openness and then get out of the way. That's the hardest lesson for interviewers to learn – assuming that they want to learn it. Whatever else it's about, writing is about ego, while successful interviewing often entails setting your ego aside. The subject is the story, and once you've gotten them to open up, you've done the most important part of your job.

The interview, then, is a curious (in all senses of the word) kind of writing, one in which all the words are not those of the author – a circumstance that I allude to in the title of this book. The authorial work consists first in eliciting quality responses, and then shaping them in a way that is at once true to the experience and gripping to read. Interviewers should guide the conversation, push it deeper and then let their subject emerge.

That's why I don't mind letting answers run long if they're compelling enough – another departure from the current fashion of keeping quotes short. I take my cues in this regard from the documentary filmmaker D.A. Pennebaker, who made the classic Bob Dylan movie, *Don't Look Back*, and the equally wonderful *Monterey Pop*. He was on a panel and someone asked about MTV-style editing in which no shot is held very long. Pennebaker explained that he followed no fixed rule about how long to hold a shot. He went strictly on the basis of common sense. He kept the camera focused on a specific shot until something more interesting came along. Similarly, I like to let someone speak as long as what they're saying holds my attention – whether that's for five or five hundred words.

That said, after years of having to cut interviews to fit acceptable magazine lengths, I decided with this book that, if I was in doubt about whether to cut a passage or not, I'd err on the side of not cutting. I've included more than three dozen interviews here, and I'm under little illusion that anyone, other than reviewers, will read every word of every one of them. And I assume that few people will start reading this book at page one and then read every interview in order. Most people, I'm sure, will read it the way I would: in descending order of interest, with a good deal of skipping around to see what catches their eye or imagination.

Keeping that in mind, I felt that people who were reading about their favorite artists would want more rather than less. Many of these interviews have been significantly expanded, and others, most notably the ones with Paul Simon, Johnny Cash, and Bruce Springsteen, have been transformed from profiles into Q&As. Some of them now lack the tight, rigorous structure that I like to achieve in magazine interviews. What they have instead is a more genuinely conversational feel. There's more air in them, they feel more relaxed, and they're easier to read. I've left in more of my own participation, and more of the digressions that inevitably come up and frequently get eliminated. My criterion as an editor was not my usual one: "Does this absolutely need to be here?" It was: "Would fans of this artist enjoy reading this?" So if one of these chats is running too long for you, feel free to jump ahead to a part that's more to your taste.

I say that because enjoyment was my primary goal for *In Other Words*. That's not because I believe that these interviews lack substance. They don't. And it's not because I don't regard some of them as definitive. I do. But reading someone's speaking voice, however demanding or challenging what he has to say might be, is much easier than reading written prose. When an interview works well, reading it is an extremely intimate experience that evokes the childlike feeling of being told a story. Personally, I can often enjoy an interview even if the subject doesn't particularly interest me, as long as he has something to say and says it well. It's like having a fun conversation at a party with someone you might never run into again. I'd like to think this book is filled with the possibility of such random pleasures.

Anthony DeCurtis
New York City
March 2005

Cash Family Values

Johnny Cash

"I didn't shoot anybody in Reno"

Between 1999 and 2002, I interviewed Johnny Cash four times – three times for *Rolling Stone* and once for *The New York Times*. I spoke to him first in person, and then three times by telephone. Cash was ill during those years, and none of those interviews lasted very long, perhaps about half an hour each. The first, conducted in person at Cash's home in Hendersonville, Tennessee, ended when Cash said with characteristic directness, "I'm really tired. I can't think. I can't talk because of the pain. I'm really sorry, but I've got to stop. It's really killing me."

That was chilling. Still, each time I spoke with him, Cash was articulate, funny, candid, alert, and reflective. Because he didn't give many interviews in his waning years – he died in September 2003 – I thought that editing these four conversations together might provide a vivid portrait of a man battling disease, eager to experience the pleasures that life still availed him, burning to continue to create great art, and intent on enshrining his legacy.

Cash's commitment to his work and his loved ones while he was ill was beyond inspiring. In October 1997, the singer grew dizzy and nearly fell after bending to retrieve a guitar pick during a performance in Flint, Michigan. He then announced to the audience that he had been diagnosed with a rare nervous system disorder, Shy-Drager Syndrome – a progressive, incurable, Parkinson-like illness. That diagnosis was later changed to autonomic neuropathy, a more generalized, less immediately frightening term for roughly the same set of debilitating neurological symptoms. After he took ill and until his death, Cash, with a handful of exceptions, did not perform live. He also underwent frequent hospitalizations for pneumonia and other life-threatening side effects of his condition and its rigorous treatment. Complications from diabetes were the eventual cause of his death at the age of 71.

During his illness, Cash worked at a pace that would have been impressive in a healthy man half his age. He recorded two new albums

– *American III: Solitary Man* (2000) and *American IV: The Man Comes Around* (2002) – and enough additional songs to fill out an outstanding five-disc box set, *Unearthed*, which came out shortly after his death. In addition, he oversaw the reissue of much of his earlier work, wrote liner notes, participated in a televised tribute show in his honor, and earned three Grammys, along with a Lifetime Achievement Award in 1999. Other than Elvis Presley, he is the only performer to be elected to both the Country Music Hall of Fame and the Rock and Roll Hall of Fame. Most extraordinarily, the jaw-dropping video that he made to accompany his devastating version of the Nine Inch Nails song "Hurt" received seven nominations at MTV's Video Music Awards in 2003.

Cash did not like discussing his illness and, in his stoic fashion, he seemed to believe that he could conquer it by sheer force of will. "It's all right," he assured the Michigan crowd after announcing that he was ill. "I refuse to give it some ground in my life." In spring 1999, he told a newspaper reporter, "I've made it a point to forget the name of the disease and not to give it any space in my life because I just can't do it. I can't think that negatively. I can't believe I'm going to be incapacitated. I won't believe that."

After the diagnosis of Shy-Drager Syndrome was withdrawn, Cash told me, "I don't have any kind of old nasty disease with an ugly name. It was diagnosed three years ago as Shy-Drager Syndrome, but it was a misdiagnosis. My doctors decided a year or so ago that I didn't have that or I'd be dead, and I wasn't dead at the time." He laughed and then insisted, "I'm fine. I don't have any disease. I'm in New York, enjoying myself. We're going to a Broadway show tonight, and I'm going to buy some new shoes after I finish talking to you. I'm enjoying myself. I'm not sick."

That attitude – call it denial, call it rock-hard determination – helped Cash make the most of the last years of his life. Through the first 40 years of his career, Cash was a road hound, touring constantly. When his illness rendered him unable to tour, he initially was crushed. But he made the best of that as well. He transformed the circumstances that his illness imposed on him into a decision, bringing it under his control.

"Since I quit the road three years ago," he told me, "I'm trying to take all that energy into the studio. The most pitiful thing that happened to me in my recording career is squeezing an album in between tours when you've got no reserve. So now that I've decided that I don't have to go on the road, I take that energy and creativity and put it into the songs and into recording. I'm much happier that way. I'm enjoying my life very, very much. I'm enjoying it a whole lot more than I did when I was on the road. I don't have any plans to go back and do concerts. I want to channel that energy into writing and recording."

Like so many of the titanic heroes of rock 'n' roll, Cash was a glorious mess of contradictions. The drugs and debauchery of Saturday night – and in Cash's case, pretty much every other night too – fought vigorously for his soul against the powerful Christian conviction of Sunday morning. That tension made him one of the more combustible ingredients in the critical mass that generated revolutionary music at Sun Studios in Memphis in the mid '50s. In early songs like "I Walk the Line" and "Big River," he articulated a fierce vision of what country music – and its bastard child, rock 'n' roll – could be. He hammered out a sound that is bare to the bone.

Cash became a superstar in his mid 20s and enjoyed an impressive run of hits between 1956 and 1958 on Sun, the label run by Sam Phillips, the man who originally signed Elvis Presley. Like Presley, Cash soon left Sun to sign with a major label, in his case, Columbia. There, his success continued, beginning with "All Over Again" in 1958 and "Don't Take Your Guns to Town" the following year.

Cash met June Carter around that time; she was performing with her mother and sisters as the Carter Family, the current version of an act that three decades earlier had helped build the foundation of modern country music. Both Cash and Carter were married, both were deeply attracted to each other, and June, at least, was terrified of Cash's hell-bent, self-destructive streak and the ardency of her own emotions. She rendered those feelings powerfully in "Ring of Fire," a song she wrote with country star Merle Kilgore. It became one of Cash's signature songs. John and June eventually married, and she played a critical role in reinvigorating his Christian faith and keeping him away from drugs.

In his own songwriting, Cash was most noteworthy for his ability – in classics like "I Walk the Line," "I Still Miss Someone," and "Folsom Prison Blues" – to distill complex existential dilemmas into the common imagery of everyday speech. It was a talent perfectly suited to his sturdy baritone voice, a no-nonsense instrument that made every lyric he sang sound as if it had been honed to its absolute, incorruptible essence.

While creating his music, Cash also crafted a larger-than-life persona. His 1971 song "Man in Black" codified an image that the singer had assumed naturally for more than 15 years at that point. Part rural preacher, part outlaw Robin Hood, part patriot, part populist, he was a blue-collar prophet who, dressed in stark contrast to the glinting rhinestones and shimmering psychedelia of the times, spoke truth to power.

The darker, wilder side of Cash has drawn generations of fans to him. He is, after all, the man who, in "Folsom Prison Blues," sang, "I shot a man in Reno / Just to watch him die" decades before gangsta rap was born. He demolished hotel rooms and smashed out the lights on the stage of the Grand Ole Opry while Keith Moon was still in short pants. Throughout his life, however, Cash pandered to no specific audience or constituency. In the '60s and early '70s, he protested the Vietnam War and performed for American troops abroad. He defended Native American rights long before it became fashionable. He has both played in prisons and supported organizations that assist the families of slain police officers.

In the '70s, however, Cash's career took a downturn. The hits abruptly stopped coming, and the weekly television show he had been hosting for ABC was cancelled. For two long decades, he continued to record to no particular effect and toured constantly with June and other members of the Carter Family. In 1985, he formed the Highwaymen with Willie Nelson, Waylon Jennings, and Kris Kristofferson, and the quartet released two studio albums and occasionally toured. By the early '90s, Cash had become one of those veteran artists who is revered, but not taken seriously.

Then producer Rick Rubin engineered one of the most unlikely comebacks in the history of popular music. Rubin had made seminal hip-hop records in the '80s with the likes of the L.L. Cool J, the Beastie Boys, and Public Enemy, and he had also done eardrum-shattering work with the thrash-metal band Slayer. Now he wanted to sign Cash to his American Recordings label.

Cash had no idea who Rubin was, but Rubin believed that he understood exactly who Johnny Cash was. "He's a timeless presence," Rubin explained to me. "From the beginning of rock 'n' roll, there's always been this dark figure who never really fit. He's still the quintessential outsider. In the hip-hop world, you see all these bad-boy artists who are juggling being on MTV and running from the law. John was the originator of that."

The two men collaborated closely until Cash's death, and the work they did together – four albums and the *Unearthed* box set – restored Cash's critical stature and brought him a new young audience. "He loves music – it is his life," said Rubin, as the two men were preparing *Solitary Man*. "On our last session, when I was leaving, he said to me, 'You know, I think this is going to be my best album ever.' Now, he's made, what, maybe 200 albums? It's exciting to be around someone who's done that much work and still wants to make his best album."

For me, being around Cash was a daunting experience. He was not merely a legend, but one of the very founders of rock 'n' roll. He was tall and, though his illness had thickened him around the middle and grayed that sleek mane of black hair, he was a formidable physical presence. As he sat in a large, comfortable chair, he would occasionally put his hands over his eyes and rub them, as if he were in pain. Those eyes looked as if they had seen everything, had absorbed all the lessons his experience had to offer, and now were hungry for more. His innate dignity informed every move he made and every word he spoke. It was heartbreaking to watch him, a giant, struggle with the burden of his sickness.

We first spoke as a party was taking place outside his house to celebrate the release of his wife June's album, *Press On*. The scene was like something out of *The Godfather*. As revelers socialized outside on a brilliantly sunny afternoon, Cash, dressed entirely in black, sat quietly indoors, and visitors were ushered in to pay their respects. The oval room we sat in overlooked Old Hickory Lake, and many doors lined the wall opposite a long row of windows. After pausing to greet some family members, Cash said, "This room right here that you're in, this is the room I moved into when I decided to quit drugs in 1968."

And it's still standing? It looks pretty good, considering.

They didn't have treatment centers like they do now. The doctor said, "If you will get off the drugs, I will be at your house every day at 5 o'clock for 30 days, and we'll get you some encouragement and motivation." And he was here every day for 30 days at 5 p.m. First few days,

I had pills hid all over this room – I was still rolling stones. I was serious – but not quite. [*Laughs*]

About the third or fourth day when he came, we sat down and he looked me in the eye and asked, "How are you doing?" I said, "*Great!*" He said, "Bullshit. You're not doing great. When are you going to get rid of them?" So I got them out of the closet, wherever I had them hid, and we flushed them. Then I started the program that he laid out for me. And I came out of here feeling like a million dollars. But I stayed right here for 30 days. The house wasn't finished. This was the only room that was finished.

What has that struggle with drugs been like for you over the years?

Everything I've done and lived through has brought me to this part in my life right now, and I like to say I have no regrets. I really don't. I could've probably been writing a lot of good songs. As it was, I wrote some taking the drugs, but if I hadn't spaced myself out and put the cloud over my mind, I could've written a lot more and a lot better. But I don't regret that because it's something that never was there. I can't grieve over a loss when I don't know if there was one.

Amphetamine was my drug of choice. I used them to escape, and they worked pretty well when I was younger, in the early to mid '60s. They worked very well.

You used them to escape the pressures of your life?

To escape the pressure, yeah. But they devastated me physically, emotionally, and spiritually. That third one, spiritually, is the one that hurts so much – separation from God. To put myself into such a low state that I can't communicate with God, there's no lonelier place to be. When I was separated from God, I wasn't even trying to call on him. There was no line of communication. But that came back. He came back. And I came back.

It's been a real struggle since then. I have chronic pain from nerve damage I've had in my face for nearly 10 years, and it will not go away. I take pain medication for it because I don't think I could handle it otherwise. I've been to dozens of doctors, and I've had about three dozen operations on my face. I refuse to have any more; hopefully, I can get by without them. The main reason for my using mood-altering drugs in the last many years is because of the pain. I can honestly say that I didn't use it as an excuse, because the pain is there. It's there right now. So nobody can fault me for not trying, because I really tried. Four times I went into treatment centers and came out handling it halfway, but not really, because the pain didn't change. It would be one pain clinic after another to try to find non–mood-altering drugs that would work. And there aren't any. There just aren't any.

You've often talked about June's role in helping you with your drug problems. Can you describe the kind of sustenance that you get from her?

There's unconditional love there. You hear that phrase a lot, but it's real with me and her. She loves me in spite of myself, in spite of everything, and I know that. She's always been an anchor for me, a tree to wrap my arms around in a storm.

She's always been there with her love. Her love and caring have certainly made me forget the pain for a long time, many times. When it gets dark and everybody's gone home and the lights are turned off, it's just me and her. And she's the same alone in the dark as she was around a crowd with me. We love each other very much, and we show it quite a bit. She has saved my life – more than once, including back in '83, when I came off the drugs and went to the Betty Ford Center. The Betty Ford Center helped, but what really helped was June Carter when I got home.

When we fell in love, she took it upon herself to be responsible for me staying alive, because she wanted me to live. I didn't think I was killing myself, but I was close to it. She saw that I was. She took it upon herself to try to make me stop the drugs. She would dispose of them and then we'd have a big fight. I'd get some more and she'd do the same thing again. I'd make her promise not to do it anymore, but she would.

She fought me with everything she had. She'd do anything. She would lie to me about it. She'd hide my money so I couldn't buy any. She really fought hard, and I'm sure there were a few times that a simple thing like hiding my money might've saved my life, because I couldn't buy any. Or flushing them down the commode might've saved my life, because they weren't handy. But I never seriously tried to take my life. I never thought about suicide – even though you're on the suicide track when you're doing what I was doing. Amphetamines and alcohol will make you crazy, boy.

June has spoken about the feelings she had about you when she wrote "Ring of Fire." What's your memory of her bringing that song to you?

She was writing with Merle Kilgore, and she had some lyrics. She had a line that called her "the fire ring woman," and then she changed that. I said, "You got it right when you called yourself a 'fire ring woman,' because that's exactly where I am." We hadn't pledged our love, so to speak. We hadn't said, "I love you." It was a long time after that before we actually ever said it. We were both afraid to say it, because we knew what was going to happen – that we eventually both were going to be divorced and we were going to go through hell, which we did. But the "ring of fire" was not the hell; that was a sweet fire. The ring of fire that I found myself in with June Carter was the fire of redemption. It cleansed. It made me believe everything was all right because it felt so good.

On a televised tribute concert for you, Bruce Springsteen talked about how you showed that breaking down the barriers between musical styles was not only something that could be done, but that was important to do. You've never shown much respect for musical categories. Where does that impulse to cross the line come from?

From the time I was a kid, I didn't know that you're not supposed to like some kinds of music. I remember loving everything that came over the radio, even the pop songs of the '40s: "When I go to sleep / I never count sheep / I count all the charms about Linda" – songs like that. All the big band stuff I liked. My favorite, of course, was what they called hillbilly then, but it was folk singing. Songs by Jimmie Rodgers, the Carter Family, Vernon Dalhart's "The Prisoner's Song," which was the first million-seller in country music.

They played them all on the same program; the music was all mixed up. There might be an Elvis Presley record, then the next one might be Bing Crosby. Then there might be a Louvin Brothers hillbilly song. They were all played on the same program. And that's the way I always thought about music. What is this separation business? Why separate them? But I started selling a few records and they had to have a category to put me in, I guess, so they called me country.

You came up at a time when country, rock 'n' roll, and rockabilly were united by an outburst of energy, creativity, and wildness. As you were doing it, did you have a sense of the impact the music of that moment was going to make?

No, I didn't. The songs that I put the most into were songs that I never even thought about selling any records on. The songs I especially liked – "The Legend of John Henry's Hammer," "Mr. Garfield," "Hardin Wouldn't Run," or "You Wild Colorado" – weren't in any way meant to be commercial. I told June a couple of times, "I like this one so much, I'm not going to let anybody hear it. This song is just for me and you." I said that about a lot of songs I wrote.

Did you feel that there was a difference between who "Johnny Cash" had become and who you really were? Did you feel a remove from the public figure you had become?

Maybe I was trying to. I didn't like that "public figure" business. I didn't like that "American Statesman" stuff. I didn't like that "Great Spiritual Leader" stuff. I was a very private person. There would be something I'd have to do that I didn't have my heart in doing, and I'd say, "All I ever wanted to do was play my guitar and sing a simple song." That's all I ever wanted to do. And that's *still* all I ever want to do.

As those songs you mentioned indicate, America and its history has been one of your consistent themes. What was your response to the September 11 terrorist attacks?

September 11 broke my heart. I watched it on television. I guess I wanted to kill somebody myself.

A lot of us did.

It was a real heartbreaker for me, because I do love this country, and I saw that somebody was taking a really good shot at it, trying to disrupt not only our finances but our morale. We were hit a striking blow that really hurt. It did hurt me. But I recovered like the country's recovering. I believe ultimately that this country will prevail and that these people will not go unpunished. I certainly hope they won't.

Every time somebody mentions it to me, I'm reminded that my daughter Rosanne lives 20 blocks from the World Trade Center. She was walking her little girl to school that morning when the second plane hit the building. It was right there in their faces, and they ran home and locked the doors and stayed in for days. I think of my little granddaughter and how it affected her, that she cried when people would pull the curtains open. She wanted to stay inside and didn't want to hear anymore about it. She would turn off the television if it came on. But I think the country is recovering.

In the wake of the shootings at Columbine high school in Colorado, some people blamed the music kids listen to and the movies they watch, at least in part, for the violence in our own country. You're the guy who sang, "I shot a man in Reno just to watch him die." Do you feel songs like that affect people negatively or make them do the things you're singing about?

Nope. I don't think the music and the movies do it. I think it's in the person. I'm an entertainer. "I shot a man in Reno just to watch him die" is a fantasy. I didn't shoot anybody in Reno. And I didn't kill Delia. It's fun to sing about it, and my music – country music – goes way back, and murder ballads go way back in country. Even the Carter Family, the first family of country music, they got some really bloody records. You know the "Banks of the Ohio" – "Stuck a knife in her breast and watched her / As she went down under the water / And the bubbles came up out of her mouth and the water turned red," and all that. Or Jimmie Rodgers: "I'm gonna buy me a shotgun just as long as I am tall / I'm gonna shoot poor Thelma just to see her jump and fall." That's right up there with "shot a man in Reno."

These songs are for singing. We always knew that, the singers did. I'm not suggesting to anybody that they even own a gun – although I do. I'm not suggesting that they even consider learning how to shoot one. I used to collect antique Colt pistols. But they weren't for shooting, they were for collecting. They were like ancient coins; I collect ancient coins too. But the coins aren't for spending, and the guns aren't for shooting.

It's a complicated thing. There's so many people saying the music and the movies are causing violence. I don't believe that. It's in the people. There's a spiritual hunger in people for goodness, for righteousness, or there's an emptiness. There's something missing that they're trying to fill. I don't know why they go about it the way they do. But I don't think music and movies have a lot to do with it.

Despite being a "private person," as you described yourself, you ended up hosting your own network television program for a couple of years, 1969–1971. You brought Bob Dylan and Joni Mitchell to a public that wasn't used to seeing folks like that on television. What was hosting that show like?

ABC came to me with a proposal to do a weekly series. I said, "I don't want to do that. It's too confining. It's awful hard. You've got to give your life to that camera." But they kept after me. They kept begging. They would come down from New York, and I would have meetings with them. Finally, I said, "June and I have been talking about it, and we'll give it a try if we can have the guests that we want on the show." They said, "Anybody. Anything you want." At that particular time, Pete Seeger was in the news again, and I said, "First of all, I want Pete Seeger on." They all looked at each other and kind of nodded their heads.

Then I said, "But the musical guest I want on the first show is Bob Dylan." They looked at each other again and said, "Bob Dylan?" I said, "Yeah. If I can't have him, I don't want to do a show." So they said, "OK, we'll try to get him." I said, "No, I'll ask him myself." I was trying to keep him from going through that hassle with the agents and the deals and all that. They did get involved, of course, but I asked him myself first.

How did he respond?

He said he didn't do TV, but he'd do it for me. He asked me if I could help protect him from people that come backstage – the press and all that. I said, "I'll do my best." So they had all kinds of security, every exit blocked, and nobody could see Bob – that was the word that went out. Nobody – that means you – you don't see Bob Dylan, you don't talk to him, you leave him alone.

But a reporter from the *Nashville Banner*, Red O'Donnell, called me at home and said, "You have to get me in to see Bob Dylan." I said, "No. I promised him I wouldn't." He said, "We go way back, Johnny."

I said, "I can't do it. I promised him I wouldn't do it." He said, "Will you ask him?" I said, "No. He's already said he won't talk to press." And he said, "Just ask him for me." I said, "I'll mention to him that you called. OK?" So at rehearsal, I asked Bob, "Red O'Donnell is the number one man with a music column in town in the newspaper. You want to talk to him?" He said, "No."

I called Red back and said, "Bob don't want to talk to you." So he said, "Ask him if I can give him 10 written questions that he can give me an answer on." I said, "No, this is too much. I don't want to do that." So he said, "Ask him if I can give him three written questions." So I went back to Bob: "He wants to know if he can write down three questions, and you can give him an answer on them." Bob said, "Oh, no, I don't think so." I said, "OK."

I told Red, "No, he don't want to." And he said, "Ask him if I can write down one question." I said, "What's the question?" He said, "I don't know, but just ask him, if you will." I said, "You're wearing me out, Red." So I went to Bob and said, "Will you answer one question that this reporter wants to ask you?" He said, "What's the question?" I said, "I don't know." He said, "Ask him what the question is."

So Red had his foot in the door. We were at rehearsal, and suddenly into Bob's room – I was standing there with him and the producer – walks Red O'Donnell, who had on sunglasses. I said, "Bob, this is Red O'Donnell." They shook hands, and Bob looked at me like, "How did he get in here?" I didn't have a clue, and I knew Bob was upset. I would have been.

I don't know what the question was, and this will be an eternal mystery. But Bob would not answer him. Red kept following him around this little bitty room. Bob would move to one corner, and Red would move in on him. He'd come out, walk to the other corner. This went on and on. Red kept asking the same question over and over, and Bob would not open his mouth. He wouldn't say a word. Finally, Red shook hands with me and said, "I'll see ya later, Johnny," and walked out. I started laughing, I couldn't help it. But Bob wasn't laughing. He wasn't happy. I said, "I'm sorry about that. I had nothing to do with him getting in here. I don't know how he did it." And Bob said, "I would've talked to him, except for one thing." I said, "What's that?" He said, "He wouldn't take off his sunglasses." [*Laughs*] I said, "I don't blame you."

You were a big supporter of Dylan's early on. What was it that you heard in his songs that made you respond to him?

I heard him for the first time on the radio somewhere, I believe in Las Vegas. I thought he was an old country singer, and then somebody told me who he was. So I bought his records. I bought *Freewheelin'* and the *Bob Dylan* album. Then I wrote him a letter, and he wrote back. We wrote each other back and forth. I just heard a fresh approach to some old themes but really done well, with an insight that had never been put on record as far as I knew. I just loved his work. I loved him. Always have. And I still do. I still buy his records. I go to the record shop with every release he has. His latest one [*Love and Theft*], by the way, is the best one yet. It's terrific.

Bob is timeless. Invariably before every day ends, there will be a Bob Dylan song that'll float through me. Walking along in the yard the other day, I started singing "Maggie's Farm" of all things. It just came out of the sky through my head, and I started singing it.

I appreciate Bob in that he has given me music. All these people that have contributed music for me to sing and feast on over the years – like Kris Kristofferson, for instance – I love and appreciate very much. Bob Dylan is one of those I truly love and appreciate. He's still the best thing out there.

In your life and career, you've had something of an outlaw image – the "Man in Black" – and at the same time a deep spiritual concern. Your younger audience in particular seems drawn almost exclusively to the outlaw side of things. Are you OK with that?

I'm OK with it. This younger generation, I find they're very spiritual people. I do spirituals in my albums. I don't know of an album I've released that I haven't had one or two. Matter of fact, one had a song called "Spiritual," which I thought was a fabulous song. The young people loved it.

I think they believe me. And I believe what I say, but that don't necessarily make me right. [*Laughs*] I think my daughter Rosanne said that: "My dad believes what he says, but that don't make him right." But that's OK, too. I respect anybody's right to believe or not believe.

It's as if one side of your personality lends credibility to the other. You're not putting yourself forward as some perfect specimen of righteousness.

There's nothing hypocritical about it. I confess right up front that I'm the biggest sinner of them all. But my faith in God has always been a solid rock that I've stood on, no matter where I was or what I was doing. I was a bad boy at times, but God was always there for me, and I knew that. I guess maybe I took advantage of that.

To me, it's not hard to justify. Roy Orbison wrote a song called "My Best Friend," and there's a line in there that says, "A diamond is a diamond / And a stone is a stone / But man is part good and part bad." I've always believed that the good will ultimately prevail, but there's that bad side of us that we have to keep warring against. I do at least. A lot of people do.

There is a spiritual side that goes real deep, and that's really personal. There's no reason to talk about it with people who are not into that, who don't want to talk about it. That's just fine with me. I'll talk about ancient Roman history if you want to.

Sam Phillips' refusal to allow you to record an album of gospel songs is one of the reasons you left Sun Records.

I could not convince Sam Phillips how important that was to me. His answer each time I mentioned doing an album of spirituals or gospel songs or hymns was, "I don't know how to sell hymns. I can't sell enough with this little record company to make it worth recording." I understand that. It was a very small company. Even when "I Walk the Line" was released, he only had distribution in 14 states. It was asking a lot of Sam Phillips to record and release a hymns album.

But I wanted to do it. It was one of the reasons I did go to Columbia, because I didn't want to be restrained. I didn't want to be held back from doing anything I felt was important for me to do. I didn't want to be held back as a writer. If I wrote these kinds of songs, I wanted to put them on record, and I didn't want anything to stop me.

Are you still in touch with many of the folks that came up with you in the '50s?

Well, most of them are dead. Carl Perkins and his brothers are all dead. Bill Black, Elvis, Roy Orbison, who was not only my best friend but my next-door neighbor for 20 years.

The ones that are still left, yeah, I talk to them. Marshall Grant, who played bass for me for so long, he and I are friends. We talk a lot. Jack Clement. I probably talk to Jack more than any of them. We're still really good friends, really close. We don't do a lot of "good old days" sessions. But when something comes up, we'll argue about who's right about this or that. I don't see many of them. I don't see many people at all since I got sick.

One of your old friends, Waylon Jennings, died recently. You roomed with him in Nashville early on, and later you were together in the Highwaymen. I was reading his autobiography, and he called you his soul mate. He said when he looked at you, he felt as if he were looking at himself.

We were that way, Waylon and I. Waylon and I are soul mates. We're buddies and everything else. Speaking of sharing music, he and I shared as much music as I ever shared with anybody onstage, as part of the Highwaymen. It was a great joy that we had, that we shared all this music together with Kris. I was talking to Kristofferson about him, and after we cried awhile, we got to talking about some funny things that happened, things that we kidded each other about. Waylon was as close as a brother could be. Just couldn't be any closer.

Do you have any good Waylon stories?

I was booked for a week at a theater in Toronto about 10 years ago. I found out the morning I was to leave that my guitar player was ill and wouldn't be able to go. I called Waylon, panicking. I said, "You've got to help me find a guitar player that can play my stuff and knows my records, someone I can give the titles and he'll know what key they're in, everything." Waylon said, "I'll find you somebody."

He called me back about two hours later and said, "I found you somebody." I said, "Who's that?" He said "Me." I said, "No, I'm not going to ask you to do it, Waylon." He said, "You didn't ask me. I volunteered. I'm going to play guitar for you." My old Luther Perkins style of guitar – nobody could play it any better than Waylon. He was really good at it.

I said, "You're a superstar, man. You can't stand out there and be my guitar player." He said, "You just watch me." So he was on the plane with me the next day. I said, "Do me this: let me put you in the dark the first part of the show, and then let the people find you. And when I see that they've found you, then let me introduce you." He said, "All right." So that's the way we played it.

"Who's that guy standing in the shadows? Who's that masked man?"

And it was Waylon! He did all five days, and not only did he play guitar for me, he wouldn't take any money for it. He said, "I won't play for a guitar player's fee!" [*Laughs*] I said, "All right, I owe you one." But how could I ever pay that back? That was really something.

What was distinctive about his music? What will he be remembered for?

He'll probably be remembered for the Outlaws albums, but he'll also be remembered as one of the Highwaymen. He had a certain growl in his singing that says, "I love you, but not all that much. [*Laughs*] I love you, but don't tell anybody." That kind of persona that he had – he'll be remembered for that.

As you look ahead, what drives you at this point? You've built this tremendous body of work. You've struggled with illness in recent years. What carries you from day to day?

There's always another song to sing. They're always there. I've got songbooks laying all over my desk and bookcases, and I'm always finding a new one. It may be an old one, but it's a new one. I can't help it. I find these old songs and I've got to record them. I love them.

You find some new songs, too. You've done a version of U2's "One." What drew you to that track?

I heard the song when it first came out by U2 and never thought about recording it until Rick Rubin suggested it would be a good one for me. At that time, I was in Tennessee and he was in California. I had been doing some recording in what we call the Cash Cabin Studio, and he had been back there working with me in the studio. The Cash Cabin Studio is a log house in the woods right straight across the road from my house. I built it in '78, and it's just one room. It's got a kitchen, a bathroom off the back, and state-of-the-art equipment. We're surrounded by goats and deer and peacocks and crows. We have to stop tape sometimes because the goats get on the porch and tromp around.

So Rick sent a guitar track for me to listen to, an acoustic, scaled-down version of "One." I listened to it and thought that might be the right approach to the song. I love what the song says, and Rick made it very comfortable for me to record it. It came out really good.

Talk a bit about your relationship with Rick. There's a sense that you really found your voice again working with him.

From the very beginning, I couldn't see what he saw in me.

Because of his background?

Yeah, right. I asked him two or three times before I signed with him, "What would you do with me if you had me? What would we do?" He assured me that we would go in the studio and do what I felt like doing. I said, "I have tried that a hundred times with producers, and nobody ever bought it. I always wanted to do an album with just me and my guitar." He said, "That's what I want to hear: You and your guitar, and the songs you want to sing."

So he convinced me, and from the first day it was easy and laid-back, and relaxed and trustworthy. We trusted each other to be honest. I said, "I'm going to sing you a song, and if you don't like it you tell me. If you think it's a bad song, you say, 'That's a bad song.' But if I sing a song that you like, you tell me that, too. And if you've got a song that you like, but I don't, you have to listen to me. I can't sing it if I don't like it." As it turned out, he came up with some really fine songs for me, and he never pushed anything on me. Rick and I get along just great.

You've also recorded Tom Petty's "I Won't Back Down."

That song says a lot of things that I wanted to say. It probably means different things to me than it did to Tom, which is great. That's the way it ought to be. I like the line in there that says, "I know what's right / I have just one life / So I stand my ground / And I won't back down." To me, that means I'll stand up to adversity and disease, to illness. I stand up on my faith in God. That is my power, and I won't back down from that. Then there's the line, "Hey, baby, there ain't no easy way out." [*Laughs*] I get to trying to analyze a song, and then there'll be a line like that that'll screw up everything that I'm trying to say.

How has songwriting changed for you over the years?

It hasn't changed for me. It seems that the words and the melody come at the same time with me. I always have it in my head before I can ever find a pencil and a piece of paper. It's always running through my mind.

I don't know, I think it's God. They come from Him through me. There's a bottleneck here though, and it's called laziness. [*Laughs*] I'm so lazy when it comes to writing. But, boy, when I get the end result, when I get a song I'm proud of, I'm so glad I did it.

Parts of this interview appeared in Rolling Stone *(October 26, 2000) and* The New York Times *(February 24, 2002).*

June Carter Cash

"All those people, I remember them"

I did this interview with June Carter Cash in April 1999, just as her album *Press On* was coming out and shortly after the taping of "An All-Star Tribute to Johnny Cash," which "later aired on TNT (and for which I wrote the script). *Press On* is an album of exquisite beauty, a rich evocation both of June's storied history as a daughter of one of the founding members of the Carter Family, Mother Maybelle Carter, and her stature as the wife and creative partner of Johnny Cash.

Press On was also June's effort, at the age of 69, to remind people of her own independent life as a singer, actress, and songwriter. The album is surprisingly personal, filled with reminiscence and elegiac depth. Like the mountain culture that produced the Carter Family, it is at once stirring, hopeful, and unflinching in its frank acceptance of mortality. It includes a gorgeous version of "Ring of Fire," which June co-wrote with Merle Kilgore, and liner notes that discuss the song's origins in her feelings about Johnny Cash when they began working together in the early '60s and fell in love while still being married to other people. They would each divorce, and they married in 1968.

The album's signature song, "I Used to Be Somebody," recounts June's brief relationship with James Dean ("I held the rose that he gave me for an hour") and her friendships with Elvis Presley, with whom she toured as an opening act, and Elia Kazan, who brought her to New York to study acting. "Gatsby's Restaurant" describes her adventures as a young woman in New York in surreal terms, and in "Tiffany Anastasia Lowe," she humorously advises her granddaughter, an aspiring actress in Hollywood, not to fall into the clutches of Quentin Tarantino, who "makes his women wild and mean."

"I'm so glad to see it," Johnny Cash told me when *Press On* came out. "I knew she had all this in her. Although she does a few other people's songs, hers are the ones that stand out. She's the most unusual lyricist I've ever known. She will throw in a line that will twist your head off. She just knocks me out – and I've worked with her for more than 35 years!"

The long interview in this book with Johnny Cash rehearses a good deal of the history of his marriage to June, so I won't repeat it here. Suffice it to say that when June died in May 2003, no one who tracked the lives of those two extraordinary people was surprised when he followed her in September of that year.

June was immensely charming to talk to. Actually, it was more like witnessing someone talking: She spoke virtually nonstop for an hour in a kind of genial, free-associative trance. Without an audio track, it's difficult to render the lilt of her voice or the waywardness of her thoughts, but I've done the best I can here. This interview took place in the dining room of the Hotel Plaza Athenée on Manhattan's Upper East Side. A country girl at heart, June still loved the finer things in life, and the sumptuous space – opened especially for her and empty save for the army of waiters responding instantly to her every gesture – seemed to suit her just fine. She wore a floor-length dress and looked both elegant and natural, delicate and implacable, a figure from a cameo or an Appalachian sampler set in motion in the modern world.

It was great seeing Johnny get on stage to perform at the end of the tribute taping the other night. I was worried when he didn't make it to the Grammys to accept the Lifetime Achievement Award recently.

John's just been doing what he feels like doing, and when the Grammys came up, he said, "I choose not to go." But this was such a special day. We have a real deep connection with everybody on that show. It was about seeing old friends, but when you see old friends who sing your songs, that really is something. It was very moving.

How have things been for the two of you since he's been ill?

Even now when John's been sick, we've had so much fun. I said, "We're going to quit for a year, and then we'll see how we feel. And we'll quit another year if we want to. Who says we have to work? We've worked long enough. We'll do exactly what we want to. We've got a lot of front porches – we'll go sit on them."

He's such a powerful man and such a good man. He's been a great father, and a great husband to me. We've been very lucky; we've had one of those love stories in our lives. So many people have been denied knowing that kind of love. God has blessed us.

I found your introduction to your performance of "Ring of Fire" really powerful. So much feeling came through, as it does on your version on the album.

I never talked much about how I fell in love with John, and I certainly didn't tell him how I felt. It wasn't a convenient time for me to fall in love with him, and it wasn't a convenient time for him to fall in love with me. One morning about four o'clock, I was driving my car as fast as I could, and I thought, "Why am I out on the highway this time of night?" I was miserable, and it came to me that I was falling in love with somebody I had no right to fall in love with. I thought, "I can't fall in love with this man, but it's like fire. It's just like a ring of fire." That's how the song started.

I wrote the first verse and the melody, and I started on the second verse. I about had gotten it finished, but Kilgore came in, and I said, "Kilgore, you and I have just written the best song we've written. Help me hone it." So we worked on the last verse, and it all came together. It was perfect.

I wanted so to play it for John, but then I thought, "He'll see right through me. He's going to know what this song is about." So I sang it to my sister Anita; she was fixing to record. She was a wonderful singer, and her version was kind of a folk ballad. It's a sound that basically comes from my years of being part of the Carter Family. My sisters and I put the voices on it to where it almost was like bells ringing in the mountains.

John heard Anita's record, and he said, "I want to do that song, but I hear trumpets on it." I was thrilled when he decided to do it, but I was still pretty frightened of his way of life. I was not into that kind of thing and I was protective of how I felt about myself and the things I believed in. I also had two little girls that I was very protective of. My mother, my sisters, and I had watched Hank Williams die little by little, and grieved.

Anyway, all these years nobody really knew why that song was written. I decided, "It's long enough. I'll just tell why."

It seems like all the musicians playing on Press On *are related to you in one way or another. It's a real family affair.*

Marty Stuart and Rodney Crowell, they were married to two of my daughters. I always say, "My daughters moved on and married other people, but my sons-in-law never left me!" I am always going to be devoted to Marty and to Rodney. I am devoted to Nick Lowe. When Rodney married again this last time, his wife, Claudia, got to be a part of our family. She moved right in. Marty married Connie Smith, and she is now part of my family. So I have got the greatest extended family.

So many of the guys at the show the other night, I've called my babies ever since I first heard them sing. Kris Kristofferson has been one of my babies for years. I had people I believed in. I believed in Kris. I believed in Larry Gatlin. I believed in Waylon Jennings. And I bugged John to death until they became part of our family.

How did you come to write "I Used to Be Somebody"? It's such a moving song.

That song comes from a lot of my life, a lot of things I never talked about. I never spoke to people about the times I worked with Elvis Presley. We were great friends. When he got his first motorcycle, I already had a motorcycle and knew how to ride one. I remember somebody said to me in Nashville one night, "Did I see you and Elvis Presley out riding motorcycles?" I said, "Oh, no, that wasn't me. [*Laughs*] That was definitely somebody else!" We also sang hymns together. He loved to sing hymns.

I was playing my solo act with Elvis. It was just Elvis and me. I played my autoharp, my guitar, and my banjo, and I introduced Elvis at the beginning of the show. We were playing Sarasota, Florida, and this guy came to the show and his name was Budd Schulberg. Afterwards, Elia Kazan said to him, "How did you like Elvis Presley?" And he said, "I liked Elvis Presley, but I am in love with this little girl that's on that show. You have got to go see June Carter." So from talking to Budd Schulberg, Elia Kazan sent me a telegram that said, "I'll be in Nashville on Saturday to see you." I didn't realize who he was. He was just this guy that was taking all these pictures of me who had holes in the bottom of his shoes. But we got to be real good friends.

He said, "I'm making a movie called *A Face in the Crowd.* Would you take me around and introduce me to people in this town?" So I took him out to see Big Jeff Bess and I introduced him to Rod Brasfield, and he hired both of them for *A Face in the Crowd.* Then he said, "I really would like to see you go to New York and go to school. Would you consider doing that? I would send you if you would go." I said, "Well, I don't think I would have to rely on you sending me. I've got a very good job. I work about ten days a month with Elvis Presley, and I work the Grand Ole Opry. I write the Pet Milk commercials, and I write the Kellogg's Corn Flakes commercials. It makes me quite a bit of money. I'd have to give up all that, but if I could keep my Presley dates, then I might consider going."

So Kazan brings me to New York and he took me to Sandy Meisner at the Neighborhood Playhouse and to Lee Strasberg at the Actors Studio. I said, "This is something I'd really like to do." I talked to my mother about it, and she said, "You really should go. This is an important man. You go to New York and do this."

I moved up to 20 East 67th Street, between Madison and Fifth, and I was very comfortable with that. I just started working on myself and trying to be a more rounded person. I went and observed at the Actors Studio. I thought that Strasberg was pretty rough on everybody, and I'm a very gentle person. I liked to go to the Neighborhood Playhouse. There was a professional class that had 17 people in it who were already working. I'd seen a lot of them on TV. I decided that maybe I would just sign up for that summer course. But I was still going to the Actors Studio and trying to see what I could learn. I did everything they told me to do. I took speech classes, but Kazan kept telling me, "Don't dare lose your accent. You can learn to do all the accents you want, but hold onto what is true to you." So I held onto that.

But Kazan stopped making movies, and I went back to go on tour, because I could make $25,000 a month at that time playing all of these country fairs. There was a part of me that wanted to come to Broadway if I could, but I couldn't make anything on Broadway. Somebody wanted to offer me something like $500 a week, and I said, "Look I've already done that, thank you." So I went out to California. I did a lot of Tennessee Ernie Ford shows. I did "Gunsmoke," anything that I could read for.

You knew James Dean, too, when you were in New York.

He did give me a rose once, and that's as much as I want to talk about that. OK?

Sure. Back to writing "I Used to Be Somebody" – and Elvis?

It was Elvis's birthday, and he'd been dead I don't know how many years. John and I were talking about it, and I was almost crying. I thought, "Oh, my goodness! Where in the world have I been? All these people are dead." These people meant a lot to me. That thought made me cry when I wrote the song.

And Quentin Tarantino – that's another story.

He's the star of "Tiffany Anastasia Lowe."

My granddaughter Tiffany Anastasia Lowe is six foot tall and gorgeous. She makes young men run into the side of buildings she's so beautiful. I taught her to play Mother Maybelle's guitar. I just thought, "I hope she doesn't run into Quentin Tarantino. I have seen *Pulp Fiction.* I know what goes on!" [*Laughs*]

How did you meet Johnny Cash?

I don't know why I went all those years and worked with everybody in the business but Johnny Cash, but the time finally came. He walked up to me and introduced himself backstage at the Grand Ole Opry. He said, "I know you'd been working with Elvis." And I said, "Elvis made me listen to every Johnny Cash record in the business! He's a fan, and, when we stop to eat something in these little cafes, he puts his nickels in and I've had to listen to a lot of Johnny Cash."

That next year, John's manager offered me 10 days a month, and he had the biggest show that was on the road then, so I could make a lot of money if I went to work for Johnny Cash. So he paid me a lot of money, and that's how I first met Johnny Cash.

Did you immediately become aware of his drug problem?

I was scared about him, like my sisters and I were scared about Hank Williams. I knew that the show always had to go on, like my mother taught me, so I would fight like a demon for it to go on, no matter what I had to do. If it was stealing his pills and throwing them away, I did that.

Later, to make a long story short, he did finally get himself straightened up. I believed in him, and we believed in each other. I wrote the Grand Ole Opry a letter and told them I wouldn't work there anymore, that I had committed my life to John and I was going to try to work with him and see if we made it. I loved him very much, and I committed my life to him. Then we got married – "in a fever hotter than a pepper sprout!" [*Laughs*]

The first time I ever saw Michael Jackson – we were introduced at some awards show – I said, "I'm so glad to meet you. I've always appreciated the fact that you're such a wonderful entertainer." And he said, "Hotter than a pepper sprout!" He said, "That's exactly what I've tried to be – 'hotter than a pepper sprout.' " [*Laughs*]

Are you going to do some live shows to promote your album?

Yes. All these young people have loved me, maybe because of the Carter Family, maybe because of the songs I sung with my sisters, but there's been a part of me that they've adored too. So they've made a place for me, and I can sing my songs for them and they're happy.

Once mother and the girls and I came and played in New York. I can't remember where – the Bitter End or somewhere – and somebody came in and said, "My goodness, you really do play the Carter scratch. You've got it down!" I remember saying to him, "Honey, this *is* the Carter scratch!" [*Laughs*]

I sure have missed mother so bad, and then Helen when she died. Actually, I kid all the time about my mother sending me money from the grave. When they sing "Wabash Cannonball," "Will the Circle Be Unbroken," and "Wildwood Flower," I say, "Thank you very much," and take my money! [*Laughs*]

Will John be well enough to travel with you and perform?

Oh, yeah. He'll be there, or I won't be there – we'll just put it that way.

June, you've made a wonderful record, and I've listened to it with such pleasure. It's been a great inspiration to me. It doesn't sound old, it doesn't sound new, it just sounds completely like you.

Everything is so slick anymore. They do wonderful pop country music, but what I do is something else. It's pure.

You've probably met the oldest antique in this business. I'm telling you the truth. I first started singing on those Texas border stations when I was a little girl, and I've never stopped working. There's never been a week where I haven't gotten a check. In all that time, I can't think of anybody who's worked longer than I have. Maybe Bill Monroe might've, but I don't think so. I remember him coming to our house with Charlie when they were the Monroe Brothers. And there were the Delmore Brothers. All those people who worked back in that time would come and stay at our house, because there was no hotels in the country. We had a huge house on the side of a mountain, and there was always beds for everybody.

All those people, I remember them. There's not anybody out there now. Even Chet Atkins, who worked with us, I've got a lot of years on Chet. I can't think of anybody that's got more years than I have. Maybe I've made a statement that's not true, but I think they're all gone but me. Maybe somewhere after all these years somebody's going to realize I'm there.

Part of this interview appeared in Rolling Stone, *July 8, 1999.*

Rosanne Cash

"I didn't have to pay the price"

I interviewed Rosanne Cash in the living room of the townhouse in the Chelsea section of Manhattan that she shares with her husband and producer, John Leventhal, their son, and her four daughters from a previous marriage to Rodney Crowell. Rosanne was about to release *Rules of Travel*, her first album of new songs in six years. The album had not come easy. She had begun recording it with Leventhal in the summer of 1998, and then suddenly lost her voice. For more than two years, it was impossible for her to sing and sometimes painful for her even to speak. Eventually her voice returned and she completed the album, which features her characteristically incisive, psychologically deft songwriting.

This interview took place in February 2003, during the buildup to the American-led invasion of Iraq. That was very much on Rosanne's mind – as it was on mine – when we spoke, so I left the exchanges about it in here. I also left in our exchange about the September 11 terrorist attacks. Our conversation, in that regard, was very much that of any two New Yorkers speaking in the wake of that horrific event. One question inevitably would arise: Were you in the city when it happened?

Because Rosanne has always paid so much attention to matters of the heart, both as a person and as a writer, she asked me some personal questions as we spoke, and I left those exchanges in here as well. She had just returned from visiting her father in Nashville, and his illness provided the emotional backdrop to this conversation –as it did to one of the most gripping songs on *Rules of Travel*, "September When It Comes," on which Johnny Cash sings with his oldest daughter. The depth and complexity of their relationship is evident in that song, as it is, I believe, in this discussion – and in the tears Rosanne shed as she talked about her father.

The interview began as I inquired about her father's health.

How's your dad?

I just got back from Nashville yesterday. He's not very good. Even before I got home from the airport my sister called to tell me he's back in the hospital. It was a stressful weekend. I'm still recovering from it.

Were you able to talk to him?

Yes, but he's very frail. It's hard to see him compared to how he was. It's really painful. But he's the most stoic individual I've ever met in my life.

I can't believe how active he's been. An album, half a dozen interviews, and people are really beginning to get excited about "Hurt."

I know. It's amazing. That's always been his way. It keeps his passion alive.

Well, you've gone on your own journey with Rules of Travel, *given that you lost your voice in the middle of making it. Did that experience change your sense of what the record was supposed to be?*

Definitely. So much time passed between when we recorded the tracks and I got my voice back – something like three years. We started tracking in the summer of '98 and I got my voice back around November 2000. Then we really didn't get back to the album till the following spring because John had to finish producing Joan Osborne. So a lot changed. I was anxious, and I'd lost my enthusiasm for it. I hadn't finished the lyrics for some of the songs, and it took me awhile to get plugged back into it.

When did you realize that your voice problem was serious?

Physically?

Yes, physically. Perfect question, though. [*Laughs*]

I assumed that when I said I'd lost my voice, everyone would think that I was speaking in metaphors: "Oh she's speaking figuratively, right?" No! [*Laughs*]

Describe what happened.

When I was about five months pregnant, I got laryngitis really bad, and I thought, "Oh, I have allergies." Then my voice didn't come back, and a couple of months went by and it was getting worse. I went to a vocal specialist, a doctor, and she put a camera down my throat. She literally stepped back from the picture and said, "Oh, my God! I've never seen a polyp this large unless someone's been smoking for 40 years." I said, "It's not cancer, is it?" And she said, "No, certainly not."

So I said that I know a lot of singers who have had polyps; it's not that big a deal. She had me scheduled for surgery after I gave birth. In the meantime, she went to a seminar in Paris about hormones and polyps. She went up to a doctor afterwards, and said, "I have a patient who lost her voice when she was five months pregnant." He said, "Don't operate. Wait until she finishes nursing. Six months after that she should have her voice back." And that's when it came back.

Isn't that weird? Apparently, I had a small polyp and when I got pregnant the hormones made it grow. Then when my body got back to normal after breast feeding, it went away. We never had to operate. Four months ago, she put the camera down my throat again, and she said, "It's completely gone." It was like science fiction.

You must have been so relieved.

I was relieved I didn't have to have surgery. I was fine with it for a while because I would have given that time to the baby anyway, so it was no big deal. But when the baby was a year old, and I still didn't have my voice, I started freaking out. But another year went by and I had it.

Then you had to deal with the issue of feeling alienated from your own songs. What was that about?

Because so much time had gone by and I had the baby, I was not interested in being out in the public. I'd gone through the whole thing: "If I don't get my voice back, will I be happy just writing and not ever making another record, not ever singing again?" And I felt really sad. I realized how much it meant to me.

I had kind of backed into singing. That wasn't my original idea of what I wanted to do. In fact, it still makes me nervous. It was classic "You lose it, then you realize what you had."

So reconnecting with the project took some time. John was more connected to it than I was, and he had to push me. Then one day in the studio, I sang something. It really worked, and suddenly, I was back into the record.

When you decided that you missed singing and recording, what did you miss about it? I recall your saying that you primarily think of yourself as a writer, so presumably you could just continue doing that.

I thought I would think that. But it was devastating. When I picked up a guitar to write, I'd just put it back down because I couldn't sing with myself. It was so depressing. I missed the joy of it. I didn't realize there was joy in it till it went away.

You talk of backing into singing. What was your reluctance about it?

I didn't want to be famous. That was it. Not everybody wants to be famous. [*Laughs*] You would think *au contraire*, but I still have anxiety about it. My imprinting was that fame meant that you had to stay away from home for months at a time, and your relationships disintegrated and you had to take substances to keep your energy up.

And all of that proved to be the case! [*Laughs*]

And all of that proved to be the case. I mean, I saw my dad, and I thought, "This is just about the worst thing that could happen to someone. Why would I ever want to court that?"

I always wanted to be a writer from the time I was little. Then when I started writing songs, I thought, "This has a lot of dignity. I would love to provide songs for other people." But one thing led to another. I made a demo. I got a recording contract. Not to say I wasn't a participant in it, but…

It must have intrigued you to some degree.

Sure it intrigued me. It's like a snake. [*Laughs*] I would've preferred to remain anonymous. But given the choice, then I would've preferred to interpret my own songs. So that's where I ended up.

So getting back to Rules of Travel, *how did you re-engage it?*

Just by doing it, by starting to sing the songs again and getting into the process of it. Then I felt enthused. It was exciting to use my voice again. I'd started writing again. I finished the lyrics to "Rules of Travel." My baby was a little older and starting to go to nursery school, so I felt I had time to do it.

As the record took shape, did your sense of what it was about thematically change much?

That didn't change so much. I'd only written the chorus for "Rules of Travel," and the verses were written after 9/11, so that influenced the verses somewhat. I grew into some of the lyrics, particularly something like "Beautiful Pain" or "44 Stories." I grew to feel more generous, like my goal was actually to glance up from my navel a couple of times on this record. [*Laughs*] These songs were in second or third person. Big leap for me. Big jump.

Were you here for 9/11?

Yeah, I was on Greenwich Street at a parents' meeting and the first plane went right over our heads. We went outside and saw the building burning, so I got my daughter and tried to get her home. There were no cell phones working, no trains. I basically dragged her to our house from Christopher Street. It was awful. But I hate to say my experience was so awful when 10 blocks south of me it was so much more awful. It did change me. I sometimes still *hear* the sound of that plane. Not just remember it, but actually sometimes still hear it. But I'm pissed off now. I wasn't pissed off then.

What are you angry about?

The whole thing. It's out of control. My poll of taxi drivers in this city says that we are going about this all the wrong way. Aren't you pissed?

At first, I was pissed at them. I believed we had to assert ourselves and show that we were not going to stand for American cities being bombed. Now I'm pissed at us. I feel that what was a righteous campaign against terrorism is now about wanting to see a fireworks show in Baghdad.

We're off subject. That's the main problem. Were you in the city when it happened?

Yes. We were supposed to leave on our honeymoon that afternoon. We'd gotten married upstate on September 8. It was magical, like A Midsummer Night's Dream. *Then we floated back to New York, and we were going to leave that afternoon for Greece. We were devastated. I don't constantly ponder it, but it's like my mother's death – it's there all the time. It doesn't get resolved. It's just part of my consciousness.*

That's exactly how I feel. It's like it slightly changed our DNA. While not directly as a result of 9/11, this album is also about living with the unresolved. That was the theme that kept running through it for me. At some point, I realized that not everything has an answer. So much in life is unresolved – more, actually, than is resolved or answered – and accepting that makes everything easier.

When you talk about finishing the lyrics to "Rules of Travel" after 9/11, did that experience affect what you had to say?

A little bit. I was very cautious about writing anything that was overtly sentimental or jingoistic, because it seemed that was the knee-jerk response. Every songwriter I knew had his 9/11 song. Ultimately, I did write my 9/11 song, but I haven't recorded it yet.

The lyrics to "Rules of Travel" were slightly influenced by it. "When do the walls tumble down / Into the sky, into the stars and the ground / It's a good day to give it up" – that's partly about all that. "It's a good day to just give it up" – the old model. But I had to put it in the framework of a relationship. [*Laughs*]

Another running theme on the album is the tug of loss, and the acceptance of it. It's not fatalistic, more just realistic. Some things go and don't come back.

That's exactly what I mean – just to let go of the energy of always looking for the answers is a huge relief.

Talk about the duet with your father on "September When It Comes."

I was reluctant to ask my dad to sing on it. The lyrics are inspired by him – when he first got sick. You start thinking about losing your parents and what you didn't get and what maybe you'll never get and living with the unresolved. I recorded it myself, and after it was done, John said,

"You should ask your dad to sing on this." I really didn't want to. I didn't want to use him. I didn't want it to appear to be a novelty. But the more I thought about it, the more I thought it was appropriate. He is in those lyrics. So I asked him, and he said, "I'll have to read the lyrics first."

That is so fabulous!

Isn't that great? [*Laughs*] So he read the lyrics and said, "Oh, yeah, I could sing this song." I took it down to him, but it wasn't clear he'd be able to do it because he was not feeling well. The next morning, I could tell he wasn't feeling well, but he went over to the studio anyway, and his energy really perked up once he started singing it. It was so sweet. He sounds very fragile on it.

Aptly. It suits the song. Did you talk with him about what the song meant?

No. There was no need to talk about it. He knew. He got it. It would've been smarmy to talk about it.

Has your relationship with him changed since he got sick?

Oh, yeah. I'm sure it's classic that when your parent gets sick you change roles a bit. I've felt much more protective of him and wanted to take care of him, much more solicitous of his well-being. For most of my life, my dad seemed all-powerful, but when he got sick and he's so fragile, it's a real wake-up, isn't it? Have you had one of your parents…?

Both. My father died when I was 23. That was hard primarily because we had a fairly tense relationship, and we were just beginning to turn the corner. I remember visiting him in the hospital near the end and he told me that he was surprised I had been spending so much time with him.

Thank God you had the presence to do that at 23, because a lot of 23-year-olds wouldn't have gotten it.

I wish I could take credit for the decision, but it just felt like what had to be done. With my mother it was more difficult. It was deeper, but I felt that there was very little left unfinished with her.

I think even though the grief is more profound, it's better that way. You feel, "I'm so glad nothing was left unsaid or undone."

It is better that way.

[*She begins to cry.*] I'm sorry. I just came from seeing my dad so it's all still so fresh. It's so hard with my dad because he still belongs to the world so much and there's so many people around. Even now when he's so sick, there's a lot of people taking care of him. I almost envy my friends who go and take care of their parent at the end – that you're the nurse and the primary caretaker, you provide that for them. I'm not needed as much. That's a little bit hard. But he's incredibly stoic. I say, "How are you feeling, dad?" No matter what's going on, it's, "I'm fine. I'm fine."

The whole process of dealing with, not only your father, but "Johnny Cash" – I can't imagine what that would be like. He's such an icon. But for all the complexity of your relationship to him, you made what he did your own. You made a gift out of it.

It would have been impossible for me if I'd been a boy. That's the first thing. The second thing is that I've always had an acute sense of my own limitations because of who he is. If I'd have just been on my own doing what I do, at some point in my life, maybe in the last couple years, I would've thought, "I'm pretty good at what I do." But I always have in front of me what I feel my limitations are because he's always there. He's looking back at his life, and he's looking at the life of a great artist. The arc of that. The transcendence of that. The suffering of that.

I will never look back at that kind of life, that kind of transcendence, because I'm not willing to make the sacrifices, to be that singular. And he was. To be a truly great artist, you have to be that singular, and I was never willing to do that. I wanted to have her [*gestures toward her daughter Carrie Crowell, who had just come home*] and this [*gestures toward her house*] and raise my own children and paint and travel for pleasure instead of just work. Sometimes it aggrieves me that I'll never be that. But I didn't have to pay the price either. Like he did.

Portions of this interview appeared in
The New York Times, *April 20, 2003.*

Trent Reznor on "Hurt"

"A eulogy almost"

When Johnny Cash first told me he was recording the Nine Inch Nails song "Hurt," I was immediately struck by how brilliant that was. Still, I had no idea it would become the phenomenon it eventually developed into. "When I heard that song, I thought, 'That sounds like something I could've written in the '60s,'" Cash said about the original version. "There's more heart and soul and pain in that song than any that's come along in a long time. I love it." Cash's spare, uncompromised reading of "Hurt" was an essential source of its impact, of course. He took Trent Reznor's tortured rendering of the agony of addiction and transformed it into a stunning meditation on mortality itself.

Then came Mark Romanek's video, which I believe is the greatest rock video ever made. Cash, withered by his illness, bravely allowed himself to be shown exactly as he looked, juxtaposed with images of him as a young man that bristle with virility and life. It is a stunning statement of his artistic integrity and his commitment to the truth.

When I wrote Johnny Cash's obituary for *Rolling Stone*, I wanted to speak with Reznor about Cash's interpretation of the song and Romanek's video. Even though the video had attracted a huge amount of attention – earning seven nominations at MTV's "Video Music Awards" and winning one – Reznor had not, to my knowledge, publicly spoken about it. I knew that he would have something powerful to say, and when I reached him by telephone, he did.

How did you first find out that Johnny Cash wanted to record "Hurt"?

I've been friends with Rick Rubin for quite a while, and he asked me how I would feel about Johnny Cash doing a cover of one of my songs. I thought, "Wow," because my songs have been my own therapy, a vehicle for me to keep sane. I've never really thought about writing songs for other people, and I've never tried to pitch my songs to people.

And that song in particular came from a pretty private, personal place for me. So it seemed, well, like that's *my* song.

But I have a lot of trust and respect for Rick. Johnny Cash had always been this mysterious figure to me. He'd been around. My grandfather had listened to him. I'd never paid that much attention to him, because I was more distracted by whatever was happening at the time. But Johnny Cash was one of the few greats left out there, a real individual persona.

Rick sent me a CD of it. I listened to it, and it just seemed incredibly strange and wrong to me to hear that voice with my song. It seemed weird from my perspective, which wasn't objective. I thought, "Here's this thing that I wrote in my bedroom in a moment of frailty, and now Johnny Cash is singing it." It kind of freaked me out.

Did you say any of that to Rick?

Rick called and asked what I thought, and I said, "You did a very tasteful job with it" – which I did think and do think. It was a big juxtaposition for me to hear it as someone else's song now. It instantly became his song after that.

Then I heard that Mark was campaigning to do a video for it. Mark and I are friends from working together. If I had to list the people that I had the most respect for in the music business, Mark and Rick would be on that list. I saw the video and it took my breath away. Immediately my throat had a lump in it, and at that point, it really struck home. It was heartbreaking. I had goosebumps, which I have right now even thinking about it. It became really inspiring to me.

What did you find inspiring about it?

I'm writing a new album right now, and it reminded me of the power of music. Something that I made in my room, that came out of my little private backyard – to have an icon like Johnny Cash juxtapose it into something that now, especially with the visual aid of that video, gives it a whole different set of scenery and a backdrop and a context to listen to it in. It works. And it probably works better than my version.

I was sad about the context with Johnny, but I felt honored to be a part of it. I spoke with Mark about this the other day, when I heard that he died. This artist deserves and demands respect from a new generation that wasn't that aware of him. It's nice that we were able to present him to a new world of fans, even though, unfortunately, it's the end of his life. The MTV exposure, even though they were cowards to not give him the awards he deserved, might open a lot of people up who weren't that aware of Johnny Cash, or of his importance. I felt greatly honored to have been involved in that in any way, but I'm sad that it's a eulogy almost.

When you say it felt "wrong," what felt wrong about it to you?

It felt invasive. It was my child. It was like I was building a home, and someone else moved into it. When I write a song, I'm only considering myself as the one narrating it. It's my voice. So it did seem very odd at first. Also, as soon as you hear his voice, you go, "That's Johnny Cash." How fucking weird is that? Never in my wildest dreams did I think that I would write a song that Johnny Cash wanted to sing. I never thought that our paths would intersect.

Rick Rubin is probably the one person who could make a connection between you and Johnny Cash.

Rick's a genius when it comes to things like that. I really admire what he's done in terms of taking Johnny Cash when his career may have gotten off track in the '80s and being able to come in and say, "Let's take this guy back to what he's really great at and present him how he should be presented" – as opposed to fluff and filler and, whatever's happening right now, let's jump on that bandwagon and modernize him to death. To be able to cut right down to what's really important, I have a lot of respect for Rick for doing that.

I've been listening to a lot of Hank Williams and Johnny Cash, just for the songwriting. There's nothing in there that doesn't need to be in there. There's a courage and a fearlessness in saying what you want to say in a pretty naked context. It's inspiring.

How has all this affected your own relationship to "Hurt"?

I haven't listened to my version since then. I've been so proud of what they've done with it that I haven't thought that much about it. I'm over my initial shock, and I realize that's what music's all about. I've thrown some things in the pot, and now it's turned into something else. It's a pretty powerful thing.

Portions of this interview appeared in
Rolling Stone, *October 16, 2003.*

Tom Petty on the Death of a Friend

"It sounds like God singing my song"

Tom Petty and the Heartbreakers were essentially Johnny Cash's backing band on *Unchained*, the second album Cash made with Rick Rubin, who also is Petty's producer and friend. Cash also recorded version of Petty's "Southern Accents" and "I Won't Back Down." When I was writing Cash's obituary for *Rolling Stone*, I called him for his reminiscences about his friend.

When did you first meet Johnny Cash?

The first time I met him was really unusual. I was with Nick Lowe, who was his son-in-law at the time. We were in Nashville, and John had invited us out to dinner at his place on the lake. We arrived and we were really disappointed because he had taken ill with pneumonia that morning and he and June had gone to the hospital.

But dinner was still going to go on! [*Laughs*] We sat at this long, elaborately set table. Then just as dinner was about to begin, someone said, "Tom, John's on the phone and he'd like to talk to you." So I went to the phone and we talked for, God, about half an hour. He was very sorry he couldn't be there. Then after dinner, he and June spoke by phone to every single guest as they left the house and asked them if they had a good time.

That afternoon, we had gone across to the cabin that he had, where he had a lot of exotic animals running around in the woods. There was an emu, and his kid John Carter said, "Do you think you could catch that emu?" We'd a few drinks, and I said, "Hell, yeah, I can catch the emu." And he said, "Nah, nobody can ever catch him. I bet you can't." So I started chasing the bird through the woods, which I found out later wasn't a good idea. I guess the emu went kind of crazy. John Carter, though he was just a little kid, had put me up to bad business. When John came home and went walking through the woods, from out of nowhere, the emu attacked him, leapt on him, and broke a couple of ribs! So I got another call from Johnny Cash: "I just want you to know that that emu broke my ribs." He started laughing and we became friends.

When was that?

That was in 1982. After that, I saw him here and there from time to time. He came to a few shows over the years. I really loved him. I remember Rick Rubin asking me at a session one day, "Do you think I should sign Johnny Cash?" I said, "Johnny Cash? Are you crazy? Sign him *tonight!*" He said, "I was thinking about it, but do you think that he would work in this kind of atmosphere?" And I said, "Hell, yeah!" While John was making that first album [*American Recordings*] with Rick, we started to see quite a bit of him. I remember him coming to the session when we cut the song "Mary Jane's Last Dance." John sat through the whole session and I was impressed that he liked rock that much.

When he came out to make *Unchained*, the Heartbreakers kind of became his band. I just love that record. I still view that as the best work we ever did. We really were having a great time. It was, like, "OK, here's the song." They'd play it down and we'd run out and whoever got to their favorite instrument first got to play it. [*Laughs*] We had a ball making that record. He had such an interest in so many kinds of songs. We played Gene Autry songs, Beck, Leonard Cohen, all over the map.

What were your impressions of him as a person?

He was the man that we all would like to be. He had such dignity and charisma, but at the same time, he was very approachable. He would put the room at ease and just become one of the bunch, which is quite a thing to be able to do. One of my favorite stories is we were at the studio, which was in downtown Hollywood, kind of a weird neighborhood. He came in with June, and he was laughing. I said, "Where you been?" He said, "We been sitting across the street at the bus stop. June and I thought it would be fun to sit on that bus bench for a while. I met the most interesting people over there." I was just trying to just picture the look on these people's faces as they came to sit on the bus bench, and there's Johnny and June.

I just treasured our friendship because he was so full of great stories. He told me a really funny story about the Sun Records days. One time, he was going somewhere in Texas and Elvis had a hit record at the time. Sam Phillips told them, "I've got to get some Elvis records over to Texas and my distributor can't get them there, so I'm going to put these in the trunk, and you guys can give them to the promoter when you get there." So John told me, "We were crossing this high ridge in Tennessee and I just had to sail one of those records off the cliff there. We wound up pitching every one off the ridge like Frisbees."

Did you pay much attention to him when you were a kid?

I'm from Gainesville, Florida, and the first time I heard of him, he had come to Gainesville with a television show called *Hullaballoo*. There was great controversy in the town that this guy named Johnny Cash has passed out during the taping, and had to be re-taped again and again. I just thought, "How cool! This guy's an outlaw." And being from a Southern family, he was just a saint to those people. So you heard a lot of him.

Did you get much of a sense of how he felt about the revival of interest in him in the '90s?

He was really excited about having a younger audience. He thought they were so much fun to play to. Me and some of the Heartbreakers played with him at the House of Blues one night, and he was so buzzed about it! I remember the night when we were finishing the Soundgarden song "Rusty Cage," and he burst out laughing. He said, "That ought to piss off every country music fan! Country radio is made for people that hate country." He might have been hurt that *Unchained* won a Grammy for Best Country Album, and it never got any country airplay. He phoned the night of the Grammy Awards – we were in the studio – and he was really excited that it had won and he thanked everyone. But later on, he made some mention that if they had played it on the radio it might have had some real sales. But he wasn't the kind of person to carry a grudge and be morose. He just went on.

Did he discuss his relationship with Rick Rubin with you?

He loved Rick, and Rick deserves so much credit for what he did for John, for believing in him and being the first guy to break John down to just the guitar and his voice. That was a stunning move. John approached that with a great deal of trepidation. He had never done it, and it made him nervous, but Rick got him to be comfortable with it.

I was really impressed when he cut a couple of my songs. The first time, I just went, "Wow, I'm a songwriter." But when he did "I Won't Back Down," I told him, "This is much more the definitive version than mine. This is the first time the song really came to life for me. It sounds like God singing my song." He was just a wonderful man.

Were you much in touch with him after he took ill?

Even when we did *Unchained*, he would have periods where he would have to go into the lounge and lie down for a while. I saw this incredible dedication to "I'm going to get this work done whether I'm sick or not." The illness came and went. I remember him talking to me about it. One night, Rick and I went down to see him when they had flown in from Australia to L.A., which is crazy in the first place, and they had a gig that night. They all had the flu and he was going to go on. He just said, "I'm not sick. I'm just going to keep playing."

I know he was very disappointed when he had to quit touring. He told me once, "You know, I have seven houses, but I feel most at home when I hit that first step of the bus." It drove him nuts not to be able to travel anymore. But to answer your question, we did talk on the phone from time to time, and I did see him a few times fairly recently. He was ill but didn't really want to discuss it. He was just trying to press forward. No one you'll talk to was very surprised that after June went he was ready to go too.

What do you think his legacy will be?

He's certainly not going to leave us as far as his music or his influence. But if you've got to bust it down to one word, it's integrity. He never lost his integrity. This guy was friends with presidents, and he was friends with people at the bus stop. He was probably the only country singer who opposed the Vietnam War publicly. He really stuck by his convictions. So integrity is what I always think of with him.

The music reflects his honesty and, being the absolute definition of icon, his music will live on and will influence people. Being honest in your music and having that incredible feeling of truth in it, I hope that inspires young people. It does to some degree already, or he wouldn't have this kind of respect.

He was quite a man. I am fortunate enough to be friends with a lot of people who are huge in the field of music, but he was a special person. With my band, he pulled the best music out of us that anyone ever has, and he'll have that influence on people whether he's here or not.

There was such charisma about him. To see a man in his 60s come to work in knee-high boots and a cloak – and that was just for a night in the studio – I thought that was so damn cool. He was just so great.

Portions of this interview appeared in
Rolling Stone, *October 16, 2003.*

Bono on the Meaning of Johnny Cash

"Nobody could be him"

I once interviewed Bono about Johnny Cash's guest lead vocal on "The Wanderer," the concluding track on U2's 1993 album, *Zooropa.* The song is a haunting saga of a man drifting through a post-apocalyptic landscape, searching for whatever truth may have survived. Bono remarked that Cash had a problem with the lyrics, a problem that Bono found revealing. The verse in question begins, "I went out walking with a Bible and a gun," and concludes with the lines, "Yeah, I went out for the papers / Told her I'd be back by noon."

"He didn't like that line about going out for the newspapers," Bono told me. "It's too cute. When he plays it live, he doesn't put it in. He said to me [*imitates Cash's desert-dry drawl*], 'Bono, I won't make light of the song with that verse.' You see – he's staring it out, whereas in that line, I looked away. It's like when you make a joke of something to get yourself off the hook. But he doesn't ever want to be off the hook. That's a very powerful place to be as an artist."

When Johnny Cash died, Bono offered some remembrances.

Unfortunately, I'm calling you on a sad occasion...

Maybe it's not that sad, when you've lived a life like that. It's sad for us, but, you know, June went off to prepare the house, and he wasn't long behind her. Theirs is quite a love story, really. In fact, I called John just a few months ago, two weeks before she died. I was talking to June, and she was saying, "How's everybody in Dublin and in Ireland? How's the band, and what's going on?" I was talking to her for 20 minutes, and she was saying, well, John's this and John's that. So I said, "Will you pass on my very best to John?" And she said, "You can pass it on yourself. He's here beside me. We're in bed." She'd been talking for him – *at* him – for 20 minutes! John just took the phone and said, "That's womenfolk." [*Laughs*]

He's going out on a high point. The video for "Hurt" is such a moving statement.

And perhaps the best video ever made, just on the basis of, if beauty is truth. The absence of vanity – it's just an extraordinary thing to see. It's an extraordinary film. But how could Trent…I mean, only Johnny Cash could have written that song. It was a great song. Now it's a *great* song.

How do you think people will remember Johnny Cash?

To be that extraordinary and that ordinary was his real gift. Every man could relate to him, but nobody could be him. I was saying to somebody, we're all sissies in comparison to Johnny Cash.

How could he have a weekly show on network TV and not compromise an inch? How do you do that? Did anyone ever think, "He's selling out," or "He's gone all showbiz?" And yet it *was* show business – and it wasn't. How do you do that? Punks, truck drivers, and church folk – it's like, what's *that?*

And he was a zookeeper! Did you know that he was nearly killed by an emu? He told me, "That emu damn near killed me. I defended myself with a post." He was laughing as he told the story, but you can only imagine. "Johnny Cash passed away after seeing off the love of his life," is such a different outcome than death by emu. We should be grateful.

Humor and bare-boned honesty. Adam Clayton and I once had dinner with Johnny and June at their house. We sat down and bowed our heads, and John said the most beautiful, poetic grace. And then he just looked at me and Adam and said, "Sure miss the drugs, though." It was just to say, "I haven't become all Holy Joe-ish." He just didn't have self-righteousness down.

He was a very Godly man, and you have the sense for sure that he spent his time in the desert when he was a wild man. That just made you like him more. It gave the songs some dust. And that voice is definitely locusts and honey.

When you discover the eloquence of his understanding of relationships and their cost, you get the sense in his music that love costs everything you have. It's the very opposite of free love. No, love is very expensive. At the time of free love, Johnny Cash was telling us how expensive love is.

Portions of this interview appeared in
Rolling Stone, *October 16, 2003.*

Meet the Beatles

Meet the Beatles

The first interview with Paul McCartney in this section and the interview with George Harrison were conducted on consecutive days in June 1987 for an issue of *Rolling Stone* commemorating the magazine's 20th anniversary. Lining up those two interviews entailed a process that in each case very much reflected its subject.

Shortly after receiving my faxed request, McCartney's personal assistant contacted me months in advance with a date and time to meet with the former Beatle at his London office. It was organized, efficient, professional.

Meanwhile, it was difficult to find a way even to reach George Harrison. At a time when any artist remotely of his stature employed a battery of handlers, it was impossible to locate anyone who could guarantee me that they could even get my request to him. I sent letters and faxes and left messages all over New York, Los Angeles, and London. Finally, I got a call, not from the hired help, but from Harrison's wife, Olivia. "You've been very persistent," she noted. We spoke for about 20 minutes, and as a result of our conversation, I was able to break the news in *Rolling Stone* that Harrison was working on a new album that would become *Cloud Nine*. Olivia explained that George was interested in the possibility of an interview and that I should stay in touch as my deadline approached. No commitment, though. I did stay in touch with her, eventually explaining that I would be coming to London to talk to McCartney. I was to call again after I'd spoken to him.

McCartney was perfectly engaging during our interview. I'd gotten off on the wrong foot by asking for a turkey sandwich when he was making arrangements for lunch – vegetarian food only, please – but things relaxed after that. He had a jukebox in his office that was playing Elvis Presley; he politely offered to turn the volume down when he noticed my worried glances toward my tape recorder. Our conversation lasted about an hour, and I found his comments about John Lennon especially candid and moving. His old friend had been dead for almost seven years at this point, and McCartney still seemed to be struggling to determine the meaning of their relationship – how so much had been good about it and how it had gone so wrong.

When I got back to my hotel after finishing with McCartney, I called Olivia again. Harrison had still not agreed to an interview at this point, and my instructions were to stay in London until he did – or didn't. She said she would call me the following morning, a Saturday. In those pre-cellphone days, that meant staying in my room until I heard from her. I remember taking a shower and leaving the door of the bathroom open so I could hear the phone ring, which it finally did.

"George will be free this afternoon, so if you can make your way out here, he'd be happy to speak with you then," she said. I got the train directions to Henley-on-Thames, the suburb outside London where they lived, and prepared to set off. (Later that day, Harrison remarked, with characteristic wryness, that he was surprised that the ever-frugal *Rolling Stone* didn't spring for a car service to take me there and back. Clearly, he had never worked as a journalist.)

I arrived at Henley at a lovely, leafy train stop, and the other passengers either headed for their cars or met family members and friends. Olivia had told me that someone would be picking me up, so I stood on the platform looking around for my ride. When everyone else had left, I resigned myself to sorting out my British coins to make yet another call to Olivia. Then I heard a voice behind me say, "You look like the only person here who might be from New York." I turned around and there, smiling, stood George Harrison.

Partly because he had always been such a reclusive, mysterious figure, it was a little shocking to see him in the flesh. He hadn't spoken to *Rolling Stone* in 13 years; really, he'd done very few interviews of any kind during that period. Moments later, I was lying in the low passenger seat of his black Ferrari 275 GTB as he drove me to his Friar Park estate. As he drove – unnecessarily fast, his fondness for racing cars much in evidence – he glanced over at me. "So, I understand you spoke to Paul yesterday. How is he doing?" So this is what's become of the Beatles, I thought: George Harrison has to ask *me* how Paul McCartney is doing.

I explained that Paul seemed to be doing pretty well. I also told him that, while McCartney had been friendly, it had been hard for me to get control of the interview. I don't know if McCartney was simply used to people being stunned into silence around him, but he was so garrulous that I had to assert myself to get to ask my questions.

Harrison was quiet after I said that, and then looked over and flashed a sly smile. I thought of the scene in *Let It Be* where Harrison bridles at McCartney's bossiness as he's attempting to play a guitar part on one of McCartney's songs. Harrison snaps, "I'll play whatever you want to me play, or I won't play at all if you don't want me to play. Whatever it is that will please you, I'll do it." When he smiled at me, it was as if Harrison were saying, "Well, that's what it was like. And that's why I'm asking you how Paul is doing."

As we drove through the gates at Friar Park, Harrison's spectacular mansion came into view through the trees, looking like something out of a fairy tale. He had bought the estate in 1971 from a religious order – it had most recently been used as a convent – and proceeded to restore the 120-room house and 30 acres of gardens, caverns, waterfalls, and ponds to its original surreal glory. The house and grounds had been conceptualized in the late 19th century by a famed English eccentric, Sir Frankie Crisp, whom Harrison immortalized in his song "The Ballad of Sir Frankie Crisp (Let It Roll)" on *All Things Must Pass*. On the cover of that album, Harrison sits on a lawn at Friar Park, surrounded by four gnomes, an arch reference, perhaps, to his former band. He eventually built a studio at Friar Park and, along with jam sessions with musician friends like David Gilmour and Elton John, recorded most of his solo work there.

As I gaped, Harrison pulled up at one of the guesthouses, which is where we would do our interview. A couple of months later in Los Angeles, when I had another occasion to interview him, he explained, "Incidentally, I wasn't sure how to handle that situation when you came out to Henley. You must have noticed that I took you to the lodge to do the interview. Partially, it was because the house is so weird. I don't normally do interviews at home, because it's such a distraction, this big Gothic heap. I always try to make people welcome there, but you can't help but say, 'What's this? Why is that there? What's that say?' There's all these Latin inscriptions and little carvings. It would have been like going to Disneyland: give me three coupons, and I'll show you this bit."

At the lodge, which, though much smaller than the main house, was a mansion in itself, Harrison prepared a pot of coffee, and Olivia stopped by with a plate of cookies – "*American* cookies," she emphasized, her California origins coming to the fore. Harrison and I then sat down at a wooden table in the dining room, smoked cigarettes, and talked for two hours, as the late-afternoon sky clouded over. It was stunning to hear how unsettling he had found his experience in the Beatles, in marked contrast to McCartney's much sunnier recollections.

That interview is the most distinct in my mind of any that I've done. The Beatles, after all, had changed my life. More than any other single factor, they are the reason why I do the work I do. Simply being able to speak with someone of Harrison's cultural importance was a rare enough opportunity in itself. But when you meet someone who got under your skin when you were a kid, the intensity is indescribable. As we sat there talking, so many images flooded my mind: the Beatles on "The Ed Sullivan Show," the videos they made for "Strawberry Fields" and "Penny Lane," Harrison's dark eyes staring out of so many album covers and photographs. It seemed impossible that, at one time in my life, I was sitting in my living room watching the Beatles on television and he was one of those four people on the screen, and now we were sitting at a table talking.

Meeting McCartney had been important to me, but it had been far less personal an encounter. And doing these interviews one after the other no doubt had a cumulative effect. But spending time with Harrison at Friar Park felt like admission into the inner sanctum not only of an artist I greatly admired, but into one of the sources of my own life's journey. It was quite overpowering.

On that day, out of pure necessity, I created the internal mantra that I repeat to myself whenever I'm interviewing someone and in danger of losing my focus because my emotions are threatening to overwhelm me. "Get excited later," I tell myself – meaning, get excited when the story is in the magazine. For now, focus, concentrate, and do your work.

As the afternoon progressed, the room darkened and filled with the smoke from our cigarettes. Sharing those smokes seemed like such a bond of intimacy then; the lung cancer that eventually killed Harrison has needless to say complicated that memory. The major impression Harrison left with me that day was of the depth of his spiritual conviction. "The danger is when you become attached too possessively to each other, even to your own body," Harrison told me, "or to your wealth, your motorcars, your fame, your fortune. The idea is to be unattached to it, but still experience it. It's all part of life's experiences. The only God we need is within ourselves."

I interviewed McCartney again more than 14 years later, this time in New York shortly after the September 11 terrorist attacks. Interviewing one of your idols a second time can be a bit of a letdown. The first encounter seems like a dream; the second, however special, like a terrestrial event. I was very conscious of the time that had passed in both our lives.

Still, the circumstances of this meeting rendered it compelling in its own way. The specific introduction to that interview provides the full context, but I will say that I was deeply moved by how visible McCartney made himself in New York during those devastating weeks, clearly in an effort to lift the city's spirits. The role suited him well and endeared him to me. "Take a sad song, and make it better," indeed.

Finally, the 20th anniversary of John Lennon's death provided the occasion for my interview with Phil Spector about his extensive work with Lennon – as well as with Harrison and, on *Let It Be*, the Beatles themselves. (McCartney had not yet rather churlishly remade *Let It Be* according to his own specifications.) Once again, the introduction to that interview provides the essential background, except for one chilling detail. The house in which it was conducted became the scene three years later of the shooting death of a 40-year-old woman, for which Spector was arrested for murder.

Paul McCartney, 1987

"I always idolized John"

With the release of the Beatles CDs and the 20th anniversary of Sgt. Pepper's Lonely Hearts Club Band, *everyone is getting to meet the Beatles again this year. You, in particular, seemed to get involved in all the hoopla surrounding the anniversary. Why?*

It's reawakened interest, that's the nice thing. What happened early this year was: I often travel into London – it takes about two hours. So I'm looking for cassettes to play, and I said to the guy who drives me, "For coming home tonight, get [the Beach Boys'] *Pet Sounds* and *Sgt. Pepper*, and we'll play them in that order on the way back." So we did, and it was a blast.

I really love the *Pet Sounds* album – it was my inspiration for making *Sgt. Pepper*, actually. And then we went right into *Sgt. Pepper*. And, I mean, I really loved it. This is before the fuss about "20 years ago."

What impressed you about Sgt. Pepper*?*

When I heard the first side of it this time, I thought it had finished. There was enough on the first side for a whole album. And then it flips over and you've got "Day in the Life" to come. So without boasting too heavily, I really thought it was a great album.

When you started out, no one was thinking about 20th anniversaries. The general assumption about rock bands was that you would make records for a few years, then disappear.

That was what we thought. You see old interviews with us now, and Ringo says, "Well, you know, I might get lucky and have a string of hairdressing salons." That was the apex of his vision at the time. And John and I are talking nervously: "There might be 10 years in this." Remember, we were 18 – 20, maybe – saying this. We couldn't see playing rock 'n' roll beyond 30. Of course, by the time we were 30, it was still all happening.

John and I knew we were writing good songs. Not in a conceited way, but you had to be an idiot to listen to what we were writing and not say, "Hey, man, this is good." So then the vision started to push forward a bit. We started to think, "Well, wait a minute, we could even do well in America," which was unheard of for a British act.

That's certainly changed enormously. Before the Beatles, the British music scene didn't exist, as far as the rest of the world was concerned.

Originally, we'd seen our top stars here go and be third on the bill to people like Frankie Avalon in America. We all thought, "God, I thought he was bigger than Frankie Avalon." People like Cliff Richard. He was *huge* over here; he was like Elvis.

One of the cheekiest things we ever did – we said to Brian Epstein, "We're not going to America till we've got a Number One record," because we knew that would make the difference. We didn't go in like all the other British acts.

Luckily, we didn't know what America was – we just knew our dream of it – or we probably would have been too intimidated. In fact, when John made his "We're more popular than Jesus" remark, that was the first time we started to see the power that could turn against us. We'd very innocently assumed everything would go with us. I'll never forget the face of a little blond kid, who must have been about 11 or 12, *screaming*. If there hadn't been a window on that bus, I swear to God he would have…he was fired up with the Lord.

What motivated you in the early days?

Basically, we were trying to get out of the sticks, like anyone to this day. That's why a lot of guys joined the service, because there's nothing else, man. It was either the service or music. In our case, national service – as we called it – had finished, almost unbelievably. It was like Moses and the sea opening. The Beatles were looking at being broken up like the Everlys, like Elvis, like everyone. And I don't know what happened, but the heavens just opened up, and God said, "No more national service. These boys need a break."

In fact, for me, it was *almost* – I do stress *almost*, because it wasn't really – a disappointment. Because our elder brothers – not my elder brothers, elder brothers of friends, George's elder brothers – had been in the service and had come back tanned and grown up. They looked like real men; they'd gone away kids. In the recesses of my mind, I didn't mind this idea. I thought, "I'll come back a man – and tanned!"

But as I said, we didn't have to do this national service. So we were just trying to get out of the sticks and become famous – all the normal aims of why anyone had ever entered show business.

In the early days, the Beatles never seemed particularly arty.

Once we'd established a certain commercial platform, we started to gather the more artistic side of it. John had been to art school. I'd been to kind of sixth-form grammar school. George had been to grammar school. Ringo hadn't, but he didn't need education. He'd been educated in life – the university of life, as he put it. We were a cut above a lot of the other groups in a way. Art school – it's such a good breeding ground for that kind of attitude. You know a little about architecture, a little bit about drawing. Little things that elevate your taste. You might go and see a play, for instance, which some guys would just *never* do.

We were in Hamburg once. We were in the dressing room. I'd been sent a volume of Yevtushenko poetry by a girlfriend. It was rather cool, all very beatnik of us. And there was a sax player with one of the other groups who was a bit more...*down to earth*, let's say. And he came into the dressing room, and we all fell in on this scam where I picked up the Yevtushenko. I can't remember any of it now, but it was [*strikes an intense pose and begins intoning*], "Yea, morning shall not be so bright, lest ye look over the..." And I'm doing this *seriously*. The rest of the group's like Rodin's *Thinker*. They're all going, "*Um-hmm, um-hmm.* Yeah. *Hmmm*." And this sax player starts creeping round, unpacking his sax, like [*whispering*], "Sorry to interrupt you." We could put people on like that.

You see, John was actually a bit middle-class. He had read the collected works of Winston Churchill. I'd never met anyone who read that kind of stuff. He was actually the only guy I've ever known to this *day* whose auntie gave him a hundred pounds on his birthday. Which was, what, $300? Now, do you know a guy to this *day* who was given in his hand 300 smackers? I don't. I'd *still* be pleased with that, I really would.

I think that's where your artiness came from. Obviously, it manifested itself later when John met Yoko and truly wanted to follow that art-school path. I think that's why he had to clear the decks of the Beatles.

George Martin said at one point, "Even Brian Epstein and I were outside that particular thing of the four of them versus the world." Were there times when the four of you felt you were the only people who could really understand what was happening to you?

When we actually got in that limo, big blacked-out windows, there were really only ever four of us in the back of that car. And what went on then, that was the real thing. That was where we drew our strength from. We were able to withdraw into this private world of our own. And it was rather a good thing, really. Someone said to me, "Oh, God, it's so strange, isn't it, when those things break up. How can it be so nasty?"

It's nasty for precisely that reason.

It's just like divorce. It's that you were so close and so in love that if anyone decides to start talking dirty, great, then Pandora's box is open. That's what happened with us. In the end, it was like, "Oh, you want to know the truth about him? Right, I'll tell you." One good thing, I'm glad I never answered a lot of John's stuff. I thought, "No, I can't handle a big battle in the media with John." Part of it was that I knew he'd do me in.

It was as if John were trying to exorcise the Beatles by focusing on the things that were wrong.

An exorcism, in one way, is what it was. A clearing of the decks of us to give space to his and Yoko's thing.

Obviously, I go over this ground in my mind. I was one of the biggest friends in his life, one of the closest people to him. I can't claim to be the *closest*, although it's possible. It's contentious, but I wouldn't...I don't *need* that credit. But I was certainly among the three or four people who were closest to him in his *life*, I would have thought, and obviously it was very hurtful.

Actually, it was really nice after John died. Yoko was quite kind in telling me that he did really love me, because it had looked like he didn't.

In a recent court case, an affidavit emerged in which John suggested that the Beatles were thinking of performing together for a movie to be called The Long and Winding Road.

It was always a slight possibility, but we never really got to the point where the four of us knew of it as a concrete possibility. I think he thought, "Well, I might do it." I know the three of them did play together once, maybe on [Harry Nilsson's] *Pussy Cats*. They jammed together, and I remember, I think it was John who said to me, "Man, it was great. We're a great band." Because that was the great thing about the Beatles; we really were a great band. I mean, *really*. I know now from playing with other people that it's not always you can sit down and actually get in a groove. With the Beatles, it nearly always was. We could sit down and do any old piece of crap, and we'd generally hit a groove. And that is something you cannot buy.

You got out from under the Beatles' juggernaut by making a very modest, homemade album – McCartney *– as your first solo record.*

That was my solution to it, and it was a very personal solution. In fact, the day the Beatles broke up, that was the final argument. Allen Klein [the band's manager] had met the evening before with John. Allen wanted to do a new Capitol deal, but he knew the group was breaking up, so he wanted to get in with this deal real quick. The night before, John had told Allen he was quitting, and Allen had said, "Don't tell them until after they sign the new contract." When we came to the meeting, we started talking about the future of the group, not knowing that there wasn't to be any future to this group.

Is this when you suggested that the Beatles do a club tour?

That simple, let's-get-rid-of-the-pressure approach was my answer to it all. Before I did *McCartney*, I said, "Let's do that with the Beatles." That goofed. I said, "I think we should get rid of all this big pressure and play little clubs and get back to our roots. I think we'll find ourselves again that way." And John said – his very words were – "I think you're daft." Then he said, "In fact, I wasn't going to tell you till after the Capitol thing – I've quit the group." Our jaws – me, Ringo, George, and Linda, because I think she happened to be nearby – dropped, and we sort of went a little pale. "Uh, what do you mean?" And he said, "I'm quitting the group, and I wasn't going to tell you till after this thing, because Allen asked me not to... But it's a rather good feeling, it's sort of like a divorce." So that was the end of the group.

What happened then?

We were all trying to keep it quiet. Then three or four months later, I came out with the *McCartney* album, and somebody said, "You've got to see the press." I said I couldn't handle it, so I decided to do it in the form of a question-and-answer thing, where the guy from the Beatles' office just wrote me some arbitrary questions. He just slipped in, "Do you plan to carry on with the Beatles?" Just casually slipped it in. There were casual little questions like, "What do you think of John and Yoko's stuff?" I had to answer honestly that I didn't like it. It was a nasty little period, all of that. Looking at it now, it seems very callous.

I actually have a talent for that. It's like when John was killed, somebody stuck a microphone [in my face] and said, "What do you think about it?" I said, "It's a drag." But I said, "It's a *dra-a-a-ag*," and meant it with every inch of melancholy I could muster. When you put that in print, it says, "McCartney in London today, when asked for a comment on his dead friend, said, 'It's a drag.' " It seemed a very flippant comment to make.

Because you didn't deliver an instant eulogy?

Exactly. In fact, I really got pissed off at all the pundits that evening who did just that. All these people who were supposed to have been John's friends. The rest of us were just gaga with grief and sitting at home crying, watching all the news and watching all the telly, watching anything we could gather, and listening to every bit of radio. It was just like Kennedy dying, only worse for us, and that had been bad enough.

Then the pundits come on, "Yes, so John was the bright one in the group. Yes, he was a very clever one. Oh, well, he'll be sorely missed, and he was a great so-and-so." I said, "Bloody hell, how can you muster such glib things?" But they were the ones who came off good, because they said *suitably meaningful things*. I was the idiot who said, "It's a drag."

Anyway, looking back on it with John, you know, he was a really great guy. I always idolized him. We always did, the group. I don't know if the others will tell you that, but he was our idol. He was like our own little Elvis in the group. Not because of his good looks or his singing – although he was a great singer – just for his personality. He was just a great guy. Very forceful guy. Very funny guy. Very bright and always someone for us to look up to.

What I cherish is that, aside from that venomous period. I know that I sat there and we wrote "Love Me Do." And I sat there and we wrote "I Want to Hold Your Hand," and we screwed around with the lyrics. I know he brought in "In My Life," and he had the first verse and the rest of it wasn't written. And I know he brought in "Norwegian Wood," and we developed the idea of setting the place on fire. I remember sitting down doing "Help," and then I'd come in with "When I was younger, so much younger than today," and he'd have the main melody, and I'd do the countermelody. I can remember where we were, how it was and just magic moments where I'd be writing, "It's getting better all the time," and John would be sitting there – "It can't get much worse." Those moments. That's what I cherish. No one can take that away from me.

In terms of your regard for the Beatles' work, how did you feel about the use of "Revolution" in a Nike commercial?

I was not pleased with that, because the Beatles never did any of that. We were offered everything. We were offered Disney, Coca-Cola, the hugest deals in Christendom and beyond. And we never took them, because we thought, "Nah, kind of cheapens it." It cheapens you to go on a commercial, I think.

The trouble is that our management at the time was not farsighted enough. Our management never had enough foresight to say, "We'll renegotiate the record contract after three years." When you did a deal in those days, it was, like, 15 years. We said, "We won't be *alive* then. What do you mean?" The year 1987 was *forever* away. But, of course, you stick around long enough and it arrives.

Since you've worked with Michael Jackson, and he owns rights to most of the Beatles song catalog, would you say something to him about it?

I really would not know what to say. I mean, we worked, and we had a nice relationship, but Michael's the kind of guy who picks brains. We worked together. I don't think he'd even had the cosmetics then. In fact, I know he hadn't, because I've got photos of me and him at our house, and he looks quite different. He's had a lot of facial surgery since then, as I think most people on the planet know. He actually told me he was going to a religious retreat – and I believed him. But he came out of that religious retreat with a smashing new nose. The power of prayer, I guess.

The thing is, we did talk. I gave him a lot of advice, and you know, a fish gets caught by opening its mouth. I advised him to go into publishing. As a joke, he looked at me and he said [*imitates Michael Jackson's voice*], "I'm going to buy your songs one day." And I just said, "Great, good joke." I really treated it as a joke. And I just couldn't believe it, you know, someone rang me up one day and said, "Michael's bought your…" "What?!"

So you know, I haven't spoken to him since. I think he thinks it's just business. It's slightly dodgy to do things like that – to be someone's friend and then to buy the rug they're standing on.

Couldn't you have bid on the Beatles songs at that time?

Well, there was a complication with me and Yoko. Yoko thought she could get it for a bargain-basement price. I imagined a price halfway – which is what it was going for – between what she imagined and what Michael Jackson finally paid for it. I said that she and I ought to go for it. And she said, "I can get it for…," and named a very low figure. And I said, "Oh, really?" I knew it was wrong, but what could I say? I couldn't say, "No, you are wrong." I just had to say, "Oh, OK," you know? So it kind of stalled at that point. And then, without really telling anyone, he just… The joke came true.

Are you bracing yourself for other commercials?

What the hell? You know, there was a point in the Beatles where you just had to let it all go. EMI owns all the recordings anyway – we don't own any of it. Northern Songs [which published much of the Beatles' music] owned all the songs. We made *fortunes* for all those people, but they never came back and said, "We think we'd like to give you back half of 'Yesterday.'" Seriously, why wouldn't they do something like that after you'd earned so much for them?

The point about Northern Songs was that we were always cheated, and I don't care who likes or dislikes that statement. From the word go, our songs were always "Lennon-McCartney." That could have been altered somewhere along the line, but it never was. Even a totally self-written song like "Yesterday," which John had nothing to do with – only I played on the record, it was me and a string quartet – there you start to think, "Well, maybe I've got a tiny right to…*something*." Civil rights, maybe, or…human rights? Isn't there one piddling little right I can claim? But there isn't. I don't have any rights whatsoever. I just get a tip. But I get a handsome tip, and I have to be happy with that.

It does have strange little quirks. For instance, there's one that has just come up. In publishing in America, you have renewals; we don't have them here. After 27 years – and believe it or not, 27 years for some of the Beatles songs is imminent – you as a composer get the chance either to go with this publisher again or not. John's renewals will all be coming up, and Yoko can get the rights back. But my renewals don't come up, because I'm still alive and we signed our renewal rights away for life. So, pretty soon, I think Yoko will own more of "Yesterday" than I will.

Are you talking with Yoko about it?

Like, what can I say? All I can say is, "You'll have more of our songs than I do pretty soon." The reason I mentioned "Yesterday" is because I *wrote* that song, but it was our deal that we'd split everything down the middle. So that is one particular case in point, and it just happens to be the most covered song in history.

But you know what? Having said all this – it's great to get it off my chest – I really don't care. I've done great, and it's just churlish to… I mean, it niggles a little bit, but generally I just think, "Aw, come on, I was part of this fabulous thing. I wrote those things. I was there with John while we did them all." So what the hell? I gave a bit too much of it away. Big deal. I can live with that and still sleep at night.

Well, in terms of your relationship with George and Ringo at this point, did it cross your mind to play the Prince's Trust concert with them earlier this year?

I was asked to do that, but then they [George and Ringo] were asked to do Live Aid, and they decided not to do it. You know, we keep getting asked. It really is funny, it's a mood thing. I was going to do Live Aid, and [Bob] Geldof really wanted them there, and they were asked, but they declined. I don't know why.

On this one, it was just all too convenient for me to pop up. The trouble is, of course, if we just pop up, it's not just three guys playing, it's the *Beatles reunion*. I'd like to play with the other guys. But only for music. Just quietly sometime.

Is there a possibility you might tour again?

To do that, for me, the criterion is to have new material that I like. You can go and do a hits tour, but I'd like to be current as well as "Remember this." So I'm working on that. Then the other thing's a band; I'd have to have some musicians that I could be confident with.

And then, who knows? The guys might feel like playing. You never know, the Beatles might feel like getting back together. But I mean, we'd do it very privately. If we were ever to do it, we'd just have to record some tracks, really. If anything good came out of it, there'd be no one more pleased than myself. "Great, *almost* some new Beatles music." Although, obviously, you can never re-form the Beatles, because of John. I hate people who ask that – just blindly like that. It's a bit idiotic. They always suggest we get Julian in, but it's not the same. But the three guys – the other two guys and myself – you think of it, we are the basic rhythm section. It is there: bass, drums, and guitar. So it's interesting that that still exists.

It's like the Randy Newman lyric: "If things loosen up." One day, he'll be president if things loosen up, you know? That's what I'm waiting for: If things loosen up, we might play together again. I'm in no hurry, but I'd like it. They're good guys, you know. I like them. Obviously you drift apart, with George into films, Ringo into this and that, doing stuff. But it would be nice. It would be fun. I think we've got to leave it there.

This interview originally appeared in
Rolling Stone*, November 5, 1987.*

George Harrison

"Those years did seem to be a thousand years long"

The Beatles are virtually synonymous with the '60s. Do you share the perception that that decade was special?

That's a bit presumptuous. The Beatles did have a quickened and heightened experience, and maybe we packed more into those years, but I think it just happened to be the '60s.

At what point did it become clear to you that the impact of the Beatles had become much greater than you ever could have conceived?

Well, it's all relative, because our original intention was to be in a band as opposed to having a job. The goals were quite small, really. Then, after a few records in Europe, this mania thing started happening. The Americans caught on. I suppose after that it started taking on this sociological – or whatever you would call it – meaning. And then we were just as caught up in it as everyone else.

Was there a specific moment when it became clear to you that people were looking at the Beatles not only as a band but as a way of making sense of their lives?

It all came in small doses, because the fans of anybody – just like we were fans of Elvis and Eddie Cochran and Chuck Berry – tend to want to be like those role models. You want to have a guitar that looks like theirs or a hairstyle like theirs, or you want to be able to strut around like them. As we began having hits in England, the press were catching on to how we looked, which was changing the image of youth, I suppose. It just gathered momentum. For me, 1966 was the time when the whole world opened up and had a greater meaning. But that was a direct result of LSD.

How did taking LSD affect you?

It was like opening the door, really, and before, you didn't even know there was a door there. It just opened up this whole other consciousness, even if it was down to, like Aldous Huxley said, the wonderful folds in his gray flannel trousers. From that smaller concept to the fact that every blade of grass and every grain of sand is just throbbing and pulsating.

Did it make you feel that your life could be very different from what it was?

Yeah, but that too presented a problem as well, because then the feeling began in me of it's all well and good being popular and being in demand, but, you know, it's *ridiculous*, really. From then on, I didn't enjoy fame. That's when the novelty disappeared – around 1966 – and then it became hard work.

It seems as if that time was incredibly compressed. Did you feel that sense of compression?

That year – you could say any year from, 1965 up to the '70s – it was, like, I can't believe we did so much, you know? But those years did seem to be a thousand years long. Time just got elongated. Sometimes I felt like I was a thousand years old.

Was it at that point that your identity as one of the Beatles began to get oppressive for you?

Yeah, absolutely. Again, with the realization that came about after the lysergic. It has a humbling power, that stuff. And the ego – to be able to deal with these people thinking you were some wonderful thing – it was difficult to come to terms with. I was feeling like *nothing*. Even now I look back and see, relative to a lot of other groups, the Beatles did have something. But it's a bit too much to accept that we're supposedly the designers of this incredible change. In many ways, we were just swept along with everybody else.

Was the decision to stop touring in 1966 part of your reexamining your lives as Beatles?

Well, I wanted to stop touring after about '65, actually, because I was getting very nervous. They kept planning these ticker-tape parades through San Francisco, and I was saying, "I absolutely don't want to do that." There was that movie *The Manchurian Candidate* [about a war hero who returns home programmed for political assassination]. I think in history you can see that when people get too big, something like that can very easily happen. Although at the time, it was prior to all this terrorism. We used to fly in and out of Beirut and all them places. You would never *dream* of going on tour now in some of the places we went. Especially with only two road managers: one guy to look after the equipment, which was three little amplifiers, three guitars, and a set of drums, and one guy who looked after us and our suits.

During that last tour, in 1966, there were also problems in the Philippines after the band failed to attend the reception arranged for it at the presidential palace by Imelda Marcos.

I'm very pleased to say that we never went to see those awful Marcoses, in spite of the fact that they tried to kill us. They sent people out there to beat us up. They set the whole of Manila on us. I don't know if you know the full story, but after half the people with us were beaten up, we finally got on the plane. Then they wouldn't let the plane take off. We sat there for…it seemed like an eternity. Finally, they let the plane go. But they took all the money that we earned at the concerts from us.

It seems that various macabre things happened with regard to the Beatles. Obviously, later on the most tragic aspect of it would be the murder of John Lennon. But things like the "Paul is dead" rumors and the "Helter Skelter" business with Charles Manson – the Beatles were linked to the underbelly of American culture.

Exactly. I was maybe just sensing what was happening or about to happen in the '60s. We were flying into race riots in Chicago. We flew into this situation where the French and the English in Montreal were having a big fight, and Ringo was threatened. It was like, "We're going to kill him." Firecrackers would go off during the show, and we'd look around and think one of us had got it. Everywhere we went it was like that. We'd go to Japan, where the students were rioting, and there'd be Beatlemania all mixed up with the politics.

Did your interest in transcendental meditation and other spiritual disciplines help you?

All the panic and the pressure? Yeah! Absolutely, I think. Although up until LSD, I never realized that there was anything beyond this state of consciousness. But all the pressure was such that, like the man said, "There must be some way out of here."

For me, it was definitely LSD. The first time I took it, it just blew everything away. I had such an overwhelming feeling of well-being, that there was a God, and I could see him in every blade of grass. It was like gaining hundreds of years of experience within 12 hours. It changed me, and there was no way back to what I was before.

Did you feel relief when the Beatles broke up?

There was a certain amount of relief after that Candlestick Park concert. Before one of the last numbers, we set up this camera – I think it had a fisheye, a very wide-angle lens. We set it on the amplifier, and Ringo came out of the drums, and we stood with our backs to the audience and posed for a photograph, because we knew that was the last show.

Another event that seems significant from the perspective of 1987 is the Concert for Bangladesh. It helped to inspire Live Aid and similar benefit concerts.

There were a lot of small charity shows, particularly in England. But Bangladesh was the first thing I'd ever heard of that was a big issue. Although it was many years later that Band Aid came about, it was definitely something that needed doing.

Were you asked to do Live Aid?

No. I was away at the time, and I got back to England the day before the concert. When I arrived at Heathrow Airport, the press who were stationed there said to me, "Are you doing this concert, George?" I said I didn't know anything about it. I don't know where I'd been, in the South Pacific or somewhere for months.

Then I read something about it in the papers saying, "The Beatles are getting together." There were a few phone calls. I think Bob Geldof phoned my office and asked if I would like to sing "Let It Be" with Paul. But that was literally, like, the day before the concert.

Well, I was jet-lagged, for a start. I saw that they had everybody in the world in on this concert, and I didn't see that it would make that much difference if I wasn't. Also, you know, I have a problem, I must admit, when people try to get the Beatles together. They're *still* suggesting it, even though John is *dead*. They still come and say, "Why don't the Beatles get together?" Well, the Beatles can't.

One of the coups of Bangladesh was Dylan's appearance, because he had done so little since his motorcycle accident in 1966. Was he initially reluctant to do Bangladesh?

He was. He never committed himself, right up until the moment he came onstage. On the night before Bangladesh, we sat in Madison Square Garden as the people were setting up the bandstand. He looked around the place and said to me, "Hey, man, you know, this isn't my scene." I'd had so many months – it seemed like a long time – of trying to get it all together, and my head was reeling with all the problems and nerves. I'd gotten so fed up with him not being committed, I said, "Look, it's not my scene, either. At least you've played on your own in front of a crowd before. I've never done that."

So he turned up the next morning, which looked positive. I had a list, sort of a running order, that I had glued on my guitar. When I got to the point where Bob was going to come on, I had "Bob" with a question mark. I looked over my shoulder to see if he was around, because if he wasn't, I would have to go on to do the next bit. And I looked around, and *he* was so nervous – he had his guitar on and his shades – he was sort of coming on, coming [*pumps his arms and shoulders*]. So I just said, "My old friend, Bob Dylan!" It was only at that moment that I knew for sure he was going to do it.

After the second show, he picked me up and hugged me and he said, "God! If only we'd done *three* shows."

That's incredible.

But he's fantastic, you know. There's not a lot of people in the world who I see from a historical point of view. Five hundred years from now, looking back in history, I think he will still be the man. Bob, he just takes the cake.

You've become nearly as reclusive as Dylan was back then. Your last solo tour was in 1974. Did anything happen on the 1974 tour that made playing in public seem like something you didn't want to do?

There was one thing that sticks in my mind. On one of the concerts – I think it was in Long Beach [California] – instead of leaving right after the show, I waited till all the audience had gone. I was just hanging around the stadium, and I watched them bulldozing. They had a bulldozer in the middle – you know that "festival seating" situation, where everybody's standing up – and they were bulldozing all the rubble left by the audience. There were *mountains* of empty bottles of gin and bourbon and tequila and brassieres and shoes and coats and trash. I mean, it was *unbelievable.*

Another thing – you know, that rock band I was in, they were some pretty heavy-duty people. We had been known in the past to smoke some reefer ourselves. But I'd go on out there, and you'd just get stoned, there was so much reefer going about.

What was your relationship with John during that period when he was living in New York?

I didn't often go to New York, but when I was in New York, I'd go see him, and he was nice. He was always enthusiastic. That period where he was cooking bread and stuff, I always got an overpowering feeling from him. Almost a feeling that he wanted to say much more than he could, or than he did. You could see it in his eyes. But it was difficult.

In what way?

Well, you'd read all these stories – and they'd keep coming all the time – about how the Beatles didn't mean a thing. That he was the only one who had a clue about anything – and the wife. There was a definite strained relationship right from the *White Album*. There was a lot of alienation between us and him. It was particularly strained because having been in a band from being kids, then suddenly we're all grown up and we've all got these other wives. That didn't exactly help. All the wives at that time really drove wedges between us. And then, after the years, when I saw John in New York, it was almost like he was crying out to tell me certain things or to renew things, relationships, but he wasn't able to, because of the situation he was in.

Did you feel the two of you might have gotten close again if he hadn't been murdered?

No, I only felt *physically* unclose to him, because we'd gone through too many things. The very first time we took LSD, John and I were together. And that experience together, and a lot of other things that happened after that, both on LSD and on the meditation trip in Rishikesh – we saw beyond each other's physical bodies, you know? That's there permanently, whether he's in a physical body or not. This is the goal anyway: to realize the spiritual side. If you can't feel the spirit of some friend who's been that close, then what chance have you got of feeling the spirit of Christ or Buddha or whoever else you may be interested in? "If your memory serves you well, we're going to meet again." I believe that.

One final thing. What's your sense about the future? Are you hopeful? Feeling positive?

In one way, I feel pessimistic. When you see the rate that the world is being demolished – people polluting the oceans and chopping down all the forests – unless somebody puts the brakes on soon, there isn't going to be anything left. There's just going to be more and more people with less and less resources. In that respect, I feel very sad. But at the same time, I have to be optimistic. Even if the whole planet blew up, you'd have to think about what happens when you die. In the end, "Life goes on within you and without you." I just have a belief that this is only one little bit, the physical world is one little bit, our planet is one little bit of the physical universe, and you can't really destroy it totally. You can destroy our planet, but the souls are going to keep on going, they'll keep on getting new bodies and going on to other planets. So in the end, it doesn't really matter.

This interview originally appeared in
Rolling Stone, *November 5, 1987.*

Paul McCartney, 2001

"That's why I always loved this group"

As Paul McCartney strolls along Manhattan's Sixth Avenue on a spectacular fall day, he leaves a trail of stunned people in his wake. Some just stop dead in their tracks and stare slack-jawed as he walks by. Some smile and nod. Others call out to him – "Hey, Paul!" – or shake his hand. Wearing sunglasses and a navy-blue V-neck sweater over a white T-shirt, with a sharp blue jacket slung over his shoulder, McCartney has a good word or a thumbs-up for everyone. He's weaving that old Beatles magic, and he knows it.

He also knows that New York needs it. He watched the Twin Towers burn on September 11 while seated in an airplane on the tarmac at Kennedy airport with his fiancée, Heather Mills. The plane never left the ground. Instead, McCartney and Mills retreated to their house on Long Island and continued to watch the devastation on TV. "There was a sense of shock being here," he says after sitting down for lunch at a restaurant on West 57th Street. "The normal ebullient mood wasn't there. It was much more somber."

About a week after the attack, McCartney and Mills quietly visited Ground Zero. "Heather and I went out to dinner," he recalls, "and when we finished, I said, 'Would you like to get a cab and see how near we can get?' So we took a cab, and we went down to Canal Street, and then we started walking. It was raining. We went up to the police lines and asked, 'Could we go down here?' A few of the guys recognized me and said, 'Well, you can come through, Paul!'

"It was that kind of spirit," he continues. "It was like, 'Good, you're down here,' and I was like, 'It's great what you're doing.' Of course, the nearer we got, the smoke was in our clothes, in our eyes. You could see all the spotlights. We just stood there, said a little prayer, and that was it. Then we went to this bar nearby, which was nearly empty; maybe a couple of rescue workers were there. I said, 'I need a stiff drink.' "

Then McCartney became determined to help revive the city, taking his cues from Mayor Rudy Giuliani. "I thought Giuliani was really good about saying, 'We've got to get back to work,' " he says. "If we don't, the terrorists achieve one of their objectives. I think he came out of this looking really good." Most prominently, McCartney headlined and helped organize the Concert for New York City, which raised more than $30 million for relief efforts. But perhaps just as important, he was a continual, visible, inspiring presence in the city, including at Yankee Stadium, where he could be seen on national television drinking Budweisers, cheering enthusiastically for the Yankees and leaping up to sing along with the chorus of "I Saw Her Standing There," which blared over the PA in his honor. "That was only my second time at Yankee Stadium," he mentions, as we walk along Sixth Avenue, adding with a wink, "though I've been to Shea Stadium a couple of times."

All that activity capped what has been a stellar year, even by the standards of a former Beatle. First of all, The *Beatles 1* went to Number One in 34 countries around the world and was one of the best-selling albums of the year. Then the double-CD Wings compilation, *Wingspan*, not only fared well commercially but served an important emotional purpose. "It was therapeutic," McCartney says, "seeing Linda in Wings. I know she wanted a record of that. Once you do that, then you do have a form of closure on it." He published a collection of his poems and lyrics called *Blackbird Singing*. And, finally, he has also just released *Driving Rain*, his first album of new songs in four years. And does anyone not know that he got engaged? No wonder, when it's said that he's had quite a year, McCartney simply responds, "Already." There are a few weeks left, after all.

You've had an amazing burst of energy this year.

Well, it all goes back to losing Linda [in 1998]. When that happened, obviously, my world collapsed. We'd been fighting a battle [with Linda's breast cancer] for about a year and a half. All our efforts, every single thing, had been to beat it. And in the end, we lost the battle. It was just staggering. Linda and I had been together for 30 years. Four kids. It was...shocking. I thought, "How the hell do I deal with this?" For about a year, I found myself crying – in all situations, anyone I met. Anyone who came over, the minute we talked about Linda, I'd say, "I'm sorry about this, I've got to cry." People had said, "Immerse yourself in work," and I said, "I don't think so." I ended up toward the end of the year doing *Run Devil Run*, the rock 'n' roll album, because Linda had wanted me to do it. That was a good jumping-off point.

You also did some work on her solo record.

That's right. Anything that was Linda-related I could just about cope with. Then, once the seasons had gone around once, I started to notice a lightening of my mood. I was coming out of my shell a little bit, because I had thought that I was going to be, like, a monk. Linda was my only love, and it was very unlikely it was going to happen again, so I thought, "I must just pull away and retire." But after a year or so, I started to think, "Maybe not." Then I met Heather, and I noticed that I liked the way she looked. I said, "Wait a minute, you're looking at other women." Immediately it was like, "Uh-oh. You can't do that." The married guilt. I beat myself up a bit about that. But I referred it all to Linda, and I started to get the message that it was OK, that she wouldn't mind.

She communicated with you?

Nothing you'd really want to go into, because it's very private, but there were strange, metaphysical occurrences that seemed to mean something. Animal noises. Bird noises. You'd ask yourself a question under the stars, and there'd be like an owl in the valley going *whoo-whoo-whoo*. Things like that. So I started going out with Heather. Started having a laugh, feeling good. "Oh, my God. Am I dating? I don't believe it. I haven't done this for 30 years! Can I do it?" And it was, "Yes, you can." I started to fall for Heather. And that was it. That reawakening brought back a lot of energy. I started to write quite a bit more, and I thought, "Ah, I'll make a new album."

Driving Rain *traces some of that emotional journey.*

But it's not obvious. I mean, someone said, "We expected it to be very somber, very serious," and I had an idea that maybe it would go that way. But I let it flow, and it didn't. Also, I hadn't had a good play in a while. When you're a musician, you do love to play, which you forget sometimes when you're doing other stuff. So it was good to just get back with a few guys and sit around and go [*moves his hands as if he's fingering a bass*] *dum-dum, dum-dum.*

You have said that you just wanted to be the bass player again.

Well, with the Beatles, I was the bass player. So it occurred to me, "What a nice, clean idea: I do bass and vocals. Let's go back to that if I'm going to make a new record." It was a bit of a release, really. I didn't have to think about much, because it's very instinctive for me.

There's a great thing about bass playing and singing. There are only a few people who do it. It's like this [*rubs his belly and pats his head*], particularly something like "Day Tripper," where I had to go [*sings the bass part*], "*dum, do-do, do-do-do, do-do, do-do-do,*" and [*sings*], "She's a big teaser / She took me half the way there." It's a very strange feeling at first. But you do it so often, you learn how.

With all the success you've enjoyed, what are your hopes for this album?

I'd like it to have the same effect on people as it has on me. You get a good feeling off it. I would like it to communicate that good feeling. It seems quite positive.

And, for that reason, very appropriate for the times.

I've approached records in millions of ways. This one was approached in a very offhand way, and I don't mean that in a bad sense. I like the result, and I believe in that approach – in life. [Painter] Franz Kline said, "Don't make so much of it," and I always liked that. That's the sort of expression I latch onto.

Of course, I'd also like the album to do well, because…I'm used to it. I'd like people to like it, on a lot of levels.

Will you be touring next year?

It's likely. I just don't know how. People are starting to talk about smaller gigs, which I like the idea of. But then you get into that vicious circle of, well, they say 5,000 people in Cleveland couldn't get in. And you go, "Oh, we should've played a bigger gig then." Then it's 20,000 couldn't get in, in New York. So it's always a trade-off against the intimacy you want, which is a little club somewhere, and people being disappointed because they couldn't get in.

But it's not a terrible problem to have. A worse problem would be, nobody shows up. [*Laughs*] So I'm definitely thinking about it. I like the idea of getting out – getting out of the house.

On another subject, there was a panic this year when a tabloid newspaper in England fabricated a quote from George Martin that George Harrison, who had been undergoing treatment for cancer, was about to die.

I spoke to George immediately after that. He said, "I suppose you're ringing about [the newspaper reports]." I said, "Not really, but I'm concerned." He said, "I just got an e-mail from George Martin, who said, 'I promise you, George, I really didn't say that. I wouldn't ever.' "

I don't really like to talk about [George's health] because I don't know enough about it. I don't really like to pry. Obviously he's had problems, and I'm not sure of the current stage of things. But every time I ring him, he's very upbeat. So I just cross my fingers and pray that things will be all right.

The Beatles 1 *collection was one of this year's biggest records. Since, unlike George and John, you never went through a phase of disparaging the Beatles, do you see this kind of success 30 years later as something of a validation?*

Like, "That's why I always loved this group?" Yeah, that's probably true. And I did always love it. Sure, you go through things – fame is very difficult to deal with. I think George once said, "It cost me my nervous system," and I know exactly what he means. But I try and rationalize things – that's my way. You wanted to get famous and rich. What did you expect? You expected it to be the same as being infamous and poor? [*Laughs*] So I accepted it.

I was thinking the other day about the achievements people want in life. It was sort of shocking as I started to think of some of mine. Let's say, imagine being the guy who wrote with John Lennon? Jesus Christ, I mean, what about that? The guy.

Let's just go over this again: "The guy that wrote with John Lennon." Are you kidding? I have such an admiration for John, like most people. But to be the guy who wrote with him – well, that's enough. Right there, you could retire, and go, "Jesus, I had a fantastic life. Take me, Lord."

There was a major televised John Lennon tribute show this year. Were you asked to participate?

No. But I do get asked to appear in a lot of John tributes. It's difficult for me. I don't have the best relationship with Yoko and, obviously, to be in those things…it would help. So I generally pass and just wish everyone well.

It's really a pointed affair for me. For most people, it's great. They love John. You go, you play a John song, it's beautiful. If I was anyone else, I'd do it. It just feels difficult.

It seemed that after John died, people often felt that part of praising him meant putting you down.

The minute John died, there started to be a revisionism. There were some strange quotes, like, "John was the only one in the Beatles." Or "Paul booked the studio" – I don't want to get into who said what, but that was attributed to someone who very much knew better. "John was the Mozart; Paul was the Salieri." Like John was the real genius, and I was just the guy who sang "Yesterday" – and I got lucky to do that. Even with John in that song ["How Do You Sleep?"], when he sang, "The only thing you done was "Yesterday.'"

I tried to ignore it, but it built into an insecurity. People would say, "Paul, people know." I said, "Yeah, but what about 50 years in the future?" If this revisionism gets around, a lot of kids will be like, "Did he have a group before Wings?" There may come a time when people won't know.

It was only after we'd stopped working together it even reared its ugly head – the whole idea of who wrote what. You remember the story of John getting pissed because he went into a restaurant and the pianist started up with "Yesterday"? Really, John once said to me, "I wonder how I'll be remembered." I was kind of shocked. I said, "I'll tell you how you'll be remembered: You're great. But you won't be here. It won't matter to you, so don't worry about it." And I thought, "Why'd he get into that?" But now I understand.

But what can you do about it?

I apologize in advance for this – this is a crazy little pet peeve of mine. I'll try and keep it short. "Lennon-McCartney" was always cool. I like it. It's a logo. But what was happening was, for example, my poem "Blackbird" appeared in an anthology, and it appeared as "By John Lennon and Paul McCartney." I mean, wait a minute, I wrote that.

Sort of like "Yesterday," which none of the other Beatles even performed on.

Same thing, but this was being reproduced as a poem. I thought, "That should really say, 'Written by Paul McCartney.' Or at the very worst, 'Written by Paul McCartney and John Lennon.' I should get front billing." So when the [Beatles] *Anthology* came out, after 30 years of always having John's name in front, I thought it should say, " 'Yesterday,' by Paul McCartney and John Lennon." So I rang up and asked Yoko. This is when Linda and I were going through our real horror times. I rang Yoko up and said, "Couldn't I, on the *Anthology*, just on this one song, put my name in front? Could we put, 'Written by Paul McCartney and John Lennon'? It would be a great favor to me." Linda actually rang her and said, "Do this as a favor." Well, it became a major issue – and listen to me talking about it, like I'm trying to make it little. But in the end, she just said no.

After that, I was in Rome, late at night in a bar. And there was a pianist's fake book in the corner. Well, I have to go and look at it, don't I? I open the page, and it says, "'Hey Jude,' written by John Lennon." There was no room on the page, and "Paul McCartney" got left off. That was the killer blow. It was like, "*Awwrrrgh!*" So I thought, "This is what's going to happen." This is what I meant when people said, "Don't worry, Paul."

So I say: Put me first, man. But, listen, I'm in deep therapy. I'm seeing a therapist every three hours about this. [*Laughs*] No, no, seriously, I do think it would be not a bad thing for me to be allowed to do that – and only when our names are used in full. When it's Lennon-McCartney, John should always come first.

How would that ever happen?

Yoko has to say, "What a good idea, Paul."

That's unlikely.

It's *slightly* unlikely. [*Laughs*] But this is why we don't have a great relationship. That, and the fact that Linda rang her personally during the height of her chemo shit and asked her, and Yoko said, "That's never going to happen."

And, you know, I don't have a hard time with her. She's a good lady. She's a great artist. [*Looks away and laughs*] I should get off it – there are more important things in the world. But it's become sour, and it never was when John and I worked together. We were the two guys who knew it didn't matter. So, that's enough gossip for one day, loves!

You talked about possibly touring. What else is coming up for you next year?

I'm getting married.

You've set a date?

Well, we did, but we didn't *tell* a date. [*Laughs*] We just said to people, sometime next year. So that's the main thing for me. You know, my nephew's wedding was a week after the bombing, which actually worked out fine because people wanted a release. You had to do the "in these difficult times…" speech, but after that, everyone was, "Ah, let's try and enjoy ourselves." Which is one of my big philosophies.

Years ago when the Beatles were with the Maharishi, he gave us a book. He wrote in mine, "Radiate bliss consciousness." I thought, "That's pretty good." And then he just put, "Enjoy." I took that to heart. If at the end of each day – or most days – you could say, "That was a good one," it builds into a reasonably successful life. So I do try and enjoy, even when things are looking grim, as they have been for the last month. If you can, try and enjoy it, because it's moving by fast. And in the meantime…[*laughs*], listen to my record!

This interview originally appeared in
Rolling Stone, *December 6, 2001.*

Phil Spector on John Lennon

"We were like brothers"

The gates open, and the long, black limousine I'm riding in moves along a driveway and deposits me in front of a stone staircase that ascends a steep hill. I get out, and a genial, well-dressed security guard informs me, "Mr. Spector would like you to walk up these steps through the front door." I eye the 88 steps and ask, "Is that the only way into the house?" "No," the guard says, "this driveway goes straight up to the back door. But Mr. Spector likes for people to enter through the front on their first visit."

I knew that getting one of Phil Spector's rare interviews would involve hurdles, but I didn't expect them to be physical. With former Beatles business manager Allen Klein serving as intermediary, Spector had agreed to speak about the making of *Imagine* when the remastered album came out earlier this year. In faxes printed in Gothic type, Spector insisted that the interview be done in person at his lavish home – which he typically refers to as "the castle" in aptly named Alhambra, California, northeast of Los Angeles.

Spector had decided to talk because of his friendship and long working relationship with John Lennon. An inductee into the Rock and Roll Hall of Fame himself, Spector had, of course, essentially invented the idea of the producer as auteur, the musical equivalent of the director in film, in the late '50s and early '60s. His signature is the monolithic – with a very definite emphasis on the "mono" – Wall of Sound, a grand architecture of guitars, strings, horns, keyboards, and percussion that combines breathtaking lyricism with Wagnerian power. Delivered by rapturously emotional singers like Ronnie Spector (with whom Phil would experience a tumultuous marriage and divorce), Darlene Love, and Tina Turner, these "little symphonies for the kids" – like the Ronettes' "Be My Baby," the Crystals' "He's a Rebel," and Turner's

"River Deep, Mountain High" – are, to say the absolute least, among the most magnificent singles ever made.

But while Spector's groundbreaking early achievements are universally known, far fewer people are aware of his extensive work with Lennon and the Beatles, who numbered among Spector's most ardent admirers. As Lennon searched for new creative partners in the waning days of the Beatles, he enlisted Spector to produce "Instant Karma! (We All Shine On)," a rhythmically driving single that shot to Number Three in America in 1970. Spector also was on board for Lennon's "Power to the People" a year later. More dramatically, between those two hits, Spector stepped in to assemble the *Let It Be* album, which had been left in utter disarray as the Beatles splintered, and none of them could face the blood on the tracks.

For Spector and Lennon, however, the end of the Beatles in 1970 signaled a vital new beginning. In that same year, Spector co-produced Lennon's ravaging solo debut, *Plastic Ono Band*, with Lennon and Yoko Ono. It is a stark deconstruction of the Wall of Sound that rubs as frighteningly raw today as it did 30 years ago. The trio also co-produced the much lovelier *Imagine*, Lennon's most successful solo album, in 1971. Lennon and Ono teamed up with Spector again on *Some Time in New York City* (1972), and during Lennon's "lost weekend" separation from Ono, Lennon and Spector collaborated on *Rock 'n' Roll* (1975), a raucous collection of cover versions of rock classics. (On top of all that, Spector also worked with George Harrison on his solo debut, *All Things Must Pass*, as well as *The Concert for Bangla Desh*.) Also, in a touching echo of *A Christmas Gift for You*, the legendary album he made in 1963, Spector co-produced "Happy Xmas (War Is Over)" with John and Yoko in 1972.

Tales of mayhem trail Spector; the rumor persists, for example, that during the drug-and-drink-fueled L.A. sessions for *Rock 'n' Roll*, he fired a gun in the studio. But today, once I have climbed those 88 steps, he is gentle and friendly, surprisingly eager to talk not only about *Imagine* but also about the rest of his work with Lennon and the Beatles. Dressed in black and playfully aware of his reputation for mystery, Spector takes a seat, looks at me through purple-tinted shades, and smiles. "What would you like to know?"

Can you talk about the genesis of Imagine*?*

We had already done *Plastic Ono Band*, and it was quite apparent it was time to make a commercial album. *Imagine* took only six days to make, and one day overdubbing in New York with the strings. We finished the whole album in seven days. Everybody had been saying, "If Spector gets involved, it's going to take six years to finish." [*Laughs*]

On *Imagine*, we knew what we were going to do – we knew it was going to be a Beatles-like album. John played me the "Imagine" lick – he had a piano lick that was very good – and I said, "Just write it – it's right." We built it around that.

Both you and John were such strong personalities. What was it like for you to work with him?

We were like brothers. I was concerned because McCartney had had this tremendous success [with the *McCartney* album] and George had had this tremendous success [with *All Things Must Pass*], but *Plastic Ono Band* really hadn't done what we expected. So I was afraid that John would get a little frightened, but he didn't.

You could tell John to change something. You could tell him to redo something. He was completely flexible. After all, I was there to make his life easier, so he wouldn't have to worry about producing. I mean, there's no animosity between us. I don't even know the guy, but George Martin is an arranger. All the Beatles know how to make records – and John knew how to make records. He just didn't want to be bothered with it.

It's difficult to produce your own records.

I remember when we did *Plastic Ono Band*, and I had to do the piano solo on "Love." It took 20 takes – I made a million mistakes. I had memorized it, I knew it perfectly. But as soon as John and Yoko were [in the control room], I started hitting wrong notes. John would say, "You don't like being on the other side of the goddamn lookin' glass, do ya?" [*Laughs*] And it was true. He said, "Now you know what it's like to be an artist." You have to perform.

What John needed was an editor. That's what the Beatles would do – they'd edit each other. Now they didn't have anybody anymore, so I filled that gap. John couldn't turn to Paul and say, "What do you think here?" They didn't have that family anymore. It was like a divorce. So who's the new cook? Who's taking care of the kids? My job was to take that off them, so they always had somebody to bounce things off. And John did do that: "What do you think of this?" "What do you think of that?" Which meant to me that he was used to asking, that he liked feedback. We worked well that way.

What did you think of the songs John came up with for Imagine*?*

I was essentially looking for a story to the album – and hit songs. That's why he had me: He wanted hits. Writing was just part of what he did, but he would write even if there was no music to it. And all that about the Beatles writing together is a myth. I don't think they wrote together after "I Want to Hold Your Hand." [*Laughs*]

In fact, one time it was John's birthday, and we were in a restaurant. One of the violin players heard John was there, so he sent for the other violinists, and they came up to John's table and as a tribute they played "Yesterday." [*Laughs*]. John was like, "I didn't write that fucking thing. I hate that fucking song." He was pissed off – you know, "The only thing you done was 'Yesterday' " [from Lennon's attack on McCartney, "How Do You Sleep?"]. But they didn't know. Lennon-McCartney, that was the myth.

So John wasn't difficult in the studio?

The most grueling sessions we ever had – of course, we were out of control at the time – were when we did the *Rock 'n' Roll* album with other people's material. When we were running around out here, we could have gotten into a lot of serious trouble. The late Harry Nilsson, I loved him dearly, but there were a lot of drugs going down. I mean, we'd be in a convenience store, a 7-Eleven or whatever, and Harry would say, "Let's try to stick it up, just to see what happens." "What? Are you fucking crazy?" Coke makes you do those kinds of things. We could have gotten killed.

As far as the album is concerned, we didn't really like doing Chuck Berry and Larry Williams. I mean, there was no stamp of personality on it. We even did "Be My Baby." It was ridiculous, because we didn't believe it. The *Rock 'n' Roll* album was really…it was good, but it was a mishmash. It wasn't the best of John Lennon. I think *Imagine* was the best of John Lennon. *Plastic Ono Band* was the best of John Lennon.

John had trouble afterward, coming up with the uniqueness of those songs. He had written his very best on *Imagine*. The next one, *Some Time in New York City*, became more tedious. It became more difficult to find subject matter. He'd try to make statements – "Woman Is the Nigger of the World."

What was it like when you came to work on Let It Be*?*

There was a lot of animosity. Nobody, other than George – and, for some reason, our relationship has become a bit strained over the years – but George and Ringo were extraordinarily helpful to me. George did have a motive: He had these 80 songs that had been rejected by the Beatles. [*Laughs*] They would allow him one or two [per album], that's it. That's why [*All Things Must Pass*] is a triple album. And every song, you could just hear John say, "I don't like that fucker at all." [*Laughs*]

But that was a very tumultuous time. McCartney leaving; his lawyers. Allen [Klein] coming in; those lawyers. It was a war zone.

What was John and Yoko's relationship like at that time?

They really loved each other. They loved each other's friendship. They were like school kids. I became best friends with John, but I always knew his best friend was Yoko. That was it. If you had told John, "You're giving the Beatles up for Yoko," he would have said, "I don't care. It's worth it." He was happy.

It's preposterous what Yoko has taken all these years. She had about as much to do with the breakup of the Beatles as Elvis Presley did. She was somebody to pick on, somebody to blame. Those were the best years of John's life, without question. They were buddies. It felt like the Three Musketeers with them.

Can you explain how John and George differed in their work habits?

I don't want George to read this and say, "Ah, he's fucking putting me down." But to give you an idea, the *Imagine* album took seven days, OK? *Plastic Ono Band* took a little longer, only because it was grueling to get John to perform. It was like psychoanalysis – a lot of screaming and crying. That album was not only his life and Yoko's, it was mine. "Isolation" – I still live that way: "We're afraid of everyone / Afraid of the sun." That tore me to pieces. "Mother, you had me, but I never had you" – I started thinking about my dad, who took his own life. It was "To Know Him Is to Love Him" [the epitaph on the gravestone of Spector's father, and the title of one of Spector's earliest songs] all over again. It was therapeutic, but very painful. And that's what took so long.

But George [for *All Things Must Pass*] – six, seven months. I mean, we did the solo on "My Sweet Lord" maybe 50, 60 different ways. It was just an insecurity he had, and I think it came from being the third kid on the block – not the hero, not the number one or two. He had an immense amount of material, but he wouldn't move one step forward until he was absolutely sure it was safe and right and finished. So we remixed and remixed and remixed.

And in the end, we'd always go back to what we did originally. When I make a record, I don't want to tell musicians, "Well, it's eventually going to sound like this – you're going to be in more echo." No, put it on *now*. You can't take the echo off "Be My Baby." You can't take the echo off "River Deep, Mountain High" – it's on Tina Turner *forever*. That's my art. That's what I do better than anyone. But George was very hesitant about it.

Did John ever talk about the impact your early work had on him?

John was very aware of everything I did, and he was a little intimidated – how would I react to his voice? When we went into the studio to do "Instant Karma!," John was afraid to sing. He loved Ronnie's voice, and he wanted to be able to do that. He wanted the tremolo; he wanted all that stuff. When he came in [the control room], and I put the tape on, he said, "It's just like Sun Records." That relaxed me. From that point on, he knew that I knew how to record his voice. Also, the whole thing about "Happy Xmas" was [*mimics John's accent*], "I wanted to make one Christmas record with you, Phil, because it would've fucking killed me not to."

Before you worked with them, what kind of impact did the Beatles have on you?

They had a major impact, because there would be ten Top 10 records, and they would have eight of them. [*Laughs*] You couldn't very well ignore that. I was very impressed with their writing. I heard a lot of Cole Porter, a lot of Gershwin, a lot of brilliant things.

But – and I told this to John – they were still second to Elvis to me. Elvis still was the King. My idea was to bring Elvis and John together – that would have been an incredible meeting. And then Elvis passed on. And then in 1980, John was gone. It never materialized, obviously, and we never got to work together again. But we would have.

Where were you when you heard that John had been killed?

I was at home. I got a call. That was something that never should have happened. John didn't believe in any kind of security. I don't know whether it was New York, or just not being a Beatle and not being under scrutiny anymore, but I guess in his last years he became much more trusting, much more carefree.

He'd stop and talk to people, and a lot of them were like the nut who killed him – "You wrote that song about me." Who wants to talk to those people? But it kind of shows you, while they hated being the Beatles, they also missed it. They missed the adoration. John missed that rapport.

When you think about John now...

And I do every day. Every day. I miss him so much. It was just a very loving, wonderful part of my life. I'm very glad that I know Yoko, and I'm very glad that I knew John.

This interview originally appeared in
Rolling Stone, *November 9, 2000.*

Songwriters

Van Morrison

"Why is it that people ask me these certain questions?"

Whenever I'm asked about the interview I enjoyed the least – or hated the most – I immediately bring up this 1985 encounter with Van Morrison. I was working at *Record* magazine at the time, and we were excited that we were one of the few publications Morrison was going to speak to. I'd been a fan of his since the days of Them, his first band in the mid '60s. I had come upon a copy of the single of "Mystic Eyes" in the rec room of my parish church, Our Lady of Pompeii in Greenwich Village. How it got there I haven't any idea, but its being part of a bulk donation by one of the local mob guys with a hand in the jukebox business is the likeliest guess.

Anyway, I'd also seen Morrison perform live in Central Park around the time of *Moondance* and been totally knocked out. I'd gone to the early show. I was still in the park smoking weed with a friend, when the late show got under way, and hearing the horn shots of "Caravan" bounce off the buildings on Fifth Avenue on that gorgeous summer night is one of my favorite New York memories.

In person, however, Morrison turned out to be a bitter, defensive guy, by far the biggest disappointment of any of my idols. He would wait before answering each question, as if he were turning it over in his mind to discover its secret, malicious intent. The exchange below about his singing – about as safe a topic as I could have imagined – went so badly that for days afterward I wondered about it. Finally, as I was walking along Sixth Avenue one afternoon, it occurred to me: He had interpreted my suggestion that his singing was part of how his words communicated to mean that I didn't think his lyrics were important. Nothing could have been further from the truth, of course, but that hardly mattered. Testy as he was, though, he did eventually muster responses.

I've thought a great deal about the lyricism and spiritual ambition in Morrison's songs and how they fit with the pinched personality I encountered. It seems to me that the uplift in his music must be a yearning for some kind of escape from the prison of himself. Or maybe he was just having a bad day.

When you started out with Them in the mid '60s, the idea of being in a band was very different from what it is now. At that time, how did you envision what you'd be doing when you were this age?

How did I envision…?

Did you think much about what you'd be doing in the future? I'm not sure many people at that time felt that being in a band was something they could do for the rest of their lives. Did you feel that, or was it something that only seemed possible later on?

Well, as far as being a singer and musician, I felt that way long before Them. Long before that. Basically when I was about 12 was when I wanted to be in a band, so from 15, I left school and went on the road. So I envisioned it long term then. Otherwise, I wouldn't have even got into it, because it's a lot of hard work [*laughs*] – especially starting off then, because it was different than it is today. Completely different. You had to sort of serve an apprenticeship then, which you don't have to do now.

What do you mean by "serve an apprenticeship"?

In those days, you had to play three or four instruments, sing, you had to do different types of material. Not rock material. That was not the big thing at that point. You had to be able to do ballads, jazz, C&W, all kinds of material. That's what I meant.

At the point at which you started having hits with Them, did you feel much of a kinship with other R&B bands from Britain?

Oh, yeah. Sure.

You had a sense that this was something that was defining itself against pop, or that the R&B movement was deeper or purer?

Oh, yeah, it was a very purist thing. You used to get these guys who had huge record collections, listening to this blues material all the time, and you got guys promoting R&B shows or jazz. It fell more into the jazz thing than it did the rock thing. But none of those people were in the least interested in pop music.

Do you feel a personal sense of the historical importance of the '60s?

I think it was historically important, sure. It's, like, what you do with it, isn't it? Really, what do you do with that? I mean, a lot of people went in various directions bouncing off of that. There's still some of that about, but it's all fragmented at this point. In the '80s, I think it's completely fragmented. I haven't really made an evaluation myself, although sometimes I'd like to. I haven't got to that point where I've taken it in and spit it out yet.

"Tore Down à la Rimbaud" on A Sense of Wonder *seems to be a song about the difficulties of inspiration, waiting for the muse. Is that something that you experience, and does it worry you when it occurs?*

I suppose anyone who writes goes through this. It's basically what I do, so if I'm not doing it, then what else am I doing? [*Laughs*]

What do you do when it happens? Do you have ways to try to get yourself going, or do you just try to ride it out?

I try to ride it out because trying to make it happen makes it worse. It's like insomnia, when you're trying to go to sleep. I tried making it happen, but for me, that doesn't work. I just have to wait until I hear something, or somebody might say something and I think, "That's interesting." Or I might read something, or I might just get it from wherever it comes from. But usually I have to wait for it. Otherwise, it's not in the flow. It's being forced.

Do musical ideas come to you first, or a lyric or a theme?

A, B, and C. "A" is a musical idea, and then you think about words. "B" is words and thinking about a musical idea. "C" is when they both happen together. "C," unfortunately, doesn't happen a lot.

Do you keep notebooks?

Oh, yeah.

Do you write things that you don't think of as songs?

Yeah, I write some prose.

Do you have plans to do anything with that, or is that just for yourself?

No plans at the moment. Not really.

Do you try to play or write every day?

That's not the way it works. I try when I have the time. I have a lot of business things that take up most of my time. That gets in the way. So whenever I've got space, I try and write. But there's not a lot of space, because I'm dealing with a lot of business.

Business like interviews?

No, like calling lawyers to find out where the money went, then calling another lawyer to check him. All that kind of stuff. That's on a weekly basis, and sometimes a daily basis. All the phone calls take up a lot of time – "I'll call you back," in different time zones, and all that. It's a lot of work.

I've gotten a sense from your interviews that you see self-consciousness as something that exists in opposition to creativity. That if you become too aware of how things happen...

Yeah, well, that's not my idea. It's as old as the hills. Ginsberg talks about this quite a bit, and various other poets.

I wasn't suggesting that you invented the idea, but that you feel it. Were there points at which you felt you were becoming too self-conscious about what you were doing and that that hurt you?

Oh, yeah. Sure. That comes, you see...well, you're just doing it naturally like breathing. You start writing songs and it's just like everything else in life, it's just the way it's going. Then you have a couple of albums out and you get these reviews, and people are saying, "This means this about that, and he was going through that when he wrote this." And you read these things and go, "Who are they talking about?" This sort of analyzation puts it all somewhere else. Then you run into other people, and they say, "I read this thing in such-and-such years ago, where the guy said… Is that right?" You get involved in all that analyzation about what it means and…the *projection*. So you get to the point where you're afraid to write anything because you know somebody's going to make something of it, and you spend a lot of time explaining it wasn't that way, it was this way. Then you say, I'm fed up with it, so what's the point? That's what happened to me, anyway.

Do you still pay attention to what people write about you?

No. I just had to acknowledge that that's something that belongs to them. I don't have to buy it. I'm not responsible for that. Then I just proceeded to get on with whatever's coming out, and not worry about what's projected on it. That's the only thing you can do, really.

What about the level of self-criticism you bring to what you do? What sort of criteria do you use to evaluate what you've done?

Just knowing that it's right – not based on analyzation, but on the magic of the thing. If the magic's right, then it's right, even if somebody played a wrong note. That way. The overall picture.

Do you have anyone you play stuff for?

No, I don't play anything for anyone. In fact, I make a point not to, because they're going to project themselves onto it, right? There's no point in doing that. I figure anybody that makes albums shouldn't do that. It's not the proper thing to do. It's like somebody writing a piece of journalism, and somebody's standing over your shoulder saying, "Keep that in. Take that out."

Do you feel uncomfortable when people ask you to listen to things?

I do actually, because I really get a load of rubbish. I get some unbelievable things that are supposed to be happening, and record companies say, "Have you heard this? They want you to produce them." It gets a bit embarrassing, because they want to know, "Well, does he like it?" And you listen to it and think, "My God, what am I going to tell them?" Not that it's so bad. It's more like it's so unrelatable to me. It's quite difficult to tell people about what they do.

Having an affinity for blues and R&B, do you have any take on the idea that physical or emotional suffering is essential to creativity? Do you feel your own creativity comes out of your pain or out of your joy?

Both. It comes out of both, really. And in between. Not so much in between. But, no, you don't have to be suffering. I don't really believe that it has to be like that. Some people do. I should imagine if you're feeling good that you'd write more, and more stuff would come out. That's my theory.

Has it been that way for you personally?

Yeah. When I write, I have to feel good. Otherwise, I don't write. I can't write if I don't feel good. For me it doesn't come out of that "you have to be depressed" thing. I've written very little behind that.

I think it's possible to write about those experiences at a point at which you're feeling good.

Exactly.

There's one thing that runs through your music: the tendency to invoke people by name in your songs. Why do you like to do that?

Like what? Like who?

James Dean. William Blake, Yeats, Joyce, Tennessee Williams...

It's also the way the name sounds. It's part of the musical thing as well. I don't think I do that very much. I mean, maybe I've done it three or four times.

A lot of singers shy away from that. You feel like, when it's right, you just want to do it?

Sometimes it's just part of the song. That's the way I do it. If it's part of the song, I do it. If I write it down that way, that's the way it's coming out.

What about particular images that come up. The radio has always...

That was a long time ago.

I guess it has diminished some, but at least as recently as Wavelength. *Do you still listen to the radio very much?*

No.

You used to?

Used to, yeah.

You feel it's gotten bad?

There's just so much crap on it, I couldn't be bothered, you know?

Many people now – a younger generation – seem to be first encountering music primarily through videos. Any impressions of that phenomenon?

I don't really think about it, because I'm not really in that marketplace at all, and I don't want to be. It doesn't interest me at all.

I understand that on A Sense of Wonder, *you had set one of Yeats's "Crazy Jane" poems to music, and the Yeats estate refused to allow you to use it. Were you personally involved in the efforts to get the estate's permission?*

No.

Did it disappoint you that it didn't work out?

No, not at all.

You just felt that they were entitled to their view of it?

I've recorded other people's songs before. My lyrics are better than Yeats anyway, so I figured I was doing them a favor in the first place. I just didn't want to piss around, basically. I don't need that – so thank you very much, good-bye. That was basically it. But it was sort of blown up in the press.

I understand that Mose Allison's "If You Only Knew" is the song you substituted for it. Any particular reason you didn't put another original on there?

No. There wasn't an original I wanted to put on the album that I had a take of that I liked – number one. Number two, I felt that that song fit the situation perfectly. I said, "Of course, this is it. It says exactly what I want to say about this situation. 'If you only knew all the problems that a man like me had to face/If you only knew all the stupid things that keep a man from his place.' " It's perfect. So that went on.

As somebody who has always had a great regard for American music, at what point did you form an idea in your mind about what America was? When you heard the music when you were younger, did that trigger any notion about the country itself?

No. None.

You thought of it just as music, independent of place?

No, I didn't think about a place at all. I was just enjoying what was coming through. I wasn't thinking about any geographical place.

What about when you first came to the United States? Were you curious to see some of the places that had generated the music you'd been listening to?

I probably thought about that, but it wasn't really part of the game then, because by that time I was writing my own stuff, so I didn't really need to go anywhere to get anything. You know what I mean? By the time, I'd come here I'd got well into writing my own stuff. I was out of the blues thing at that point.

So that just didn't loom as large for you?

Exactly.

Having lived in the U.S. for different stretches, when you get back here do you have much of a feeling of coming back to a place that once was home, or do you feel removed from it?

I don't feel removed from it. What's the question?

When you come back to America, do you think about it as a place where you once lived and that's part of a musical tradition that was once really important to you? Does it have those kinds of resonances?

I think of it as somewhere I'm familiar with. I think of it that way. It's different than going somewhere you absolutely know nothing about and you're trying to suss it out. I feel like I'm coming somewhere that I know what's happening.

Does it feel like a former home?

I'm not quite sure. I'd have to think about that. I don't really know.

Do you go back and listen to records you've done before?

I just tend to leave them. I'm more interested in what I'm doing this week or tomorrow or today. So I don't really tend to do that. Sometimes though, if I want to remember a song. But usually no.

There are particular songs of yours that have risen to an important place in a lot of people's thinking, even if they're not the types of things you'd do now. When you look back, are there any particular albums or tunes you feel especially good about, or ones that you don't think are as successful artistically as you would have wanted them to be?

No. I'm perfectly OK with the way everything is. I don't think about it. That's for other people to decide. It's not for me to decide. It's for the people who buy them, I suppose.

Obviously your lyrics are really important to you, but part of the way they communicate is the way that you sing them, your vocal style. It seems that a lot of times you're almost rebelling against...

What? Tell me something. Tell me something. I've been wondering this for a while. I just realized maybe I should ask somebody: Why is it that people ask me these certain questions? This is just for me personally. Journalists are always asking me different questions than they ask, I notice, other people in my profession, other people that would be, say, in a similar marketplace, or whatever you want to call it – you know, peers. I've been trying to figure this out for a while. I figure I should just ask somebody and get it that way, because I don't know. It seems like the interviews that I do, people ask me...I mean, you ask me completely different questions than you would ask Dylan, for instance.

I'm not sure I wouldn't ask Dylan that question.

Really? Because, you see, I'm very unanalytical about what I do. But people seem to want to get in there and find out...and these are things that I really don't even want to think about, because it's taking away what that is. Do you know what I'm saying? Still, that seems to be what people want to know, so I'm wondering why me in particular, or writers in particular. Because I don't think about it that way at all, because to me that's an indulgence. That's indulging. That's not something I care to do. Because it's not that way for me.

In other words, you sing it as it comes?

I'm just doing it as naturally as it comes within the flow. And to take it apart takes away from that. If I start analyzing why did I do this...you're into another area. I am, anyway.

That question, since you mentioned Dylan, is the sort of question I'd ask people who are really distinctive singers, whose voices are more than a blank medium for their words, whose voices seem in a way to convey a lot of emotion as well as just a statement. That's the only reason I brought that up. It's almost as if your voice is a kind of instrument itself. I was wondering if, in listening to your own stuff, do you sometimes say, "Well, this particular vocal is not emotive enough. I'll try it again."

Sometimes you do that. Yeah, sure.

One thing that's become more pronounced in your work is an interest in and fascination with a tradition of romantic and mystical poetry. Is that something you were interested in your whole life, or how did you discover those writers?

Who do you mean?

Blake, Yeats, Wordsworth, Coleridge. Obviously people you've read and care about.

My particular connection is with Blake, because I connect with him, with various things he's written. Wordsworth to a certain extent. They're describing actual states in words, or coming close, because you can't really describe them in words. But they're coming close to describing them in words. That's my connection with that.

It seems in your singing that you're trying to convey something that's beyond words, beyond speech, beyond anything you could just say. Something deeper than just the words – is that how you feel your particular vocal style works?

It's also the way the words are being said. It's never exactly what it is on a page. Shakespeare is not Shakespeare. Shakespeare is an interpretation of Shakespeare, or whoever wrote the things. The oral tradition is the closest to what something actually is, because it's the way somebody is saying the thing. It's also the way it's being said. For instance, I'm saying things now which in print are going to look completely different, because you don't see my facial expressions, you don't hear the tone, all of that. Words on a page are as close as you can get to the thing, but it's not the real thing. It's a description of something else.

There seems to be a renewed interest in social, political, and humanitarian concerns among a lot of artists. Have you thought very much about those issues?

If I had the time I would sit down and think about it, but I don't. I suppose I feel the same way that everybody else feels. Why are people starving, for instance, in the world where there's all this money? In various countries, even in this country, why are people starving? Not only Ethiopia, but in America, people are starving, and in other countries. What can you do about that? You do whatever you can do. Everybody thinks about this. I don't have an angle on it.

What kinds of things would you say to a young songwriter who wanted to know what your years had taught you?

I'd probably tell him what people told me, and I didn't listen: You need something else as well. You have to have something else. You can't just rely on that.

Something else being...

Anything. Another job, another hobby, another interest, another angle. Something else other than just that.

What about your influential stance as an independent force in an industry that encourages conformity. Is that something that gratifies you?

Basically what I'm saying, in terms of all that, is I'm somebody who has "made it" – so called, quote, unquote, in brackets. Well, that doesn't exist. To me, through my experience, "making it" does not exist. It's another word. It's like when you're at school, and they have words for things, classifications for different people. Also, society's got terms for things, and "making it" is just a term. It doesn't mean anything. It's not a reality. So what I'm saying is, I've gone through this process early on, the mill, what have you. I've gone through this, and it's not something that I think is desirable, all right? That's basically what I'm saying. But that's just my personal opinion. Now, whether that's going to influence people or not, I've no idea. But all I can do is talk about it, through my own experience. That's all I can do.

A shorter version of this interview appeared in Record, *October 1985.*

Bruce Springsteen

"You have faith in what you do. And then you do it"

When Bruce Springsteen enters a room, he fills it up – even when it's just a room in the guest house turned studio on his own property. His eyes shining and his face red from the fall air, he greeted the people who work for him as if he hadn't seen them in months and makes visitors feel like long-lost family. A mountain of sandwiches, prepared to the specific instructions of Springsteen's wife, Patti Scialfa, sat on a catering tray in the middle of a long farm table. The sound of Scialfa's solo album, *23rd Street Lullaby*, which was being mixed in the adjoining room and which would not come out for nearly six years, wafted into the kitchen.

It was late October 1998, and through the studio's many windows you could see the bursting colors of the trees beyond the nearby fields – peak foliage in southern New Jersey. The entire scene was Dickensian in its warmth, redolent of two of the most important elements of Springsteen's life: family and music.

Springsteen, who had just turned 49, was in a good place. He was psyched about the Yankees' World Series triumph the night before – it was the sort of season that makes you "glad to be alive," he said. He proudly talked up Scialfa's album. While he and Scialfa had retained ownership of the palatial home they had built some years before in Southern California, they and their three children (Evan James, Jessica Rae, and Sam, ages eight, six, and four, respectively) now were spending most of their time on this farm, which is shouting distance – and several tax brackets away – from the Jersey Shore haunts Springsteen immortalized on such early albums as *Greetings From Asbury Park, N.J.* (1973), *The Wild, the Innocent & the E Street Shuffle* (1973), and *Born to Run* (1975).

Springsteen had had plenty of recent opportunities to look back and consider how he'd come to be where he was. He was just about to release *Tracks*, a sprawling, four-CD retrospective that consists of 56 unreleased performances and 10 B-sides spanning his entire career. *Tracks* opens with the voice of legendary producer John Hammond, announcing an audition by Springsteen in May 1972. Springsteen performed riveting, Dylanesque versions of "Mary Queen of Arkansas," "It's Hard to Be a Saint in the City," and "Growin' Up," accompanied solely by his acoustic guitar. The set also includes material recorded as recently as 1995 during the sessions for *The Ghost of Tom Joad*. In addition, a lavish coffee-table book called *Songs* – which includes the words to all the tunes on Springsteen's studio albums, reproductions of his handwritten lyrics, a lush photo history, and his revealing comments on each of his records – was about to be published.

Taken together, the box set and the book constituted an eloquent and thorough celebration of 25 years spent making music that has moved, inspired, and lit a fire under millions of people. That frenzy of memorializing also set the stage for Springsteen's induction into the Rock and Roll Hall of Fame the following March. Later, in 1999, Springsteen would reunite the E Street Band and launch a powerfully emotional tour.

The *Tracks* compilation by its nature provided an occasion for looking back on his entire career, and I was particularly moved when Springsteen began to describe the period between writing *Tunnel of Love* (1987) and *Human Touch* and *Lucky Town* (both 1992), when he was exploring, as he put it, "the relationships between men and women." As gripping as Springsteen's more public tales of social and political redemption are, his unflinching looks at the fears that cripple people's attempts at intimacy are no less intense and unsettling.

Bruce Springsteen is one of my personal heroes and, while I'd had the chance to interview him for a television show, this was the first time I could really speak to him in depth. He lived up to my expectations, and more.

Let's start by talking about Tracks. *Why did you decide to assemble a set like this now?*

I came home after the *Tom Joad* tour – and I had really enjoyed that tour a lot. I love performing in that format. I wrote a lot of music on the road, sort of in the same vein, and I came home with the idea of continuing maybe for another album like that. I cut about half of it, and then I got stuck. I felt like I had some really good things, but the overall feeling wasn't quite as formed as I would have liked. And maybe it didn't quite extend itself from the *Tom Joad* record. So I put that aside.

Then I began to write and record a lot of electric music, just making demos here at the studio. I did about half or three-quarters of a record like that. I thought I had some good things, and then I hit a spot where I needed to write some more and there wasn't anything coming. So I ended up with these two records I liked very much, but that were only partially finished.

About a year or so ago, or maybe it's two now, I had some time on my hands and I had Toby Scott, who engineers for me, send me tapes of all our outtakes. It was, like, "Just send me everything. I'm going to just listen to everything."

Was this for fun, or were you already thinking of doing something with it?

I knew we'd recorded a lot of music over the years that we didn't use. But I didn't know what state it was in or how finished things were. So he sent me boxes of DATs that had probably 200, 250 songs. In the morning, I would just put one on and listen through it.

I figured I take so long between records, what I should do is put out some of this music for fans to enjoy. I wasn't sure what I was going to do, but I wanted to have some things that I could release. That was where the idea started.

So I listened to the stuff, made some quick notes on everything, and put it away. Then when I came upon the exact circumstance that I told myself earlier I was going to come upon, which was that I had half of an acoustic record and half of this electric record, and both of them felt very open ended, I said, "I should look into releasing some of these things." So I collected the tapes again, and I had Toby make up an edited list of probably 130 songs.

Based on your earlier listening?

Based on what I'd listened to. You'd come on things that weren't finished and things that obviously didn't work or weren't very good. Then you'd come on things that were completely finished and you couldn't figure out why they didn't come out on the record they were supposed to have come out on. So I said, "Great. I'm going to release some of these things while I'm working on my newer stuff." I hung out with [producer] Charlie Plotkin and we threw a quick sequence down. It was like, "This is going to be ready to go in no time." And then [manager] Jon Landau listened to it and said, "None of these things are mixed." And I said, "Yeah, that's their *charm*. [*Laughs*] People are going to get to hear it in its raw state."

Right – "That's what we were going for."

But there were things that we had mixed, and they were more focused and had more impact. As soon as Jon said, "I think we should mix these," I was like, "You're talking about 80 mixes. And what if we have to mix them twice? Then you're talking about 100 mixes. That's going to take us forever." But he was right. The stuff did need to be mixed, and I realized all of a sudden that I had gotten myself into making a record – which I thought I was trying to avoid.

But it was good. It got me into focusing on the stuff in a way that increased the impact of it. It was a big job. I like to go slow and be very controlled: We'd put something up when I was making *The River* and it would be a week before we had a mix – and then we'd do it again later! Thankfully we've dropped some of the neuroses that made all that necessary, and we were able to get this done pretty quickly. Within probably a month or six weeks, we mixed the whole record.

How did you end up feeling about the final shape of it?

We were left with a real record that has an arc and a story of its own. Like I said in the liner notes, it's the alternate route to the records I've released. It takes you to the same place, but by a different way.

I didn't have the burden of being overly conceptual with it. I was very concerned with creating a point of view on my records. That was a way I'd sustained my own identity and the integrity of what I was trying to do. So you get *Darkness on the Edge of Town*, where I edited it very severely and maintained a particular emotional and musical tone throughout the record. Now when you hear the outtakes from *Darkness*, there's party songs! There's all this laughing. The band is playing like it's the third set in a bar at 2 a.m. That's why those things didn't get on at the time, but it was fun to go back and allow them to come out, because it's terrific stuff.

It's like you're encountering them on their own terms, not within a context in which they don't fit.

"Give the Girl a Kiss," in the middle of *Darkness*, might have sounded… [*Laughs*]

Like "Where's he going with this?"

But it comes up on its own, and it's just, "Hey, we're in the studio and we're having a great time."

I used the studio as a place to test my ideas and do my editing. You wrote a particular song, you went in and maybe you only played it once and got it out of your system. Either it was going to stand or it was going to fall and you put it away.

I conceptualized the records as we went along. I'd have two or three songs that I really liked, and then I followed those songs like a map, trying to find the other ones. And on the way to the rest of the record, for every song I'd keep, I might cut two or three. Some we recorded just to have fun or to blow off the tension from the seriousness of some of the other material. Not so much the first three records, but certainly on *Darkness*, *The River*, and *Born in the U.S.A.*, this is how we used the studio. It was the records where I went in not knowing exactly what I was going to do, where we recorded a lot of material.

The first record [*Greetings from Asbury Park, N.J.*], we had three weeks to cut the material I had and that was it. The record was done. It was the old-fashioned way of doing it. There actually were quite a few outtakes from *The Wild, the Innocent & the E Street Shuffle*, and they are all very much in that vein – "Zero and Blind Terry," "Seaside Bar Song." All those things could have been on that record. At the time, we just made the choices, based on what I'm not sure now.

There were only so many songs you could fit in those days. Forty minutes was a long album.

The record company didn't *want* to put 40 minutes on there. They would say 36. It was very tight.

And all your songs were like five minutes long.

Exactly. I was writing these long, strange stories – these little funky epics. I don't know what they were. [*Laughs*] So all that stuff got left off just because of the time constraints. Then you moved on to a different sound picture on your next record.

When we went to *Born to Run*, it had a very specific sound picture and a very limited amount of material. From what I can recollect, there were maybe two outtakes from *Born to Run*. One we put on, and one was the only song we couldn't find the master to. It was called "Walking in the Street," and it probably should have gotten on *Born to Run*. I really regretted not being able to find it. But that record was tight and we had a limited amount of material.

It was in my first records after having gotten some success that you began to feel that what you were doing had implications. You had gotten in the door. OK, now what did you want to do? What did you want to say? Where do you want to go musically? Who did you want to be? What did you want to represent?

At that point, it just seemed that there was so much on the line. People were watching.

That's right. There's nobody watching earlier. Now that's the circumstance you found yourself in, and so you moved cautiously. And some of the things that were the most spontaneous got left off. At that particular point, I was very concerned with having a lot of focus. There are always spots along the way where you see people lose their focus or drift away from their initial ideas. This is where people get lost, I thought, and if I can make this step without that happening, I'll have moved down the road. So *Darkness* was an important record for me. And we made the right record. But we left off some nice things, so it's nice to see them get out.

The River is the same thing. The only thing I knew was I wanted to make a less constrained record than *Darkness* had been. I wanted to make a record that had room for the fun and didn't have to take itself so seriously throughout.

Those two qualities are exactly what I think about The River. *There are the serious songs like the title track or "Point Blank" that have the same kind of stringency as the songs on* Darkness, *and then there's party songs like "I'm a Rocker" that seem to me like the kind of songs the characters you're singing about would listen to.*

That was the idea. I wanted to strongly identify the people I was writing about, and I did that in "The River" and "Point Blank" and those parts of the record. But I also wanted to capture a certain spirit and essence that came out of the rock music that we put on that record. It was such an integral part of what I was doing live that I had to find a way to have it represented on a record. It was like the soundtrack of those people's lives on Saturday night.

After *Darkness*, I didn't want to let go of the characters I had. These were the people whose lives I was going to trace and follow, along with my own. So I tried to find a way of both holding on to those characters and incorporating the kind of excitement that comes when you're out and you see a great bar band or a great live show and it's just pure enjoyment and fun. That's how that material ended up forming itself.

Right. It's like, if the album is about marriage, what sort of music would they listen to at a wedding?

That's how we ended up with two records. And in the course of making a double record, we probably made three or four records. That's why you have an entire record that's basically outtakes from *The River* on *Tracks*. And most of that is rock music. I had a certain amount of space for those types of things, and I made my choices at that time. I don't know what they were – probably just what I liked at a given moment. You know, "I like this song, but I don't like the way my voice sounds," or whatever. All the minutiae that later on just doesn't mean very much.

That's why it's sometimes so annoying to talk to musicians when they've just finished working on an album. You'll hear a song that's amazing and you'll ask about it, and the artist will say, "I really felt that we never got the bass sound right in the second chorus." And you're like, "What are you talking about?"

[*Laughs*] That's a big problem, and it dogs most musicians. I get to a point where I would make so much out of a single line. And if there would be a word or two in there and you're just not singing that word right, you get pretty crazy about it.

What was the emotional experience of putting this set together? Was it complicated to go back and reencounter so much of your past?

Initially the thrill was that I was going to get to make a record where I wasn't going to have to do any writing. [*Laughs*] That really made me happy!

It was fun to be able to hear things without sweating the details. Even the initial things from the John Hammond demos that start the record were interesting. That was a taste of the record that maybe Hammond would have liked us to make. While it obviously wasn't folk music, they're a link to folk recordings, just the sound of the voice and the guitar. Very austere.

That was a powerful evening for me. I'll never forget being in that studio. Stepping up to that microphone. I came up on the bus. I had a guitar with no guitar case, and I was carrying it around the city that whole day. I was kind of embarrassed. I'd auditioned in his office. He said he wanted to see me play. We went down to Greenwich Village and went from club to club asking who would let me play for 30 minutes that night. There was a guy at the old Gaslight. He said, "Yeah. It's an open mike. You can sing for 30 minutes."

After he'd seen me play, we had to record an audition in Studio E at Columbia. The engineer had a tie and a shirt. Everybody was dressed with a jacket. I stepped up to the mike, sang these songs, and I had everything on the line. It was tremendously exhilarating – a big, big moment.

That's Hammond's voice at the beginning of the first disc?

Yeah. I was 22, I guess. So going through this stuff was fun. [Drummer] Max [Weinberg] was here one night and we were listening to this stuff from *The Wild, the Innocent*, and listening to [Vini] Mad Dog [Lopez]'s drumming. Max was like, "Mad Dog was great! He had an amazing style." If you go back to *The Wild, the Innocent*, Vini is playing constantly, these little foot things, drum fills, but he is very in tune and responding to everything else that was happening around him. It was an eccentric group of people. We were folk musicians in the sense that people's playing was very free and original, and it came out of their experience and who they were.

It was fun hearing the freeness and the lack of preconception that you brought into the studio, because, as you said, nobody was watching. Nobody was listening. And you had never listened yourself to know what you were doing or how you sounded. You just went in and did what you'd always been doing.

Even the writing. It was a combination of my own experience – what I felt in Asbury at the time, the group of characters there – and then my own imagination and my abstract take on those things.

It was like you wanted to get everything you had to say and every musical idea you had into every song.

We weren't satisfied until there were two or three endings. I thought they were all good, and I wanted to use them all. [*Laughs*] Plus this was your shot. You didn't know if you would ever get in a studio again. Hey, I had a record contract that said I could make two records, so it was very possible that this was going to be it. I was just trying to do it all, right then and there – all my arrangement ideas for the band, all the stops, the starts. And I wanted to tell the biggest stories I could think of. It was really before your realization that you were going to have breathing room and be able to continue and develop your ideas.

I was excited at how much good stuff there was sitting around. It's the dark matter of my work. There were like a hundred songs initially, and I edited it down to things that were directly related to records I'd released. Part of what I wanted to do was – if you liked *Darkness*, if you liked *The River*, if you liked *Born to Run*, if you liked *Tunnel of Love*, if you liked *Nebraska*, there is a reference point for where a lot of the music is coming from.

It's like a shadow career. I was struck in your liner notes for Tracks *when you specifically cited* Darkness, Nebraska, *and* Tom Joad *as the records that seem most clearly defined to you.*

They're the records that had a real hard focus to them, and maybe they form some inner core of what I've wanted to do that the other records extend out from. That might just be my own point of view of it. Other people might feel like other records do that. They were records where I got to what I was really thinking about and what I wanted my music to be about. They were very clear. Because they were limited in tone, they had a certain clarity to them.

I forget – how did I refer to them actually? [*Laughs*] I'm trying to think what I was saying about them.

It was much along the lines of what you're saying now. You mentioned that as you were discussing the criteria for why the songs on Tracks *didn't end up where you originally intended them to go. And you said that any substitutions would have been harder on those three albums than on some of your others.*

Right. If we go to *The River*, obviously I could have pulled half a dozen of these and put them on and taken some of the things that were in the same vein and switched them around. Whether it was "Out in the Streets" or "Where the Bands Are," they performed a similar function and, while I'm sure I had my reasons, the choices at that time were idiosyncratic and personal. If I'd made switches, it wouldn't have fundamentally altered the essence of what the record was. Whereas those other records wouldn't have taken substitutions as easily. On those records, the editing I did created something that was very clear and realized.

What was the most fun to hear?

I had the most fun with the wild stuff from *The Wild, the Innocent*, where I just enjoyed hearing the eccentricity of both the band and myself at the time. That song "Thundercrack" was my showstopper. You'd pull it out at the end of the night and it was a big, long production. We played it once in the studio, and I remember listening to it and saying, "This is too much work." So we put it away and never went back to it until this record. I pulled it out, and we didn't have the vocal parts. So I called up Vini and I said, "Vini, it's about 23 years later, but I got some singing for you to do." So he comes in and, of course, he remembers his part *exactly* with no coaching whatsoever. He just steps up and sings all those high notes, and says, "Hey, thanks, that was fun," and walks out. You realize once you've done it, it stays in there!

You come across things and wonder, "Wow, when did I do that?" "Give the Girl a Kiss" – I love that. I don't remember writing it or recording it. It was just totally spontaneous. I got a note from some fans about this song "Iceman," which I didn't even know existed. I had no recollection of it. So we dug it up.

On *The River*, there were a lot of things that I enjoyed hearing again. "Restless Nights" was a psychedelic mixture of the Animals, Strawberry Alarm Clock, the Byrds, all in one. I got into a couple of things simultaneously when I was working on *The River*. Earlier, I had gotten into country music and John Steinbeck. And I had just deeply gotten into Woody Guthrie's records for the first time. Then I was listening to all of these power-pop records, like the Raspberries. So I was thinking about three-minute singles. We'd go in and I'd write my three-minute single before the session. "Restless Nights," "Dollhouse," "Where the Bands Are," "Loose Ends," "Living on the Edge of the World," "Take 'Em as They Come," "Be True," "Ricky Wants a Man of Her Own," "I Wanna Be With You," "Mary Lou" – they are all like three- or three-and-a-half minutes.

The last disc articulates a little clearer some of the things I was trying to get at when I began to write about relationships between men and women. That was a time when I felt like I had to sort through these things. Those intimate connections, that's how you ultimately root yourself someplace. That's your kids, your faith, your hope made real and physical, your tangible connection to tomorrow and to what happens in the world. The inability to do that leaves you very loosely tethered. In some sense, those relationships are ultimately the core of your politics. When I began to try to figure these things out in my own life, when I began to write about them – *Tunnel of Love*, *Lucky Town* – there was this music, which is almost another record.

The series of records where I wrote about those things, I was trying to make it clear for myself. It was an issue that was a natural extension of the things I'd written about earlier – community, people finding their place. Finding your power within family and friends, neighborhood, the country you live in. Ultimately that power is nurtured by these essential relationships that give meaning to your actions, your ideas, and your work. I went into that very intensely. I dogged that trail as hard as I could.

It was extremely compelling.

When you watch the end of *The Searchers*, you see a classic moment where John Wayne is in the doorway at the end of the film. He's reconstituted this family and he comes to the house, and then he steps back and moves away. That's a very powerful moment, and a great failure. Artists create in a good deal of isolation, and your isolation may have been what initially spurred your imagination and your creative life. You needed a world to go into. But if you get lost in that world, then that's what you are – you're lost. There are plenty of people that that has happened to.

How do you walk through that door then? How do you walk through the door that leads into the house? And what do you do when you get in there? How do you behave? How do you treat one another? What do you create? That was real important once I got down the road myself. It was an essential link in the things I had been writing about.

So this last CD [on *Tracks*] is about fear, paranoia, mistrust, doubt, the lack of faith people have in themselves to be capable of creating those kinds of relationships. And also making your peace with it and finding your place in it, which happens toward the end – in "Happy," "Back in Your Arms." I don't know how well I've articulated it, but that was the arc of the albums I released and it's also the arc of this material. Hopefully, it will give my audience a little broader take on those ideas and the connection between this part of my work and the earlier stuff I did.

You mentioned how much you enjoyed the acoustic tour you did in support of The Ghost of Tom Joad. *What made it so rewarding?*

I enjoyed its clarity. It was something I'd thought about doing for probably 15 years, since the *Nebraska* album. Obviously when I came up with the *Tom Joad* recording, it made sense.

The way I bring my music to my audience is still fundamentally through performance. I don't know how well I fit into the way records are presented these days. Basically, I'm pre-video, you know? We're into making a record and touring it. That was how you connected with people: You went to their town and they saw you. I think that's still a fundamental connection for me.

Initially I didn't know how long I'd do it. I didn't know if I'd enjoy it – you know, you're out there on your own. But right from the first night, I felt good. I felt a very direct communication. Over the course of 130 shows, I found the audience for that music and that particular presentation. And they came. So it was very satisfying.

I've had an incredible audience in Europe the past 10, 15 years. At the end of the night, you'd have 14-, 15-year-old kids, 60-year-olds, all right in front of the stage. I was shocked at how it connected, because basically there's a guy strumming a guitar and singing a lot of words in English. [*Laughs*] So I spent a good amount of time over there. I got to some places I hadn't been before – the Czech state. Václav Havel came to the show. That was a real honor. He's an incredible writer and an amazing person.

It was just something I got a lot out of. It really fed me. And it wasn't physically consuming, the way a show with a full band is. When you're playing with a full band and you have days off, they're rest days. Those are days where you need to be open, but you may feel closed because you're tired or you can't speak. When I'd come home from this tour, I had my voice left and I wasn't exhausted. I could speak with my wife and kids.

So it was exciting. I loved going on stage every night. I loved the freedom of being completely self-contained. It improved my acoustic guitar playing a lot, and my slide playing. It was just a very whole experience. I really look forward to doing it again at some point. I like that idea that 15, 22, 23, 25 years down the line, I'll be able to find a way to represent what I do.

These days, you don't see a lot of rock 'n' roll at the top of the charts. I'd be curious to get your read on what's going on out there and how you feel you fit into it.

The trendy part of the music business is fun. I enjoy it. That's always an essential part of pop music – its disposability, its being of the moment, right here, right now. It just didn't fit me. I had a different take on it, just because of who I was, what I wanted to do, how I saw myself, and what I thought.

And what had made an impact on you.

When I was young, in my teens, I was probably more in tune with trends. That's when it's important to your identity, when having the right shoes and the right haircut is essential. It's everything. Later on, it's not everything. It can be something you want to do or don't want to do, but your life changes and you're not living in that same context.

I've created a long body of work that fundamentally expresses who I am. That's what I go out to present. That's the only way I know how to do it, and the way I approach it now isn't any different to when I started.

I haven't really had a work life where I tried to fit myself into what's out there. When I started, I didn't feel like I particularly fit into the mid '70s music business. I try to do my best job, and think as hard as I can about the things that interest me, and write and perform as well as I can and then try to find the audience that's out there for it. I am interested in presenting what I do to anybody who wants to hear it.

What's different for somebody like me today is I have less access to the mainstream music business. I'm never going to be on MTV, and there are a lot of radio stations you can't get on. That's the reality. You have to deal with that, and what I've generally done is go out and perform when I can. You find who's interested and where you can go and you go there. But that doesn't fundamentally alter anything I do at this point. I'm not going to make a particular kind of record so I can get on a particular kind of station. It would be foolish for me to attempt that at this point.

Basically, I've been pretty consistent with my approach since I started. Hey, you have faith in what you do. And then you do it. You go out and do it.

Are you here full time now? Do you still have your place in California?

Yes. We have a place, but basically we are here a lot of the time. The kids go to school here. We've had this place for five or six years now. It's great. We have a big family back here – a 60-, 70-member family.

I grew up like that. I grew up on a street where we probably had six houses – all relatives. It was an L-shaped block. There were a lot of nice memories. Plus your children are exposed to different talents and abilities. It's not all about music. One guy fishes, another guy works doing something else. They're exposed to a lot of different things and a relatively normal life. They get a lot of support from people. It's just been a great experience.

There is something very resonant about standing on that same street corner with your kid where you stood holding your dad's hand or your mother's hand. I like that. It broadens your view of what you're doing here. You can already see over the hill, over the rise. You can see where it's going and what's next and you can see your job clearly. I find that to be a great comfort. You have a place. You know what it is. You make choices you stand by. You have your job that you do. You understand why your hope and faith are important. It helps the day make sense.

Portions of this interview appeared in
Rolling Stone, *December 10, 1998.*

Paul Simon

"We can't say the deepest truths"

I had three long interview sessions with Paul Simon in fall 2000 – one for a story in *New York* magazine, the other two for a *Rolling Stone* feature. When I first met with him in September, Simon had recently completed *You're the One*, his first album since *The Capeman*, the 1997 Broadway musical he co-produced, co-wrote, and scored – and that closed after a disappointing 68-show run. Unlike *Graceland* (1986), much of which Simon recorded in South Africa, or *The Rhythm of the Saints* (1990), on which Simon collaborated with a host of Brazilian musicians, *You're the One* is a quieter collection of songs, and it marked a dignified return to the sophisticated, folk-rock art songs of his early solo work. Elements of all his musical experiments drift through tunes like "Senorita with a Necklace of Tears" and "Darling Lorraine," but more as subtle coloration than predominant style. I met with him two additional times in November during a tour stop in Los Angeles.

Simon had been in the news for other reasons than his new album. In *Almost Famous*, which had come out earlier that year, Frances McDormand, playing the mother of *Rolling Stone* writer Cameron Crowe, points to the moody portrait on the cover of Simon and Garfunkel's 1968 album *Bookends* and insists, "They're on pot!" In an interview in *Revolver* around the same time, Bono described his song-writing standard: "You stop thinking about who's hip and you start thinking about 'Bridge Over Troubled Water.' " At a meeting of the nominating committee of the Rock and Roll Hall of Fame, Bruce Springsteen's manager, Jon Landau, had delivered an impassioned brief on behalf of Simon. Soon after, Simon was nominated for induction into the Rock and Roll Hall of Fame as a solo artist, and he won election early in 2001. Simon and Garfunkel had been inducted as a group a decade earlier.

Simon interrupted rehearsals for his tour at a midtown studio to talk about *You're the One*, the *Capeman* controversy, growing up in public, the critics, and his friend Bob Dylan, with whom he toured in 1999. Wearing an orange T-shirt, black jeans, and a light brown cap, he sat, a bit anomalously, among equipment cases and other studio detritus. "I find the rehearsal process a bit anxiety-filled, whereas I don't find that to be true at all about performing," he said. "Performing's easy. But until everything is settled and prepared, I'm not thinking about anything other than, 'Let's get prepared.' "

Simon's shows at the Wiltern Theater in Los Angeles a couple of months later proved that preparations had produced the desired results. For the last song on the opening date of his three-night stand, Simon hauled out "Mrs. Robinson." Powered by three percussionists, Simon's 11-piece band was a mighty rhythm machine, and the song was transformed into a roiling R&B workout. But the real surprise came when Simon arrived at the song's final verse – which took on powerful new meaning in the wake of the battle then raging over the Gore-Bush presidential election, which at the time still had not been resolved.

"Sitting on a sofa on a Sunday afternoon," he sang, "Going to the candidates' debates / Laugh about it, shout about it when you've got to choose / Every way you look at this, you lose." The jaded Angelenos roared – and the night ended on a rich, complex note nicely in tune with the impact Simon's music has had for the past 35 years. In a time of far more one-dimensional sounds, it was like finding a fine, rare wine on the menu of a fast-food restaurant. Call it the shock of the old.

"Yeah, that was shocking, wasn't it?" Simon said in his dressing room before the next night's show. To say that the room was bare-bones would be to grossly overstate the elegance of its well-worn couches and lumpy chairs. Seated in one of those chairs, Simon sipped chai tea. He was dressed this time in gray slacks, a maroon shirt, a blue windbreaker, and the ever-present baseball cap. He is not given to large emotional gestures – moving his fingers gracefully in the air is as animated as he gets. But he was obviously pleased with how the previous night's show had gone. "That was the first time we sang that song on this tour," he said. "As I approached it, I thought, 'Oh, my gosh, here we go!' Until it was just about to happen, I didn't know."

While the crowds at his shows were impressively receptive to the half dozen or so new tunes Simon had been including in his shifting 30-song sets, they came for the most part to hear their favorites.

Fortunately, Simon's songs retain an ability to shed new light as they make their way through time. For example, the original version of "Mrs. Robinson," released in early 1968 on the soundtrack to *The Graduate*, wistfully captured the yearning for lasting values and unvarnished heroism in a country that was splitting apart at the seams. Meanwhile, the song's current, more aggressive arrangement seemed well suited to these more cynical contemporary times. Longing for heroes seemed pathetically naïve given the decidedly unheroic nature of the candidates battling over chads, dimples, and butterfly ballots in the first presidential contest of the 21st century. Even Joe DiMaggio, the symbol of unquestioned integrity and valor to whom "a nation turns its lonely eyes" in the song, had been rudely knocked off his pedestal by an unflattering biography published earlier in the year. "Joltin' Joe has left and gone away," indeed.

In the '60s, as the songwriting half of Simon and Garfunkel, Simon deftly traced the decade's inexorable slide from innocence and hope to alienation and disillusionment. In the course of that work, he left behind a collection of songs that stand with the greatest popular music written in the 20th century: "The Sound of Silence," "America," and, of course, "Bridge Over Troubled Water," among them. As a solo artist in the '70s, he caught that era's unsettling freedom and casually unsatisfying pleasures in songs like "50 Ways to Leave Your Lover," "Slip Slidin' Away," and "Still Crazy After All These Years." In the '80s, the propulsive, world-embracing rhythms of *Graceland* rebuked – by example, not explicit denunciation – not only the soul-crushing brutality of the apartheid system in South Africa, but the vicious xenophobia of the Reagan-Bush years.

The '90s proved more difficult for Simon, though. The decade started off promisingly with *The Rhythm of the Saints*, but, as Simon himself admits, that album was more an extension of *Graceland* than a departure from it. He enjoyed the critical acclaim and commercial prominence that *Graceland* had restored to him, but he needed to move on – and move forward. Determined to venture off in a new direction, he spent seven years writing, producing, and staging *The Capeman*, a musical based on the youth gang warfare that plagued New York in the late '50s and early '60s. The production attracted massive attention – and helped launch the crossover success of Latin singer Marc Anthony, who had a starring role. But the notoriously enclosed and ego-driven Broadway community perceived Simon as an arrogant interloper, and the show closed after a barrage of hostile reviews and a disappointingly short run.

While eliciting a far less contentious response, *You're the One* had its problems as well. It drew generally favorable reviews but it did not sell well. It's a problem that many artists of Simon's generation – now 63, he was 59 at the time – face. He will always have a following as a live performer because audiences both young and old will never tire of his hits. But it has become increasingly difficult to expose listeners of any age to his new music. The video music channels and print publications are youth-obsessed, and even radio cannot define a format suitable for older artists who are determined to remain creative and not succumb to the living death of being an oldies act.

In the meantime, however, Simon's personal life had become more stable than it had ever been before. He's married to Edie Brickell, the former lead singer of the New Bohemians, and they have three children, two boys and a girl. Still crazy after all these years? Not likely. But, as you'll see, even Paul Simon couldn't resist the temptation to ask the Delphic Bob Dylan the meaning of it all.

One additional note: At one point in this conversation, Simon refers to my writing for "a magazine that doesn't do what it pretends it once did." He's talking about *Rolling Stone*, of course, and it's a critique that comes up from time to time in interviews. I usually don't include it in published pieces, because it's insider-ish and rarely gets at the issues of how and why a magazine evolves. I've left it in here, though, because as part of a larger discussion of aging in popular culture, it makes some sense.

In Los Angeles, Simon and I started talking casually about our mutual fascination with the old New York in which we had grown up, and I just switched on the tape recorder, easing into the interview.

I know what you mean about old New York. I used to ask my parents about growing up there all the time.

New Jersey is pretty interesting to me too, because I have roots there. I was born in Newark. They were born in New York, my parents, but my father got a job playing live music on a radio station in Newark, so they moved there for a year. Now I have this blemish for the rest of my life. [*Laughs*] I'm not actually from New York. I'm from Newark.

Your father was a bass player?

Yeah, but he was a bandleader, too.

What do you remember about him and his band from those days?

The first thing I remember is this radio station he worked at. I was around four. The whole band was playing. They were reading their music on the stand, and when they would finish with the sheet they were reading they'd drop it on the floor and go to the next page. I didn't understand that. I thought they dropped it. So I came over to bring it back, which everybody laughed at. They probably thought it was adorable. I thought it was unbelievably embarrassing.

Then he got a job playing at…I think it was WOR in New York, so we moved back. Then he had a band at Roseland – starting at the old Roseland on Broadway – for 25 years. He used to play there every Thursday afternoon, and some Saturdays. I was seven or eight. If we went to visit my father, we'd say we were going "into the city." To go into Manhattan was a big deal. It was a big deal just to get on the subway. We were going to be with my father, who was going to be in a good mood. Actually, my father was pretty much always in a good mood.

Did all of this make the life of a musician seem alluring?

That's funny, I never thought about it. I liked all his friends. The musicians were always laughing; they all seemed to get along. It didn't seem alluring; it seemed like a job.

He bought me my first guitar, and he showed me the chords to rock 'n' roll. He couldn't stand rock 'n' roll, but he was, "Fine, the kid should play." He would play dances in playgrounds at night around the city for kids. He would have his band and they would play fox-trots and "Won't You Come, Bill Bailey" and all that stuff. Then he would book me to play rock 'n' roll. I played with his band, and they would follow me. I was 16, and I knew all the tunes the kids wanted to hear.

What would you play?

Whatever was a hit. Frankie Lymon. Louie Lymon and the Teenchords. Elvis Presley. I knew them all. Those were my first jobs, really, and it was fun to be around my father and the guys. They kidded me, but they were happy to have me.

Playing for the kids must have been exciting. Were they digging it?

Oh, yeah, the kids were digging it. It was, like, a little bit of screaming. Girls coming after you. All that stuff. I also remember playing some jobs that my father booked me on – like weddings, bar mitzvahs – in wealthy people's homes where I saw the way musicians were treated. Wealthier places in New Jersey, where the social secretary would tell you, "Do this" and "Do that." You had to go in the back way, and eat in the kitchen. I could see that musicians were a good bunch of people who weren't always treated particularly nicely.

The most exciting thing was that for a while my father would do television shows. He did "The Arthur Godfrey Show," Gary Moore. For a while, Jimmy Dean had a morning show. He had to get up at four every morning. We'd be watching, and every once in a while they'd show the orchestra, and you could see my father on television. Back then – even now – for a kid to see his parent on television was a huge deal. He was as interesting as anybody I ever met.

Then when he got into his 50s, he got bored or scared or whatever and he went back to school and got a Ph.D. in linguistics.

Really?

He had a second career. He taught at City College, and he got up to associate professor, which is pretty good. He was extraordinary. He died in '95, and I really miss him.

So coming up to the present, what was on your mind when you started working on You're the One*?*

Always the same thing on my mind: Sound.

Like the first line on the record: "Somewhere in a burst of glory/Sound becomes a song."

That's right. I heard a sound and I wanted to know if it was just an imaginary sound, or could I make it? That was two years ago, in September, and the band came together in October. By May, we had completed five tracks: "Darling Lorraine," "That's Where I Belong," "Love," "Look at That," and "Hurricane Eye," which we called "Banjo." They didn't have titles, and I hadn't even thought about words. The songs were called things like "C Minor," "Mystery Train."

That's a good title; somebody should use it.

"Mystery Train" is a good one. I'm always trying to make "Mystery Train" – it's my favorite record. And that's what I mean. You get this sound in your head at some early point in your life and you love it so much. Then you spend your whole career trying to make that sound.

And over the course of that time, you move in and out of it.

Closer to it. It's elusive. There are a lot of different elements that I always thought were part of "Mystery Train." Why does that rhythm work? Why does that emptiness sound so full? Why can you accomplish it all with three instruments? How come there are no drums, but it sounds so rhythmic? Those are all interesting questions with very big answers.

And you find as you start to ask those questions that other musicians are also asking them. Their metaphor isn't "Mystery Train," but they're the same questions. I'll hear drummers breaking something down: Why does it swing? You can ask people all over the globe and they'll never agree on what's swinging, but once you do agree, you're in the same band. You don't, you're not. You might as well not even be friends, because if you have a disagreement about rhythm, you can't be friends. [*Laughs*] What, you like *that* record? OK, see ya!

It's funny to hear you talking about sound so much. You're often thought of as a word guy.

If you don't have the sound right, it doesn't matter if you have the words right, because the ear isn't available to hear them. Edie, my wife, hears the words way before I do. She'll listen to some song and she'll say, "Did you hear that?" But I didn't hear it. I wasn't up to the words. I'm listening to, "What's that drummer playing? What's the bass playing?"

So much of it is subjective, too.

Everybody's got different taste. That's why there's all different music. When I hear musicians play very loud and angry and abrasive, I don't relate to it at all. But they're deeply into it, and I'm sure they understand just how to be abrasive and why it's satisfying and they're playing to an audience of people who are connoisseurs of abrasion. They're talking to each other and having a good time. That's what I'm trying to do when I make a record. I'm trying to make a record that is so pleasurable for people who like what I like that they can just swim in it.

You're the One *is a more conventional album than you've made in a while. Did you feel that you had to get back to basics after the debacle of* The Capeman*?*

No, I wasn't thinking of *The Capeman*. The reality of *The Capeman* is, outside of New York, nobody heard of it. It was a non-event. It's like, "Where you been?" "I spent seven years working on *The Capeman*, and it was gone in three months." "Oh, I didn't hear about it." It was a big New York story, but it's not a big story in St. Louis or Tampa. Broadway's not a big story, unless you have a big hit and everybody comes into town and goes to see it.

Were you surprised by the level of vitriol directed at The Capeman*?*

The harshness? Yeah, I was. [*Long pause*] I was surprised by a lot of stuff about that. One thing, though, bothers me. I was widely quoted as saying that I could care less about Broadway, I'm only doing this for me, and I never said that. People thought I had a real attitude, when I didn't have any attitude.

I didn't feel, "I should be unbelievably grateful to be here," or "I feel far superior." I was just working my ass off with people I was crazy about. Then it got beat up. I didn't read most of it. Why should I get hurt? I think that somehow the Broadway community thought I felt superior. But I didn't. I was happy to be there. I didn't come from that tradition, but I didn't know that you had to.

Actually, I thought *The Capeman* was very good, and I was proud of it. It was flawed, and I would have done some things differently. But the idea that I came in with an attitude wasn't true.

Going back a little further and thinking about Graceland *now, did you imagine that it would have anything like the impact that it did?*

I thought, "I wouldn't be surprised if this was a hit. I think it's great. I love it." And also, "I wouldn't be surprised if this was a flop. I could imagine that people wouldn't get it at all." It's not unusual for me to be in love with a sound that nobody else can hear. I think that's what happened with *The Capeman*. I was crazy about those sounds. Those voices – Latin, doo-wop, Marc Anthony, Rubén Blades. It didn't have any effect on critics at all. They didn't hear it.

Once you get into a recording studio with musicians, especially if you don't know them, you either capture their imagination and they're interested, or they're not. With *Graceland*, those guys were into it. And we didn't know if anything was going to happen. I could do whatever I wanted because there was no expectation. I'd just had *Hearts and Bones*, and it was a flop. The record company wasn't breathing down my back, "When are you going to give us a record?" Not interested at all. Nobody was looking at me.

But I was invited to South Africa with the thought, "Well, maybe this guy'll make a hit and the world will hear our music." That was their thought. I didn't even get the whole picture until I got there, and then I said, "Whoa, this is an unbearably tense country, and these guys are desperate to get their music out.

And the criticism that came – "cultural imperialism," when they really meant "cultural colonialism" – they don't even know what they meant. You must have ripped them off, because you're white and they're black, so it's got to be a bad deal for them. It wasn't. It wasn't a bad deal for anybody. Everybody had a good stake, everybody had a ride, everybody was having a good time, and everybody knew it was special. I thought those musicians were incredible and I really tried to write good songs so that they would be proud.

Recently Bono said that he uses "Bridge Over Troubled Water" as a standard for songwriting. It must be gratifying how songs like that one and "The Sound of Silence" continue to resonate for people.

I was 21 when I wrote "The Sound of Silence," and I'm amazed that it has lasted all this time. "Bridge Over Troubled Water" was the most mature song of that period, although there were a couple of others that

I think are mature for a young person's work. "Old Friends" and "Bookends" are touching. "The Boxer" is a touching song. Of course, I didn't think about how long anything would last. You don't think that way when you're in your 20s. "I wonder if this will last 30 years?" It was inconceivable that you were ever going to be that old.

But "Bridge Over Troubled Water" came so fast, and when it was done, I said, "Where did that come from? It doesn't seem like me." Then I gave it to Artie, and for decades it didn't seem like mine. First, it was beyond where I was when I wrote it, and then I didn't sing it, because it was Artie's signature song. So in a strange way, I didn't identify with it. I didn't feel like it was mine. On the last tour I did with Bob Dylan, I found a way of singing it that felt right to me, and I felt like it was my song again.

There were two great versions of that song. One is Artie's and one is Aretha's. I imagined Aretha's when I wrote it. I was influenced by the Swan Silvertones, and I heard it as a gospel song. Artie sang it the white choirboy way, which was extraordinarily beautiful. But neither of those voices are my voice, so in a way that song's a mystery because it sort of drifted out of my hands.

What was it like touring with Dylan?

Oh, that was fun. We played two shows in Minnesota, and they were both fabulous, particularly in Duluth – the affection for him, what he means in the Midwest, particularly in Minnesota and in his hometown. We were playing at some fairgrounds, about 40,000 people were there. We were onstage, and he said to me, "I grew up about four blocks up there." It was really touching.

He's my age, and he's a songwriter who knows how you do it. We used to laugh together. Many times we were close to laughing uncontrollably. Every once in a while, we would sing something that was just so good, some verse. I don't think we ever sang an entire song that was good. [*Laughs*] We couldn't remember the words.

I have a lot of affection for him. When I was younger, I was wary, because I didn't want to be him. He was so good. Frankly, I never would have written "The Sound of Silence" had it not been for Bob Dylan. But soon after that, I said, "You can't be that. He's that. You are…we don't know what. But you're not that. Don't be that."

It seems like there was so much pressure on songwriters of that time because of Dylan.

It wasn't just Dylan. It was because Dylan and the Beatles and Stones all happened a year and a half to two years before Simon and Garfunkel. I remember thinking at that time, "There's no room to be original here. They've got the whole pie." It was like if I could just get a tiny little slice and get in there, I'll be happy, because they seemed like, between them, they had every idea. They were so powerful.

When you look back on it now, you can say that generation was pretty remarkable. At the time I thought that's just the way it is. There's always going to be four or five people who are amazing. "Look, here's Stevie Wonder – he's the next generation." It's going to happen again. But it didn't.

How emotionally invested are you in You're the One *being a hit?*

It's much more fun if it's a hit. *The Capeman* was a very rich experience, but it wasn't...*fun*. It's one of the things I think about all the time, really. What does any of this stuff mean? And then I say, "You've got to stop thinking about it, because you don't know." The easy answer that seems to satisfy that is, "It's what you do."

I remember standing backstage and talking to Bob once. We were thinking of extending the tour, and I said, "I don't know. What actually is the point?" And he said, "This is what we do." That seems to be the answer. There's not really a point. You've got to do something. You're bored if you don't. Now, you're going to say, "Is this important?" That's a whole other question. I don't think it's important. You make it up. It's not important. It's just not. It's what you do. But it's not important. It doesn't mean anything. Nothing.

Still, you seemed really relaxed onstage during the first night's show in Los Angeles.

I've always been relaxed, but I used to have a completely different theory about what I was supposed to do onstage. I had an anti-entertainer mentality. A lot of that came from my reaction to leaving Simon and Garfunkel, because that was more of an entertaining act. I used to talk a lot and be funny, and when I left that, I said, "I'm finished. I don't have any desire to be funny."

Why was that?

I wanted to be a musician and I didn't want to be an entertainer. It wasn't until I went out with Dylan that I started to say, "The audience has a strong desire to be joyous. I'm going to do that. Anyway, why am I out here if not for that?" So after many years, I changed my mind about what the purpose of my performance was.

Do you have any idea why you would change your mind at this particular point in your life?

[*Simon's eyes fill up.*] I became very aware of how grateful I was to be alive and what a blessing it was. I had a great feeling of gratitude and awe. It was a powerful realization, a spiritual thing. I don't want to trivialize it by describing it when you can't describe it.

I can understand that.

It loosened everything up, like, "This is a big old jingling universe, and you're just jingling along with it." I had this thought that the only thing that God requires from us is to enjoy life and to love. It doesn't matter if you accomplish anything. You don't have to do anything but appreciate that you're alive – and love. That's the whole point. All the rest of the stuff is... You like to make music? Fine, go ahead. Make sure that if you do that, what people get from it is joy.

When I quit about seven or eight years before that – I didn't announce it, I just quit – I was in the middle of a performance at a benefit, and I said to myself, "I don't know what I'm doing here. This is so bogus. I don't know what the audience thinks I'm doing, but this is an imitation of a musician. I don't want to be that. I'm out."

What brought you to that point?

It was an epiphany. It occurred in the middle of a song: "This is ridiculous."

Do you remember what song it was?

I think it was "You Can Call Me Al."

Extraordinary.

"You Can Call Me Al" is a very powerful song because I've never had any song that came near to its ability to make people get out of their seats and dance.

I remember your playing it twice in a row one time at Madison Square Garden.

We used to play it twice. The Africans taught me that. You know how that came about?

"Well, they liked it the first time, so..."

No, it was even funnier than that. We were playing a *Graceland* concert in Zimbabwe – it was filmed, in fact. We finished "You Can Call Me Al" and everybody was doing some kind of unison cheering. I was taking a bow and getting ready to count off the next song. Hugh Masekela says to me, "They really like it. They want you to do it again." I said "Well, that's nice..." [*Laughs*]

"But we just played it."

Yeah, "We just did it. Now we're moving on to the next song." He said to me, "You don't understand. They're not kidding. They want you to do it again." So I said, "*Oh-kay...*" [*Laughs*]

"The next song will be 'You Can Call Me Al.' "

It's kind of an African performance...whatever you want to call it...oddity, trick.

But you were saying, the song has a certain kind of power...

And, for me, because it does, I have something in me that says, "Don't play that."

Why?

It's the same thing that made me not sing "Bridge Over Troubled Water" for years. They want it – "Don't do that."

Like, it's too easy? It's so obviously what they want to hear?

I don't know. It's not that I don't like it. I don't like the power of it, and what it does. It peaks everything. It bores me that a peak is predictable.

The fact that it's predictable makes it less of a true peak?

But on the other hand look at opera. The great aria comes, and that's the great aria.

It's also the whole reason why songs are hits.

They have power…

When you hear "Pledging My Love," you feel something, whether you've heard it a hundred times.

It's really powerful. But in the middle of "You Can Call Me Al," I could easily say, "You're not playing the song anymore. The song's gone. They took it. It's not an expression of anything anymore. It's only an expression of a peak in a performance. It's all about the performance." Anyway, that's what I thought at that point, and I said, "I'm very uncomfortable with this. That's not what I meant to be." But when I came back to do it with Dylan, I had a complete change of mind and said, "I'm perfectly happy. You want to hear that? Great."

It sounds as if you've been able to recapture the heart of what it means to be onstage.

The whole performance is all about heart. And the realer it gets, the more powerful its impact. The error of heart is sentimentality, just like the error of being cerebral is pretension. Nothing wrong with cerebral, but if you go over the line, you're pretentious and it's bullshit. Same with heart. It's from the heart, but all of a sudden it's sappy and you're Judy Garland.

Or Elvis Presley. There's a guy: from the real to the surreal. And you don't even notice it. It's like, "That'll never happen to me," but it could happen to anybody, because that's what happens with repetition.

Audiences like repetition, and I'm not particularly an audience guy. It's like when I was on tour in England recently, I went to visit George Harrison, whom I like a lot.

I remember you performed with him on "Saturday Night Live."

Yeah, we sang together. I hadn't seen him since he was stabbed. Jeff Kramer, who manages George and me, said to him, "It's a great show, come down and see it." George said, "Yeah...I'll try to." And I said, "Whatever you want. You don't have to come and see me. There's no new news for you about performing." Either it's going to be so good that it's aggravating or it's not, so you say, "You think that's exciting? You should've been at Shea Stadium." You can't freshen it up, and that's just the way it is. So I'm not particularly an audience person in popular music.

Speaking of audience, I wanted to get back to a point you made earlier, when you described that you'd defined a new aesthetic as a solo artist, in opposition to what you were like as part of Simon and Garfunkel.

That's too strong a contrast. I was a big Lenny Bruce fan, and there was a certain talking comedic thing that co-existed with the beginning of folk-club performances. You had to talk, and there was a lot of comedy in it. There was a lot of give and take.

Right. It also counterbalanced the seriousness of some of the material.

And it distinguished itself from the rock 'n' roll of that period, which was going through a very teen corporate phase. The talking was a way of saying, "We're not stupid. We're clever." We weren't clever, but we were trying to learn how to have observations or wit.

But when I left Simon and Garfunkel, that was one of the things I left. I was more impressed with Miles Davis turning his back on an audience – "I'm not begging you, 'Please love me.' I'm playing. You like it? Great. You don't like it? Leave." It was coming from that place, even though I hadn't earned the right to that.

You embrace a premise, and then you really don't question that premise for a long time. Like I decided when I was 12 or 13 that I was going to be a rock 'n' roll singer, and here I am 45 years later. I say, "Well, that was a 12-year-old's premise – are you sticking with it? Because it was a great idea, but you made it up when you were 12!" [*Laughs*]

Did that sort of thinking lead to The Capeman *– a desire to move in a different direction?*

I began thinking about *The Capeman* before I decided to stop performing live. It was, like, that's what I can do because I like writing and I like making up stuff and I like recording. What I don't like is …I don't want to be Paul Simon of *Graceland*. I've been it for enough time. I took a lot of bows. It was a big fight, but I ended up winning, and at a certain point, that's the end of that. Be something else. *The Rhythm of the Saints* was really a companion piece to *Graceland*. It wasn't a new statement.

All that coincided with this idea that I could write *The Capeman* and I wouldn't have to perform. I could write a wider spectrum of song and have it performed by people that really could do it justice.

So what do you do now?

Here's the irony for me: There was a time not too long ago when everything I made was not only a hit but won a prize. Then the industry reorganized itself and you can't even get played on the radio. It's not a rejection. It's not as if they say, "If you really do a great one, we'll play you." It's got nothing to do with that. "Love it! My favorite album! Can't play it."

Then your choice was either make what the marketplace wants or get out – unless you're somebody who's really famous and been around a long time. Then they don't really know how to say, "Get out." They don't even *want* to say get out, because if they say get out they're also saying, "We have to give up your catalog, which sells at a constant rate. So don't get out. Stay. But we don't know what to do." [*Laughs*] You represent a value system that, although it's been to a great degree abandoned, is still revered. So you say, "If you revere it so much, why did you abandon it?"

It's spun itself into this place where you and I are talking about a thing that doesn't exist, and you're going to write about it in a magazine that doesn't do what it pretends it once did. And we try to be purposeful when we can't say the deepest truths. Maybe we could, but they would be lost.

We could say some of them. Whatever Rolling Stone *may be, I had a 6,000-word story on Johnny Cash a few issues back, and an interview with Phil Spector talking about working with John Lennon. Not to mention doing this interview with you.*

That's the reverence for the other value system.

But it's still going out to the same 1.25 million people who are reading all the other stuff. It's still available to them to read, if they want to.

And they do. They have reverence for that value system. Except they don't understand the value system anymore; they just know you're supposed to have a reverence for it. The reason they don't understand the value system is that the system has ceased to have an opportunity to evolve, so it's like some dead religion. Each generation loses further contact with where God was, and now it's just a ritual.

I don't know. I think people can still encounter...

Maybe Radiohead has that value system.

There's stuff around now that connects. And there are young readers who want to discover what came before them, the way I discovered Muddy Waters when I heard the Rolling Stones. I think that still continues. It's not necessarily the page-one story, but...

I guess I'm saying that I personally think that *is* the page-one story. But it's not.

Culturally it's not.

So if that's the case, how do you engage that discussion in any way other than wringing your hands and saying, "Oh, boy, we're entering the dark ages"? How would you begin to represent that value system? Assuming you think it's worth defending, how do you defend it? The first instinct is to say, "Well, this group stinks, that singer stinks, this record stinks, that's just hype, that's nothing, that's zero." But that attack is a waste of time. Attack itself is a waste of time. The value system is not an attack value system. It's a non-aggressive value system that is now at war with an aggressive value system. It's Gandhi.

Yeah, well, Gandhi won.

That's the way to win, if you think it's worth winning.

And the way you attack is…you do it. You make the music you want to make, and you play it for the people who want to hear it. You put your point of view out there.

I agree with you: That's the answer. You just put it out there. The thing is, you need to get enough back for you to feel like you want to keep putting it out.

You're generally perceived as a "sensitive" guy, but there's a feistiness and a toughness about you. Do you recognize those elements in you?

Makes sense. Not feisty, but when I was a kid I didn't mind getting in a fight. I didn't mind getting punched, and I didn't mind punching somebody. It was a phase. I think the feistiness is I'm from New York, but I'm not from Manhattan. It's just a New York attitude, from the boroughs. [*Laughs*]

Here's the other side of the feisty thing, though. The huge dread of an interview is that you're going to be faced with boring questions. But I really don't like to hurt people's feelings, so I would indulge boring questions rather than say…

"I'm not going to bother with that."

Right. And I always think, "Would Bob?" He can do the opposite, and everybody says, "That's fabulous!" [*Laughs*] But if I do it they say – and they used to always say – "He's an arrogant guy." I used to see that a lot. But I don't think so. I think it's New York. I don't really feel like indulging in certain kinds of bullshit.

It could be a projection about size, too. Size is an interesting question. Somebody once asked me, "Do you think that because you're short, that's why you're ambitious or competitive?" I said, "I don't know, man. John Lennon wasn't short. [*Laughs*] Bob's not. The Beatles weren't. The Stones weren't." It's a generation of guys who are a very competitive group of people. I try to not be, but I am.

It's hard not to be.

I don't find it of great value. When I feel it, I say to myself, "Move off that. It's an irrelevance. Don't beat anybody, and don't think you got beat. It's not true." The world will tell you the opposite: You're a winner, or you're a loser. I don't want to buy into that. I don't want to beat anybody, and I really don't like to lose. [*Laughs*] Either way, I don't like it. But if push comes to shove, I'm not afraid of a lot of things.

When your tour's over, what will you do?

Get back into the flow. Get back to the kids. Get back to Edie. Relax into life. The misleading thing about a tour is that it has an extraordinary amount of ego involvement – people looking at you, people cheering for you, people interviewing you. You've got to stop that, and it takes a while. It's not going be about me; it's going to be about everybody else. And that's better. When that slips back into place, we hum along and it's nourishing.

Then for me, the question always is: Will I get another idea? And there's also, Am I coming to the end? What about age? We're on the edge, this generation. Are we going on like B.B. King or…not?

For what you do, I don't think there's any particular issue. You can keep on going the way you've been going.

The thing is, as far as the world's concerned, it doesn't matter.

You do have an audience, though.

I suppose that's true.

Oh, come on, man…

My view is like – if somebody disappears, they disappeared.

So if Dylan just went away, you wouldn't think about that?

I wouldn't. A lot of people would. I wouldn't. Look, I'm crazy about him. He's fun, and we probably will play together again. But much as I like him, if he went away, would it have any effect on me? No more effect than my going away would have on him.

It wouldn't affect your day-to-day life, but you'd think, "I wonder if Dylan's going to make another record, or if he's going to play again."

That's really the question. At his level of ability, if he wants to make another record, I'd like to hear it because I'm curious. And I suppose that's how people feel about me: "If he wants to do it again, I'll listen."

Portions of this interview originally appeared in New York *(October 9, 2000) and* Rolling Stone *(February 1, 2001).*

Billy Joel and Elton John

"That was my life in words and music"

Billy Joel was the subject of the first cover story I ever wrote for *Rolling Stone*, in 1986. The afternoon we met – in midtown Manhattan at an Italian restaurant, natch – we got merrily drunk on Sambuca, and then he brought me back to the studio expressly to meet his producer, Phil Ramone, who had also worked on Julian Lennon's second album, which I had recently trashed. It was a typical Billy Joel performance all around. The brashness, the drinking, and the rough-edged camaraderie all made the singer a very recognizable New York type to me, like one of the guys I had grown up with. We've understood each other since then and I've had a number of subsequent opportunities to write about him.

I'd never met Elton John before doing this story, but when he and Joel were about to play three shows together at Madison Square Garden in 2002, I thought it might be a perfect occasion to do a songwriters discussion piece I'd been talking about with *The New York Times*. So I went to see the two men perform in Hartford, CT, and then, a few days later, met them backstage before an arena show in Philadelphia.

I spoke with them together for about an hour. In addition, I talked with Joel for a while before John showed up, and again for a few minutes after John left. This was fortunate, because Joel seemed reticent, and even a bit deferential, when John was present. Part of that, I'm sure, is because John speaks in torrents that tend to reduce everyone else around to silence. Also, as this interview suggests, I think Joel felt uncomfortable because he had essentially stopped writing pop songs, while John had recently released a critically praised album of new songs. It seemed to me that John's energetic – and obviously well-intentioned – encouragement of Joel to begin writing again only made Joel feel more put on the spot. Talking about songwriting under these circumstances seemed to put a strain on Joel.

Shortly after this interview ran, Joel imploded onstage during the opening night of the duo's Madison Square Garden run, ranting incoherently about a variety of issues that had little to do with why anyone had come to see the show that night. Not long after that, he checked himself into a rehab clinic to address a drinking problem. While I never could have predicted any of that, none of it surprised me.

I'm not sure I understand the real reasons why Joel stopped writing songs – and, to be honest, I'm not sure he does, either. But I do believe that decision is related to some of the other problems he's had, and that the tensions he was feeling about it are evident in this conversation.

It's easy to imagine someone wanting to learn how to play an instrument or be a pop star. But how do you go about becoming a songwriter?

EJ: I was in a mediocre band called Bluesology, playing behind an English blues singer named Long John Baldry. We were doing cabaret, because he'd had a couple of pop hits. I'd been on the road since I was 17 or 18, backing people like Patti LaBelle, Major Lance, and Billy Stewart, and that was great fun. But this cabaret thing was killing me.

So I thought, What can I do? I sang a couple of songs with the band, but I wasn't really a singer at the time. I figured the only thing I could do is try to write songs. So I answered this advert for Liberty Records. I went there and said, "I like to write songs, but I can't write lyrics." And they said, "Well, here's a bunch of lyrics by this guy in Lincolnshire." And history was made.

Music came naturally for you, and the words were a struggle?

EJ: Yeah, and that led to me writing to other people's lyrics – Bernie's mostly, of course.

Billy, you've called songwriting "the world's loneliest activity." Have you ever tried collaborating?

BJ: I tried it, and the only thing worse than doing it by yourself is doing it with somebody else. You can't share the responsibilities. There's got to be one captain of the ship.

Now, I've seen him write to Bernie's lyrics. He looks at the lyric, and he sits down and starts writing music. I do it the other way around.

I write music first, and then I jam lyrics on top of it. So there's a totally different dynamic to how we work.

I don't think Bernie's there when you're working on his lyrics.

EJ: No, but he can be in the same building. [*Laughs*] I wrote "Your Song" in the living room while he was in the bedroom. But I couldn't have him in the room – it would be too distracting – especially now that he's become more musical over the years, and plays instruments and has made records.

I really don't want him there. It's that sacred, selfish piece of it, where this is my part of the baby. Sometimes, and I think Billy would agree, when you've first written a song and you've got it right, it's the best it will ever sound.

BJ: Yes.

EJ: Because it's naked. It's not adorned with anything. And it's fresh. That moment is sacrosanct to me.

BJ: It's that Promethean thing. It didn't exist before. You were there at the birth. And then you go through the postpartum depression.

In the early days of rock 'n' roll, and certainly before that, it was perfectly acceptable to be an interpretive singer and exclusively sing songs written by other people. After Bob Dylan, that essentially became impossible. What are your own ideas about the relative importance of singing, playing, and writing?

BJ: People who play instruments tend to look at singers as people who scream in key. It's like, most people can sing, but playing an instrument, you have to learn the thing. You have to study it. You have to sleep with it. You've got this whole other understanding of music.

Writing is another level. Some people can sing. Some people can play. And then there are the people who can write – and that's the wellspring of everything. For me, there's a great legitimacy to being able to write and play and sing. But singing is the least of it. It's the changing-the-light-bulb part.

EJ: I started off as a piano player who wrote my own songs, and now, 32 years after the *Elton John* album, I consider myself as good a singer as I am a piano player. It's taken me awhile to catch up.

But I'm glad I write my own songs and don't have to rely on other people. Where would I get songs from? It's a shame that we've lost that arrangement where people wrote for other people. I think the only person that does it now is Diane Warren. There's no Holland-Dozier-Holland, no Goffin-King, no Leiber-Stoller.

BJ: For a while, songwriters like that were seen as maestros. People like Leon Russell, who wrote songs that other people had hits with – they were masters. Then it fell out of favor. It was seen as too much of a craft – too studied, not primitive enough, not the rock 'n' roll animal thing. So it's disappeared.

EJ: When Bernie and I signed our contract in the U.K., we were told to write songs for people like Tom Jones and the Hollies, and we were very bad at it. We never got any songs properly recorded. Then when we started recording the songs ourselves, people started recording them, too. That *Elton John*, *Tumbleweed Connection*, *Madman Across the Water* period, we had a lot of covers. After that, the songs and lyrics became so personalized that people found it hard to record them. Lyrics became far more complicated, far more angst-driven.

The great songs of the '50s and '60s, you can still sing them now. Those lyrics were like poetry, but they weren't overcomplicated. People could sing them easily. You can't actually think of someone going down the road singing a complete Alanis Morissette lyric – it's impossible. And it's the same with some of our songs.

If you look at the Top 10, say, even 15 years ago, you could probably sing most of those songs. Now, you're not going to be singing Ja Rule in five years, or Jennifer Lopez.

BJ: Actually, "song" is almost a misnomer for what's on the charts now.

Certainly hip-hop and sampling have called into question the very idea of what a song is.

EJ: There are only two or three chords, and it's just a riff.

BJ: I talk to my daughter about this all the time. She's a good pianist, and she wants to be a songwriter. She goes, "I feel like I should be singing like Mariah Carey or Christina Aguilera," where they never settle on a note. I said, "Just sing the song." And she says, "But nobody does that anymore." And she's right.

EJ: There are very few singers in that vein who sing the song. Mary J. Blige sings a song. She is a proper singer. You can't really judge the others. I mean, Angie Stone's got a great voice, but they're not really songs. They're just kind of riffs. It's nice, but in a way it's annoying because she's an incredible talent who's capable of singing…anything you like. Kelly Pryce, Jill Scott – they're great, but I wish I could hear them sing a proper song.

BJ: Alicia Keys. She's the hottest thing since sliced bread. She's talented. She's got potential. She's got the voice. She knows how to arrange. She knows how to sing. She knows how to play the piano. I listened to the album and I said, "I'm not getting blown away." I'm sorry, I'm not. And kids my daughter's age, 16, 17, ask, "Well, Dad, is it good?" Is it as good as what we had? No, it's not.

EJ: You need to go back and listen to "I Never Loved a Man" by Aretha Franklin. The great song that Alicia Keys did ["Fallin' "], it's James Brown's "It's a Man's Man's Man's World." But I do think that she has incredible potential. This girl knows a melody.

BJ: She does. She could have longevity.

EJ: Absolutely. It's her first album, for Christ's sake. My first album was *Empty Sky*, and hers is far better than that.

Who are some of the songwriters who inspired you?

EJ: The thing is, when we started writing songs, we had a well of great songwriters to draw on. You mentioned Leon Russell. You had Neil Young. Bob Dylan. Leonard Cohen. Cat Stevens.

BJ: Lennon and McCartney.

EJ: Jagger and Richards.

BJ: Joni Mitchell.

EJ: Brian Wilson. In the folk vein, you had Tim Buckley. Tim Hardin – "If I Were a Carpenter" is a fucking amazing song. People who write songs today, their reference point is really…what?

BJ: I don't know.

EJ: U2 write great songs. Sting writes great songs. But you're talking about the Rolls-Royces. When you come down to the assembly line, there ain't too much happening.

Actually, there are new people I do like. I still listen as much as I did, and I'm encouraged. It seems that the tide is turning. There's so much crap and mediocrity, but there is some quality out there, and I'm going to champion it until I die.

One artist I like is Ryan Adams. He's brilliant. There's a boy from England called Tom McRae. There's Pete Yorn. There's John Mayer, whose album is called *Room for Squares*. His influences are Sting, Eric Clapton, Stevie Ray Vaughan. Great references. I mean, he's going back to the people who wrote great songs. And that's what Ryan Adams and Pete Yorn have done as well. They're influenced by…

BJ: Quality.

EJ: We had so much quality around when we started to write. It was frightening.

Paul Simon once told me that he was almost daunted by Bob Dylan, the Beatles, and the Rolling Stones when he was starting out. They seemed "to have every idea," he said. Did you feel similarly?

BJ: You looked to them, but I didn't see it as daunting.

BJ and EJ [*together*]: I saw it as inspirational.

EJ: Absolutely. Totally inspirational. We'd listen to Simon and Garfunkel. We used to listen with our headphones on to a stereo album and look at the gatefold sleeve and listen to the different sounds that were being created. There was a well of things to discover.

And we went on the road. Billy played in bars. I played in bars. I'd done my apprenticeship with a band. That helps your experience, and gives you all that wealth of knowledge for writing songs. I played with Leon Russell. Derek and the Dominos. People like that. They inspired me because every night I went onstage and said, "Fuck, you're not going to follow me." And every night, they followed me and did better, and it was inspirational. It made my spirits soar.

BJ: I see it happening with my daughter. She recently discovered Stevie Wonder. It was like an epiphany, like St. Paul on the road to Damascus. And it's influenced her writing. She's becoming more syncopated. She's experimenting with jazz chords. This is all good.

Stevie Wonder seems everywhere as an influence these days.

EJ: India.Arie is an example.

And Alicia Keys.

EJ: India.Arie's album is better than Alicia Keys's. It's got warmth to it, and style. I was very excited by it. I gave it to Sting and said, "Listen to this fucking album. It's incredible."

You've both been writing songs for quite some time. What is it like to hear your songs change their meanings as times change?

EJ: I've been very lucky the last couple of years. I've had *Almost Famous* come out with "Tiny Dancer" and "Mona Lisas and Mad Hatters," and it's gotten lots of younger people coming to my shows. They hadn't heard "Tiny Dancer" before. This is a whole new age group. I mean, we've been around 30 years.

There's a boy band in England called Westlife, and they did "Uptown Girl" last year to raise money for a charity. And it was Number One. Since then, I've noticed people in England have been discovering his records again. That's a great song.

BJ: Imagine if they heard the Four Seasons.

EJ: Every musician is influenced by somebody. We all pinch things.

BJ: Absolutely.

EJ: And we do it out of love, out of respect. I mean, Brian Wilson changed my life. I pinched the first chord of "God Only Knows" for "Someone Saved My Life Tonight." You used to buy 10 or 12 albums a week that were good. Carole King. Fucking *Tapestry* was, like, the album of reference when I started writing.

BJ: I remember hearing James Taylor when his first album came out. He got all this attention as the first singer-songwriter star. But that was the same era that you were out, and Cat Stevens. For some reason, "Fire and Rain" had this resonance. It was so personal and tragic. She was in an insane asylum, they were shooting drugs, she killed herself – it was the ultimate singer-songwriter song. But James was a marvelous singer and a great guitar player to boot. I learned a lot from him.

He's right. We had these people – kicking our asses.

How much attention have you paid over the years to each other's work, and can you comment on it?

EJ: What I love about Billy's music, and I realize this the more I hear it, is what I loved about the Beach Boys – that they were so American. It's all about where his soul is, and his heart. That's why I loved the Band and Crosby, Stills & Nash. Randy Newman. They could have only come out of America. That gives them an identity. It gives them personality.

I can always pick out a Billy tune, because it's got character. Things like "Scenes From an Italian Restaurant," "Movin' Out." "It's All About Soul," "Allentown." It's got a complete identity of its own, and that's the hardest thing for an artist to achieve.

When Billy first came out, people said, "Oh, he's just America's Elton John." I never got it. I used to say, he doesn't sound anything like me. I always thought he sounded perfectly like Billy.

And anybody who plays piano's got my vote anyway. Seventy to seventy-five percent of the great songs, starting with the Cole Porter era, were written on piano.

BJ: I was just going to go there about his stuff. There's something about piano-based material. Even the Beatles, their earlier stuff, OK, was guitar-based. But then when they got more interesting, piano was introduced into the music. It became more sophisticated.

His music is piano-based music, and it's eclectic. It's all over the place. Some of his songs are in keys I'm not even familiar with. They're difficult keys. This is a strange comparison, but I love Chopin because he wrote in untypical keys. A guitar player will play an E, an A, a D, or a G. Piano players like C, F, and G. He plays in these flat keys.

EJ: I think in flat keys; things sound better on the piano in flat keys.

BJ: When I first learned "Your Song" by ear, in D, there was something missing. It wasn't as good as when he does it. Then when it was time for me to really learn it, he said, "It's in E-flat." I said, "Oh, shit." It's difficult if you're not familiar with that key.

EJ: That's why all my guitarists hate me!

BJ: E-flat is a horrible key for a guitar player.

I wanted to get back to the point about songs taking on different meanings over time.

BJ: He's had a good deal of that from movies. He's had songs that were hits resonate again with a new generation of people. That's a wonderful feeling, maybe one of the most gratifying feelings for a songwriter to know…

EJ: …that their song lasts.

BJ: It has gone beyond him, your time, into a whole other time. And that means, after you're gone, that song will still be alive.

EJ: "Candle in the Wind" has been a freak. It's been a hit three times in England. And then, of course, there was the Princess Di thing. It's proof of what music can do. The reason I did "Candle in the Wind" at the funeral was because people were writing the lyrics in the book of respect at St. James' Palace.

Songs mean something. They mark different periods of my life, whether I was happy or sad. It's the same for everyone. When you can affect people like that, it's a very joyous thing. It can also be a millstone around your neck. It was two years before I could sing "Candle in the Wind" again. People were saying, "Oh, for fuck's sake, don't sing that," and I can understand why.

BJ: I kept pushing him to do it.

EJ: I'm a very big lover of sad music. When I was a drug addict and at the depth of my despair, I used to listen to "Don't Give Up" by Peter Gabriel and Kate Bush, and also a track called "Lost Soul" by Bruce Hornsby and Shawn Colvin, and cry. That was my life in words and music. When I was at my worst, I still clung to music. And there are times when I hear "Brown Sugar" or "The Weight," and I just light up. That's what songs do to people. Music for me is the most magical thing in the world.

We've talked a lot about composing music. What about lyrics?

EJ: When I was younger, I listened to the sound and the playing and the melody. I didn't particularly listen to the words. And that's what I still do. If I like the vibe on a record, or the atmosphere, then I'll cotton on to the words later. Lennon used to say, "I never listen to the words first. I say, 'Fuck, what's that sound?' " You hear the first three chords of "Brown Sugar" and you think, What the fuck is this?

BJ: That's how I write songs – when I used to write songs.

EJ: Listen, I've been on him forever. I genuinely miss his songs. I say, well, maybe you should do an album of standards, just as a way of easing back into it. He's the greatest mimic. He can do Otis Redding, Ray Charles, Elvis Presley. And when he sings someone else's song, he knows how to interpret a lyric. While you aren't writing, go ahead and do that.

I think a lot of it with Billy has to do with fear. It's like, I can't write again. And that's nonsense. But I can understand the fear, because as soon as you go into the studio, you think, Can I write?

BJ: You may be right about the fear thing. I haven't really thought about that. But as far as writing goes, I have to want to, and I haven't wanted to. I've wanted to write the piano pieces that I wrote.

How did you end up feeling about the classical album? Do you think about it in commercial terms at all?

BJ: You can't. It's not realistic. I mean, it was the top-selling classical album, which is kind of ironic. I knocked Yo-Yo Ma out of Number One, which I actually feel bad about. But I've been blown away now by Pavarotti, so it's poetic justice. Elton even said to me, "You're a genius. You've figured out a way to sell only a few records and still be Number One." And I didn't even play on it.

But I'm glad I tried it. I'm glad that people who might have been curious about that kind of music listened to it. I'm sure that classical purists don't find it as satisfying as Chopin or Beethoven, but I didn't pretend for it to be anything like that. And I'm sure there are a lot of people who like pop music who just don't like this kind of music. For a few people, maybe it's expanded their ideas of what kind of music they can appreciate. If that's happened, then it's successful, I suppose.

But I wasn't even compelled to record it. All that was important was composing it. The important thing is the idea, not necessarily the execution. That's how I feel these days. It's not important for me to be out there. The important thing for me now is to feel that I'm being productive, and it doesn't always have to do with record sales or hit singles or the music business at all.

EJ: I can't make him write again. But I can certainly…

BJ: He keeps nudging me.

EJ: He says he's got to want to, and I agree with that. But there's a fear factor there. I think he will write again, and when he does, it will be really special.

BJ: I always wanted to be a better lyric writer than I was. I wanted to write like Bob Dylan or Leonard Cohen. Those are the kinds of lyrics I've always loved, because they weren't so bloody literal. Surrealistic lyrics that Bowie would write, or abstract lyrics like Dylan, or philosophical lyrics like Leonard Cohen. That's what I wanted to write.

I actually made a big stretch on the last album, *River of Dreams*. I began to write more in metaphor, more surrealistically. I got a great deal of satisfaction out of that. And I said, OK, I proved that I could do that – *phew*. Now I want to do something totally different. It's interesting, because it will be going on 10 years since I've actually written a song.

EJ: For me, the biggest thing is, I'm so fucking competitive. With this album, I'm really proud of it, but I've had to work three times as hard to promote it, because a 54-year-old is not going to get the same amount of airplay as he used to. It's a real battle. I don't think I can do this again. I mean, I've been promoting it since last May. I've just got to cut the umbilical cord and say, I'll just make records, and if they don't sell, they don't sell. I can't spend the rest of my life doing chat shows. It's ridiculous.

BJ: It's all about sales. You're a salesman.

EJ: And I don't enjoy it anymore.

What's gotten easier and what's gotten harder about songwriting over the years?

EJ: When I made *Songs From the West Coast*, I tried to do away with being influenced by so many different things. As a keyboard player, you sometimes get fed up with playing the piano. You think, "Ah, a synthesizer, a different sound." I had gotten away from playing piano on my records and writing on the piano. I would write on synth. And there's something about a song written on the piano that's got so much more soul to it.

I had pressure from my record company: We need a hit single. We never used to do that. I used to just write albums, and then the record company would choose a single. That's gotten harder because as you get older, you need the hit to sell the album, and I got waylaid by that during the '80s and '90s, and it affected my writing.

With this album, I just said, I'm going to write the song that's going to start the album, and the song that's going to finish it, and to hell with it. That cleared my mind a bit. Now I think my writing will become not easier, but clearer. That's as honest as I can be.

[*John leaves to "get a massage" before going onstage.*]

BJ: I've always looked at songwriting as an evolutionary process. I'm never going to stop creating music, but am I going to continue writing pop songs? I saw the way the business was going, which pretty much started in the '80s with MTV, and it was visually oriented, image oriented, hit oriented. It was about narrow demographics. There weren't the same reasons for writing songs as there used to be. There was a sense of community before that, something that united us all. All that silly, clichéd stuff about Woodstock – we really believed that, and it seemed to have gone away. The music business became so big and, as he said, the hit single became so important, that the album shriveled in comparison.

I owe a great deal of whatever success I've had to album tracks, as much as hit singles. People who just know Billy Joel from Top 40 singles may not like me, and I can't say I necessarily blame them. I don't think that represents the sum and substance of my work. But the album tracks got played less and less as time went on. Radio changed, and would only play what was created for their format that demographic. Writing songs stopped being fun. Writing songs became writing singles, like he said, and I stopped wanting to.

I want to write songs for my own enjoyment, as part of an album. If it becomes a hit single, it becomes a hit single. It was always a matter of serendipity. A lot of my hits were almost novelty songs. "Uptown Girl" was a joke. So was "Tell Her About It" – that was my take on the Supremes. Even "Piano Man" was a wacko song – I mean, people thought it was Harry Chapin. But as long as it was a hit, that was all the record company cared about.

So when I got to that last album and wrote that last song, which is called "Famous Last Words," I really meant, "These are the last words I have to say." But I gave myself an out. I said, "Before another age goes by." I left the door open to write songs again. And I may. I'm not saying I definitely will. But I'm not saying I won't.

Do you feel any pressure about it, from your record company or anyone else? Do you feel a twinge when someone like Elton says he wants you to do it?

BJ: No, because if I did it just for them, it wouldn't be any good, and I don't think they'd want that. I think people may want me to re-create something that they liked before – say, "Scenes From an Asian Restaurant," "Piano Man II," or "We Didn't Start the Fire, Take III." I don't want to do that. I hate repeating myself. I'd like to do something completely different.

I've done this piano album. I've learned a whole new discipline by composing these pieces. It took me eight years, and I'm interested to see where that takes me next. Maybe I'll take that discipline and put it into another type of songwriting altogether. I'm not afraid to write lyrics, but I want to write totally differently from the way that I used to. I'll have to be saying something totally different.

Part of me is feeling like I went through this very fruitful, productive songwriting stage, and now I have to step out of it and leave it alone for a while. I have to want to come back and say something meaningful, not just about my personal experiences – you know, me and my girlfriend and what happened with Christie or my daughter or my dog. I have to feel like I've really got something to say. I suppose I was a lot more arrogant when I was younger. I really thought what I had to say was very important, and needed to be said.

I look at the work that the Beatles did after they split up. Some of it was good, and some of it I didn't like much. Some of McCartney's stuff I didn't think was up to snuff. Lennon, when he's talking about "Yoko and me" and "me and Yoko," I didn't care. And he was this great figure.

So Lennon should have stopped writing?

BJ: Maybe it's what Elton said, he's competitive as hell. That may be the key to why he continues to write. And it's true – he is very competitive. I don't have that same drive. I don't feel like I need to prove anything. Only to me. What satisfies me. What do I want to do for me. What interests me. And my musical interests are all over the place. I'm interested in jazz again. I'm interested in classical music. I'm interested in strange music that I don't even know about. What form will that take – if it takes any form – I don't know. And no matter what everybody says, you know, "Come on, we really want to hear some new stuff," that's not going to make me write.

So what makes you go out and play your pop songs?

BJ: [*Long hesitation*] That's a good question. You know, playing them with Elton is different from playing them on my own. If I was doing my own tour, I would be sick of doing the same thing the same way. Working with Elton brings a different dynamic.

If I had been a band, I would have broken up a long time ago. But I can't break up – I'm a solo artist. So how do you break up? Well, what you can do is join something. That's fun. So I get to play his stuff. I get to play with his musicians. His musicians play my stuff, and he gets to play my stuff. And then we play together. So it's almost like a piano band. And that makes it interesting. It wasn't just a matter of packaging – although the money is unbelievable. It's crazy. But that's not it alone. There's more to it than that.

When this tour ends, I don't have any plans to tour again. I'm not making the big announcement – "I'm never going to tour again." I'm not retiring. I just don't want to tour the way I used to. I'd like to spend more time composing. I'm going to be building a house. My daughter is 16. There's only a few more years until she goes off and lives her life. I want to be around for that. And I guess I'll see what I'm going to do.

I don't have this compulsion to put something out to the public. I feel like I've had an unbelievably successful career and great years in the major leagues, playing in the big stadiums, in the spotlight. There are new people coming along – let them have their day in the sun. I've had my day. I almost have that Greta Garbo thing going. I would kind of like to fade away. It doesn't bother me. I don't have this driving need to be famous. I don't have that Judy Garland thing where I need the audience to love me. I don't have that at all.

Maybe in the music business, that's not good. The record company can't understand it: "Do you know how many millions of dollars we'll give you if you'll deliver an album?" And I'll say, Yeah, but I just don't want to. "What do you mean you don't want to?" It just goes down the line. [*Incredulously*] "He doesn't want to." "He doesn't want to."

I mean, when you read *Catcher in the Rye*, it's like, Jesus, how do you follow that? Maybe that's what it was. Maybe that's all we needed. The Beatles, how many albums did they put out – 10, 11? That's all. That's all we needed. Of course, we want more. We're pigs. But I don't think they should have done more. When it was time for them to stop – good. Stop.

A much shorter version of this interview appeared in The New York Times, *March 10, 2002.*

Lucinda Williams

"Sometimes you already had it, and you just didn't know"

Making records used to be an epic undertaking for Lucinda Williams, but the self-described "late bloomer" is starting to get the hang of it.

Lucinda Williams's eighth album, *World Without Tears*, will sound immediately recognizable to anyone familiar with her work. In particular, it combines the rock 'n' roll muscle of her most successful album, *Car Wheels on a Gravel Road*, with the obsessive introspection of her most recent one, *Essence*. But even the quiet songs on *World Without Tears* sound raw. Recorded live in the studio, the album bristles with immediacy. An unsettling restlessness coils at the heart of its most peaceful moments.

Williams and restlessness go way back. Born in Louisiana, daughter of poet Miller Williams, she has called many places home over the years, but just long enough to get the itch to move on to the next place. In the '70s and early '80s, she lived in Texas, finding her voice in the fertile songwriter communities of Austin and Houston before migrating west to Los Angeles and then back east to Nashville in the '90s. Just over a year ago, she moved back out to Los Angeles, which is where she calls from for this interview to talk about her new album. For the moment, at least, she sounds content with her new surroundings; the L.A. music scene is lifting her spirits. "There's great stuff happening right now," she says, "music that hearkens back to the outlaw country of Waylon Jennings and Merle Haggard. It's mostly people in their 30s who have rediscovered that music. Somebody called it 'Stone Country,' and I like that. And then there's 'Canyon Country,' stuff that's more like Neil Young and Gram Parsons."

On the day we speak, Williams is just four days shy of her 50th birthday [January 26]. How is she dealing with that landmark? "Oh, God," she groans. "Try to get it right, because *Entertainment Weekly* listed my age as 51. It's like, give me a break. Don't push it past where it needs to be!

"But I'm taking it all in stride for the most part," she continues. "I'm a late bloomer – and I'm blessed with good genes. Everybody is surprised when I tell them I'm going to be 50. They all compliment me – 'Oh, you don't look it,' and 'I'd never know if you hadn't told me,' and all this stuff. My last couple of boyfriends have been quite a bit younger than I am, so that tells you something right there. And I feel like, as an artist, I'm still learning and growing. I'm not over. I haven't finished anything."

Did you start out with a specific plan for World Without Tears*?*

I was thinking somewhat consciously about wanting to do more of a rock record, especially since *Essence* was so low-key and mellow. But just because I want to do something a certain way doesn't mean it's going to happen. For the most part, I just got lucky.

Way before we even went into the studio, I had been talking to Greg Sowders, the drummer in the Long Ryders who I used to be married to, and he was saying, "C'mon, Lucinda – you can do it. This could be your *Exile on Main Street*." And then I delved into the process, and it just started unfolding that way.

You recorded with your road band this time around.

That was a real part of the organic process. Normally we would have had outside players do overdubs and stuff, but at a certain point, we decided, "Let's just do it ourselves." We'd been playing the songs on the road, so for the most part they were already arranged. And we did all the recording live.

We worked with Mark Howard, who'd done [Bob Dylan's] *Time Out of Mind* with Daniel Lanois. He also worked on [Dylan's] *Oh Mercy* and Willie Nelson's *Teatro*. We ended up with just the three guys in the band, me and Mark – just the five of us for the whole record in one big room.

And you recorded in L.A.?

We did it at this place called the Paramour, which is a 1920s mansion on four acres on the top of a hill in the middle of Silver Lake. It's real atmospheric. Mark discovered it. He lives in the neighborhood and just stumbled upon it one day and made a deal with the owner. Mark has a remote studio, so he set it up in what's called the Ballroom, this huge room where they would entertain, so the acoustics were originally designed for live music.

Did it freak you out to record live?

I was skeptical in the beginning. I was nervous. I kept saying, "I don't know if this is going to work. What if I need to redo my vocals?" Mark just said, "Humor me. Let's see what we get. If we have to redo something, we'll do it. Don't worry." So we put "Ventura" down live. Then we all listened back to it, and looked at each other and went, "Wow, this sounds really good!" Long story short, we ended up doing the whole record like that.

It sounds like you worked up a nice communal vibe.

One of the reasons that happened was we started doing these listening parties at the end of every week on Friday night. We would invite people to come in and listen to the tracks – not like a business thing, just friends, people we wanted to hear the stuff and who would be excited. We started out with a few friends, and then it grew into this regular weekly thing. It really became an important part of the process because it enabled us to hear through other people's ears. And if people would react excitedly to a particular track, they'd make comments, so we were able to learn from that.

Were there any songs you had a difficult time with?

There were a couple where we kind of, what we called, "chased it" – like second-guessed it, tried to do it over again. "Those Three Days" is one that we were having trouble with. The version on the record is one that we went back to, one of the initial takes we did of it. When we first put the song down, I approached it with kind of a half-assed attitude, like, "Let's get through this and then we'll do it over again later." I was in a bad mood, and I was tired. So we spent a couple of days chasing that track, trying to re-cut it. I said, "I'm going to really nail it now! I'm going to put some attitude in it." And all that happened was that it sounded overdone.

What I've learned, now that I'm becoming a veteran at recording, is that it doesn't always work to make a conscious effort at trying to better something. Sometimes you already had it, and you just didn't know. That's one of the things Mark told me. He said, "Lucinda, I know you don't realize this, but a lot of times you get your best performances when you are at a disadvantage."

What did he mean by that?

Well, what he means is, like…this is what's so hard about recording to me. If I'm feeling tired, it's hard for me to get outside myself and be objective. Every time I listen back, I think it's not good enough, because I remember how I felt. But now I think sometimes when you're at a disadvantage, something comes out from inside of you in the performance that you're not aware of. That's one of the hardest lessons that I've had to learn – and I still haven't bought it completely. I still tend to go back and…anyway, you could go on and on, analyzing it to death. That's why I've always had trouble making records. The whole process has always been so difficult for me.

What made you call the album World Without Tears*?*

We were going to call it *Fruits of My Labor*, but then when I started reflecting on it after the dust settled, I started leaning towards *World Without Tears*. It just sounds better as a title for the whole body of work. It's more universal. It also seems to fit with the mood of things in general right now in the world.

What's your sense of what's going on in the world right now?

Where do you start? That's what I wrote "American Dream" about. That song was a reaction to the knee-jerk patriotism that was going on after September 11, with all the little American flags all over the place. I had so many mixed feelings about all that. I mean, it's a great country and I do love it, but we still have problems.

I am overjoyed at the whole antiwar movement. I haven't seen that kind of activity in 35 years. So that's a good thing. Then there's also an apathy that I see among younger people that's disheartening. I was at a party the other night and there were three guys standing there, and we were talking about who voted and who didn't. And two of the guys said, "Oh, I never vote. What's the point?" And the other guy said, "I always vote." So I ended up hanging out with him – I don't go out with guys who don't vote!

Well, that should incite a rush to the polls.

I hate that kind of apathy, and that's what I've seen over the past 15 or 20 years. I've always wanted to write more topical songs in the way that Dylan did, and people like Phil Ochs and, of course, Woody Guthrie. But it's so hard. Steve Earle's good at it, but I've found it difficult.

But your songs do seem to suggest the impact of larger events on the lives of individual people.

Human politics, that's more what I do. Individual lives and compassion for another person. Feeling empathetic. Being able to see someone else's point of view and how everything affects everyone else, how we're all connected. It seems that things have gotten to be like every man or woman for him- or herself: "As long as I have mine, the hell with everybody else. That homeless guy can go get a job – fuck him." It really gets to me, that lack of compassion. That's what I find so disturbing. And that starts with the individual. I guess maybe that's my statement.

This interview originally appeared in Texas Music, *spring 2003.*

Sting

"The impossible things that we simply can't understand"

Although this interview ran when Sting received a humanitarian award from the National Academy of Recording Arts and Sciences in early 2004, it was done earlier in the year as part of a documentary, *Sting: Inside the Songs of Sacred Love*, which aired on A&E and later became available as a DVD. Working on the documentary was one of the most fun jobs I ever did. It entailed a week in Paris as Sting was finishing up work on his album *Sacred Love*, and a week at Sting's house in Malibu – a dream right on the shore of the Pacific Ocean – as he rehearsed his band for the show featured in the documentary.

I first interviewed Sting when I was living in Atlanta in 1983 and the Police, the biggest band in the world at that time, were playing there. When I reminded Sting at dinner one night in Malibu that we had met that long ago, he cringed. "Was I an asshole?" he asked. "That's what I ask everybody who met me back then." Over the years, I've had many occasions to interview Sting, and it's always been a pleasure. He's smart, articulate, and loves the challenge of a good conversation.

✦ ✦ ✦ ✦ ✦

"You know, this is our world, we all have a stake in it," Sting said, while he was finishing up the recording of his latest album, *Sacred Love*, in Paris. "So that's the only way peace will be achieved: if we're given our rights, as human beings, all of us. I have a great deal of privilege in my life, a great deal of good fortune, but I'm a rare exception. Most people don't. And until most people do have those freedoms, the world will continue to be in this turmoil. We need to figure out a new way so that peace is more important than war."

Those words have a strong contemporary resonance, needless to say, but helping to find a way for people to live together in peace has been a consistent theme of Sting's since his career began with the Police 25 years ago. "One world is enough for all of us," he sang with that band. On *Sacred Love*, he articulates a vision of love – spiritual, personal, erotic, communal – as a force that can triumph over the greatest evils and most destructive ills. For these reasons – and many others – Sting was an inspiring choice as MusiCares' 2004 Person of the Year.

Of course, Sting has done a great deal more than simply sing about a better world. He has worked hard to make our world a healthier, more nurturing, more beautiful place. Amnesty International awakened his social consciousness in the '80s, and made him aware that the loss of essential human freedoms anywhere in the world diminishes the lives of all people. From that understanding grew his commitment to the rain forest, an environmental issue that relates directly to the human rights of indigenous people and, more broadly, to the very survival of our planet. Sting and his wife, Trudie Styler, have helped make rain forest preservation and restoration a cause that people who live nowhere near primeval jungles can comprehend and support.

Then there is the music itself. In the course of selling tens of millions of records around the world – and earning 11 solo Grammy Awards (as well as five with the Police, who were inducted into the Rock and Roll Hall of Fame last year) – Sting has woven new wave, jazz, Anglo-Celtic folk, world music, and Tin Pan Alley into a sound that remains immediately identifiable as his own. He has starred in movies and acted on Broadway. In his latest artistic leap, he has written a memoir, titled *Broken Music*, which is a reminiscence of his childhood and young adulthood, before the success of the Police. *Broken Music*, too, became a best-seller.

On accepting his award from MusiCares, an organization that aids musicians in medical or personal crises, Sting once again demonstrated his abiding concern for the world community, saying, "I'm deeply proud to be the point person tonight to raise funds to have a safety net underneath musicians, because they nourish the world, and I thank them all for that now."

As you've built an audience over the years, many people have taken a good part of the journey with you. What do you think those people expect and want from you?

I'd like people to recognize a certain progress in the work, which is the result of my desire to get better – to be a better singer, songwriter, musician, arranger, producer. Person, even. That's a grand ambition but it's nonetheless the intention, and each record should reflect this process. I don't think people would come to the concerts and buy the records if they weren't enjoying the process, and they are very much a part of it. They feed my ability to create music, and I take that seriously. I'd never want to put something out for the sake of filling the market place. There's enough noise out there. When you put something out, you have to mean something.

You once said – and it also came through in your memoir – that, while it looks like the Police were instantly successful, you had a long period of slogging it out with other bands before you broke through. How does that make you feel about the success you now enjoy?

I served a long apprenticeship as a musician before I became celebrated. I was 26 before I had a hit record. I'd spent the previous 16 years teaching myself to play an instrument, playing in bands, learning to play different kinds of music, dragging gear up and down stairs, driving for hundreds of miles to the next gig in a van, sleeping in the van, sleeping in fleapits. That apprenticeship is something I value greatly because it makes me appreciate my lifestyle now. I can fly in a private plane if I want to after a show, go to a five-star hotel anywhere in the world. But I remember where I came from and it's not something I'm blasé about. I'm rewarded beyond any expectation for what I would do for nothing, really. That life makes this one meaningful. So I'm grateful for those years. They made me who I am, and I'm proud of who I am.

With the Police you were inducted into the Rock and Roll Hall of Fame last year. What did it mean for you?

Personally, I thought it was a little early. This first act inducted in this particular ceremony was the Righteous Brothers, whom I love. And it was just the right time for them. Twenty-five years doesn't seem that long to me. I'm still too close to the Police to be able to have perspective on it. Of course, it was a great honor and it would be churlish to turn it down. I just wish it happened a little later. Do I want to be in the museum? Not yet, but I'm there. I can only say I'm happy.

Let's talk about Sacred Love. *The duet with Mary J. Blige is reminiscent of a Marvin Gaye–Tammi Terrell duet. I was wondering if you thought about any of those songs, the energy that comes out of duets like that?*

Mary J. Blige was the right singer for this duet. The song is about finding solace in the world through love, through finding that one person. "Whenever I say your name, I'm already praying": That's not just romantic gobbledygook, it's real. If you really love somebody, it's a religious experience when you're with them, think of them, speak to them. Certainly, the only connection I have with religion, apart from music, is this sense of love with someone else. So Mary and I are playing these roles, a relationship that is codependent and necessary. And she is just so passionate that it brought passion out in me. I'm not the most passionate person – I'm English! We find it very difficult to express passion, so we need some help. [*Laughs*]

"Send Your Love" addresses a lot of the issues you're talking about. When you sing a line like "No religion but sex and music," it raises notions about what religion means in the West, what religion means in Islam, what people do in the name of religion, and what could be done more productively in its name. At the same time, the record is soaked in all kinds of religious imagery. So much of your writing is.

I've always been fascinated by religion. Although I don't belong to a denomination, I regard myself as highly religious. I just felt that, in light of September 11 and the subsequent struggle, religion had a lot to answer for. And religion needed to be redefined. It's been used in a very narrow political sense of closing down who we are. In other words, if you belong to my religion, then you are family; if you don't, then you're not: them and us, black and white, good and evil. People imagine that God looks like they do. Well, I don't think God's Episcopalian, Catholic, Islamic, or Jewish. I think He, She, or It is bigger than all of that. And religion needs to address that. It shouldn't be so petty.

There has to be a larger thought. So I had to redefine religion for myself. What are my religions? Music is one of my religions, where I can sense the infinite. And the other is love – sexual love, romantic love. My relationship with my wife, for example, I regard as a devotional practice. It's a way of approaching eternity, infinity, the impossible things that we simply can't understand. Love gives us a window onto that. So the album is really about that – defining religion. I say a very polemic statement: "There's no religion but sex and music." It might embarrass some people, it might insult some people. I don't mean it to. God created both.

Along similar lines, you've got "The Book of My Life," a track that I was particularly affected by. Its elements of introspection and self-examination encourage listeners – willing or not – to come up against some of the events of their own lives.

In the period before I started writing this record, I was engaged in writing an autobiography about the early part of my life – from childhood through young adulthood up to the eve of success. I didn't really want to write about success, fame, or having dinner with Elton – all sorts of celebrity nonsense. I wanted to write about a normal person who becomes famous and what happens to him. I'm writing about my parents – who were very young, 20 and 25, when they had me – from my perspective as a 50-year-old man with a certain amount of wisdom and life experience. And in the process, I learned to forgive them and to love them again. It did bring up a lot of stuff I probably would have preferred to bury. I remember being very depressed at the end of writing the book, because all of this stuff was welling up. So I decided to write "The Book of My Life." There are no secrets in the book. There's lots of stuff that needs to be examined and it's not all good, but it's good to reflect. I get very reflective sitting in front of a fire. The thoughts that come, the memories that come. The song attempts to bring that feeling into somebody else's life, to be reflective, to remember.

At this point in your career, where does your inspiration come from?

I'm not of these guys who waits around for inspiration. I don't sit in the lotus position, meditate, and hopefully I'll channel some God-given message. What I do is put the hours in. I work. I practice music and plod through the piano. I'm a terrible piano player, but I plow through. I'm learning all the time, learning as a guitarist. That's what feeds my inspiration. I learn something from someone better than me and that sparks me: "I could write a song based on this idea." I'm not waiting for a message. Life's too short. You have to work. So I put the hours in.

You've talked about the way September 11 and some of the subsequent events have made you reexamine the role of the artist, the role of music, the role of creativity in general. Obviously, it's a job like any job; on the other hand, it is one that communicates to a lot of people.

I've always considered my job to be important. It's certainly important to me to sing songs, to express ideas, provoke people's interest, enjoyment, or thought. After September 11, it kind of recalibrated everything and made you reconsider it. Something you may have been doing unconsciously for a number of years, suddenly you were alarmed into thinking, "What is it I do? Is it important? How do I justify this?" In a sense, it woke me up. It woke a lot of people. We're still in the process of figuring out what it means. Every single human being on the planet is connected to these events. How does an artist reflect that? I don't say I've an answer, but this record is part of the process of trying to figure it out. I don't think I'll ever get to the end of it, but certainly my intention is to try to understand it.

What drives your involvement with organizations like the Rainforest Foundation or Amnesty International, and what problems arise for a singer addressing social issues?

For most people of my generation who are influenced by, say, Dylan and who became singer-songwriters, that was part of the job. So I suppose it began there. Practically for me, it began in the very early '80s. I was invited to do an Amnesty show in London, and at that point I learned about their work. I remember going to Chile with the Police – this was during the Pinochet regime – and Amnesty gave me information about his regime. There were arguments about whether we should go or not, and I decided that it wasn't like South Africa. It was a society that needed to be kept open for change to come about. So in that sense, I was supported by Amnesty. We went down there, played in Viña del Mar, where a lot of people were murdered, and we had a hateful time ultimately. But that got me going.

Then Amnesty got me to do a world tour with Bruce Springsteen and Peter Gabriel, and if you ask any of them what their favorite tour was, they'll tell you that one. It had a great many memories, but we also raised the membership of Amnesty by a huge percentage, so we had a direct result. At every press conference, I read an Amnesty story. I think the man's name was Fitaram Maskey. He was a political prisoner in Nepal and I read his story in every country. At the end of the tour, I was told he was released. It's because of the embarrassment that governments go through when the spotlight is put on them. Amnesty's one of those civilizing organizations, shaming people to behave in a civil way.

What sustains you through long involvement in a cause?

Knowing that it's not a flash in the pan. This is something that I will consistently support. I got the most flak for the Rainforest Foundation; that was in '89. I have a backseat in that organization now. I mean, I helped raise funds for an infrastructure that is getting on quite nicely, thank you, and they don't need a rock star to be distracting from the real work. But just to consistently do that, it basically silences the critics. So there's satisfaction in that.

The initial impetus was that I visited the jungle and was asked by some people if I could help them demarcate their land. I said, "I'm a singer, I don't know how to demarcate land." They said, "You can help." So my idea was to have one of them tell the story of what was happening to his people, especially the human rights issue. People criticized me like I'm hugging trees or whatever, but it's basically human rights. We met the Pope, the king of Spain, and the prime minister, and I think we generally raised consciousness. But God, I'd got it in the neck. [*Laughs*] I was being stabbed a lot, and I thought, "Well, I'm not sure what I'm doing wrong here." Eventually, we demarcated this piece of land, and we did that by creating a real infrastructure, and that took a while. I've been helped by my wife, who's an extraordinary organizer and who kept me going when I was flagging and thinking I should just give up. She was the engine behind that really.

What do you see as the most pressing issues facing people today?

I think all of these problems are related. You can't separate the environment from human rights. You can't separate the environment from the imbalances of economic power. All these problems are connected. It's all about trying to balance the world. It is completely out of balance in terms of justice, economics and resources.

More personally, how does it feel to publish your first book?

A little scary. I feel like I've just landed on a planet, and I'm not sure whether it's friendly or not. I'm excited about the prospect. It's all new to me. You know, I'm not expecting too many kindnesses from the press. I'm a little anxious, but at the same time, I really wanted to do this. I'm proud of it. I look at it as an artifact and I think, "I wrote that." I wrote every word, and it's not a normal celebrity bio. I think if I've achieved anything it's that. It's something different. I wanted to do something that was going to help me understand my life – and not enumerate how many Grammys I'd won. [*Laughs*] I don't need to do that.

Did it work?

Yes. It made sense of a lot of issues that had been buried, deliberately or unconsciously. Ultimately, it was good to give it an airing and then have a better understanding of why you behave the way you do or believe certain things. I was writing about a child from my perspective, and hopefully soothing and comforting that child. Coming to terms with that as a 50-year-old man was a good thing to do.

Published in slightly different form in
Grammy Magazine, *spring 2004.*

Director's Cut

Director's Cut

For a while at *Rolling Stone*, I was doing interviews for a run of stories that the magazine called its "Directors Series," and four of those interviews are in this section. It was fun for me because while I'm not nearly as well versed in movies as I am in music, I got to speak with people whom I genuinely admire. A couple of them, Al Pacino and Robert Redford, are far better known as actors than directors, but that only allowed me to broaden the scope of the interviews further. In every case, while directing provided the focus for these conversations, the talk certainly didn't end there.

Woody Allen

"The real world is a place I've never felt comfortable in"

He refers to it as "the year" – the maelstrom of events that swept Woody Allen out of his carefully constructed private realm and into, of all things, the national debate on family values. From being perceived, along with Mia Farrow, as half of the perfect modern couple – charmingly combining family and work, glamour and seriousness, commitment and independence – Allen was suddenly a tabloid sensation, no longer being compared with Ingmar Bergman, but with Roman Polanski and Fatty Arbuckle.

The more lurid aspects of the story have resolved into cold facts. After 12 years and 13 movies together, Farrow and Allen have split up, and Allen continues to see Soon-Yi Previn, Farrow's adopted 22-year-old daughter from a previous marriage with conductor André Previn. Farrow was awarded custody of her three children with Allen: their natural child, Satchel, and their two adopted children, Dylan and Moses. An investigation produced no evidence to support Farrow's charge that Allen had sexually abused their daughter Dylan. Farrow is now trying to have Allen's adoption of Dylan and Moses overturned.

Of course, as with all emotional issues in post-'80s America, there is also a business angle. Allen recently split from TriStar – which produced, distributed, and lost a bundle in the United States on Allen's most recent movie, *Husbands and Wives* – and signed a three-picture deal with Sweetland Films, a company headed by one of his oldest friends, Jean Doumanian. Despite persistent rumors to the contrary – and the fact that Sweetland has yet to arrange a distribution deal for Allen's films – both Allen and TriStar deny that Allen's decision had anything to do with his personal problems or the potential of a public backlash against him.

So now, perhaps, the time is right for a few laughs? Allen's new film, *Manhattan Murder Mystery*, is a smart, funny comedy that reunites him with his former lover Diane Keaton for the first time since

Manhattan in 1979, Keaton's cameo in *Radio Days* notwithstanding. Keaton, with whom Allen co-starred in five movies, stepped in when it became clear last fall that Farrow would no longer be appearing in Allen's films. *Manhattan Murder Mystery* is Allen's 24th movie since his debut as a director in 1966. His swift, steady pace of nearly one movie a year has covered an ambitious range of stylistic ground: from early slapstick comedies like *Take the Money and Run* (1969) and *Bananas* (1971) to more mature comic studies of contemporary manners like *Annie Hall* (1977) and *Manhattan*; and from stark psychological dramas like *Interiors* (1978) and *Another Woman* (1988) to troubling examinations of moral corruption like *Crimes and Misdemeanors* (1989) and *Shadows and Fog* (1992). *Annie Hall,* Allen's most celebrated and popular film, won four Oscars, including Allen's awards for best director and best original screenplay.

This interview took place in the course of two 90-minute sessions in the screening room Allen maintains in a Park Avenue hotel, a short walk from his Fifth Avenue penthouse apartment. The room is dimly lit, done in dark tones and rather drear. Allen, who is now 57, sits in a corner of a couch. He fiddles absently with a throw pillow in his lap and leans over or rests his elbows on the arm of the couch as we talk. I sit in a chair immediately to his left.

Instantly recognizable, Allen looks and dresses exactly as you'd think – a plain white shirt the first day, a light polo shirt the second, khaki pants, the glasses. But he doesn't stammer, doesn't hesitate, doesn't tell jokes, doesn't try to endear himself. He looks healthy, fit, even strong. He's polite and thoughtful, considerate in the way a host is considerate of a guest he has admitted into his world – a protected world that in the course of "the year" had been at war, in tumult, under siege, but that has now been painstakingly restored to the appearance of order.

Was it a struggle to make Manhattan Murder Mystery *with everything that was going on in your personal life?*

It was not hard. When all my personal woes began, I was determined not to let all that nonsense become the focus of my entire life. To suddenly find myself not working and obsessing over…a court date or something would seem to me the height of self-destructiveness. So I worked. I increased my physical exercise.

People who were in concentration camps learned that it was positive for them to shave every day and be disciplined, eat their food. Certain things were important under those ridiculously horrible conditions for keeping their sanity and health and their best chance of survival. I felt that this was true here. Even though I was going through terrible things, I wanted to keep a focus. I never missed an evening playing clarinet at Michael's Pub. It would be an easy step – downward – to let myself be too overcome or preoccupied with my problems.

So it was not hard. I went into work every morning, and it was an easy picture. We finished it nicely, on schedule and under budget.

What's the genesis of the movie?

I've always wanted to make a murder mystery, just for pure self-indulgent fun. Years ago, when I did *Annie Hall*, I wrote a version of it that was a murder mystery. It began the exact same way: I met Diane Keaton in front of the movie house, and we went home that night and met our next-door neighbors, and they have us in, and then one of them dies. It was the same story. And then I thought, "No, I don't really want to do a murder mystery, because it's too self-indulgent, it's a genre piece." So I changed it, and we did *Annie Hall*.

Then about a year ago or so, I spoke to Marshall Brickman and said, "Why don't we try and whip this into shape?" I had some of the story, and he came in, and we plotted out some other points. I thought I would just do it, finally get it off my chest after all these years.

To me, it seemed like a comic murder mystery filtered through the imagination of someone who had made a movie like Crimes and Misdemeanors.

That's unintentional. The difference is that in something like *Crimes and Misdemeanors*, I'm trying to use the crime to make a larger point. Here I'm trying to use it for fun. It would be the difference – I mean, this will sound pretentious, it's an extreme example – between something like *The Maltese Falcon* or *The Thin Man* versus something like, you know, *Crime and Punishment* or *Macbeth*, where the murder becomes a vehicle for a very profound author to hang all his philosophical ideas on.

What was it like working with Diane Keaton again?

It was great because we're very close friends, and we hadn't worked together for a pretty long time. I really believe that there is a genuine chemistry between Diane and myself. I don't know why, it's just the mixture of the elements, who she is and who I am. It's a pleasure to work with her.

I think, along with Judy Holliday, she's the best screen comedienne we've ever had. After the movies she did with me, she has not chosen to pursue an out-and-out comic agenda in her films. If she had wanted to, she could be as giant as Lucille Ball. She moves funny, she ad-libs funny, she sings, she dances, she's hilarious.

When she's in town, we spend a lot of time together, and we speak on the phone once a week or so. We have remained close. I love her.

Why did you go for such a long time not working with her?

After *Manhattan*, she started dating Warren Beatty, and he was using her in movies. She wanted to do *Reds* – that took a couple of years – and then she wanted to do more dramatic films. Eventually, I started dating Mia, and when there was a female part, I always offered it to her first because I was with her, and we liked to be together and work together. But as soon as I wasn't going to work with Mia again, I called Diane and explained, and she said, "Great, I'd love to." I'd love to do an out-and-out comedy with Diane, because this one I had not written for her. I'd love to start from scratch and write for her.

The role was originally written for Mia Farrow. Did you have to alter it significantly?

No. I didn't do any changes at all, and Keaton made it into the dominant role, because her screen personality is so large – certainly larger than mine. Mia would have played it differently. Mia's naturally – in life – a more sober character than Diane. She's a very fine actress, Mia, but a more serious person. Keaton has a more naturally funny personality. Mia is very good at creating different characters; Keaton's always the same – and great.

I wrote it for an aspect of Mia that I knew – where I was sort of the jerk, and she was the sharp one. And when Keaton did it, I didn't change anything at all, absolutely nothing. I said: "Look, this is a straighter role. This was going to be funny, with Mia being straight and me being the comic persona. I have all the jokes." But when she came in and did it, she became the comic persona. Her personality is so large, it's hard to see anything else on the screen. It's like you're dancing with Fred Astaire, and you may be a decent dancer yourself, but your eye goes to Astaire. Your eye goes to Keaton. She has such a natural gift, she eclipses everyone.

Why have you chosen in the past to work with the women you're involved with?

I was dating Diane Keaton and then Mia, and it just seemed like a natural. They were two actresses. They're both very good; it was easy for me to write for them because I knew them well. It was a logical thing; I saw no reason not to. I knew that Mia could play that character in *Broadway Danny Rose*. I don't think anybody else would have known that, but I knew it because I knew her, and we talked about it. And I can always give Keaton good things to do because I've known her so well for so many years. Apart from that, if I was dating a woman who was an agent or a writer or a producer, I would just cast my movie and not think about it.

But it's one factor that contributes to autobiographical readings of your movies – for better or worse. Do you feel that Husbands and Wives *got overwhelmed by all your personal issues or that people stayed away from it because they disapproved of you?*

I felt that was their loss. *Husbands and Wives*, from my point of view, is a successful picture. It had absolutely zero to do with my private life. Before I shot *Husbands and Wives*, I offered Mia either part. It had nothing to do with my life with her. I asked her if she would rather play the part that Judy Davis ended up playing or the other part, and she read it and said it would probably be easier for her schedule if she played this part. She could have just as easily been the other woman. It was conceived and written before any problems occurred. It was a meaningless, fashionable cliché, the path of least imagination and resistance, to say, "Hey, this is his private life."

I don't feel any really bright or perceptive people would stay away from a movie based on public-relations things. I mean, if someone hears it's a good movie, they would go see it. And if not, that's their loss. They miss what would be entertaining for them. I can't even imagine how the chain of thought would go, someone saying, "This movie's come out, and I hear it's a good movie, but it's about his personal life, so I'm not going to see it."

I've put out pictures – *Broadway Danny Rose*, for example – where people said they didn't do as well at the box office because they were black and white. And I think to myself, "The kind of mentality that would think, 'Gee, I don't want to see this movie because it's black and white,' I'm better off without that person seeing it." If that's the level of their imagination or perception, then I'd just as soon they didn't see the picture. And I feel the same way here. The picture has to be judged on its merits completely and nothing else.

Now, in terms of *Manhattan Murder Mystery*, it will be very interesting to see what happens. If it gets good reviews and people don't come to it, I guess I'll think, "That's their problem." I don't know what else to do. All I can do is make the film and do the best I can. I know that years down the line, people will be watching *Husbands and Wives* and enjoying it. And with *Manhattan Murder Mystery*, if most people writing about it say, "It's funny and entertaining," I'll just feel people are making a self-punishing mistake not to see it.

Was the fact that Husbands and Wives *lost so much money any factor in your decision to leave TriStar?*

Not at all. TriStar has been very good. They promoted *Husbands and Wives* well, and I think they're doing an excellent job with *Manhattan Murder Mystery*. I have no negative feelings about them. But the situation with Sweetland is so seductive, because I love the idea of an isolated, controllable mom-and-pop store for my movies.

I have a situation where my closest friend in the world has started a film company, and it operates out of New York, and this person is partners with my sister. I mean, it's people who have only my artistic interests at heart. They're interested only in allowing me to make any kind of film I want to make, whether it's black and white or color, dramatic or a comedy.

Now, I had a very good deal that way with TriStar as well: It was 90 percent friends and 10 percent the parent company, who were very nice but still had obligations to stockholders and other responsibilities. But you never can tell what can happen – you're still out in the commercial world. Here I don't have that. It's a 100-percent self-contained operation.

What's your attitude about your audience at this point?

The healthiest focus is not to think of the audience, not to think of the critics, just to do what you want to do and put it out there, and pray that they like it. That's why it's very important for me not to read criticism of myself – positive or negative – because I don't want to be influenced when I'm thinking of my next project. And the same with the audience. I'm not trying to elude them – or to pander to them.

I don't mean to sound callous or cavalier. I love when the audience likes the picture, and I like it if critics like the picture – that's pleasurable and fun. But that's something you find out down the line somehow. It doesn't happen to me that often, incidentally. I have not had a lot of commercial hits over the years. I've had enough success, so that at the price I make movies, it's a reasonably good bet. The thing that has saved me over the last 15 years or so has been Europe. Even a picture like *Husbands and Wives* or *Alice* – *Alice* made more money in Paris than in all of the United States. Just in Paris, not France itself. So it saves me.

Your attitude toward your audience became an issue around the time of Stardust Memories, *where it seemed that you were perceiving your audience as these Fellini-esque grotesques.*

People hated me, they got so angry at me when I did that movie. But that was their misconception. First of all, it was a complete work of fiction. I was writing about a fictional film director who had had all kinds of success and was still suicidally depressed. If I had gotten somebody else to play that role, they may not have even made the association or made it more tenuously.

But they confuse everything I do with my life. They think my life was *Annie Hall*, they think it was *Manhattan*, they think it was *Husbands and Wives*. But it was a fictional story about a film director who had become suicidal. He was seeing life as encroaching upon him in a way that made him feel depressed and unsatisfied. It had nothing to do with me. I wasn't depressed and didn't feel that way. It was just an interesting story to me.

But you write the movies, direct them, often act in them. Your girlfriends appear in them. You have a set of issues that you explore consistently. Isn't there any basis for looking at your movies in autobiographical terms?

People have difficulty conceiving that another person has an act of imagination – an *act of* imagination, not an *active* imagination. For some reason, they feel at sea if they can't relate it to something real. These things are made up. Charlie Chaplin was not a little guy who was inept and beset by things. Clark Gable used to say he'd go for a drink in a bar and some guy would come up and say, "You're not so tough," and want to fight with him.

When I did *Stardust Memories*, I was making up a story. If I did feel that way about the audience, which I didn't, I certainly would have been too smart to do it in a movie. I mean, I'm not a dope. But I never had those feelings. Everything was fine. I had just done *Manhattan* and I was happy. I didn't feel at all suicidal. I didn't have any of those thoughts.

But if it causes so much confusion, why do you act in your movies?

I'd just as soon not. I couldn't care less. When I made my film deals, they wanted me to be in the movies. It was always hard to get a contract that let me not be in a portion of them. The movie that I'm starting to shoot in September I'm not in, and I'll be happy not to be in it. Every once in a while, there's a part I can play because it's right up my alley. One of the advantages of being in it, when the part is right, is that I know how to do it. I wrote it, and it saves a lot of time. Otherwise, I'd be honored and thrilled if I could have Dustin Hoffman play it or something. I'd much prefer it.

Which of your movies do you feel best about, and in which movies do you feel that you didn't achieve what you wanted?

The three best ones to me were *Husbands and Wives*, *Zelig*, and *The Purple Rose of Cairo*. Those are the ones that I felt I achieved what I set out to make. I've had other films that were successful, but I'm aware of the compromises I made – and they were tremendous.

Artistic compromises?

Yeah, where I screwed up things. I ended *Hannah and Her Sisters* too happily. I ended *Alice* incorrectly.

Why did Hannah *end too happily?*

The original ending was that Michael Caine still loved Barbara Hershey. She had married someone else, and though he had gone back to his wife, he still was crazy about her and was going through the motions. That's the way it ended. And it was so down for everyone that there was a huge feeling of disappointment and dissatisfaction every time I screened it. People went away with a bad taste in their mouth. Where I screwed up was, I didn't properly prepare for that ending in the body of the film. So I had to put a more benign ending on, and it dissatisfied me.

In the case of *Alice*, I had an inspired ending that enraged everybody: She flies to India, goes to work with Mother Teresa, and you actually see her doing that. People were enraged by it. They said, "You've got to be kidding. Mother Teresa is a joke name. It's terrible. There's so many problems in New York City, she's such a cop-out to go there" – I mean, 10 million excuses. Everybody I showed it to was outraged.

Who did you show it to?

When I'm finished with a film, I usually show it to friends here and ask them what they think – groups of six, eight, ten, who give me feedback. I always ask them to be as brutal as possible, not to spare me anything – and they try. And that was the problem.

In retrospect, you would prefer the movies with the endings you originally wanted?

I would have preferred it, but I think it would be not enjoyable at all to anyone else. When everyone, unanimously, is so put off by the same thing, I start to think, "I've done something wrong. That's not the feeling I wanted them to have and they're having it."

This being Rolling Stone, *I feel I have to ask: What's your problem with rock 'n' roll? Your references to it in your films are always so disparaging.*

I'm willing to say this is a deficiency in me, because many people whose taste I completely respect – musical people as well – go so crazy over it. I don't know what it is that I'm missing. After like 1950, I tuned out somehow. I have no appreciation whatsoever, zero, for stuff that came after that. I don't know how to explain it. I mean, the Elvis thing escapes me 100 percent. I don't want to knock the guy, but to me, it just didn't mean anything. And nothing that came after it meant anything either. So much of it sounded like just eardrum-busting noise – and the incredibly self-conscious lyrics, message lyrics, whether they were social or psychological. The whole drug thing completely eluded me; I've never taken a puff of marijuana in my life. I have no idea what it's like and not the slightest curiosity. So people are always referring to what turn out to be these major rock groups, and I have no idea who they're talking about. I'm like a dinosaur.

Interestingly, Mia and I, we always used to joke that we had nothing in common. I love New York, she didn't love it; I liked sports, she didn't like sports. It was right down the line. The one thing that we had in common was our musical taste, because for some reason she also just never warmed up to that kind of music.

When people criticized Spike Lee for making movies that focused on the black community virtually to the exclusion of whites, he asked why nobody asks you why there aren't more black people in your films? Why aren't there?

There's a difference between putting them in the movie and writing about them. Normally speaking, I shoot on the streets of New York, and who gets in the background is who happens to be there. And when we have extras, we always try and specify that we want blacks and Hispanics. But in terms of writing about the lives of people – in his case and my case – it's not what we could do best. I don't think I could do it well at all, and I'd be surprised if he could. I see no evidence that he could write a story about the problems of a Jewish family in Brooklyn and really get an authentic feel to it. In the same sense, I can't really write a story with any kind of authenticity about the problems of the black community.

Now there is an aspect of black culture that I could write about: I think I could do a great New Orleans jazz film and might one day. One of the reasons I haven't is that the concept I have in mind for that kind of picture is substantially more expensive than the budgets I get. Otherwise, I don't know what goes on in the hearts and minds of the black community in Watts or Harlem. When I see *Boyz n the Hood* or *Menace II Society* – and I love both of them – it requires a much greater depth of perception and experience to make those pictures. I wouldn't know where to begin.

You've always been obsessed in your work with death, aging, mortality, and a lack of moral certainty. How has your attitude toward those issues changed as you've gotten older and had more experiences yourself?

Well, it's remained terrible. I can't say it's gotten worse with the years; it was terrible when I was younger, it's terrible now. I've always had a very pessimistic view of everything. And I still do. I find it very hard to shake.

Is humor part of what makes it bearable?

No, humor is involuntary with me. It doesn't make it bearable. It's just something that I can do, so I do it for a living. I don't feel, you know, that feeling of, "Heck, what can you do but laugh at it?" I feel it's terrible, and one wants to say, "Why are we laughing? Does nobody realize what's going on out there?"

In Manhattan *and elsewhere, you seem to suggest that people create enormously complicated emotional lives for themselves as a way of avoiding having to look at those bigger issues.*

Yes, I think that one is always creating problems for oneself in life that to the outside eye seem silly and trivial – because indeed they are. They're irrational and foolish. But they keep you busy. They keep you from focusing on the other kind of problems. I don't know what it's called – existential boredom or just the sense that you are going to eat that day, you have money, you have clothes, but you come face to face with, "Well, then what?"

In Husbands and Wives, *the choices seem to be either crazy passion or monotony.*

That's what I see around me. When I look around, I see an unsettled feeling that everybody has, certainly in the area of their personal relationships. Imperfect, you know – and they make these patchwork things. It's like Sydney Pollack and Judy Davis, they have the sexual problem and they, you know…

Sweep it under the rug.

Yeah, it rises up, and it falls, and because they don't really want to break up, they sweep it under somehow and go on. Whatever jerry-built accommodation they can make, they make. Everybody I know has problems with their romantic relationships, their marital relationships. The demons of romance and marriage and sex and all of that are very rough on people.

One of the consistent elements of your movies is the decline from some romantic ideal into an almost unbearably compromised real world.

Right. The real world is a place that I've never felt comfortable in. I think that my generation grew up with a value system heavily marked by films. There was no television, we didn't read books. Your values and everything you thought about life, you got from this overwhelmingly powerful image of the movies. You'd go into a beautiful movie theater; even the neighborhood movie theaters were beautifully carpeted, chandeliers, brass, they were gorgeous. You'd go in, and suddenly on some ugly, broken-down, sun-drenched street in Brooklyn on a summer afternoon, suddenly you're in a totally different world and there's a pirate ship off Spain. You saw all of that as real as could be. Then that picture was over. And there were six people living in a penthouse on Park Avenue and going to nightclubs; and all the women were beautiful, and all the guys were attractive, and everybody always had the right thing to say. This is overwhelming when you're a kid. And it forms your value system, and it's hard to outgrow.

Now you do outgrow it because you see the world is not really like that. But my tendency, like when I made *Manhattan*, was to portray things very romantically. People are always telling me that they just don't know the New York that I write about, that they don't know that it really ever existed. I think it did. It may have only existed in movies, I don't know. But for me, that's all derived from a childhood of moviegoing. My ideas of romance came from movies. I mean, I speak to adults my age, and they're constantly telling me that they still are hurt in life because they can't get their mind around the fact that things are not the way they were led to believe when they were growing up.

Is all of this related to your fascination with magic and magic tricks and illusion?

I always loved magic as a boy, and I feel that the only way out of things is magic. Everything is so glum, so really depressing, that the only hope you have is…it would require magic, you know. There's no way, short of a magical solution. All the rational solutions are finally degrees of workable but not thrilling.

People are always extolling "truth" and "real life" and "truth is beauty." I don't think that; I don't think that's beauty. You can't really come face to face with reality too frequently or for too long a time because it'll wipe you out. It's too brutal; it's too terrible a thing.

Sometimes I've had the thought that to try to make films that say something, I'm not doing my fellow man a service. I would be better off not asking the audience to try to come to grips with certain issues because those issues ultimately always lead you to a dead end. They're never going to be understandable, they're never going to be solvable. We all have a terrible, fierce burden to carry, and the person who really does something nice is the guy who writes a pretty song or plays a pretty piece of music or makes a film that diverts.

It's great when people can go into a movie house for an hour and a half and just see Fred Astaire or Abbott and Costello. They laugh, and they're a little refreshed. They've had a breather from the storm, and that should be the function of films – not *The Bicycle Thief* or *Grand Illusion* or Bergman.

It's similar to the aliens' message in Stardust Memories *– that if you want to help mankind, you should tell funnier jokes.*

Yes, it's a case that can be made – and I do make in the privacy of my shower very often. What is the point of doing a film like *Crimes and*

Misdemeanors? Yes, you're trying to reflect on the fact that there's no God, and if you commit a crime and nobody catches you, if you have no conscience about it, you won't go punished. And there is no real justice in the world: Terrible things happen to nice people, and not-so-nice people do very well, and even an attractive and bright girl like Mia in that movie will finally, as the Alan Alda character says, "They don't pay off on trying." What is the point of showing people that? They know it already.

After all that's happened, do you feel that you're at some sort of crisis point or defining moment in your life or career?

Not in the slightest. So many people in this last year have said to me, "How did you get through the year?" I think, "God, I know several people who died of AIDS during the year." That's a problem. What I went through? It's a pain in the ass.

I never think of career in any way at all. See, for one thing, I couldn't care less if I ever made another movie. I have enough money to live. I'm a writer. I'd be very, very happy just to sit home and write books, write plays. People used to say to me, "All this publicity, what if…?" but it never meant a thing to me. I just worked the same way I worked. I did *Husbands and Wives*. I did *Manhattan Murder Mystery*. I'm on to my next film. If people want to see them, fine. If they don't, they won't.

I have just made a deal to make three more films. I'm going to make the same kind of films I've been making. My feeling always is that if the films are good, people will find their way there. And if I'm wrong, and let's say nobody ever wanted to come to a movie of mine again, it wouldn't matter to me that much. I mean, I almost – almost – wouldn't mind it, because a decision that I'd like to make and don't have the nerve to make would be taken out of my hands.

What do you say to the person who has liked your movies in the past, but who now says: "How am I supposed to watch that scene in Manhattan *where he stands near the skeleton and compares infidelity to naming names before a senate committee? How am I supposed to see his movies after what's happened?"*

I say…that's fine. They ought not to see the film is what I say. If it doesn't give them any pleasure, they should not see them. I don't want this to sound callous...but I don't care. It doesn't mean anything to me whatsoever, whether they come or don't come. I don't...that sounds much worse than I want it to sound.

Nobody has any right whatsoever to any judgment of my private life. They're not entitled to know anything about it. What they know, they know 10th hand from tabloid newspapers. I do what I want, and they can take it or leave it. It sounds harsh when I say that. I don't mean it harsh.

All I can say is, if there is any impediment to them enjoying the movies, then they ought not to come and see them, because they're not going to like them.

What's ahead for you at this point?

Well, unless there's an external change, pretty much the same thing. I have had a very terrible year, and if that really were to reflect in responses to my work, if I was not able to work or something...but I don't really see that, because I still get so many offers from all over the world to make films. So I guess what I'm probably going to be doing is just making films.

I don't know, maybe I can get lucky, get blackballed from the industry, live out my dream and write books and stay home. But otherwise...

What is your frame of mind at this point? Are you content?

No. My frame of mind is still unsettled because there are unresolved issues in relation to me and my children. And that's tough. That's the source of great pain. But apart from that, I feel fine. I'm in good health, and I've got a million ideas. Everything is going very smoothly. Once I get the paternal situation resolved, I'll be fine. The worst of the storm is over.

It all began last August 4, and those first few months were incredible. But I say "incredible" – it's only the problem seeing the kids that's really hurt. The actual experience itself, apart from that, wasn't very hard for me.

But it must have been ravaging. You and Mia had been together for so long – to be suddenly in the thick of something that was so full of anger and recriminations...

Oh, it was terrible. But terrible within the parameters of that level of terrible. It's like when you put out a movie and it gets bad reviews – it's terrible. You worked a year on it, the critics don't like it, the public doesn't come – it's terrible. But it's not really a terrible thing.

And the same thing here. This was terrible, but it's not terrible like the person who goes in and sees their X-ray, and the doctor says, "You see this little spot on your lung?" There's degrees. So it was terrible, but I have it in perspective. Believe me, I suffered much, much worse – much worse – on one or two occasions in my life when I became convinced that I had a brain tumor. This was right after I made *Manhattan*.

What happened?

I had lost the hearing in one ear, and it's more natural to lose it in both. So the doctor said, "Well, we should watch that." I was editing *Manhattan*, and we had this huge book of Gershwin music and lyrics. But in the book, of course, is the biography of Gershwin as well. And you know, he had a brain tumor. Every day I would read it, and I started to become convinced that I had a brain tumor. I finally went to the doctor, and he didn't give me comfort. I didn't hear, "Oh, get out of my office." He said, "All right, we'll give you a series of tests on Monday." And that weekend was terrible, much worse than all of last year put together.

That happened to me one other time. I went to a skin doctor for something and he said, "It's nothing, but let me ask you a question: How long have you had that black dot on your face?" I said, "A couple of weeks." He said,"I want to take it off and do a biopsy. I don't think it's anything, but I want to be safe." I went home and immediately looked in my hypochondriac's manual and found the word *melanoma*, and I spent, again, a much worse three or four days till the labs came back with nothing – much worse than all of last year put together.

You know, "the year," what are you dealing with? Publicity and stuff that's nonsense: Newspapers, domestic quarreling – it's all bullshit. But this other stuff was terrifying to me, absolutely terrifying. That's really the scary stuff. I don't wish that on anybody.

This interview originally appeared in
Rolling Stone, *September 16, 1993.*

Jonathan Demme

"I root for the underdog"

It really shouldn't surprise anyone that Jonathan Demme would defy Hollywood taboos to direct a movie about AIDS, homophobia, and social justice or that the movie Philadelphia would earn over $40 million in its first two months and nab five Academy Award nominations. *Philadelphia* was fueled by three of the director's staunchest convictions: that helping out people who are having a hard time is less a duty than a pleasure; that bigotry is more the result of ignorance than evil; and that for all the country's political outrages, goodness is deep in the American grain. Despite his impeccable downtown New York credentials, Demme, who just turned 50, is less a card-carrying member of the cultural elite than a suburban product who, however astonishingly, believes what he was taught in civics and is determined to act on it.

Certainly little about Demme's early history – first on Long Island, where he was born, and later in Florida – would indicate either his idealism or his eventual success. His ambition to be a veterinarian evaporated when chemistry class at the University of Florida proved insurmountable. He was writing about movies for local papers when his father, then head of publicity at the Fontainebleau hotel in Miami Beach, introduced him to studio mogul – for once, the term can be used unironically – Joseph E. Levine. Levine glanced at some of Demme's reviews – a rave over *Zulu*, one of Levine's movies, natch, proved especially persuasive – and Demme was offered a job as a press agent in New York.

A few years later, while working in Ireland as a publicist on the set of a film by B-movie titan Roger Corman, Demme was invited to write a screenplay for Corman's new company, New World Pictures. The result, *Angels Hard as They Come* (1971), a motorcycle movie based (very loosely) on *Rashomon*, began Demme's film career in not exactly earnest. He continued working for Corman, making his debut as a director in 1974 with *Caged Heat*, a quite literally revealing look at women behind bars, and following it up with *Crazy Mama* (1975) and *Fighting Mad* (1976).

Demme's uniquely sweet American vision began to manifest itself after he split from Corman. He directed *Citizens Band* (1977, retitled *Handle With Care*), an eccentric, bighearted exploration of CB-radio culture, and later, *Melvin and Howard* (1980), about Melvin Dummar, the working-class Nevadan who claimed that Howard Hughes had named him the heir to his fortune.

Demme's baptism by fire came with *Swing Shift* (1984), which he conceived of as an exploration of the lives of working-class women in factories during World War II, but which Goldie Hawn, the film's executive producer and female lead, saw as a star vehicle for herself. Hawn played the heavy, and faced with adding 30 minutes of scenes he couldn't stand, Demme walked.

Following that debacle, Demme delivered a run of films that established him as a significant new directorial voice. *Stop Making Sense* (1984), a splendid rendering of Talking Heads' exultant 1983 tour, won a National Society of Film Critics Award for Best Documentary. Then *Something Wild* (1986), a comedy of urban manners that veers into a violent suspense plot, managed to capture every nuance of life in New York in the mid '80s, from bohemianism to stockbroker paranoia – all set to a fun and friendly, if dauntingly in-the-know, soundtrack.

Swimming to Cambodia (1987), a documentary of performing artist Spalding Gray's riveting monologue about his experiences in Southeast Asia on the set of *The Killing Fields*, seems indistinguishable from Gray onstage. All of Gray's intelligence, neurosis, humor, and sheer humanity are palpably, and somewhat eerily, present. *Married to the Mob* (1988) features Michelle Pfeiffer as a mob wife looking to go straight. In its affectionate sendup of gangster movies, the film, like *Something Wild*, demonstrated Demme's ability to be simultaneously parodic and unapologetically emotional. Even when his characters are cartoons, he seems to love them.

Demme became an industry powerhouse himself – Goldie Hawn, beware! – with *The Silence of the Lambs* (1991), based on the terrifying serial-killer saga by Thomas Harris. The film racked up five Academy Awards (including Best Director for Demme, Best Actress for Jodie Foster, and Best Actor for Anthony Hopkins); particularly estimable was

Hopkins's gripping portrayal of Dr. Hannibal "the Cannibal" Lecter, which lifted the grisly character into the pantheon of American film roles. Despite criticism from gay activists over the depiction of gender-bending murderer Jame Gumb, *Silence* earned more than $130 million.

With *Philadelphia*, Demme took on the story of a gay lawyer with AIDS (Tom Hanks has been nominated for an Academy Award for the role) who is fired by his firm and wins a wrongful-termination suit with the help of an initially homophobic lawyer (Denzel Washington). The film has realized Demme's hope of bringing a gay-oriented AIDS drama into the heartland, though again, not without generating fierce controversy.

Some gay activists – most notably Larry Kramer, author of *The Normal Heart* – have attacked what they consider to be *Philadelphia*'s avoidance of gay sexuality (between Hanks and his lover, played by Antonio Banderas) and its too rose-colored view of Hanks's extended and supportive family. Few people with AIDS are quite so fortunate, they say. In addition, the family of a lawyer who died from AIDS in 1987 has brought a $10 million lawsuit against the creators of *Philadelphia*, including Demme, for allegedly basing the movie on the lawyer's life without acknowledgment. TriStar Pictures, the studio that produced *Philadelphia*, has denied the claim. Demme has refused to comment.

Both as a director and a producer (through his company Clinica Estetico, which roughly translates from Portuguese as "beauty parlor"), Demme has had a hand in a number of small-budget documentaries focused on social issues, including the ongoing series *Haiti Dreams of Democracy*; *Cousin Bobby* (about the director's cousin Robert Castle, a radical clergyman in Harlem); and *One Foot on a Banana Peel, the Other Foot in the Grave*, an AIDS film directed by Demme's late friend, the artist Juan Botas.

Demme has been busy for a man who now says that he hopes to cut back his activities in order to better enjoy life with his wife, Joanne Howard, an artist, and their two children in Nyack, N.Y., where the two interviews for this story took place. His unstoppable enthusiasm, torrent of words, quick, explosive laughter, and energetic engagement of any idea put in front of him suggest that any slowing down of his pace might prove undetectable to the rest of us.

Why did you want to make an AIDS movie?

My friend Juan Botas became sick. Juan was my wife Joanne's soul mate. They had the kind of friendship that was completely without restraint. Juan and I also became good friends – you can see him in his documentary, *One Foot on a Banana Peel.* So when Juan said that he was HIV positive, I reacted in the only positive way I could, which was to try to work somehow.

I talked to my partner Ed Saxon, who was very keen on the idea, and also to Ron Nyswaner, who had done the shooting script for *Swing Shift* – a wonderful writer. That Ron was gay didn't hurt. Anyway, the desire to do a film on AIDS was born of Juan's sickness.

We looked for a story for a long time, and we decided it would be pointless to make a film for people with AIDS. Or for their loved ones. They don't need no movie about AIDS. They live the truth. We wanted to reach people who *don't* know people with AIDS, who look down on people with AIDS.

You made a conscious decision about that?

When I read in the papers that *Philadelphia* was "targeted for the malls," part of me goes, "Oh, my God, that sounds so calculated." But we *were* calculated about it. We calculated what audience we aspired to.

How exactly did you do that?

We started off with angrier scripts, very politicized. Scripts that were informed with the rage I felt when confronted with society's not only indifference but hostility to my sick, courageous friend. Ron and I were pissed, and we were not only aggressive, we were *assaultive.* There was a desire to just, like, stick AIDS in your face and say, "Look at it, you scumbags."

Tom Hanks's character displays conviction and intelligence, but very little anger. Where did that aspect of the story go?

If your immune system is imperiled, the best way to stay alive is to strive for as much serenity as possible – stress is debilitating and will hasten the onslaught of the illness. We made a choice to get spiritual. We had scenes of Tom meditating to tapes, things like that. We felt this guy is so committed to staying alive, at least long enough to see his name vindicated, he is going to identify rage as a wasted emotion. Maybe we went a little too far on that side.

I find it admirable that he isn't more actively angry. The whole time we're talking, though, I keep picturing ACT-UP demonstrations – and I admire that, too. People who are afflicted with this disease are entitled to all the anger they feel like venting. Our choice for this particular guy was he was going to avoid rage.

What about the charge that the gay couple in the movie doesn't get a bed scene?

We had one scene showing the guys preparing to go to sleep. It was like, "We've *done* it! They're in *bed* together! Sure enough, one of them wears pj's, the other doesn't. And, gosh, they're a lot like you and me." But then you're back in court, and all this other shit's happening. So we made a choice. The film was edited, finally, to tell its strongest story in the best possible way. And that was the story about the fight for vindication. The film is richly permeated by feelings of love and attachment between Tom and many people in his life, including Antonio. Their scene together toward the end of the picture in the hospital is one of the most intimate, beautiful scenes between two people I've seen in a long, long time. I think it's stunning.

But didn't Denzel Washington reportedly tell Will Smith that whether you play a gay character or not, you never kiss another man onscreen?

I wouldn't fault Denzel for telling Will Smith that. That's Denzel responding to the same concern that Ron, Tom, Antonio, and I had. It's a real concern. When we see two men kissing, we're the products of our brainwashing – it knocks us back 20 feet. And with *Philadelphia* – I'm sorry, Larry Kramer – I didn't want to risk knocking our audience back 20 feet with images they're not prepared to see. It's just shocking imagery, and I didn't want to shoehorn it in.

Denzel ain't a homophobic guy – he had difficulty understanding some parts of his character's extremes. I think he was saying: "You'd better watch out. With the kind of climate that exists, you don't want to be identified as the guy who makes out with other guys. It could work to your detriment in seeking other roles."

It also becomes the only issue that gets discussed. The movie is two hours, but it becomes the movie in which two guys kiss.

Well, in *Prelude to a Kiss*, which I didn't see, Alec Baldwin kissed an old man – wasn't that considered the *coup de grace* of that movie? We found that there was no way people were going to pay to see that.

There was also a lot of speculation that you made Philadelphia *to atone for offending the gay community, which perceived* The Silence of the Lambs *as homophobic. Did that whole flap have much of an impact on you?*

I hadn't been paying attention to the absence of positive gay characters all that much, so I came away from the protests enlightened. And it made me happy that I was already working on *Philadelphia* before *Lambs* came out.

By the way, maybe you can explain something. Who on earth would get the shit kicked out of them and then turn around and do something nice for the people who kicked the shit out of them? I don't get that.

Well, the reasoning runs, "Jonathan so much wants to do the right thing, to advance the cause of people he sees as oppressed, that it would sting him to get criticism from them."

Right.

"So whether he believed it was justified or not, he would in some way try to make up for it."

Well, I try to be nice – but not *that* nice. [*Laughs*]

The thing about *Philadelphia*, targeting the malls and everything – I didn't have some *better* version, some deeper, more complicated version – of this movie that we turned away from. We set out to make a movie dealing with AIDS discrimination, and there it is. And I've got to tell you: When I sit in a theater, and Denzel says, "Let's talk about it, our fear, our hatred, our *loathing* of homosexuals," I'm like "*What?* An American movie is saying *that?* Holy shit! I love that."

You started out making films with Roger Corman. What are some of the things you learned from him?

As the years slip by, my mind goes to this luncheon I had with Roger, one week before starting my directorial debut. That was Roger's ritual – this unbelievable 60 minutes of *rules*. It remains quite vivid. My favorite – because it has the word *organ* in it – is this one: "Jonathan, never forget what the primary organ is for the moviegoer. It's the eye. You must keep the eye interested." He goes: "Have a lot of foreground action. Have interesting things going on in the background. Move the camera – always find some motivation, don't *just* move the camera but find motivation to move it. If you're in a room too small to move the camera, get a lot of different angles, so you can cut a lot. And don't forget, your actors are the greatest source of inspiration for the eye. Choose actors who look tremendously interesting."

You've earned a reputation as an actor's director. How much do looks affect your casting choices?

It's imperative. I need to want to see their face a lot. If I can't be interested for 15 minutes, how can an audience be expected to go with this person for two hours?

Another imperative is that the actors take full responsibility for the characters. I can't work with actors who look to the director each morning for guidance, actors who ask historical questions – you know, "Where did my guy go to college?" I'm like, "Uh-oh."

Has anything else from the early years stayed with you?

Roger used to refer to himself – and we heard this *endlessly* – as being 40 percent artist and 60 percent businessman. That was *soooo* Roger – to have a formula, even for that. But I'll be damned, 20-some-odd years later, boy, he's right. You'd better be 60 percent businessman, because if you don't have an eye, a *passionate* eye, on getting the picture done at the right cost, you just ain't going to get to make a whole lot more of them. So the terror of going over budget remains happily with me to this day. It's a healthy aesthetic.

Corman also stressed that movies should contain an element of social critique, something that's obviously stayed with you. Even in a jail-girl titillation like Caged Heat, *you had a plot about the medical exploitation of prisoners.*

This is before *Cuckoo's Nest* came out. I thought [*laughs*], "It may only be showing in drive-ins, but it shows what's going on in prisons: We are lobotomizing patients to make them nonviolent." It's true, that's Roger's formula: Your picture must have action, nudity, humor – and a *little bit* of social statement, preferably from a liberal perspective. I'd love to get in deeper with Roger, as to "Is the social statement there because audiences like it? Or, *finally*, is that a little bit of you getting in there?" [*Laughs*]

Another way that has played out for you is that you've always created strong roles for women.

I just admire that extra something that women bring to getting through the day, faced with all of the hassles that we males put in their face. I'm appreciative of that, and I'm glad my movies reflect that.

I root for the underdog. One of the things that made us think *Philadelphia* might have a chance of succeeding was that we came up with the David-and-Goliath one-liner. It's the little guy going up against the big guys. I'm much more interested in that than the eminently capable guys vanquishing their lessers. I mean, my Stallone movie would be *Rocky*, not *Rambo*. Rambo's better armed, he's smarter – superior firepower doesn't interest me.

Also, as someone who's been force-fed things European and male, I long for more variety – in my own life and in what I see onscreen. I'm not interested in boy movies, and I'm not interested in white-people movies. I want to see movies that reflect the country I live in.

People have found fault with *Philadelphia*: "Oh, look at this. You got the noble gay guy who goes to the black lawyer and who lives with a Latin. How PC." *Excuse* me – that's America. We got black attorneys now. We got tons of Latins. The ongoing melting pot has a lot of appeal to me.

It also makes for texture in your movies. Something like putting Michelle Pfeiffer at the center of a gangster comedy helped make Married to the Mob *distinctive in an overwhelmingly male genre.*

What really made me excited about *Married to the Mob* was the same secret theme as *Silence of the Lambs.* A woman wants to go straight, and the men just won't let her. The bad guys won't let her. The good guys won't let her. And she is able to carve out a positive trajectory through other women.

I think every picture, however light, needs to be saying something. I need that for my work – just something, just some kind of theme. *Something Wild* also had that, showing how awful violence is when it occurs. It's not fun. It's not exciting. It's slow and awful and tragic.

Something Wild *also had that "when worlds collide" element that you seem to be drawn to. Even in* Swing Shift, *you have a World War II movie and a factory setting, and suddenly women are introduced into this otherwise alien environment.*

My grandmother, by the way, worked on the assembly line, making fighter planes during World War II. So a story like that had great personal resonance for me. That's one of the reasons it was devastating to have the picture changed so much. I loved that theme of women going up against adversity and rising to the occasion. And this was *true.* You know, we looked at the documentary *Rosie the Riveter* a lot in preparing for the movie and always walked away blubbering. The goal of our fiction was to try to match the emotional impact of that documentary. And in the first version, we did a pretty good job.

That's the sort of thing that got cut out of the picture. I was sad when it got all chopped up.

There's been talk of your version of the movie being released. Any chance of that?

The agents I work with talked to the folks at Warner Bros. to see if it would be possible. We were told that all the outtakes and supportive material of the other version had been destroyed. So the material doesn't exist to do that.

How did the Swing Shift *experience affect you?*

I emerged from it exhausted and damaged, because it was a long, drawn-out fight. I wondered what it was about making films that made it worth trying again and risking a similar experience. It's the opposite experience of what I love about making films. I thrive on collaboration. I thrive on trust. When people are trying to hurt and damage you, that's a face of human beings you don't really wish to see.

Luckily, I committed to *Stop Making Sense* before the shit hit the fan on *Swing Shift*, and we were too deep into preparing for *Sense* to not do it. It boiled down to three days where I was sort of…not directing so much as *officiating* these new scenes that I hated for *Swing Shift*. And at night, I would go to the concert and direct the cameras for *Stop Making Sense*. It was literally going from hell to heaven.

Oh, what a thrill it was to be doing those concerts! Even as I was having the horror of the animosity with *Swing Shift*, I was enjoying the intense collaboration and trust with the Talking Heads and my crew. That really helped me get through the whole thing. Then I moved back to New York – I'd been living in California – and went out to make *Something Wild*. It really felt like a first film. I was clean as a whistle. It was like a student film.

In situations like Stop Making Sense *or* Swimming to Cambodia, *how do you capture a performance?*

It's a simple discipline. I know how transcendental this performance is live. With Spalding Gray, there's no impediment to your enjoyment of what he does, that he's just sitting in a chair, talking. In fact, it's part of the magic. So the discipline is simple: Help the moviegoer get that whack. And you have some added tools. You have the camera, which can provide emphasis. You can bring in sound effects. You can bring in music. The way you make it work onscreen is honoring the material and the artist, not trying to make it cinematic. Trust the source.

You've been inventive in your use of music. What do you see as the role of music in films?

I love manipulating the viewers' emotions through music – and I think it's fair. Music is such an inescapable part of reality – our lives are infused with it. We go to the cleaners, and there's a certain aural mood there as a result of whatever's on the radio. You go home, there'll be a different mood. You've got to honor that dynamic. It's just another tool to try to suck people into the experience.

Like you're watching the scene between Denzel and Tom in the library. One guy is poised to extend himself, overcoming certain hurdles to do so. The other guy is daring to think that maybe someone who had rejected him is reaching out to him. It's OK for a movie to now send you some musical signals to reaffirm that this is a significant moment.

There's also the now-famous opera scene in Philadelphia*, where Tom Hanks uses an aria that's playing as a way of confronting his impending death. It's very long, and it's one of the most controversial scenes in the movie. Did you foresee that response?*

No. It wasn't until I watched the first cut of it after the picture was finished that I… You know, there's two schools of thought on this. There are those who can't believe this overly theatrical, ludicrous sequence and are completely untouched by it. There are also those, myself included, who have a big emotional epiphany through that scene. I mean, I was *devastated* the first time I saw it cut together – tears coming down my face. I was so moved, I couldn't believe it.

But back in the script, I never knew. I knew nothing about opera. I wasn't sure how it should be played. But I always trust great actors. Truthful actors will discover the truth of the scene. Tom and I never discussed how it should be played. Denzel – we didn't talk either. That's Take One in the movie.

Was the scene in which Hanks and Banderas wear sailors' uniforms a joke about gays in the military?

No. That was just for elegance. Having a party hosted by gays, now you're in a minefield. Are you going to have drag or not? Then I realized, they're an elegant couple, they would throw a swellegant, Cole Porter–type party. So the idea of the guys in dress naval – they'll look so handsome, they'll look so elegant. The gays in the military thing came after that, and we were chortling.

It had a timely resonance.

When we showed the picture at the White House, shortly after the shot of the guys dancing in uniform, President Clinton left the room – he had to relieve himself. But I thought that was kind of…interesting timing.

What was it like to screen the movie at the White House?

I'm greedy. It wasn't enough that the movie was seen at the White House – I hoped that with the 50 or so guests, there would have been 10 minutes devoted to a discussion about AIDS in our country. Instead, President Clinton took the guests on a guided tour of the White House. I was disappointed by that.

The enormous success of Silence of the Lambs *really put you on the map as a major director. You probably couldn't have made* Philadelphia *without it. Has that success affected you in more personal ways?*

At certain points, I was afraid there was something – a missing chink of skill – that was going to prevent me from having a movie that was financially successful. That frightened me. So when *Silence of the Lambs* became an unqualified success, I took a huge sigh of relief. I mean, I can't tell you how wonderful that felt.

How do you account for the fear?

I didn't go to film school; I didn't work toward being a filmmaker. I stumbled into writing movie reviews so I could get into the movies for free. Then my father introduces me to Joseph E. Levine, and Levine offers me a job in the movie business. "A huge stroke of luck" doesn't catch it.

Then I wind up crossing paths with Roger Corman, and Corman has just started New World Pictures and needs scripts. My best friend is Joe Viola, one of the most gifted storytellers I've ever known. So Joe and I write a script for Corman, and then, because Joe directs commercials, suddenly Roger wants us to make this motorcycle movie. Again, "an enormous stroke of good fortune" doesn't fully characterize it. I mean, people bust their butts for decades to get to make a picture, and I fell backward into it.

Maybe that's one of the reasons I work so hard, I'm still trying to justify that luck. It's also why I'm amazed when I get to actually finish a picture, because I'm still afraid of being found out: "*He* can't direct! Look! What? *Look!* He's...he's a *phony!*" So there's that still, but I try to use it healthfully – "But wait, I've made several pictures, now surely I'm entitled to..."

Well, before Silence of the Lambs, *people were always predicting breakthroughs for you that never seemed to happen.*

Yeah. Sometimes my pictures would get good notices and, with *Melvin and Howard*, even a lot of notoriety. That's one picture I can go, "That is truly a good movie." Again, luck goes into all this: Thom Mount, who was the head of production at Universal in those days, would open his door to people who weren't happening, such as I. Thom had seen *Citizens Band* and liked it. Mike Nichols was supposed to direct *Melvin and Howard*, but he couldn't cast it to his satisfaction. Thom thought of me as someone who might do a good job on *Melvin and Howard.* Thom went from *Mike Nichols* to a *zero* and trusted me with that picture.

On such things do careers hinge. I will never forget, I was calling Mike Medavoy, trying to persuade him to give a "go" to a little script I had found after we'd done *Married to the Mob.* And Medavoy goes, "Oh, gee, you in your office? I'll call you back in five minutes." Hang up, five minutes later, the phone rings, and Mike goes: "I'm going to send you a book. See what you think of it. It's called *Silence of the Lambs.*"

Actually, as we sit here discussing these things, I get very terrified of the whole bizarre process. [*Laughs*]

Speaking of good fortune, how did you get Bruce Springsteen and Neil Young to write original songs for Philadelphia*? Each song has been nominated for an Academy Award. Did you expect them both to write such introspective ballads?*

I thought, "Let's reassure people. Let's get these guys who, if anything, are identified with a testosterone, machismo kind of thing." Like, "Hey, if Bruce and Neil are part of this party, it's going to be something for the unconverted."

I thought: "What we need is the most up-to-the-minute, guitar-dominated American-rock anthem about injustice to start this movie off.

Who can do that? Neil Young can do that." So we edited a title sequence to "Southern Man" to help him see how his music could power the images we were working with. He said, "I'll try." Six weeks later, "Hi, it's Neil, I'm sending a tape." So in comes this song. We were crying the first time we heard it. I went: "Oh, my God, Neil Young trusts this movie more than I do. Isn't that pathetic?"

But now we're back to square one. Even as I'm going, "He trusts the movie more than I," I *still* don't trust it, because now I'm going to call Bruce Springsteen! The same exact dialogue goes on – "So we still need to kick ass at the beginning." Then one day, this tape shows up. Again, it was not the guitar anthem I had appealed for. Springsteen, like Neil Young, trusted the idea of the movie much more than I was trusting it.

So after Philadelphia, *what's ahead?*

Well, the great thing about documentaries is that if you're interested in social issues, you don't need a $20-million budget to put them onscreen. We made *One Foot on a Banana Peel* for less than $30,000. It's wonderful. It sheds light on the experience of having AIDS in a very different way than *Philadelphia* does. We're also working on *Haiti Dreams of Democracy, Part IV* now.

That's taken away my fervor to do big-budget versions of social issues – unless they offer the possibility of making some wild *magilla* of an entertainment, like the project we're working on based on Taylor Branch's biography of Dr. Martin Luther King, *Parting the Waters*.

What do you have in mind for that?

I'm picturing a cross between *Nashville* and *Battle of Algiers*! But I couldn't be more excited by anything than making the next Tom Harris book.

I'm probably not as open to full-tilt entertainments – "Never mind the message, let's just have a ball" kind of films – as I might have been five, certainly ten years ago. I'd rather read books and be a lazy person than just make a movie anymore. That's probably a function of age and the fact that I've got a family life. I don't need to make movies.

This interview originally appeared in Rolling Stone, *March 24, 1994.*

Robert Redford

"Are we going to find some way to express our outrage?"

Robert Redford aspires to be casual, but doesn't quite get there. Whether seated on a conference-room couch or behind a desk in the Manhattan office of his production company, Wildwood Enterprises, he strikes the postures of relaxation – putting his feet up on a coffee table, leaning back into the couch with his hands behind his head – but they never ring physically true.

Apart from the looks, you would never believe that Redford was an actor – which is, of course, why he's so effective onscreen. Being with him in a room, in fact, oddly produces the same effect as watching him act: It's tempting to assume the handsome exterior and affable manner tell the whole story, but his edgy grace signals that he's holding something back. He is more earnest than publicly introspective – more is going on than he is willing, or able, to reveal. He is the literal definition of reserved.

Redford is dressed in jeans and a T-shirt, the shirt's dark blue just happening to provide a splendid foil to the sky-blue gleam of his eyes and the rich glow of his blond hair. At 57, he no longer looks perfect – his weathered features attest that he has lived an actual life, not a movie-star life – but he looks perfectly himself. Married to Lola Van Wagenen in 1958 (they divorced in 1985) and the father of three children, Redford does not own a home in his native Los Angeles and essentially divides his time between Utah and New York City.

"I always distrusted California quite a bit because I grew up there," he says. "It was not a place you went to, because I was there already. It had no magic for me. I was born at the end of the rainbow, so I didn't see the rainbow. Whatever was wonderful about California for me was slipping away with freeways and concrete and pollution. For me it was a place to leave."

Redford has acted in nearly 30 films since his screen debut in 1962. Appearing opposite Jane Fonda in *Barefoot in the Park* (1967) – a reprise of the role he had successfully played on the Broadway stage – made him a star, and then two years later, *Butch Cassidy and the Sundance Kid* propelled him into the stratosphere. But instead of walking through an endless series of charm-'em-till-they-drop roles, Redford began portraying darker, more troubled American heroes in movies like *Downhill Racer* (1969), *The Candidate* (1972), and *Jeremiah Johnson* (1972). If *The Sting* and *The Way We Were* (both from 1973) – not to mention last year's *Indecent Proposal* – demonstrated Redford's daunting appeal as a handsome leading man, his roles in *Tell Them Willie Boy Is Here* (1969), *The Great Gatsby* (1974), and *All the President's Men* (for which he was also executive producer; 1976) indicated that he had far more on his mind than that tousled head of hair.

Anyone doubting the seriousness of Redford's artistic intent has had those doubts dispelled by his career as a director. He made his debut behind the camera in 1980 with *Ordinary People*, a sympathetic but staunchly unsentimental portrait of the psychological dissolution of an upper-middle-class Midwestern family. The film won him an Academy Award for Best Director and was also named Best Picture.

Instead of instantly cashing in on that success, Redford spent the better part of four years finding practical applications for his aesthetic and political convictions. He established the Sundance Institute in Utah to encourage the development of quality independent films, and at the same time, he founded the Institute for Resource Management to advance research in the field of environmental protection, a passion of his since the late '60s.

In 1988 came Redford's second effort as a director, *The Milagro Beanfield War*, a sweet film that drew on the literary techniques of magic realism to tell the story of the battle between a small Mexican-American community in the Southwest and avaricious developers. *A River Runs Through It* (1992) continued Redford's exploration of humanity's relationship with nature. In that film, which is set in the early decades of the 20th century, fly-fishing becomes a kind of emotional language that the members of a Montana family can speak when little else seems able to hold them together.

Now Redford has directed *Quiz Show*, a gripping look at the quiz-show scandals that rocked the television industry in the 1950s, shaking the country's confidence in the newly prominent medium. Redford centers his film on the story of Charles Van Doren (played by Ralph Fiennes), a hypereducated, upper-crust WASP who became a national hero – the anti-Elvis, proof that not all young people had been corrupted by rock 'n' roll – through his rise on the brainy quiz show "Twenty-One."

It turned out that the show had rigged Van Doren's ascent so that he could replace the reigning champion Herbie Stempel (played with nervous brilliance by John Turturro), a clearly ethnic working-class Jew from Queens, N.Y. Rob Morrow plays Richard Goodwin, the congressional investigator who is determined to get to the bottom of the scandals for his own complex and not entirely idealistic reasons.

In *Quiz Show*, Redford unravels the densely interwoven issues of class, ethnic identity, and the media's manipulation of reality in post–World War II America. And he makes a case for the quiz-show scandals as the beginning of a slide into moral indifference that our country has yet to stall.

"Van Doren's fall from grace had a lot to do with shame," Redford says. "That he would come forward and say, in effect, 'I am ashamed,' had great power. And shame doesn't exist anymore – except maybe some cosmetic company will come up with a product called Shame.

"We could look back and say, 'Oh, my God, we've come that far in that short a time?' " he adds. "If you just look at this subject on the face of it, you say, 'Big deal, what's so special about that?' But in the context of what's going on today, it has a lot of significance to me."

Do you have memories of watching the quiz shows on television?

Yeah, I do. I arrived in New York when all this was hitting. I was 19 years old. I guess you could say the country was still enjoying its age of innocence. I remember being absolutely caught up in the mass hypnosis of these shows. It was irresistible. And the reason you knew it was irresistible was that you found yourself resenting the fact that it was irresistible. You hated that you were watching something that there was something bogus about, but you didn't know what it was, and you watched it anyway.

That feeling persists, unfortunately.

Now it's a fact of life. But I remember my feeling was, I don't believe Van Doren. I believe this is a performance. Like most young actors, I looked at other performances with an extremely critical eye. I remember thinking, "This guy's giving a bad performance. But he is giving a performance." The paradox was that I never doubted the show. I should have gone all the way and said, "Well, then the show is rigged." I just couldn't bring myself to that point. I couldn't go that far.

It was probably just inconceivable.

If it were to happen now, that would be your first assumption, and you would shrug it off. But in those days the combination of our innocence, the new technology of television, the fact that the merchants of our business hadn't quite gotten the grip on it that they now do, I had this odd reaction. I didn't believe Van Doren, but I didn't doubt the show.

But I didn't get involved with *Quiz Show* for any of these reasons. I got involved with it because it gave me some opportunities I was looking for as a director. I wanted the next thing I directed to be urban in nature because I had done rural pieces. I wanted it to be edgy and fast paced because what I had done had been slower, more lyrical. And *Quiz Show* also had elements I had been wanting to touch on for quite a while: greed, the manipulation of truth, and the fact that our lives are controlled by merchants. The merchant mentality dominates my industry, and I've wanted for some time to get at something that would illustrate that.

When you say that you wanted to make an urban picture, was that simply for a new challenge?

That as much as anything. *The Milagro Beanfield War* and *A River Runs Through It*, the rhythms of those films were tied very much to nature – the rhythm of the river, the flow of the river. *The Milagro Beanfield War* had to do with the rhythms of a culture that had no information access, that had no television or radio. They just lived as they had for 400 years.

I enjoyed making those films, but I thought I'd like a change of pace. I wanted to do something that relates more to my experience living in New York. I have two halves in my life. I live out west, in the mountains, but I also love living in New York. That energy is part of my life, and I wanted to be able to work with it.

Were you concerned about the commercial prospects for Quiz Show *at all?*

This is dangerous, I guess, in a commercial sense, because we're living in a time when action runs the show. It's not a time for subtlety or shading or even thought for the most part. Still, I was attracted to it. I'm not that far gone that I would do something *knowing* it wasn't commercial. It's just that it's my own arrogance to think, "Yeah, this is offbeat, but I'm going to try to make it work for people." The challenge here is to convert this into something dramatic enough, emotional enough, that it is almost like watching an action film. What the film tries to illustrate is simply that this was the beginning of a loss of innocence.

The movie does depict the quiz-show scandals as a cultural watershed, the first time it became clear that we couldn't accept what was right before our eyes at face value.

The quiz-show scandal was the beginning of that – it shocked the public. People could not believe they had been ripped off that bad. The effect was shattering. Then, historically, we go right down the line with the deaths of J.F.K., Bobby Kennedy, Martin Luther King, and then Watergate, Irangate, BCCI and S&L, and then [Senator Robert] Packwood and O.J. Simpson – it just keeps going. Each one gets a little worse, and we get a little number each time. And now we're in a place where we just sort of shrug.

But again, what drove me with the film was not the historical event – as it wasn't with *All the President's Men*, either. *All the President's Men* for me was about investigative journalism and what it took to get that particular job done. I just didn't think it had ever been touched before. We'd seen *Front Page* and movies like that, but there had never been, to my knowledge, a film that said, "This is about hard work." What those guys did is they just worked harder – and that still has a payoff in our society.

All the President's Men also was a character-driven piece from the standpoint that these two guys were so different. One guy was a Jew, the other guy was a WASP. One guy was a liberal, the other was a conservative. They were so totally light and dark – that's good stuff dramatically. So it wasn't about Nixon – history took care of that one.

As the man who made All the President's Men, *how did you feel when Nixon died?*

I had no remorse. I did not think he deserved the kudos he got in death. There was this weird revisionism that went on. You feel for the family. There's some sympathy for that. But for me, it was not the passing of a great man. He was a man who dealt us some pretty undignified blows. He did not symbolize the better part of ourselves at all. Look, I admit to some prejudice here because I grew up in California with him as my senator, and I remember at close hand some of the dirty tricks he was doing even back then. He had such a disregard for other human beings.

Watergate is often seen as the source of the contemporary disillusionment with politics; disillusionment has been an important theme in your movies for a long time.

The first picture I produced was in 1969, *Downhill Racer*. It was meant to be the first part of a trilogy that would deal with the same theme – the Pyrrhic victory at the end of someone's ambition in the fields of sports, politics, and business. Three subjects with the same theme: What price the victory? I wanted to take on those subjects because they influence our lives so much.

I only got two parts. I tried for 10 years, but I couldn't get a script on the business picture that was like *Downhill Racer* or *The Candidate*. In a way, *Quiz Show* is maybe a version of it.

My fascination with these subjects through the years connects to the so-called American dream and how it was presented to us and how much of it was true, how much of it was possible, as opposed to how much of it was fantasy perpetrated by advertising agencies to sell things to us. Television was the conduit that pumped this juice into our veins, and what greater example than the quiz shows?

The Candidate *seems remarkably contemporary in that regard also.*

That movie was about my anger and my cynical view of our system. I thought I'd make a very dark film about how we get people elected in this country – it's all about cosmetics, purely about image and cosmetics. And that was 1971. I had no idea it would have that kind of carrying power – to be here in 1994, and nothing has changed. That you'd end up with Dan Quayle.

Quiz Show *essentially has three main characters. Do you see yourself in any of them?*

A little bit of Goodwin. And something of Van Doren. Goodwin is the part of you that senses you're being bullshitted, and you want to cut through it, get to the core of the truth. There's something very chauvinistic about me and this country, about the strengths of this country, because that's what I was given as a kid. I grew up trusting that until I realized that it wasn't quite so true, and the anger that comes from being disillusioned gets played out in my work. Goodwin represents the embodiment of that disillusionment.

With Van Doren, it's simply what celebrity can do to someone, the threats of celebrity on your soul. The temptations that come your way. The struggles with moral ambiguity, the struggle within yourself. Are you going to continue on this path, where things are irresistibly tied to wealth and fame and privilege? Or can you stop, reorient yourself, and redirect yourself for the sake of your own soul?

Also, what it feels like to have iconography become part of your own life, where you're treated differently than you were before just by virtue of who you are. What does that feel like? What pressures does that put on you? So in that regard, there's some connection to the Van Doren character.

How hard was that for you to sort out in your own life?

Well, it's an ongoing struggle that maybe never will be fully resolved. It's resolved enough for me to go on with my life, but it continues. It takes different shapes as you get older. If you stay in the public eye, if you remain a celebrity, it's always there. So that's an ongoing thing.

On the other hand, I'm pretty comfortable going about my business and doing what I'm meant to do. I'm not going to adjust my life for fashion. I'm just going to go forward as an artist and a citizen, and if it gets approval, fine. If not, that's OK, too. The only part I can't control is that persona that's created by some mix of media and the public that becomes like having another person walking around with you, a shadow self. That's tough because I don't control that.

At what point, did you first encounter this persona?

It went across a line. The line first showed up probably when I was in *Barefoot in the Park* in New York, a Broadway play that was hugely successful. That was the first time I moved out of a sphere of my own. And *Butch Cassidy* was where it went beyond, into an international situation.

What was your reaction to that at the time?

It confused me because it happened so quickly. And so *magnificently*. There was something so magnificent about it; it was huge, you know? And it was so quick that it was really hard to adjust to it. The only way I remember being able to deal with it was with humor, to make a great, grand game of it. So I remember playing mad games with my new celebrity. Changing my name, saying I was an exchange student from Bogotá, wearing disguises to a Knicks game, wearing a disguise on a ski hill, only to have the disguise slide halfway up my head and me not know it and have people look at me like I was from outer space. The humor of all that, using get-away cars and passageways and playing with the public as they came to you, playing back to them. Finally, it just got tiring, and I realized I was eating up a lot of my life playing this game. Then I got fearful about the loss and I had to make a big adjustment.

Fearful about the loss?

Fearful about the loss of yourself, your own self – as opposed to your persona. Your persona begins to take over, and you begin to fear the loss of yourself.

Did you begin to feel entrapped by the particular brand of celebrity that came to you – the movie star, the matinee idol, the dashing leading man?

Well, it was a mixture of feelings. On the one hand, you're only human. Who wouldn't, at least in the initial stages of something like that, be flattered? How could you not be? I didn't grow up being told I was good-looking. I was a freckle-faced, kind of redheaded kid that people made fun of because my hair had so many cowlicks. I was out of control as a kid, and people would always tell me, "Slow down," or "Sit down," or "Stop." Or, "Where have you been?"

Then suddenly, you're referred to as a glamorous figure, and it's flattering. Then shortly after that, you begin to realize that what's also coming with that is reduction, that you're then going to be seen in only one light. So, Redford's a movie star, and therefore that's all he can be. I mean, you feel like there's more of yourself to play with, to work with. It begins to unnerve you that you see yourself actually reduced, that you are this, therefore you can't be that. Then another kind of struggle begins.

Was there a point at which you felt that you had to actively combat that?

Yes. *All the President's Men* was one effort. Producing that movie took a long time; it was not easy. It was a three-year effort and a real commitment – it went way beyond just being an actor.

Actually, it started before that with *Downhill Racer* and *The Candidate*, but somehow it never quite sunk in with people that I was producing those movies. I was just "the actor." *All the President's Men* was the first real shift, and I suspect a lot of *All the President's Men* had to do with fighting for the more serious side of myself.

The first movie you directed, Ordinary People, *seemed like a really ambitious project to take on – attempting to dramatize issues like suicide, divorce, psychoanalysis.*

The movie was about a character who could not get in touch with her feelings and the consequences of that to her family. I had never seen that character on film, but I'd seen that character in life a lot – the person who shuts down rather than ride the emotional roller coaster that needs to be ridden. And it dealt with youth, that painful place of not being understood. It was a little bit like *Catcher in the Rye* – I loved that book as a kid. Then there was the look, an area of the Midwest where a strong ethic still exists but that really is most interested in money and comfort and breeding. Those are the things that attracted me to *Ordinary People*.

That movie was a turning point in my life. I was about to turn 40, so there was that decade coming to a close as well as a full decade of work as an actor and producer. There was a confluence of those two things. I thought, "Now I want to direct."

I was beginning to get frustrated with having to put so much body English on the films I was doing. I thought, "I wish I could have total control of this situation. Why not just do it?" I remember talking to a person who worked for me and saying, "I'd like to direct something now, and I'm looking for something that has to do with behavior and feelings." That person then sent me *Ordinary People*. I got it and said, "This is it."

But *Ordinary People* was turned down by a lot of people. Then, Barry Diller, who was at Paramount, said, "Do it." He was very stand-up about it. So I was left alone. It was a little movie, only $6 million. No one gave a shit. And then it was out.

What was directing like the first time?

It's going to sound funny, but it came naturally. There were no great surprises. It's a lot of work, but I enjoy being able to control the whole scene, all the parts. What was difficult was that I didn't have the language of a director. As an actor, I had purposely blocked out learning about the technical parts of my industry. I thought it would get in the way of my performing, I thought that what I owed a film was a performance completely inhabiting the space I was in. If I was splitting my head and being calculating, thinking, "They've got a 50 on this lens now, where are they cutting me?" – I just didn't want any part of that. I said, "The director will shape all that." So I had purposely stayed away from learning the vocabulary of the camera.

So suddenly, I'm directing, and I found myself asked these questions – "Do you want us to put a 25 on it or a 50?" I thought, "Shit, what the hell's that?" And I got into trouble, because I had to try to express myself, and I didn't have the language. So, in frustration on *Ordinary People*, I whipped out a piece of paper and sketched what I had in mind, and the director of photography understood. I ended up doing a whole storyboard because that's how I could communicate with him. By the end of the film, you damn well know I learned a lot. And each time out has gotten easier.

What about working with actors?

That was one thing I felt almost arrogant about – I knew I could communicate to the actors. I knew I would know a good performance and could work with an actor to get one. There's probably very, very little I wouldn't endure from an actor simply because I am one, and I know what the inside feels like.

Are any types of actors hard for you to work with?

The hardest thing for me are actors who think they know but don't. Like an actor who thinks, "Let me do this because this is funny," and it isn't. You have to let them play it out. Meanwhile, the meter's ticking, you don't really have the time. So that's one thing. Maybe an actor who has no sense of rhythm.

What do you mean by rhythm?

Timing. There's a sense of timing some actors have, mostly actors who have been involved with music or athletics. They know when to say the line. They know when to get off it. They know when to move to the next thing. Actors who are not coordinated that way, you have to guide them. They'll take forever to say the line and have no concept if the scene is going down the tubes because they're taking forever. That's frustrating.

Oh, and the actor who won't listen. To me, that's one of the most important things an actor can have – the ability to listen. I felt that very strongly from the time I first became an actor, that listening was as important as speaking. An actor who doesn't listen either to the rhythms of life or to direction does nothing for me.

Were there, among the directors you'd worked with, people who served as models for you?

I've had different relationships, the oldest one with Sydney Pollack – he and I go back to being actors together. That was a very collaborative relationship. I was always comfortable with Sydney being the director and my being the actor because he knew what he was doing. I never paid much attention to what he was doing with the camera – unless we'd be somewhere, and he'd have the camera pointed, and I'd say, "How come you have the camera pointed over there? Isn't this a better view?" And he'd say, "Would you mind? Go have a coffee. Go sit in the woods for a while." [*Laughs*]

George Roy Hill, I learned something from. He really understood the importance of telling a story visually. He wouldn't allow any fat anywhere. He told me he had been influenced by comic strips because there were only four or five panels to tell the story. Punch and payoff – he took that approach in his film work. His storytelling was related to simple editing rather than a lot of meandering, self-indulgent stuff that was very much in vogue in the '60s. I was impressed by that.

Has directing affected your own acting?

I'm much more patient with directors, because now I know what it's like to juggle so many balls, make so many decisions. I always was very impatient with directors who took too many takes because to me it was a sign of insecurity – "You're doing 25 takes when you got it on the fourth one. Are you that insecure?" I would be very arrogant – in my head.

Now, I'm much more tolerant of that because I know what it's like when you're really looking for something, and you're going to stick there until you get it. So that's changed. Directing has probably made me a better actor technically. Directors used to complain about my inability to match, particularly Sydney Pollack. He'd say, "Jesus, you're driving me crazy. You've got a peach in your hand in the first part of the scene – what happened to it?" I'd say. "I'd be more concerned if I didn't have a peach in my hand in the beginning of the scene and I suddenly had one." [*Laughs*]

How do you square your political activism with your acting and directing?

I've always felt if you look at the work, it's there. It's there in *Jeremiah Johnson*. It's there in *The Milagro Beanfield War*. But I've never believed in agitprop because I don't think it works. People don't like to be preached to, treated like children. I do believe in working politically in film, but I also believe that it has to be entertaining, because that's your medium. We're not in politics here.

Right. So A River Runs Through It *is not about cleaning up a river.*

But we couldn't shoot on the river where it took place, because it's polluted. So there's a point to be made. I look at that film and realize that in my own history, rivers flowed like that, clean and fresh and pure. Now it's hard to find one that's not polluted. It's worth thinking about. So there's a kind of subtextual point you're making by saying, "Look how beautiful this was. How is it now?"

Has directing affected what you look for in acting roles?

No. When I first started as an actor, I selfishly only thought of my part. I seldom thought of the movie, the large context. Then when I started to produce, I saw how a role fit into the film. I began to play parts that sometimes were sacrificial to the theme of the film, as in *The Candidate*. Purely as an actor, I would rather have played the campaign manager. It's a better part. But it was better for me to play the candidate because it was more suitable. I could help the film by being the candidate. So I sacrificed an impulse as an actor for a better film.

Then there began to be more and more of those parts. I didn't want to be in *All the President's Men*, but because the bidding got so high on it, I had to be in it. Ostensibly that was not a very exciting part, because the character had a bland exterior. Actually, Bob Woodward used that as a ploy to get information out of people by appearing to be bland, almost boring. I began to think about it and said, "That's actually a pretty good character to play, because underneath that is a kind of killer instinct." Then it became something else. But that was for the sake of the film.

So I guess I changed. But now, I've gone back to the other way. As I've gotten older, I think more about character. For me to spend that kind of energy and time on something, you want to be rewarded, and the reward is not just the sheer commercial success of it. That matters but not that much. What's more interesting is to be satisfied that you've gotten ahold of somebody to put on the screen, that you have a chance to deliver a profile of someone rather than just running around with a gun in your hand.

Any lessons you've learned along the way?

Just two, really: follow your instincts and recognize that this is a business.

What do you mean by that?

Don't expect art to have much currency. It's a business, and that's foremost what it's all about. Don't delude yourself into thinking that art plays that major a role. Art only plays a role insofar as it helps the business. A small film that might be perceived as an art film really only matters if it makes money. That's the business world. I don't think anything profit oriented is easy to change because that's the kind of society we are. It just helps you personally to understand it and not delude yourself.

So that you don't confuse artistic success and commercial success?

No, I try to. I'm a producer, a director. I have Sundance, and we try to help filmmakers get quality product into the marketplace. So I try very much to achieve that balance. But in the end, the great satisfaction I get… I mean, *Milagro Beanfield War* didn't do very well at all. I got tremendous pleasure out of making that film. So, finally, that's a big factor. What kind of pleasure do you get out of your experience?

So what do you want people to take away from their experience of Quiz Show*?*

My own arrogance is that I could hopefully entertain in a way that's also provocative in terms of the lives we're living in our society. That would come in the form of questions the audience would ask themselves.

Maybe out of *Ordinary People*, someone may ask questions about whether they're really in touch with their feelings, particularly involving people they love. For *Quiz Show*: Is this moral ambiguity that we're in going to lead to no morality at all? Is the issue of ethics going out of our culture? Are we going to find some way to express our outrage, or are we just going to continue being numb?

I don't know. Those are issues I can't do a whole lot about, but I can put them out there. The quiz-show scandal in the '50s, that's not what this is about. It's about that scandal being the genesis of where we are now. That's the scandal. So that would be a hope, that we just look at where we are now. I couldn't ask for more than that.

What about where you are now?

I'm doing OK. I don't have any regrets – possibly a few as an actor. It's clear to me that as the business moves toward high tech, toward formula, less toward literacy and more toward visual action, I will have to develop stuff myself that I would want to do as an actor.

But I have no regrets about my career. I'm doing the pictures I want to do, even though they might not be in the mainstream of things. As long as I can continue to do films like the ones I've been doing, I will be happy. I've been doing it for 25 years, and I have no desire to change it. And there's enough subjects out there for me as a director – God knows, five lifetimes couldn't cover all the stories to be told. So I'm fine.

This interview originally appeared in Rolling Stone, *October 6, 1994.*

Al Pacino

"I didn't know that that was showing"

"When I first met him, I was really intimidated," says Oscar winner Kevin Spacey. "I mean, this was Pacino, man." No kidding. A series of images – the ruthless, inscrutable Michael Corleone from the *Godfather* movies, the viciously explosive Tony Montana from *Scarface*, the swaggering, intense salesman Ricky Roma from *Glengarry Glen Ross* – assaults my brain as I come face to face with Al Pacino for this rare interview.

We are here to talk about Pacino's directorial debut on film with *Looking for Richard*. This freewheeling documentary, in which he also stars, presents him in a completely different light: an engaging, maddeningly obsessed quester in search of the meaning of Shakespeare in our everyday lives. A scruffy-looking Pacino wanders the streets of his native New York, asking passersby for their feelings about the Bard and one of his most riveting characters, the fiercely ambitious hunchbacked king, Richard III. You can imagine the responses he gets.

Those zany encounters alternate with behind-the-scenes looks at readings, research, rehearsals, and performances for a film of *Richard III* that Pacino is trying to get under way with such stars as Spacey, Winona Ryder, and Alec Baldwin. "It's the first time that Al has ever revealed his own process, and it really does show him for the ham that he is," says Spacey, laughing. "We're pleased to finally break down the brooding *Godfather* image and show him going for cheap laughs as much as he can. It's kind of delightful." But it's not all joking around. In particular, a seduction scene in which Pacino's Richard weaves an erotic web around a stunned and stunning Winona Ryder as Lady Anne is a spellbinding realization of theater on film.

A four-year labor of love, *Looking for Richard* is one in a series of offbeat projects Pacino has taken on while also starring in such big-ticket items as *Scent of a Woman* (1992) – for which he won his first Academy Award after eight nominations – *Carlito's Way*, *Heat* (with

Robert De Niro), and *City Hall*. Since Pacino's role as a hard-drinking cop in *Sea of Love* and a comic turn in *Dick Tracy* restored his box-office clout after the commercial and critical beatings taken by *Cruising*, *Author! Author!*, and *Revolution*, he has been determined not to play it safe.

At the moment, Pacino is playing to full houses on Broadway in *Hughie*, an obscure one-act play by Eugene O'Neill that Pacino also directed. And he's completed his film of *The Local Stigmatic*, a brutal one-act play by the British playwright Heathcote Williams that has been Pacino's pet project for more than a decade. He still refuses to release it commercially, though the short film (less than an hour long) appeared at New York's Whitney Museum for a few weeks in 1992. Pacino prefers to arrange occasional screenings for pals and journalists.

"I really admire the way he's running his career just the way he wants to," says Sidney Lumet, who directed the star in *Serpico* and *Dog Day Afternoon*, two '70s films that helped establish Pacino as one of the preeminent actors of our time. "They make it very tempting to do what they want you to do," says Lumet of Hollywood studios. "For one thing, the money is ridiculous."

For both sessions of our interview, which are separated by a day, Pacino is improbably dressed in an unconstructed sea-green suit and a black, ribbed tank top that dips low on his chest and under his arms. Accessories include a gold chain and a yellow scarf around his neck, and a pinkie ring. In short, he looks like a styling Italian kid from the Bronx, where he was raised. Born in East Harlem in 1940, the only child of Salvatore and Rose Pacino, Al was two years old when his parents divorced and he and his mother went to live with her parents in a tough Bronx neighborhood. Young Al enjoyed going to the movies with his mother and later playacting all the parts for his grandparents. There he was, age four, mimicking the alcoholic whom Ray Milland portrayed in *The Lost Weekend*. At 17, he dropped out of high school and earned money for acting lessons that would lead to stage roles and his 1971 film breatkthrough as a junkie in *Panic in Needle Park*. Today, the never-married Pacino (he has a daughter, Julie, seven, who lives with her mother) continues to approach his vocation with the fervor of a monk. "In acting," he has said, "you could find some peace, you could get away from the loneliness."

Pacino sets our chairs close together in his Manhattan office, facing each other, on the same side of a long wooden table. From where I sit, I can see over all of Central Park, up into Harlem, nearly to the distant Bronx. He slouches in his chair, listens carefully, and never responds without thinking first. Once he starts talking, he's voluble. He's never glib, nor is he wary or nervous. He just seems to want to get things right.

"I'm easy to talk to," Pacino says as we shake hands after our first meeting, seemingly pleased that I thought so, too. I found myself thinking of something Lumet told me, "Al is so completely dedicated to the truth of what he's doing that he becomes a barometer of truth for everyone else on the set, including the director."

After *Looking for Richard*, Pacino will co-star with two young pretenders to his throne – Johnny Depp in *Donnie Brasco* and Keanu Reeves in *The Devil's Advocate*. More than a quarter of a century into his career, Pacino is still fully in motion. "He's still on this search," says Spacey. "He's on this hunt. And it never ends. You have to keep pursuing it." Here's Al Pacino, in pursuit.

You directed and acted in Looking for Richard *onscreen, and you're directing and acting in* Hughie *onstage. Why take the reins now, for the first time, at 56?*

If you're still hanging around, why not direct? [*Laughs*] I mean, I'm still here, what the hell? Why not try this? I do think, though, when I see the work of directors I admire, it doesn't feel like it's anywhere in my range of talent. I see great directors and what they've done, and I feel humbled by it. However, I do direct as someone who's lived in these worlds for 40 years. I use what I've picked up, what I've come to know. I have 25 years of making movies, and I've worked with some real masters. Even though I wasn't aware of their directing while I was working with them, subliminally I must have picked up something. So it's not like I'm a novice.

Is it a hard switch from acting to directing?

I look at the world from an actor's point of view. I look at you, and I see you not as someone I want to paint, not as someone I want to write about, not as someone I want to direct, but as someone I would act.

There has been a lifetime of that; that's how I see things. With directing, it's like I'm suddenly playing the oboe or something. How the hell did I get to do that?

How did you?

There's reasons for it. The reason I directed the film is, I was out of my head – who else would direct it? [*Laughs*] The reason I directed the play is, I had an idea about how to do this O'Neill play. I thought, "By the time I express it to another director and go through that, I might as well try doing it myself."

What are the qualities of a great director?

I know it when I see it. The world that Coppola got in there in *The Godfather* was indescribable. I don't know how he did it, what was on his mind. You can't call it. I can't tell you when I'm on a set with somebody how the picture's going to turn out by the way they behave. It's only when I see what they've done. It's like a painter, and you're behind the canvas: You can't see what he's painting; he can be drunk or he can be singing. You don't know what he's painting until you see it.

One exception: I do know when directors are unsure. I can feel that. They don't know where to put the camera. Or you see setups being repeated, and you get a sense that the director has not given a lot of thought to the scene. But it's not my place to dwell on it. It doesn't do me any good or the film or the director.

My point is, with certain directors, you can feel their control – they're in charge. They've got a sense of what they're doing, and it just permeates the crew. Then, some directors know how to work with actors better than others, some tire you out, some give you energy, some never say anything, others are enthusiasts. I've worked with them all, all kinds.

Looking for Richard *is a documentary about making a film version of* Richard III. *Why did you decide to take that approach?*

I try to set the stage for you, so that when you get to Shakespeare, you can get into it a little bit more relaxed. Some of the scenes have given you a chance to understand what the characters are doing and why they're doing it, so you're then able to receive the vintage Shakespeare, the real power of his vision.

Why Richard III*?*

Richard was familiar to me because I had played it three times onstage. I understood the play.

The movie invites audiences in. It shows that it's possible to have a variety of views about Shakespeare – there's no "right" view.

We have Shakespeare, and we have a documentary about Shakespeare, two things that people don't want to go see. [*Laughs*] I guess we hope they cancel each other out and serve each other so that they can make the film more popular. It's an experiment – and also, hopefully, it's fun. I try to keep it entertaining.

What about the character of Richard? In certain ways, he's not that dissimilar from other characters you've played. He has this willingness to do anything to get what he wants. Do you feel the connection between him and other roles you've played?

I don't feel that. When you look at it, though, I guess there's a certain similarity, just by the nature of the character. Sometimes I do use certain characters to help play others. Look at *Arturo Ui* by Bertolt Brecht. I did that play many, many years ago, and some of that character turns up in Big Boy Caprice, in *Dick Tracy*. Now what would Bertolt Brecht and *Dick Tracy* have in common? But there are commonalities; you find them.

Looking for Richard *and* Hughie *are hardly blockbusters, and probably the film closest to your heart is your version of* The Local Stigmatic, *which you rarely show. How do you balance such work with box-office projects such as* Heat*?*

It's changed over the years. It has to do with where you go as you go on in life. Right now, I feel like things are exploding all over the place for me. I thought, for instance, that what's going on now was going to be happening 10 years ago. But it wasn't. I found myself not doing anything for four years. So here I am in a place where I have an opportunity to do all these things. I'm not going to do them? In a world where you always feel as though you have to produce – you're a "professional," you've got to come up with the goods – what happens is that you can start repeating yourself or playing it safe, because that's what's asked of you. *Required* of you.

That's restricting. Growth is hard to have happen there. So you have to find a way to experiment, to get a perspective that isn't just about success or failure: "Oh, my next one's got to be a whatever." That kind of thing. To avoid that is liberating – to get into a *Stigmatic*, where it doesn't matter if it even comes out. Just the idea that you're doing something for the sake of what it is, to try to accommodate the vision of the play. To be freed of having to score, having to make something that a lot of people go to or a lot of people like. Just something that you're doing because you have a connection to it.

But then, I'm in the entertainment business, too. I got here because I was lucky enough to be in a very successful commercial movie, and I'll never forget that.

You first made your mark in the early '70s. Did you feel much of an identification with other people like Martin Scorsese and Robert De Niro who were mining similar terrain?

They came after me, so I didn't know them. Francis [Coppola] had mentioned Martin Scorsese to me as being a great artist – I hadn't even heard his name. Of course, I know Bobby from the street. I'd seen him around, and I remember seeing him in a movie that Brian De Palma did called *Greetings* and thinking that he had a real energy and talent. Then he popped up in *The Godfather, Part II.*

Did you and Scorsese ever talk about working together?

There was one time years ago – he was working on *Modigliani*, the Dennis McIntyre play about the painter, developing it with me. The script didn't turn out. He would be someone I'd really want to work with. He's tops. As Bobby once told me, Scorsese can't help making a movie that comes right out of himself – he just can't help it. He's a great filmmaker. I marvel at his stuff. Anything he does.

Obviously, in Heat*...*

Bobby and I?

Yeah, exactly. What was that like, working together even in one scene, since you had no scenes in The Godfather, Part II*?*

It's hard to say. I mean, I hardly saw him. For the scene in *Heat*, we got together and didn't rehearse much – I don't think we rehearsed it at all. We read it through a couple of times; then a month or two later, we were in this coffee shop filming it. He was there; I was there. We just did it. You know, you read a score and play your duet together. It was easier with Bobby because I knew him; we have a relationship we feel mutual about. We get along – it was just kind of an extension of that.

How did the director of Heat*, Michael Mann, handle that situation?*

Fortunately for both of us, Michael made the pressure less. It probably would have been even less pressure if Bobby and I were doing the whole movie together. But this setup – one scene, the two of us – it was just sort of built to make you feel a little uneasy. But Michael Mann made things real easy.

How?

I just really, really like Michael. I think he's a great director. Great. There's an example of a guy, when you're around him, you feel that sense of his control. That's a Michael Mann set, that's his film, and you are in it. And it's a real comfortable milieu. You can let it go and just be whatever your guy is. He allows that.

That's the thing about directing: control. There is a certain comfort when you are directing a film yourself, and you have control – it's just a bloody relief. Just for that control, it's worth directing. Just for that.

Do you feel more control acting on the stage?

That's where I'm most comfortable, because it's where I started. The best way I can think to describe it is walking up on the wire – it's the wire without a net. And because of that, it requires your metabolism to do another thing. It requires the chemicals in your body to go through the kinds of changes that can accommodate the high wire. It's that kind of action. There's a magic there.

I never feel that in movies ever – never, no matter what. So when I dream, daydream, whatever, I usually daydream about the theater.

I wanted to talk, a bit about some of the other directors you've worked with. For example, you did Scarface *and* Carlito's Way *with Brian De Palma.*

I love Brian. I don't know what the rap on him is, but he's got real quality and depth. These directors you're mentioning – Marty Scorsese, Michael Mann, Brian De Palma – I mean, that's directing. Sidney Lumet. That's what it is. They've got that thing, that touch.

Is there something in particular they bring out in you?

I'm tied to the playwright, the text, the writer. That's who my relationship is with. Directors are more exotic figures to me – that's probably why I'm slightly in awe of them. But the writer is somebody I'm with. It's the actor and writer. Shakespeare was an actor and a writer. It's that classic relationship; it's real symbiotic.

Scarface*, which was written by Oliver Stone, has become a kind of cult classic. Has its ongoing life pleased you?*

Oh, sure. Especially because when it first opened, it was ridiculed. So the fact that it has lasted is wonderful. It's the only movie I've ever been in where someone will stop me in the street and quote a line, and they're always the oddest lines. You never know what they're going to quote. You would think, "Say hello to my little friend," or something like that. But sometimes a guy will just turn, look at me, and say [as Tony Montana], "Can I go now?" I mean, it's thrilling when people do that.

"See what you made me do" is my own favorite, from the assassination scene in New York.

That's vintage Oliver Stone – Oliver Stone and his anarchic wildness.

Weren't you and Oliver Stone talking about doing a movie about Manuel Noriega?

Yeah. We were going to do it. Then we read it a couple of times, and much to Oliver's credit, he was able to see that while there was some great stuff in it, absolute magic stuff like he can do, it wasn't quite formed yet.

You were also supposed to star in the film of the David Mamet play American Buffalo, *which you'd done onstage. The role ended up going to Dustin Hoffman. What happened?*

There's an example of a movie I was asked to direct, but I didn't feel I could. I had played it for four years on the stage. As far as I was concerned, John McNaughton was going to direct, and Jerry Tokofsky, who produced *Glengarry Glen Ross*, was going to produce it. That was my understanding. It just didn't work out. The part was offered to me, but I felt an allegiance to Jerry. We had done *Glengarry* and, with McNaughton, we were going to do [*Buffalo*]. But some political stuff was going on, and something got lost. I truly don't know the details.

Are you disappointed?

I guess in part I am. In doing something that long onstage, I would have liked to have done the film. It's a great play. It should be done. And as long as it's been done, that's good. I look forward to seeing it.

How do you respond to criticism of your performances?

I try to avoid reading it or hearing about it. If it's good, it makes you conscious of the good things. If it's bad, it makes you conscious of the bad things. Sometimes in retrospect it's interesting, but it can be really upsetting when you're in the middle of something. It can hurt you. Mentioning *Scarface*, there I was doing *American Buffalo* on Broadway, and somebody comes to my dressing room and says, "Oh, could you please sign this for me?" I said, "Sure," and I took a pen, and this woman wanted me to sign a headline that read, "Al Pacino Fails Miserably as Scarface." [*Laughs*]

I had an experience once in the theater in Boston. I was in the dressing room while this guy was looking at a review of our play. For everybody else in the play, there was – what's the word? – adulation. With one exception: me. The guy didn't want me to see it, of course, but I said, "What's that?" He had a look on his face, but it was too late – there it was. And the moment I saw that review, on the speaker in my dressing room came my cue to go onstage. Maybe I was young or whatever, but it struck me really funny. It was very liberating. I went onstage, and it was really fun. I wish I could say I always felt that way.

How much of a perspective are you able to maintain on you and the character you are playing?

I remember the very first time I saw myself in a film, my reaction was, "I didn't know that that was showing."

What did you feel was "showing"?

When I looked at myself, or the character I was playing, I thought, "Gee, that guy looks really" – what's the word? I thought he looked kind of lonely. After that, I said I cannot cope with the film thing if I'm going to be subjective, so I have to say that that's an actor doing a part. That's how I approach it. I look at it as an effort I made, and I feel it's no longer about me. I remember when we were working on *Dog Day Afternoon*, we had to do some retakes. I had been working on it intensively for about 11 weeks – but *intensively*. Then we were off for a couple of weeks, and I had to do a couple of pickup shots. I could not get it. A friend of mine was in the scene with me, and he said that he saw the character leave my body.

Was it a big adjustment to go from stage acting to movies?

Someone once called actors "emotional athletes." They're dealing with that experience every night on the stage. In movies, it's strange because you've got to stay in a state for 14 hours a day. After you've made enough movies, you start to understand that there is a technique for film. You develop a way of accommodating the frame and working to that – something I've always been reluctant to do, since I am a stage actor. I try to not pay too much attention to how it's coming off in the frame, but just to feel it. But what happens with film is that almost unconsciously, you develop a certain camera sense.

Early on, in the films with Lumet, I never knew where the camera was. As I went on, I became more aware of its presence and what I could do with it. But even to this day, I try not to be too aware of it.

Does that affect you as a director?

Directing, now, makes me aware of a frame: What's in the frame? What's being said when you look at it. Where do you put the camera? That's the first thing you think about. It's a nightmare. I have this memory of Brian De Palma in Florida. We were making *Scarface*. One morning, I'm having coffee on this beautiful deck overlooking the ocean at the Fontainebleau hotel, and I see a crowd of people all looking out toward the sea. I'm thinking, "What's going on? Did something wash in, some dead sea lion or something?" Then the crowd parts a little, and I can make out De Palma standing there with about 200 people staring at him. They're all looking at him, and he's looking at them, and you know he's thinking, "Where do I put thc camcra?" And they're all looking at him, saying, "Where do we put the camera?" He looked so lost, and I completely know what he was feeling. It's impossible. It's just impossible. Everybody is waiting for you to make up your mind.

I can't sit in a room with you and not ask about the role with which you're most closely identified, Michael Corleone. What was the impact of that role on you?

The first two *Godfather* pictures were beautifully made movies by a master, and it was my unbelievable good luck to be in them. Because, as someone said to me the other day, "That picture would have been good even if you weren't in it. It didn't need you to be good." [*Laughs*] It's true. It just happened that I was in it. I feel good that Francis always wanted me to play Michael, even when I didn't see myself in it.

The movies, unlike the book, became Michael's story.

That's who Francis was. As writer, as director, in his expression, he was mostly Michael. He's got a bit of Fredo and Sonny in him, a bit of all three sons – I felt that. But I always felt that he understood Michael very well, and he was able to communicate that to me. I don't know if I would play it the same way again, the earlier films.

Do you see Michael differently now?

At that time, he was someone who was trying desperately to change his fate, a destiny that he could intuit. That's what gave him the sense of tragedy. He was a beautifully etched character in terms of the writing. Beautiful. He's the symbol for the second-generation Italian-American or any group that's felt that pull from the family. *The Godfather* had that kind of span. Mario Puzo and Francis, they could taste it in themselves. I felt a bit naïve at the time, but I must have felt these things unconsciously, because they came out.

There was a thing nagging in the back of that character. At what stage did he put the blinders on and say, "I go in this direction"? His curse was that he didn't have the old country to support him, his father's sense of things. He had to desensitize himself in order to go on, so Michael became an isolated person. And a brutally sad character when you think of him being that locked up.

Palpably there and absolutely unknowable.

At the time, doing it, I didn't particularly think that. To me, it was like, "There's nothing to play here." Sonny's got all the [*makes dramatic arm gestures*], so what do you play? But as it went on, especially in the second one, the contradictions, the conflicts, the emotions... And in the third one, trying to finally find a way back to humanity for Michael – that was complicated.

What are your aspirations at this point?

I'm coming to a point now where I understand what doing something for the sake of doing it is, and what doing something because you have to do it is. Occasionally one hopes that something will come along that stimulates aspirations, something that will transform you. Here I am in the middle of so much stuff, and in a way, I'm trying to get loose of it. But then something else comes up, another movie that's interesting. There's a movie now about that guy who was a spy for the Russians, Aldrich Ames. It's a fascinating script. You're tempted to go into that world, but you know that's going to take six months or a year of your life.

I used to say, "Just one thing." Now I don't feel satisfied unless I'm doing two or three things. They feed each other. Then there's the life in between those things.

The discipline is good. The discipline is important. In the end you find that if you are an actor, that's where the fun is. The Flying Wallendas said, "Life's on the wire. The rest is just waiting." That's your purpose. That's why I'm here. In the end, it's a plank and a passion. That's the name of the game. And as long as that's there, I'll keep doing it. When that goes, I quit. I've been pretty lucky. That's all I can say. Pretty lucky.

This interview originally appeared in
Rolling Stone, *October 17, 1996.*

Beyond Irony

In Other Words

Beyond Irony

As even a cursory reading of any part of this book will no doubt tell you, I'm not much of an ironist. Irony too often seems merely cute or smug to me. Apart from becoming a pervasive rhetorical strategy in the culture at large, it's been epidemic in writing about popular music for many years now. In that context, it's primarily a way of suggesting that you're smarter and hipper both than both your audience and your subject. Unfortunately, for most practitioners of that particular form of irony, none of that is typically true.

The artists in this section have characteristically used irony as a means of subverting musical styles or, as I discussed with David Bowie, the very notion of authenticity itself. My impulse when I interview such artists is to try to find if there's a firm grounding somewhere beneath their ever-shifting shapes. That was certainly one of the issues on my mind when I spoke to these subjects and, in every instance, I was pleased – and sometimes surprised – by what I found.

David Byrne

"We felt we had discovered a new synthesis"

Since emerging from the New York underground in late 1977, Talking Heads have set the standard for progressive music that rocks both the mind and body. Their debut LP, *Talking Heads 77*, fused catchy, wound-tight rhythms drawn from soul music and white pop with edgy lyrics that depicted love as a dangerous distraction from work, extolled the virtues of civil servants, and celebrated a polyglot "psycho killer" incited to violence by boring conversation and bad manners. Clearly, a weird new day had dawned in American music.

Four subsequent studio albums have consistently refined and developed the compelling synthesis the Heads' first record forged. Singer-guitarist David Byrne, keyboardist Jerry Harrison, bassist Tina Weymouth, and drummer Chris Frantz seemed driven to repel complacency; the band pushed to greater avant-rock heights with each release, while deepening their funk groove.

The Heads' artistic breakthrough came with the 1980 masterwork, *Remain in Light*. Under the guidance of all-purpose experimentalist Brian Eno, who had produced their *More Songs About Buildings and Food* (1978) and *Fear of Music* (1979) LPs, the band expanded its four-person lineup to incorporate more percussion, a fatter bass sound, richer keyboard textures, and a host of ideas derived from an intense immersion in African and other tribal aesthetics. The result was satisfying on virtually every level. Not only was the concept intellectually visionary, but the Heads' live shows with the 10-piece band were raucous, funked-up stomps that left audiences in sweat-soaked wonder.

Commercial success finally came in 1983, when the dance-groove "Burning Down the House" soared into the Top 10, carrying *Speaking in Tongues*, their fifth studio LP, along with it. This popular recognition came not a moment too soon. *Speaking in Tongues* arrived on the heels of a spate of solo projects that had Heads fans concerned about the band's possible break-up. Byrne had collaborated with Eno on the theory-laden, ethno-disco LP, *My Life in the Bush of Ghosts*, composed the score for choreographer Twyla Tharp's performance piece, *The Catherine Wheel*, and produced records by the B-52's (*Mesopotamia*) and Fun Boy Three (*Waiting*). Frantz and Weymouth headed for the tropics with Tina's sisters and some friends, invented the Tom Tom Club, and scored a hit with the street-music soul homage "Genius of Love." For his part, Harrison delivered an ominous, darkly textured funk study, *The Red and the Black.*

Speaking in Tongues draws life from all these sources, and has left the band not only richer but more unified than before. And sitting at the heart of the Heads' unity like a tense, art-boy Buddha is 31-year-old David Byrne. Wrapped in a long, black coat that made him appear even paler and more attenuated than he is, Byrne sidled in for our interview at precisely the appointed time. After scouring around for an ashtray and some black coffee, he was ready to begin work. Cooperative, gracious, and painstakingly thoughtful in his responses, Byrne continuously rearranged himself in his chair, as if physical comfort were an ideal he believed one should ceaselessly strive for, but could never seriously hope to attain. After each question was presented, and occasionally in midsentence, he would think silently for extended periods, seemingly considering both exactly what he wanted to say and what his questioner's justifiable expectations were.

When he felt his answers were complete, which was not always apparent by any means, he would simply stop speaking. If I hesitated too long against the possibility that he might want to say more, he'd eventually look up with a benign expression that implied it was perfectly fine if I wanted to sit with him in utter silence, but another question would be OK too.

Byrne would occasionally chuckle and glance over shyly when he said something humorous: His obvious, if controlled, delight at these moments suggested that he inwardly believed these remarks to be hilariously funny, but thought it might be immodest to take too much public enjoyment in his own wit.

All in all, I can't really agree with Byrne when he brays in "Burning Down the House" that he's an "or-di-na-ry guy." He's still pretty strange, folks, and very special.

When Talking Heads first formed as a trio in 1976, with you, Tina Weymouth, and Chris Frantz, did you have any ideas about why you were forming a band and what you felt you could add that was missing from the musical scene?

Like a lot of other bands at that time here and in England, we weren't hearing the kind of music on the radio that we felt spoke to us, or we were hearing a lot less of it than we wanted to. So we felt we had to make it for ourselves and for each other. Why a band rather than something else? I suppose it probably runs through a lot of people's heads in our generation to be in a band at one point or another when they're growing up. Chris said once that if we didn't at least try it, even if we failed, we'd probably kick ourselves. So we tried it. We grew up with the notion that it was something you could do and be creative on your own terms, and yet speak to a real mass audience, speak to your peers, speak to people who were older than you and younger than you. There was no set audience or set lines you had to follow. It was a pretty free and open area to work in. I must say, for me the big attraction was that it was mass produced and part of mass culture, yet it has the kind of creativity in it that's as good as anything going.

You spent a great deal of time in the early days, when the Talking Heads were beginning to get some attention, distinguishing yourself from other bands like the Ramones, Blondie, and Television on the new wave circuit in New York. At this point, can you look back and see some of the similarities among the things you were all trying to do?

Yeah, there were a fair number of similarities, not so much in the directions we were going in or what we were trying to do musically, but in the fact that at the time a lot of the major rock bands had gotten very big and pompous. You couldn't go from nowhere to being big and pompous. You couldn't go from practicing in a loft or in your basement to being a huge act. That just seemed totally improbable. The major acts seemed to be making a kind of music and presentation that was really distant and inaccessible. I think a lot of bands wanted to bring their music down to a closer level that was maybe more intimate with the audience. A lot of the bands got lumped together at the time musically, but it was obvious to the musicians that, given their druthers, they'd go in very different directions.

Many people seemed to feel that Talking Heads 77 *overrefined the band's live sound at that point. Were you happy with it when it came out, and how do you feel about it now?*

At the time, we thought it was OK, but I don't think we were completely *thrilled* with it. Hardly, anybody's thrilled with their first record, because their first record represents everything they've been doing and everything they feel they are. I mean, it's their first shot at getting across what they represent or what they feel is in their soul. And if it doesn't say *all that* in one record, they're disappointed. Looking back on it now, it seems a lot more quirky and peculiar than I thought it was then.

How did your working relationship with Eno come about?

Just before that first album was released, we had a single out that he had heard in England. We went over to play there as a support act for the Ramones, and on one of their off days, we played a date in a little club in London, and he and John Cale came and saw us. We had known John Cale before, but that was our first meeting with Brian, and we quite liked him and hung out with him for a while. Then he came to New York on a vacation, and we chatted and hung out together. So we sort of just got to know him. It might have been almost a year that went by before we got around to making another record, and it seemed natural to ask him to produce, since we already knew him and liked some of the things he'd done. We were still a little unsure of ourselves, and it would have been difficult for us to work with someone else who maybe was a very good producer, but who overpowered us.

Do you feel Eno's involvement with the band eventually became divisive?

It's hard to say whether it was just him. When we were making *Remain in Light*, he and I had formed a close relationship, because we had already been working on the *Bush of Ghosts* record. So that set up some sort of split between us, who had a close working relationship, and the rest of the band, who weren't so close to the main songwriter and the producer anymore. So that made things a little difficult. It didn't *have* to, but it did. We were both very excited about what we thought was this new kind of music, this new kind of synthesis that we were working on, and we were fairly determined that that was the future, and we wanted to keep going in that direction with the band. And the band did too. At the same time, we sort of felt that it was "our idea" or something like that, which was probably a bad thing.

You once said you and Eno felt at that time that you were on some kind of "mission."

We felt we had discovered a new synthesis, using very modern sounds and very modern working procedures – writing and improvising in the studio with studio sounds and what not – but with a lot of the structure in the music being based on ancient forms and forms that were closer to the third world. Those musical structures implied a very different attitude than was common in rock 'n' roll at the time, and implied a union between the mind and body, no longer a split between the two. We felt the music was very transcendent and ecstatic, or it could be, and very ancient and modern at the same time. Oh, that seemed really exciting! To some extent, we were rediscovering the wheel. I mean, we listened to a lot of travel music and worked on things by layering little pieces of rhythm and sound and building up a rhythm piece by piece that in the end sometimes sounded like one good funk drummer, or one *mediocre* funk drummer! But it's very different to discover something by starting from the bottom and *re*discovering it and putting all the pieces back together than by looking out the window and just seeing. It's like kids who take their car engine apart and then put it back together again. You have a very different relationship with the automobile if you've done that than if you just look at an old car and go, "That's a great car."

Were you ever concerned that there might be a kind of easy exoticism in your interest in African and other third world music, almost a kind of cultural imperialism?

Yeah, sometimes it occurred to me that there is a danger in just being exotic for the sake of being exotic. There's a danger in doing something that uses Arabic scales that ends up sounding like Hollywood Arabic music. Then in the course of listening to a lot of pop records and ethnic records from other countries, *they're* more guilty of it than we are. If you listen to the most popular music in India, their film soundtrack music, they use riffs from Western pop songs and somebody'll sing a little melody from a Bee Gees song that then has an Indian backing to it. There's a story we heard about some groups, I think in Nigeria or the Congo, where Indian pop music was very popular. They loved the music, but they couldn't understand what the words were. So they'd redo the song and put African words to it and put an African rhythm into it. That kind of thing seems great; that's the way new things happen. As much as possible, we tried to always acknowledge that that's what we were doing. We *were* stealing; we were putting this thing from here with this thing from here. We tried to give credit to our sources, which is a little bit different from other people taking, say, a Jorge Ben song and rewriting the words and having a hit with it, but never giving him credit.

How did you go about making the decision to expand the band for purposes of recording and touring?

We had toured quite a bit up till then, and I didn't want to do it again the same way. I either wanted to go out with a vastly different lineup, which we did, or go out with the same lineup but play all new songs or improvise onstage in front of people, find a way of improvising that didn't sound like jazz. I just didn't want to get into the rut of going out there with four people trying to reproduce a recorded sound and just slogging it out. One thing that helped was that the feeling of *Remain in Light* was very different from the others. It was much more about a lot of different sounds that popped in and out and a lot of people working together. It seemed much more a communal sound and much more an ecstatic and transcendent kind of sound, which wasn't the kind of feeling that is generated by a small rock group onstage. So in order to reproduce the feeling that the record was trying to generate, we had to have a different kind of stage presentation as well. And it worked. Whether or not you liked the performances, they did generate a different kind of feeling than what we had done before. To me, it wasn't rock 'n' roll anymore; it had gone over into some other category.

Why were the band members' various solo projects necessary and how successful do you feel they turned out?

Those [projects] gave us a chance to do things that no one would have expected to be on a Talking Heads record. *The Bush of Ghosts* record, we thought some of the numbers were quite danceable. I heard some of them played at discos, not the rock discos, the real discos, which was pleasing, although the record never really was all that successful. Malcolm McLaren really did that a lot better, doing something kind of bizarre, but then having a mass success with it. The record did go over real big with dance companies, I guess because they're not quite so locked into a rock beat or a disco beat. They find other ways to move to it that aren't the kind of moves that you would do in a club. I think everybody – I don't mean me, I mean everybody in the business – was surprised at how good the [first] Tom Tom Club record was. Even *they* [Frantz and Weymouth] were. They originally thought they'd just make a single and see how it did. And originally, their single was just to be marketed in France; it was "Wordy Rappinghood," and they had some French lyrics on it. But it did so well, they had time, and they kept working and came up with a hit record. And it was really amazing. I think it did everything they dreamed would happen, things they never expected. Chris listens to quite a lot of rap records, and so it was sort of a dream come true that people would take that riff from "Genius of Love" and rap to it. And it was a real honest success as well; it was a record that just took off on its own, fairly spontaneously. [Jerry Harrison's *The Red and the Black*] was a more difficult one. There were some good songs on it, although they weren't so pop-oriented as Tom Tom Club was. So it didn't sell as well, but I think quite a lot of people liked that one.

Since you worked on The Catherine Wheel, *it seems to me that the Talking Heads' live show has taken on a number of aspects of performance art.*

That was somewhat influenced by things other people were doing, but mainly by the fact that I had seen some theater from other countries, from Japan, China, Bali, India, Africa, their own popular theater or rituals. I had to acknowledge that performing onstage is theatrical and dramatic; it's not just a bunch of musicians standing up and playing. If you just get up as a bunch of musicians and play, then that's the statement you're making. Whatever you do, you make a statement that's theatrical in one way or another. I realized that it was a very natural impulse to get dressed up for a performance and to act in ways that you wouldn't in normal life or on the street. From there, I made the decision to start incorporating a greater awareness of the way I moved and the way I looked and the way the stage was set up, so that the performances got more involved with being a stage presentation.

Is that how you came up with the idea on last year's Speaking in Tongues *tour of having all nine musicians enter the stage separately, adding one at a time for each song in the first set, and then having the entire band come on together for the second set?*

Uh-huh. That was done specifically for that tour, because we did a lot of dates in outdoor amphitheaters, like Forest Hills in New York and the Greek Theater in L.A., places where the seats are in sort of a shell around the stage. The shows would usually begin when it was still twilight, so we couldn't make a dramatic entrance with lights. I also felt that, although it's very nice to have an opening act and present a local band or a somewhat unknown band, they generally are not very well received. Although they think you're giving them a big break by having them open for you, they end up feeling lousy after the show because your audience can sometimes be pretty apathetic to something new. So we thought that we'd make it with no opening act, that we'd do the whole night. Then it made sense to just build the stage during the first half, and then, when it was dark, use the lights for the second half.

It also seemed a good way to introduce people to each of the sounds that each musician in the band contributes.

Yeah, I heard that. That didn't occur to me, but it does do that too. You really see how each element adds to the total sound.

You've made interesting videos for "Once in a Lifetime" and "Burning Down the House." What do you think about most of what's being done with rock videos? What is their purpose, aesthetic or otherwise?

Well, the purpose for me, for the short ones, is to do something that, on one level, serves the function of promoting the song, the way all rock videos are supposed to do. On another level, I would hope that it stands by itself as another piece of creative work that holds its own as well as the song, and that is independent of how well you like the song, or what the song means, or anything like that. It's sort of a parallel kind of thing. I don't think it's that for everyone. For some people, it's really just a way to promote the song. In most cases, the performers or the writers of the song are not involved in creating the video. And I don't think *everybody* should be; some people should stay clear of it. Some bands who are great on record or great live should never do videos, because they don't need them. There are other bands who may make songs that work very well on video, but are sort of boring on record. It would be nice if videos developed into a really separate creative entity, other than just being a support mechanism to sell records.

Have you seen any videos recently that seem to you to indicate some of the directions in which videos should go?

Boy, I haven't watched 'em in a while, so I'm not really hip to the latest videos. I haven't been to clubs, where they show a lot of them. So I'm really not qualified to say, especially since I just finished shooting one the day before yesterday for "This Must Be the Place." Generally when I'm doing that, I stay away from watching them. I haven't seen the rushes yet, but I was pleased with the way it went. Half of it'll be Super-8 movies and home movies, and then the other half is slicker.

Is there any particular kind of music that you've been listening to lately?

Opera. I went and saw *Carmen* last night, the one staged by Peter Brook. I have one, *Parsifal*, from the film by the German director Hans Syberberg. When we were on tour, I went to the Smithsonian, and they have this huge collection of country music, a boxed set of about 10 records. It's really amazing stuff. It goes almost up to the present, but there's hardly a bad song on there, and there's some that are really quite bizarre! Ones I hadn't heard before. Sometimes it's really surprising how people's images have changed from what they did 20 years ago to what they're known for now.

What kinds of projects are coming up for you and the band?

If all goes well, we're going to film a show, and Jonathan Demme is slated to be the director – *Melvin and Howard* is what he's best known for so far. I'm doing some music and getting involved in the production of a long theater piece by the avant-garde director Robert Wilson [who staged *Einstein on the Beach*]. I'm doing the music for one section of it, and helping out with the stage direction.

It's generally believed that the upbeat feel of Speaking in Tongues *had a lot to do with positive developments in your own life. Are you still feeling pretty good?*

Yeah, I guess so. I guess so. Yeah. I have more confidence in my abilities and my work's been accepted over the years. So that's all pretty good. Of course, you never know how long it'll keep up. The music business is pretty notorious for people rising and falling.

On that note of caution, do you think much about the larger political and social framework in which Talking Heads, and all the rest of us, operate?

I'm worried about this country, I'll tell you that. The quality of life and the quality of manufactured goods, and politically, everything seems pretty poor at the moment. When you see the manufactured goods and the way people live, when you compare this country with Japan, and the educational system and all those kinds of things...it's *hopeless*. Unless really radical things are done, this country is gonna be down there with the third-world nations we're invading. I don't have any foolproof solutions. From our point of view as a band, I suppose our political statement is that we're evidence of people working together and doing something that has, we would hope, some kind of quality in it, and yet isn't elitist. That's the best we can do as a band at the moment: be a living example.

This interview originally appeared in Record, *February 1984.*

Bryan Ferry

"My parents were the best people I ever met"

In spring 1993, shortly before the release of his album *Taxi*, I interviewed Bryan Ferry at one of his favorite restaurants, Il Continori, an Italian spot in Greenwich Village. I'd never met him before, and I was struck by the sturdy, masculine figure he presented. The persona Ferry creates in his music, as epitomized by his quavering vocals, is of a man teetering on the edge of emotional collapse – haunted, enervated, obsessed, bereft.

The man I saw standing at the bar was broad-shouldered, smiling, and engaging. He shook my hand firmly and invited me to join him for a drink. He was dressed beautifully, but subtly. The colors of his jacket, shirt, and tie were all dark and muted, flowing seamlessly one into the other. Only at arbitrary points through our dinner would I notice the elegant cut of his jacket or the rich cotton texture of his shirt. He wore clothes that were not meant to call attention to themselves, but that would reward attention when it was paid.

If Ferry's physical appearance surprised and impressed me, I was even more struck by the emotional tone of our conversation. We met to chat for a short Q&A for *Rolling Stone*, and those pieces are almost by definition light and fun. Partly for that reason, they don't come naturally to me, and because Ferry had always intrigued me, I wanted to do something more in depth.

That's what ended up happening. A more or less perfunctory question about the album's dedication led to a powerful conversation about Ferry's relationship with his parents – and, ultimately, about coming to grips with mortality. Often in interview situations I share aspects of my own experience, if they're relevant. Even though I don't like to think of that as a strategy to elicit deeper revelations from my subject, it functions that way, at least in part. After all, I'm the one who ultimately gets to decide how much of what I had to say about myself gets into the published piece. Here, I've restored almost all of it.

Consequently, this longer-version interview is a much more accurate rendering of what our encounter was like. I learned a good deal about Ferry that I hadn't previously known – principally, how different his background is from his image. It's a point that resonated with me. While *Taxi*, on which Ferry sings other people's songs, is not one of his must-have albums, it's a good one. It also provided the occasion for some comments about interpretative reinvention, a subject with implications for the personal parts of this conversation as well.

Taxi *is dedicated to your mother, who died a few years ago. What was your relationship with her like?*

Very, very close. She was a great, self-effacing character. Everybody who knew my parents loved them so much. Both my dad and my mother were one-offs. They destroyed the mold.

I had the best childhood you could imagine: very poor, no telephone, no car, none of the luxuries you people [Americans] knew – [*laughs*] as the violins come up. But she was marvelous, my mother. She was a great worrier about detail: "Oh, there's a speck of dust on the wall, get rid of it!" She encouraged me to do well at school and go to university and pushed me, along with my two sisters.

My parents were very old; they came from a different era. My father was like a country yokel farmer, from a much earthier world. Where we lived in the north of England, my mother lived in a kind of town, so she was street smart, very quick, and bang-bang-bang. My greatest fan in every way. My dad, he didn't know about music at all. He'd say, "What is this? Why do they have so many guys playing violins?" She lived in the big village; he lived in the countryside. He was very proud of winning prizes for his plowing. Four horses pulling the plow, and he was walking behind in a straight line. It was a different world, like from the 19th century.

They courted for 10 years before they got married. My dad on a farm horse riding every day to see her in a bowler hat and spats, like from Thomas Hardy. When I was young, I was embarrassed by this. I thought, "This is so awful, terrible. Poverty. We don't need this." Now I look back with such fondness and affection. My dear dad was a hero to me. And my mother too. I just wish they were still here. But you can't have that. As you get older, these things happen to you. [*His eyes fill.*] I'm very emotional and, like, Italian in that way.

As you were speaking, it reminded me of my parents. My father was a macho Italian guy. My mother was sweeter, gentler.

She dealt with the world, my mum. She learned how to use a telephone. My dad never knew how to drive a car or use a phone. He was really in a different, primitive place. But I loved him, and everybody else did. He had a wonderful charm and…I'm going to start crying now… [*Pauses*]

It takes a long time to get over that grief, when people you just want to be with all the time aren't there anymore. I was very lucky, because I became successful, a great hero figure, a star, a celebrity.

Did they enjoy that?

My mother became my greatest fan. My dad didn't quite know about it. He used to smoke his pipe and have a chuckle about it. For the last 10 years of their life, they looked after my house in the country in the south of England. We came from the north, which was a different world altogether. But if I'd said, "I want to go live on the moon. Would you come look after my house?" they'd have said, "Oh sure, Bryan." [*Laughs*] I was very fortunate to find this wonderful house in the south of England – an hour or so outside London – with a wonderful garden and a stream running through it. My dad was the best gardener in the world. For 10 years, he was in his element – "Oh yes, this is my place."

When he died in '84, that was a huge blow. That was the first time anything had really left my life – "Please come back!" It was awful. Then my mother died two years ago. I found it very hard to deal with. I was very emotional. It's strange. After a year or so, the physical absence turns into a spiritual presence, so you just feel they're with you all the time. That's the only way you can deal with it. And when your children do something funny, and you say, "I wish my mother had seen it," I think, "Well, she is seeing it, because she's here." It sounds stupid, but this is how you deal with that kind of grief.

My father died when I was 23. My mother died about six years ago. It was a similar sort of thing. When my father died, it was devastating, because before that I never understood what mortality was. But I got over it and went on. My mother lived 10 more years, but her death turned out to be a loss that is even more profound. It's inseparable to me from the very idea of what it means to lose someone. With my father, I felt we were two forces struggling with each other, whereas with my mother, being around her was more like swimming in the ocean or breathing the air. Her being there was that elemental.

I agree with you. It's like she's so much a part of you that you don't think of her as a separate person. That's very interesting.

I will still have dreams that my mother is alive. And I'll wake up...

Where they talk to you. That's a wonderful thing...

Waking up from it is, at least momentarily, a shock. I'll go to a place in the dream where we go through, "I thought you were dead," and "No, no, here I am," and it will all seem very natural. Then boom, it's Tuesday and you're up and ready to go to work and reality comes back.

Everybody has to do that; I don't feel I'm special in this regard. My parents were the best people I ever met. I was very lucky. So many people have problems with their parents; they didn't like them. I loved them.

OK, so from my mid-teenage years to my early 20s, I said, "Right, I've got to go away now for five or ten years and find myself. I'll see ya soon!" But I did see ya soon. After I'd been around, the first people I wanted to tell, "Life, this is how it is," were these two people. Parents – you have to come to terms with them. It's one of the most important things you ever have to deal with.

Did Taxi *begin as an album of interpretations?*

Four years ago, I did a tour, which I hadn't done for six years. I thought, "Fantastic, now I've found myself. The audience – I can see who they are. I love them. They love me. Wonderful." Finished the tour, went into the studio, started writing. Within three to six months, the music was all there. It was wonderful, some of the best tunes I'd ever come up with.

But I was trying to do an album too quickly, really. I was trying to do an album in six months and then go back on tour. It backfired. I hit my usual lyric block in a very hard way. At that time, I had no producer, no manager. I was on my own. A lot of things went wrong. It's a terrible shame.

I believe in inspiration, but I also think you have to work hard, and I was working very hard at this point. Looking back with perspective, I should have just moved out of the studio, written the lyrics, sung the songs, and got on with it. But I've always had this problem of writing lyrics. You've got to get the lyrics to match the music perfectly, otherwise it doesn't work. It was very problematic. It got to the point where I'd worked on the album for three years. I thought, wow, at one point I was working on my best ever record, done in the fastest time. But it didn't happen like that. It got to the point where I was nearly finished, and after the horrors I'd been through – I was having a lot of litigation problems with my ex-managers at this point – which was…

…not what you need.

…not very funny. It was something I'd thought I was immune to. I thought, "I'm smart – that's never going to happen to me," like Chuck Berry or Bo Diddley. But everybody in the whole industry now – even Don Henley now with Geffen. It's funny.

I had a handshake deal. It was stupid; it didn't make sense. So that was all going on, which is not the perfect background – too much turbulence. It reached a point where I said, "I'm going to start looking at some other songs for this album." In America, you call them covers. I hate that term. To me, a cover is just changing the vocal performance. I like to redesign the song, like the way Billie Holiday or Charlie Parker would take a song and say, "This is my way of doing it."

A great example I always think of is Jimi Hendrix's version of "All Along the Watchtower." It's a tribute to Dylan and a masterpiece in its own right.

Exactly. So when people say, "OK, you've been away for five years, why a covers album?" and eyebrows raise like it's a B-movie, I think that's strange.

Also, that kind of interpretive singing has been a consistent thread throughout your career. You're a singer as well as a songwriter.

That's very true. An interpreter. You've got to remember that the biggest singers we've had in the 20th century were Sinatra and Presley, and they never wrote a bloody song. In the '70s, I did a lot of songs by other people, which took the pressure off my songwriting. Sometimes you feel like you're on a production line: "OK, write another album. That's fine, but do another one." Wait a minute, this is my life! This is me. I want every song to be special. I want everything I do to represent me in the right way. There's nothing worse than being on a production line and feeling that you have to write an album, whatever the quality.

It's a very modern idea that...

That you have to write all your own songs, that's right. I came into music from the art world, where the only thing you have is a sense of quality. You don't want to do something bad and let it go out. You only want to put a song out if you think it's saying something or has a quality to it. And I did like Dylan's latest album [*Good As I Been to You*], which was an interpretive album.

It was an interesting move for him at a point at which people were...

...beginning to doubt him...

*Beginning to doubt him, and also there was that tribute concert at Madison Square Garden and the album from it [*Bob Dylan: The 30th Anniversary Concert Celebration*] of other people performing his songs, essentially honoring him as a songwriter. Now, he's singing songs he didn't write, saying, "Well, there is this entire folk tradition, this other way of approaching things." It was a perfect Dylan move.*

Strangely, they didn't ask me to go to that [concert]. Not that I would have. [*Laughs*] "A Hard Rain's A-Gonna Fall" – I think it's a very good homage to him, as was "All Along the Watchtower."

Didn't you also record "Don't Think Twice, It's All Right"?

No, I did "It Ain't Me Babe" on another album. [Ferry would later record "Don't Think Twice."] I like Dylan because he has very good lyrics. He and Lou Reed are very good lyricists, two whom I respect – and there are not many in the repertoire of popular music. Gerry Goffin of Goffin and King, who wrote "Will You Love Me Tomorrow," which is on this album, is another one. There's a delicate sensibility there. I've never met him, but I met his daughter, Louise Goffin. These past few weeks I've been working with her. She's on my video for "I Put a Spell on You," the first single from this album. I went to Europe to do playback performances of "Will You Love Me Tomorrow," and she came along. So I'm doing "Will You Love Me Tomorrow," and the daughter – the union of the two writers – is there with me doing it. It's so ironic.

She's a wonderful girl. As we were doing the song, you could see a tear in her eye. Her divorced parents wrote the song, and she's there playing rhythm guitar, and I'm singing it. She told me that her father wrote the lyric, which is quite interesting, because most people say it's a very female song. It's great that a man can see a woman's point of view like that. I think it translates vocally to a man perfectly.

You mentioned Lou Reed. What made you choose "All Tomorrow's Parties"?

The Velvet Underground were such a great influence on me and Roxy Music. Their musical anarchy. It's the vibe of that song. Sometimes music speaks louder than words, as Charlie Parker said. You hit on a song through a vibe, a feeling. To me, it sounds very European, medieval, with this droning sound and muffled drums. It was where John Cale and Lou Reed met in the best place.

And Nico...

And her doom-laden voice. You think, "How in hell can I do this?" But you can always find a way of doing a song, if you love it. You think, "I feel this, so maybe I can find my way of doing it."

"All Tomorrow's Parties" helped spawn a tradition of music that you are part of, and "Will You Love Me Tomorrow" is one of those eternal pop songs. But how do you approach something like "Amazing Grace"?

That's different. "Will You Love Me Tomorrow" – I had the 45 when I was a teenager and played it all the time, so it's part of my life.

"Amazing Grace," I never really took much notice of. When I was looking for songs for this album, the TV was on in the corner of the room, and Meryl Streep was singing it in *The Deer Hunter* [actually *Silkwood*]. I said, "Oh, that's a lovely song. Traditional. Earthy. People relate to it. Can I find a way of doing it? Is it too much of a challenge?" It's a beautiful lyric. Hundreds of versions have been done. But you always look for something new that you haven't said before.

It's amazing to me how that's one of the most popular tracks from this album. In that respect, it's a success. Singing those words is very nice. In this world of hideous rap, decapitating people, the horrors of the modern world, it seems old-fashioned, quaint, and beautiful. There's something splendid about it. Noble. Religious. Pure. When you do songs like this, it's like being in a studio with a few great collaborators. Goffin and King are there saying, "This is the tune, this is the lyric, have a go."

When people write about your work...

Poor things, what do they know?

...often they'll talk about your readings of songs as subversive or ironic. Do you experience them that way?

I have a strong sense of irony, but that doesn't mean I put the song down or that I'm being supercilious about it. I do recognize that the songs I choose tend to be more down-to-earth than the ones I would write, which are more..."esoteric" would be the wrong word. "Introspective," maybe.

I don't have an ego problem about writing my own words, but there's no contemporary lyricist whom I prefer to myself. This is the awful truth. This is where I've gone wrong, perhaps, in not finding a collaborator who writes lyrics, because that's where all my albums have been slowed down. I feel very strongly about my catalog, my repertoire. I want only to do good work. My audiences are good people. They are clever people. They know if I'm doing bad stuff. I don't want to do that. That is the story. The record industry says, "Why can't you do an album every year?" I can't do that. I just can't. Maybe I could in the '70s. As you get older you get more precious perhaps, more fussy about what you'll let out. It also becomes harder.

The last 10 years were very grim for me. The '80s, I did not like. I tried very hard. I didn't stop even though I had four children and built a family. I was always a semi-professional father. I was away in the studio all the time.

At the moment, though, I'm full of hope. I feel I've gone through a very dark phase, but now things are much more optimistic. I sincerely hope that's true.

Over the years you've built up an impressive body of work. How do you look back on it yourself?

I'd say my favorite albums – I tend to look at albums, rather than singles – are *For Your Pleasure* in '73 and *Avalon* from '82. Those were interesting points, when I made big changes. They were turning points. There has been one or two tracks from other albums that I felt were good, too, but those were the most complete, rounded pieces.

Were you aware when you were making the early Roxy records what a departure they represented?

I felt it was very different from what other people were doing, yeah. As the writer and director or whatever you want to call me, I felt that I'd found my thing. I thought, "This is great. This is what I want to do." I love that early work. It's great that people now – the younger ones – are rediscovering it. That's thrilling to me. That work has a quality you could never achieve again.

I was struck before when you mentioned how hard you find it to write lyrics. You always seemed…

…prolific?

And literary.

I am, but that's my problem. I'm so fussy about letting the lyric go – "Sorry, this isn't quite right. [*Laughs*] Eliot wouldn't let it go through. Sylvia Plath. Ezra Pound. I'm sorry. Just wait here for a second – or another six months." This is the problem.

Still, you sound sanguine about what's ahead.

So many things I want to do. I want to finish off that other album and have it out next spring. Do some dates in the fall here and in Europe. And now, I've got my own studio in the basement of my office in London, and I want to go there and work on the next album. Possibly a Roxy record. People keep asking me about that. They're so keen on it.

What is Roxy Music at this point?

It's a name that people are very fond of, is what it is.

Do you and Brian Eno communicate at all?

Oh, yeah. I saw him two weeks ago. We hadn't seen each other in many years. We got on very well. Very well, indeed. I'd like to work with Brian very much. Him producing me, or co-producing me, because that's what he does best.

I never really understood what happened between the two of you.

I think it was the press that split us up. Perhaps my ego was overfertile. [*Laughs*] I was very proud of the work I did on the first two [Roxy Music] albums. I wrote the albums, directed them, and so on. Brian was like the co-producer really. If I'd known that then, there would have been no problem. I was very conscious of being the artist, that's all. It's role definition. Now, we don't have any problem about roles.

Do you attribute that to maturity?

Yeah. The perspective of time. We got on really well. Splendidly. It was extraordinary that we haven't really been together for 20 years – apart from one meeting about six years ago, which was a few hours – where we also got on well. It felt very nice. I thought, "Oh, yes, he's sound" – common sense, words of wisdom. He's very bright. I'm more mercurial, perhaps. I'm sending out lots of ideas. He would always say, "Oh, that's the best one," or "What about this take?" He's a producer.

How did you happen to see each other?

We ran into each other while on holiday in the Caribbean with our respective families. I heard he was on the island, and I said, "Oh, I must call him." So I did, and we had lunch together with our wives. It was very funny.

Two Englishmen in the tropics.

[*Laughs*] It was very Somerset Maugham.

A shorter version of this interview originally ran in Rolling Stone, *July 8, 1993.*

Iggy Pop

"What is it like to be a human being?"

The first time I met Iggy Pop I literally bumped into him outside a New York club called Webster Hall before a Hole show in 1994. I had been talking to some friends and when I turned to go inside I accidentally knocked into someone – hard. When I saw it was Iggy, I rolled my eyes. He's probably going to turn this into some kind of crazy scene, I thought. Instead, he couldn't have been friendlier. He flashed a huge grin when I apologized, nodded, touched my arm, and went on his way. Pretty gracious.

The next time I met him was in a club late one night. A mutual friend introduced us, and, being drunk, I went on a long jag about his role in American culture. "You're the new William Burroughs," I distinctly remember saying several times. Burroughs had recently died, and I think I meant that, like the author of *Naked Lunch*, Iggy had achieved an incredible degree of mainstream acceptance, despite his work's still being deeply subversive. Iggy seemed to be listening intently – maybe he was flattered, maybe he was bored – and then we both moved on to other conversations.

So when I interviewed Iggy in 2001, as he was promoting his album *Beat 'Em Up*, I wanted to prove that I was neither clumsy nor a complete blowhard. We were in a studio being videotaped – the interview was for "The A List with Anthony DeCurtis," a show I hosted on the GetMusic.com website for a couple of years – which heightened the sense of exhilaration. We sat close together on stools, and Iggy seemed at times as if he were going to leap out of his skin. When he got excited about his topic, he could not contain himself – exactly what you want from an interview subject.

The first time I saw Iggy perform was in 1970 at a club in New York called Ungano's. He hit himself with the microphone, scratched his chest until it bled, and leapt off the stage onto audience members. Johnny and Edgar Winter were there with two or three tables full of hangers-on and groupies, and I noticed that, as wildly out of control as he seemed, Iggy didn't go near them. As Iggy crawled across the audience toward where a friend and I were standing, I decided it was time to check out. I'd found the performance disturbing, frighteningly self-destructive. He became much more compelling to me as a live performer in the late '70s, around the time of his albums *The Idiot* and *Lust for Life*. While no less disturbing, he seemed at that time to channel his unruly urges into his art. A show I saw him do at the Palladium in New York in 1978 remains among the most memorable I have ever seen.

The key to this interview is a hidden track at the end of *Beat 'Em Up* called "Sterility." It made a huge impression on me the first time I heard it come blasting out of my speakers, and I wanted to discuss it in some depth. You never know how an artist is going to respond when you devote more time to a song they didn't even list on the album than to just about anything else, but when Iggy said he thought "Sterility" was the best track on the album, I knew I could go for it. So I did.

Beat 'Em Up *is a raw record with strong ideas. What were you setting out to say?*

I started with the musical foundation, which had a lot to do with moving out of New York City to Miami, a secondary American town where there's still car culture. So instead of making music in my apartment with candles on and the blinds closed and fear of the neighbors, there was a more expansive feel. I had a garage again, and the next thing I know, I'm throwing my guitars in the garage and then I'm throwing my guitar *player* in the garage! So the first theme was to come up with some sort of handmade, modern classic rock that would sound good cruising around in my car, because that's what I do there for kicks.

Then in conference with the execs in charge of my project at my record company, the idea was broached that I needed to make a commercial rock record that would appeal to the new demographic – *bwaaaaaa!* Of course, I flipped out. Then I thought, "That's an interesting challenge." It was like, OK, you throw that down. I throw down, no, I'm not going to do that. But I'll do something else mindful of the new demographic and mindful of youth marketing as it's being applied to selling music in the digital world and of the state of modern American rock as man meets machine. Basically, what you have in modern

American rock is guys getting their dicks hard with machine aid. You press a drum machine and sample an old Sting song and you've got instant catchy macho. The female equivalent is a little push-up, a little surgery, a few dancers, a producer, and you've got instant titillation. That's what I heard, and I started painting what I heard.

Where I was coming from was to make music that could compete for the people listening to that current stuff. I didn't want to make a loud folk album, which is what you're in danger of making when you're 54 and stay true to your school. On the other hand, I did want to stay true to my school in that the music's handmade. It's played in real time. Most of it's live. Some of the beats are so regimented that people think it's a loop, but it's not. It's real guys playing. And then the themes come up, which are basically masking, deception, blood-sucking, ugliness…

Sterility…

…sterility, right. "Sterility," that's the one…

It's tucked away at the end…

It's tucked away at the end, because it resisted production. It was one of those cuts where the rhythm guitar player made a mistake on the best take, my vocal was distorted and the bass should have been replaced. But every time we tried to improve it, it lost the spark. I listened to it after I had the rest of the record mixed and done, and I thought, "This is the best thing on the record."

It's got a lot of force.

Yeah, so we stuck it on as a bonus track. It's unmixed, and we didn't even master it. The statement on it is…there's a little Britney. There's a little Janet. There's a little about the experience that an artist goes through when it's suggested that you be produced, and you meet professional record producers who are basically…

…sitting "on top a mountain pile of shit…"

…and they're able to make you a star, but you're going to have to bite the Vienna sausage to get that help. More than that, I'm talking about the whole landscape. I get into that in "Ugliness," too. I really believe that Columbine and this little trend of kids shooting each other – not only can you not blame it on music and popular culture, but I'd say the reverse: The popular culture isn't rocking enough. If the rock was more rocking and gave the young listener something to feel good about every day, there would be less of that.

Absolutely. It's precisely the blandness of the culture that's the problem.

The brutality, the bullying in school – I went through that, and it's a lot of what made me become Iggy Pop. I got the blankety-blank bullied out of me in school. But that was in the '50s, and in the '50s, America wasn't paved over yet. There wasn't the same McDonald's on every corner. And so you could run away and hide in the woods. Now, there are no more woods. There's nowhere to hide. Almost every neighborhood looks the same. Almost every experience when you're eight, nine, ten years old is experienced at a right angle. There are no curves.

No shadows.

Yeah, no shadows. I wanted to sing about stuff like that. And music, in its turn, is becoming more sterile and rigid. You hear clever musicians give in to that candy bowl of technological possibilities. It's like making a deal with Satan: This will really rock if you use that 808 beat. The problem is you're going to run into the problem that came up with ZZ Top and Billy Idol records. Once you turn on the sequencer and make that your whole sound, down the line when you don't use it, people say, "Wait a minute, where's that sound? Where's that little thing we liked?" The rigidity is impressive at first, and some of these records are really meticulously made. It rocks like hell in a way. The downside of it for me as a listener is that it doesn't give me joy. I don't hear the beauty in it.

So I ended up talking about the music industry a lot on the album, but not entirely. There's a lot of stuff about moral dilemmas – the impossibility of being innocent, and the worst people usually being the ones that come on the most like...we're working for vegetables, or whatever. Stuff like that.

"V.I.P.," near the close of the album, deals with a lot of this as well. But when "Sterility" comes roaring out at the end of the record, it feels like

a kind of hidden thesis statement. When you sing "I tell you people what I see," it almost has a prophetic quality. It has an authority that I wonder if you would have felt when you were younger. I was very affected by it.

Well, it's interesting. The second song I ever wrote, it's on my first record, is "1969," which has a very bold statement: "Another year for me and you/Another year with nothing to do." Everybody was, like, "What do you mean? We're having a great time!"

I remember that very well.

That was interesting, but when I wrote that line in "Sterility," I was basically writing this stuff like, "Robot doll is singing shit/I can't believe I'm watching it." I do mention that I'm watching it, too – like, what am I doing here? Then at some point...what is the old painter cliché? "I paint what I see." I thought, what's the justification for this? Well, this is what I see, and I'm supposed to be representing something to the people: "I'll tell you people what I see." So there is an implicit...

...sense that that's your job.

Yes, there's a recognition of my role, and that's self-conscious in a way that maybe I wouldn't have been capable of, or maybe that wouldn't have been necessary, early on.

Now, the conversations you're having with record company executives...

Which are fine. You have to start somewhere.

No, I understand. It's a reality. But obviously a lot of the young bands they're talking about owe a debt to you. I wonder how that irony looks to you, and does it register at all in those conversations?

Not exactly. Only in that the basic way the industry is going to look at somebody like me, first off, is they're going to say, "Well, that's all great and his stuff's getting popular and people who are selling a lot of records were influenced by it, so let's get them to play on his record, and then put his name on it." That's been happening to me for the past 15 years. It was suggested, "Let Nirvana write your record," when Kurt Cobain was big and told somebody, "I like Iggy." Suddenly, it's, "Oh, we got Kurt in the office and he wants…" I like Kurt, and I'm glad he likes me. *Ciao.*

It comes up again and again, and for this record it really came up. There were all sorts of suggestions. There were suggestions broached from a number of places about an all-star band comprised of members of certain key popular youth groups…

…who evidently shall remain nameless…

…and a youth marketing producer, and so on. And I just couldn't do it. I couldn't do it, because…that leaves you, it leaves you Vanilla Iced at the end of the day.

How is that?

It leaves you somebody that's only as good as the studio guy that can put together your record. Then you've got to go out and play those songs with a bunch of guys who will be laughing at you in the dressing room, because they didn't play on the album. The most important thing I say to anybody who's really interested in this whole game is that it isn't as cool as the reality that should still be behind it. A person should have some dynamic by which he can make music and take it straight to the people, be it a folk guy with his guitar or somebody with his little beat box in a club. That's independent of the game that you're going to get involved in later. If you've got that going for you, you'll have a great experience. Otherwise, once you get sucked up into the vortex of "The hit is to have the big record," or "The hit is to make something that fits into the system," you're lost.

In this case, it worked out. Slowly, it became evident that the thing to do was to make my own record my way. So I did it myself. I produced it myself. And I think it's of value. It's not perfect. Nothing's perfect. Hell, it doesn't have any Beatles on it – I missed that possibility. And I didn't have Dr. Dre produce a cut, and he's great, too. But it's got something else. You get your own thing. That's how I feel.

Of all the albums you've done, which ones stand out for you?

It shifts, because I don't listen to them unless they're pushed at me. For a long time, I never listened to any of them, because neither did anybody else. But then, all of a sudden in the '90s, I think after *Brick by Brick*, I'd be walking down the street in New York or L.A., and I'd hear something from *Raw Power* coming out of a bar. Now, when *Raw Power* was made, it was too fast, too mean, too hot to handle, too crazy. Now, I thought, whoa, this is where regular people go to get drunk after work and chat and try to pick each other up or network, and they're listening to my music. Cool!

And little by little, I started hearing it more. The best is when you hear it somewhere – like you'll hear the bass through the wall at a party – and you go, "That's cool, who is that?" And someone says, "It's you!" That's great.

As for actually examining them, like, *Soldier* always made me wince. I thought, what an example of a wayward, wasted, middle-aged youth gone bad – ranting, screaming, raving. But then we did a remaster, and they wanted me to hear some new tracks and listen to the whole thing for the rerelease. And I heard it, and it was pretty good. I thought, oh, damn!

I always thought that *Fun House* was good, because it's a complete musical set. It was like a jazz band. It begins with a kind of syncopated, white James Brown beat and ends in chaos, and it's what you would have seen if you had gone to our show at that time – in that order. I thought *Raw Power* was good because it made a big step. Musically it was much more ornate, and the constructions are more difficult than on *Fun House*. Also, "death" is a word that got used, and "destroy." Some key words like that first surfaced on that record. And then maybe *The Idiot*, for experimentation.

I wanted to talk to you about your lyrics. There's a simplicity that you seem to go for that must involve a lot of paring back. Can you describe what that process of writing and editing is like for you?

As background, the first thing to say is that I love Bob Dylan's work, but he's also responsible for hundreds of bad lyricists who think they *are* Bob Dylan and can write ornate verbiage, and it's just rubbish. It's just an embarrassment.

As a listener, when I was a kid, really listening to music, I'd think, "That is shit! That is shit! They must die! Why is this on my radio? Ah, *that* one." That's the feeling a kid has – "That one! *That's* the one! Yes!"

Anything that had one false word or one false sound instantly turned me off, so one tries to avoid that in one's work. That's the idea.

I had certain key writers: Chuck Berry for creating a scene that had a macrocosm and detail work. In "Sweet Little Sixteen," he mentions the girl's age. He mentions that she goes to school. He mentions what she wears, and that she's in the U.S.A. A whole national group is invoked. So that's really interesting.

Then there is a group called Them, with Van Morrison. He had a couple of songs on that first American release that weren't songs at all. It was just tone poetry put to a crazy rhythm track. One was called "One, Two, Brown Eyes," and the whole lyric was, "I went out last night walking / I heard someone talking / You better stop staying out late at night / Straighten up and fly right...You got one, you got two brown eyes / Hypnotize." That got me going – wow, tone poetry.

I started listening to old blues records from studying Rolling Stones releases and old Dylan folk-blues tracks – like, who are these guys? That's when I started hearing John Lee Hooker and Muddy Waters, and basically used blues vocabulary and tried to twist it and update it. "I Wanna Be Your Dog" was a big song for me, sort of saying, "Okay, you've got this stuff, chick, I give up. I'll be your dog." It was twisted from blues lyrics that used to say, "Before I'll be your dog, I'll walk the floor," or "I don't wanna be your dog," "I ain't gonna dog for you," "Mama, don't dog me around."

So all that's going in, and then you're pouring in the Beats. Allen Ginsberg, which is where Dylan gets a lot of the voicings for his flow. Ginsberg is like a cantor. He's like a preacher. He's like John the Baptist, saying: "Moloch, Moloch, Son of Moloch, shame!" And then William Burroughs, for the way he dissects something really precious in society, like love, and says, "Well, that's just a racket. Basically, these women have this little green ooze that they can put on you and get your money out of you." That sort of thing.

So those are some of the ingredients. Then the idea is mainly that I wait until there's a piece of music or some moment, some experience that shocks me out of being my normal self and puts me into another self and words come out. Some little phrase spits out, and often I won't know what it means. Some little key. Or I'll hear somebody say something, and I'll go, fuck, what is that? Then I'll sit down and try to make sense of it and give it structure. You use what you learn in Creative Writing 101: Try to be universal. I always thought the stuff would last better if it was well built in a way that had to do with human experience and didn't go too heavy on the current brand names, because in a few years nobody's going to know what you're talking about. Try to keep it basic.

Then there was a little bit of advertising, what they used to call jingles. Something catchy and simple, repeated over and over. Good old garage rock does that too. So those are the things that would be going through my mind while I would be writing something – and then trying to pare it down to very few words. The repetition helps a lot. And then sometimes, as a male bird will display his plumage, sometimes you want to whip out the verbiage! [*Laughs*] You have to show them, "I can spill that!" You want some nouns? Pronouns?

So that's some of it. The first one on this record that I did was "Mask." That happened from hanging out at a Slipknot show. They wear masks, and they did a great show. After the show they were back to *au naturel*, and a young woman came up, a type. She looked as if she'd hung out at a few other shows, too.

All too likely.

But she was interested, and she came up to one of the guitar players and said, "Hi, which mask are you?" Wow, which mask are you? There were a lot of implications in that. It fascinated me and haunted me. I thought, "This is good. There's something here." So it started from that. And then I was listening to the Last Poets – you know, "Wake Up, Niggers." For people who don't know, the Last Poets were like an acoustic, Black Panther–esque, '60s rap troupe, formed of a couple of poets and people who hung out with them in Jersey. So I was listening to that, their cadences were sticking in my mind. And I came up with this little, "Are you wearing a mask? Are you wearing a mask?" I had that much. Yeah, that could be a song, but it needs to tell…what is it like to be a human being? For some reason, I don't know why, it seemed to call for that. And because it had come from watching a contemporary rock band, I wanted to just in one swoop describe the whole fucking scene. I tried to get everybody in there – bing, bang, boom!

Masks are an element of anybody's performance, and in your own life, there is this persona that you've created: Iggy Pop. What is your relationship to that character? You must go into a million situations where people have expectations for you to be Iggy Pop.

It grosses you out. Basically, the simplest way to put it is when I'm open I'm Iggy Pop, and when I'm closed I'm not. Sometimes people expect you to be open, but, baby, I'm only open for business. But having said that, it got to a point where I'd been Iggy longer than I had not been Iggy. Things started to get kind of fun, and it didn't really matter what people expected of me. At this point, for some reason, they seem to be curious about whatever rolls down – there's not any particular expectation.

The one thing that's good to do, if you would like to maintain some sort of interest, is to steer clear of… For example, VH1 will call and say, "Would you like to be a commentator on our new "Sex in Rock" series?" Well, I don't think so, because then you're Poison or somebody, one of these bands where everybody thought they were sexy, and then when they weren't sexy anymore, boy, they *definitely* weren't sexy.

Other than that, all I did was come up with a little more bold of a stage name a little earlier than a lot of other people did. At first it used to just sonic boom a room if somebody said that name. Like at a party – "Hey, Iggy" – people would go [*makes animal noises*]. I used to get sneers. I used to get threatened for my name by big American regular guys in the '60s and early '70s. "Iggy? Iggy what? Iggy Pop?" All that sort of thing.

Once, the Stooges played a gig with the Allman Brothers' roadies who had a band, and they opened for us in Nashville. They chased us around backstage, yelling stuff, "Hey, y'all have pussies, too?" Real crude – until they saw us play, and then they said, "Hey, y'all rock – OK!" So I think what's in a name is what attaches itself to it by your actions. And probably the more you open your mouth in any particular way, the more dangerous that is, because later people tag you with that. "Oh, aren't you the one that hated queers in the year 2000?" Or, "Aren't you the one that said you were more popular than God in Seventy-something?" Bang. Shit really happens.

I couldn't tell you much about it except that I had a really funny name in the '60s, and then by the end of the '70s it wasn't so funny. By the end of the '80s, it was kind of all right. And in the '90s, it got positively advantageous! Now, we're in the new millennium, and it fits right in. There's all sorts of funny names.

It's like Mick Jagger's comment, citing Jean Cocteau, when the Stones were inducted into the Rock and Roll Hall of Fame: "Americans are funny people. First you shock them, then they put you in a museum."

That was exactly what was going through my mind, but I didn't open my mouth to say it. But, yeah, absolutely. It's like that. But, you know, I like museums. They're okay. I'm not, like, rushing to get there. But I'm okay with that.

A much shorter version of this interview ran in video form on the GetMusic.com website in 2001.

David Bowie

"That's the shock: All clichés are true"

For this interview I met David Bowie one afternoon in June 2002 – a day before my birthday, in fact – at Looking Glass, the studio in the NoHo district of Manhattan where he was finishing up work on his new album, *Reality*. I'd interviewed him once before, in 1995, when we'd discussed his album *Outside*, which was about to come out, and the'70s, which was the subject of a five-part series I was working on for VH1. That conversation was so fascinating that I had great hopes for this one, hopes that were totally realized.

Bowie was 56 at the time, and he still looked like the unshakably confident, instinctively provocative rock star who had altered the course of popular music when he burst on the scene in the early '70s and many additional times since then. He walked into the control room at Looking Glass, not far from where he lives, promptly at noon, looking fresh and completely composed, even though the weather was wiltingly hot and humid. He was dressed casually in a tan denim jacket and a jaunty cap, a brown T-shirt, off-white jeans, and low-top sneakers. He plopped down his bag, seated himself on one of the rundown, ramshackle couches seemingly common to all recording studios, and asked one of the studio workers to bring him a strong French roast coffee. After it came, I mistakenly grabbed his cup and began drinking from it. He burst into laughter, warned that it would probably be too sweet for me, and ordered another for himself. Then he was ready to get to work.

Bowie is one of those rare people who is able to convey his thoughts in perfectly formed sentences that are filled with shadings, nuances, and wry asides. This, despite the fact that his remarks never come off as preconceived. Unfailingly polite, he takes questions thoughtfully, as welcome opportunities to revisit and hone his ideas. When he considers what he is about to say, he assumes nothing, either about what people might want to hear or what he may have said about the subject in the past. He does not fear contradictions. Just as he made his reputation by dramatically changing personas and images – from Ziggy Stardust to Aladdin Sane to the Thin White Duke, from gender-crashing androgyne to smoothly seductive cabaret singer – he treats even his most deeply held convictions as provisional. What he believed yesterday may not be what he believes tomorrow, so everything is subject to examination and analysis. His mind, then, is as dynamic as his music.

Before *Reality*, Bowie had put out *Heathen* (2002), a record that reflected a spiritual crisis brought on by the terrorist attacks of September 11, 2001. Bowie, his wife, the model Iman, and their daughter, Alexandria, who was born in 2000, live less than a mile from Ground Zero. He spoke movingly about the impact of that day and its aftermath, stopping at one point in the midst of all the seriousness to declare, "Oh, what do I know? I'm a fucking rock singer."

As sardonic as that sounds, that blunt definition reflects something real about Bowie's attitude toward himself at the time. He seemed interested in conveying as genuine a sense of himself as he could, both in conversation and onstage. The shows I saw him do around that time bear out this impression. They were smart, stripped-down affairs, with Bowie playing songs from every stage of his career – some well-known, some obscure – with an effortless sense of command. The everyman identity with which he'd grown so comfortable now seems all the more poignant after the heart attack that forced him to cancel months of touring in the summer of 2004.

The first time I saw Bowie live was in 1975. Three of us drove 130 miles of winding Indiana roads from Bloomington to Evansville to see him after the release of *Station to Station*. That show remains one of the most mesmerizing performances I've ever seen, a stunning mixture of intelligence, rock 'n' roll force, and aesthetic daring. Having had the opportunity to interview him a couple of times since then has only deepened my admiration.

Talk about making Reality. *It was a pretty quick turnaround. You released* Heathen *just last year.*

I got tired of not being able to put out albums when I want. During the '70s I would put out one, or sometimes even three albums a year – and not just by me. It was astonishing. One year, I put out a couple of my own, plus an Iggy [Pop] album. There was another point where I did the *Transformer* album with Lou [Reed] and another of mine. So there were often multiple albums within the course of a year, which is what I love doing. I really enjoy writing, recording, and working like that.

Things slowed down as the industry started to take itself more seriously. It started to be 18 months and then sometimes two years, which is the most I've ever gone between albums. It was frustrating because I'd get blocks of material that I couldn't do. And with my attention span, I'd get tired of the things by the time it got round to being able to make an album again. A lot of stuff would go by the by, which was unfortunate. I'd lose songs en route, or lose interest in songs.

What do you think the impact of that change has been on the music industry? It seems now like making a record is just something that's part of a marketing cycle.

That's right. The phenomenal numbers that some artists seem to sell these days became a very provocative carrot for the industry. But it swings in roundabouts. I wax nostalgic about the days when one felt the companies would nurture the artist, but I'm not completely sure it's true. [*Laughs*]

It certainly didn't seem like it was true then. But it does now.

What fucking bastards they were then. "They don't listen to me." "They don't...blah, blah, blah, whine, whine, whine!" As much whining went on back then as now. Actually, I think there were a number of cowboys in the companies who really loved the music. There were always guys who would hang out and be in the studio and come to gigs and all that. Now, we're kind of lonely. [*Laughs*]

You've had big-selling records in the past, but it's conventional wisdom now that someone your age can't have a hit. Does that matter to you?

I'm not so desperate for that. I've been incredibly fortunate in having a loyal audience for almost 35 years now. And, honestly, what I sell hasn't changed much over that time. I've had a couple of anomalies, but my basic audience has been the same, and as long as I keep working, I would predict that it always will be.

It would be nice to get played on the radio, but those days are way over for a number of us at my age. But that's OK. The more interesting factor is that there really seems to be a coalition of record collections between older and younger record buyers. When I look at my record and CD collection – because I have both, I'm *that* old – I still have about 2,000 vinyls from the old days. With 2,000 albums, there must be something you can throw away, but *nooo*. I just can't bring myself to do it. I did throw a bunch away, but they were real dogs [*laughs*], because I've got all my good stuff.

I look through the CDs I collect and what a lot of younger people are buying, and we really overlap now. A lot of young people are also going back and buying stuff that we liked. That's an extraordinary situation, because it always was that kids never listened to what their parents listened to. But that is over – because of my generation. We cut our teeth in the '60s and feel that we can do whatever we want. Our approach to getting older and our independence of thought are different from any generation before us. A whole bunch of my kids love the Dandy Warhols, Grandaddy, Flaming Lips, and Mercury Rev, and those are the bands I like listening to. They buy my albums and see some continuity that makes sense to them.

That's one healthy aspect of what's going on, and that's because of the fragmentation. You can't really say it's us or them anymore. Somebody can listen to Neil Young, and then listen to South African music and also to Eminem, and it doesn't mean that they don't have integrity. It means their taste is very wide, which is fantastic.

That's how I felt as a creative artist when I began. In whatever I did, the chemistry was my wide musical likes, which ranged from Jacques Brel to the Velvet Underground, with Little Richard somewhere at the top of it all. I felt that each genre of music was as important as any other. It's great because I've been able to do that all my life and not have to be, like... "Oh, I've got to be R&B now." [*Laughs*]

Although there was that moment, of course.

Well, all those moments. That's the thing: I was able to experiment in all those areas and try to come up with hybrids involving one form as the lead edge of the album, but then amalgamating or juxtaposing it with some strands that would push it over to the edge somewhere.

Your reputation rests on that kind of unpredictability, your willingness to reinvent yourself constantly.

There was a sense of aesthetic irony in the early '70s, and it was coming out of that art-school mentality. We were all suddenly aware of postmodernism, and we'd read our George Steiner and [Charles] Jencks and thought, "Hmm, pluralistic society. Hmm, rock 'n' roll doesn't have to be just rock 'n' roll, and it can now *talk* about rock 'n' roll." All these arty ideas, which got leveled out with a loud guitar and a crazy image.

But underneath that, there was – at times unwittingly – a need to harness this new idea of dualism, this feeling that nothing is black and white, that maybe there are not as many absolutes as we thought. Maybe those absolutes are just security devices, ways that we maintain our survival. We wanted it to be like that, because it made things exciting. But now we're at this age, do we go back to "Is there a God?" [*Laughs*] Was I wrong? Was I really naughty? Am I a heathen? It was terribly exciting.

It also upset a lot of people.

Oh, yeah.

You took a lot of heat at any number of moments.

Any number. [*Laughs*] Oh, God, it was good. It was a hailstorm. "Hail to the thief" – I could definitely appropriate that one.

Does it feel strange then to go from being so controversial to now being such a revered figure?

[*Laughs*] By some.

Don't be modest. You're pretty much acknowledged across the board as someone who helped create the modern sensibility.

I won't shun that particular idea. But I must include others, obviously. We were the class of '72. Even though it wasn't as tightly bound as most movements seem to be – like the punk movement – there was some sort of tenuous movement going on to bring about change. And people were quite aghast at the methods we were employing – appropriation, hybridization, juxtaposition – that we were seemingly not loyal to any style.

And challenging ideas about authenticity.

You're quite right. I've never particularly felt that I had any other statement to make, so the shock lessens. Those just happen to be the methods I chose as an artist. And they still are. I'm just perpetuating the same ideas I always have, so there's nothing to shock. I hope that I'm producing enjoyable and invigorating music. But I felt that in 1972.

The things we were doing in the '70s now seem quite modest. But that's all right. Of course, after a number of years, one doesn't have the need to be that provocative. You become more sure of yourself. I know that a lot of my more provocative stances came about either through my own insecurities or my questioning of things so assiduously. Like every young person, I knew everything, but I had to question it and push my argument forward to see if it stood up to what those absolutes had been. But when you settle into the Buddha-like state of knowing you know nothing, your needs change.

And the needs of your audience. But you convey the sense that you're still searching.

That's important. I see it in Neil Young. I see it in Bob Dylan. I see it in quite a number of my peers. [*Pauses*] Actually, they're all slightly older than me [*laughs*], so they have their own problems. But that's critical to some type of artistic longevity.

And now, after all these years of unsettling absolutes, you're calling your new album Reality.

It is ironic. You haven't seen the artwork yet, but there's a fakeness to the cover that undermines that to a certain extent. It's the old chestnut: What is real and what isn't? It's actually about who's stolen this world.

Do you feel like your thinking about those questions has changed or deepened?

I honestly believe that my initial questions haven't changed at all. There are far fewer of them these days, but they're really important ones. Questioning my spiritual life has always been germane to what I was writing. Always. I don't think that's changed at all, because it's not a question that can be answered. It can only be re-posed again and again throughout one's lifetime.

It's because I'm not quite an atheist and it worries me. There's that little bit that holds on: "Well, I'm *almost* an atheist. Give me a couple of months. [*Laughs*] I'm almost there now. I've nearly got it right. There's just one niggling thing. Once I shave that off, we'll be fine and dandy, and there won't be any questions left." It's either my saving grace or a major problem that I'm going to have to confront.

Describe the process of making this album.

Very simple. I'd just written some songs, and I amalgamated them with a couple of covers I'd wanted to do. I've always had a list of covers that one day I intend on doing. I wanted at one time to do a *Pin Ups II*. This time, one of them was "Pablo Picasso" by Jonathan Richman, who's a wonderful writer. I hope he doesn't mind the license I've taken with it musically, because it doesn't even resemble the original. It's such a great lyric that I basically deconstructed it and gave it a different impetus for this particular time – and it rocks. I can't wait to play that live.

I didn't approach this with any kind of through line involved. It wasn't a conceptualized piece at all. It was just getting my stage band into the studio and making the most of their talent. We'd been performing particularly well last year, and I just wanted to harness all that strength.

Heathen was very different. It was written as a deeply questioning album. Of course, it had one foot astride that awful event in September. So that was quite a traumatic album to finish. This one hints at that, but it's not really trying to resolve any trauma. [September 11] did affect me and my family very much. We live down here.

Were you here on September 11?

My wife and child were. That was the awful thing, because I was up in Woodstock making the album. It was just unbearable that day – well, actually the next two or three days, coming back down and coming up against the cordon around that part of town. I had to get my wife to come to the barricades with a passport, so I could show the guy that I lived there, in *that* house. He said, "I'm sorry, I know who you are, but I have to see…," and all that. It was really weird. And that fine silt dust everywhere.

The silence of that day. Walking out into the street and hearing the city so quiet. Not to mention that awful sense of precariousness and violation.

Yes, violation was particularly strong in this town. They're not used to being fucked like that. It really got everybody.

I never had seen New York so off its axis. What do you feel has been the aftermath?

I think there's a new awareness in New York about our isolationist stance in the rest of the world. I say that as a New Yorker. There is a sudden realization that even though this is one of the most important cities in the world, others are watching us. I don't think we ever felt that before. There's a slight unease. We really felt freewheeling and that "tomorrow belongs to us," anything can happen. Now, there's not quite that swaying surge of hopefulness. There was a sense of abandon about people here before, a lack of inhibitions. That has slightly closed off, slightly pulled back. It's a little tauter here.

I still love this town. I can't imagine living anywhere else. We've been here now, my wife and I, for 10 years. That's a long time. I realized the other day that I've lived in New York longer than I've lived anywhere else, even when I was a kid. It's amazing: I am a New Yorker. It's strange; I never thought I would be.

You never thought you'd be a New Yorker specifically, or that you'd live anywhere that long?

Either. Both.

You always seemed rootless, a citizen of the world.

I kind of thought I was. I had this romantic notion that "wherever I lay my hat," and all that. But, frankly, that changed when I met Iman. We got nesting! Also, I'm not sure if I have the energy to do what I do now and travel to the extent that I used to. I used to travel an awful lot and fit in writing and recording en route. That was quite tricky. You really have to be a bachelor to do that. It's unfair to a child. You can't start moving a child around. These poor kids that see 10 schools before they're seven – I'm not going to do that to my daughter.

Can you describe how your life has changed in recent years?

What's my day like? Don't you dare say, "David, what makes you tick?" [*Laughs*] That's the one I'm *not* going for. Any interview – not mine, but any one I'm reading – I can't wait for that question to come. I love it. It's such a funny question: "But, Jack, what makes you tick?"

Well, one thing that's different is the extent [to which] I travel. That's changed an awful lot. And the periods of loneliness. I don't have that sense of loneliness that I had before, which was very, very strong. It became a subtext for a lot of things I wrote. A lot of things I wrote had a yearning quality, and these days I put that down not so much to a sense of abandonment – I never felt that precious about myself – but I did have an intense sense of being on my own. That was something I had given to myself. I have nobody to blame.

But what is the source of it?

I never had a willingness to share myself with other people. I was closed emotionally. I always got afraid of close relationships.

I don't know. I've never been keen on the whole analysis thing. I've had too much family mental illness to feel comfortable with that kind of situation. Anyone in my family who went into that ended up madder. Madder or dead. So I never really became part of it all.

In your work, you always seemed like someone on a mission.

It kind of replaced inner life. There is some seriousness in that. Work became my life, to take the place of my life. You find that a lot with workaholism. Any addiction takes the place of life, or puts the denial factor up, not having to inspect one's own life. It can be empty because I can fill it up with work, and if I do that I'll be OK. And you do throw yourself into it. So that explains an awful lot. But what came out of it was good. The work was good. But I don't think I could go through it again. Too damaging.

Those times encouraged extremeness. Nobody knew where the lines were.

But I don't think they do today, either. I worry. Oh, I worry. We've got a lot of really good young people that are being disenfranchised. Their sense of importance has been reduced. They don't really have a say about anything. Events seem to pass them by like these great juggernauts of political ambition or media despotism. They kind of override the human being, plow people – the electorate – back into the soil of consumerism.

People just don't feel they have the strength of being an individual, and that's not good for a nation. It's not just an American thing; it's the same in Europe. I worry about the vast segregation that's going on in this country between black and white, which seems more and more to be two completely separate worlds. Some elements meet at the musical level, but other than that, there's a vast chasm. And I don't see how bridges can be rebuilt. It's all economically ordered. That's the terrifying thing. The economic house is out of order in this country for sure. Again, it's reflected in Britain. We have the same problems there as well.

[*Pauses*] I worry about my luggage. [*Laughs*] I can worry about anything. I am a terrible worrier.

I never would have guessed that.

You have no idea. I can become a sweatball of worry about anything. Set me a little problem and I'll nibble away at it for hours.

Well, you're going to be going back out on the road. How does that feel?

The crack is in it for me because I'm enjoying this band. I thoroughly loved the performances last year. It was an absolutely simplistic show, just interpreting the songs, and feeling comfortable and confident in that role. I don't know what it is, but I no longer feel that appearing onstage is a life or death decision, and that's given me a sense of ease, because I didn't give a fuck. I was a fucking singer singing some songs, and that's all I'm doing out there. My job is to entertain people for a couple of hours. No big deal. It was such a relief to be able to go onstage thinking I didn't have to change the world.

That's interesting, because obviously you've explored all kinds of different personas.

All kinds of distancing techniques.

But even simplicity is an aesthetic decision.

It is a decision, because it really is a synthetic situation when anybody steps in front of people. It's that old adage about Bruce [Springsteen] – is he real? Can you consider it a blue-collar thing for him to be this one man in front of 20,000 people? Can he still be a blue-collar guy? All this is aspect of theatre. But I'm losing that. I am going on as near to some representation of who I really am as I can get to in that two hours. I'm depending on my voice and the strength of my songs – and some good lighting. [*Laughs*] And that's it.

One final thing, what do you see yourself doing in the next few years?

My priority is that I've stabilized my life to an extent now over these past 10 years. That feels healthy and comfortable for me. I'm very at ease, and I like it. I never thought I would be such a family-oriented guy; I didn't think that was part of my makeup. But somebody said that as you get older you become the person you always should have been, and I feel that's happening to me. I'm rather surprised at who I am, because I'm actually like my dad! [*Laughs*]

All those old chestnuts? They're all true. That's the shock: All clichés are true. The years really do speed by. Life really is as short as they tell you it is. And there really is a God – so do I buy that one? If all the other clichés are true... Well, if there's a 50-percent chance there isn't one and a 50-percent chance there is, why not just believe in Him? Hell, don't pose me that one.

So I'd like to think that in 10, 20 years time, I've been able to maintain a responsible and secure harbor for my child to grow up in, and that I can still retain the closeness that I have with my son from my first marriage. And that I'm good to my friends and I'm good to the few members of my family that didn't top themselves. And that I can keep that kind of stability. That for me is my priority.

Work hopefully would bring more light and joy into that life, but the life itself is the most important thing. Great if the work also comes along, if I'm still writing. But if my writing takes a nosedive and I either don't want to do it or I feel I'm not good at it anymore, I'll just stop. I don't have a problem with that.

I want to relearn how to be of some use. That's very important to me. I see so many other people who are useful. I've got to find some kind of use for myself.

Parts of this interview appeared in the September 2003 issue of L'Uomo Vogue.

The Spiritual Life

The Spiritual Life

Any number of the interviews in this book address spiritual issues – the ones with George Harrison and David Bowie immediately come to mind – and could have found an appropriate home in this section. But in the case of Bono and Marilyn Manson, the interviews were done with the express intention of focusing on spiritual matters. You never know what you're going to get when you open that line of questioning, which can sometimes prove deadly. Both men proved up to the task, though from widely divergent points of view. Funnily enough, Bono even references Manson at one point. Both those interviews were originally done for Beliefnet.com, an excellent web site devoted to matters of faith from all perspectives.

The interview with Robert Fripp is another matter entirely. While Fripp doesn't go into great detail on his elaborate mystical and social views in here, his conviction about the power of music is undeniably spiritual and that comes through powerfully. In that regard, the Fripp interview reminds me of my conversation with Trey Anastasio. While completely different in their personal styles as players and individuals, both men are visionary guitarists who view music as a kind of Platonic ideal, a reality that pre-exists its expression in the world and that must be discovered rather than created.

A number of the interviews in this book also discuss the process of interviewing itself, and one of my favorite exchanges on that subject occurs in the beginning of my chat with Fripp. His manner of speaking is simultaneously crisp and deadpan, and perfectly suits his incisive, understated sense of humor. It's always intriguing when your subject begins questioning you, as Fripp did in this case. He took a similar personal interest in me when I interviewed him some years later in the context of one of his guitar classes. He looked me straight in the eye that afternoon and told me that he could tell if someone had ever used drugs just by looking them in the eye. *Hmmmm.* He never offered his conclusion about me, nor did I ask him to.

After we finished our conversation for the interview included here, Fripp and I shook hands on a midtown Manhattan street corner, and he promptly turned around and walked down the stairs into a subway station. I was impressed.

Robert Fripp

"The disciplines of the hands, the head, and the heart"

"And, of course, what is the use of the interview if it's meant for entertainment?" asks the owlish, natty English guitar master Robert Fripp, minutes after the tape begins to roll. What, indeed. Having set our meeting for the distinctly un-rock-star-ish hour of 11:30 on a Sunday morning, the ever-inscrutable Fripp has apparently also decided that being a reporter is too good a gig to pass up. So he's been popping all the questions.

A polite and rather academic opening gambit ("What is your interest in me, Anthony?") kicks off a series of increasingly philosophical queries from Fripp ("Do you think musicians lack the objectivity from their work to see it separately from themselves?") that threatens to obscure some basic issues. Like the fact that Fripp and his mates in King Crimson – guitarist Adrian Belew, stick man / bassist Tony Levin, and drummer Bill Bruford – have released a new album, *Three of a Perfect Pair*, along with a new single and video, "Sleepless." And that the most stable Crimson lineup in recorded history is also launching an extensive tour.

But first, Fripp must know if and why I "enjoy doing interviews." Fortunately, I am able to execute a deft reverse on this question, just in time to get the Fripperspective on such topics as the English music press, punks, and dinosaurs, the magical year of 1969, Eno and Bowie, frustration and satisfaction in the current Crimson, and the rewards and rigors of discipline.

And, as a special treat, some exclusive, soul-savaging samples of Crimson "humor."

Do you enjoy doing interviews?

I would have to say, which interview did you have in mind? Do I feel a personal need to do interviews? Not at the moment. There have been times when it's been an opportunity with a penetrating critic to find insights into the work I do, to discover things I knew, but wasn't aware of. I haven't really done interviews for three or four years, so I have at the moment no interview chops.

When I was doing interviews in great number, I looked upon them as being in some senses more important than the music I was playing. This was the Frippertronics tour of 1979, which went on for four months – two months in Europe and two months in America. In America, I was traveling every day, doing four hours of interviews and one or two improvised shows. A lot of the interviews I did were with very nice, well-meaning guys from college who were appallingly bad interviewers. And that was a remarkable strain, remarkably hard work. It was staggering how many were a waste of energy.

Is it different with the English music press?

In England, interviews are generally loathed. In America, it's not even a question that one is innocent until proved guilty. One's innocence is assumed. The feeling I have from the English music press, or the "comics" as they're called in the business, is that one is guilty until proven guilty.

So the interview is just self-incrimination?

That's right. I don't know any professional musician who has a good word to say for the English music press. Other than myself, funnily enough. I liked the acrid, biting wit that cut through performers' pretensions in about 1975. I'm by and large embarrassed to be a member of the musical generation I was part of. It's a movement which went tragically off course. The "lifestyle" of musicians I knew I found to be just insultingly egotistical.

What were the components of that lifestyle?

Cocaine was one of them. Big cars, pretensions. So when punk came along, there was a dialogue with the audience, even if expressed only by gobbing. The spirit moved, and I became very excited. One could detect the same spirit stirring in the music press, too. The fact that they would refer to successful rock musicians as "boring old farts."

Or, using one of your own favorite terms, as "dinosaurs."

I was very happy to see the ruling elite of musician-hood being chewed at. But that biting wit became cynical and nasty. Finally, wholly negative and, guilty until proved guilty, it was a verdict on all artists.

The other characteristic of the English music press is it reflects an English preoccupation with the rhythms of fashion. In England, if one assumes that to be a performer you have to learn the codes of music, it's really a mistake. Learning how to dress, how to express yourself in a fashion code, is infinitely more important. To be able to sense the prevailing mode of haircut.

Between your work with King Crimson, your solo efforts, and your collaborations with people like Brian Eno and Andy Summers, you've covered an extremely broad musical spectrum. Is there an "essential Fripp" who feels the need to keep his musical context shifting?

As a quick answer, it's a way of dealing with expectation. Expectation is a prison. I have a distance from most of the things "Fripp" does. I see "Robert Fripp" as a creature that I inhabit. The very best work I do has nothing to do with me. Gary Snyder put this very nicely in talking about when a "poem springs out unaided."

It also seems that many of your projects define a specific, explicitly stated goal. Along with this, you talk about the importance of letting unanticipated developments take you in new directions. Is this a source of tension in your work?

It's giving credence to hazard. You create a situation in which something can happen. Now, if you can guarantee the outcome, well, it may or may not be worth doing, but it's not likely to be a very creative situation. For example, knowing what you're going to do in a solo down to the last note, as in Western art music, isn't very exciting. But improvisation is something entirely different. Improvisation is where you introduce a mobility into the structure of music so that there's room for the entry of the spirit.

Now in terms of what I do, whether it's Frippertronics, King Crimson, or whatever, you create a situation where you have givens. You have four members in the band, you have a tour plan, you write a repertoire. Then it depends how much you're going to pin down the mobility of all the givens. So, yes, there's a level of definition and a level of hazard, and the relationship between the two varies. But you do need the two. Security is death.

Do you feel people don't pay enough attention to your sense of humor?

Do I find it limiting to be viewed as a really, really serious person? Yes, but I have fun with it as well. Humor and being serious are kind of the left and right foot of walking.

One of the little manifestations of humor within the band, which comes largely from Bill, is to rename the albums. Bill's accepted classic is for *Starless and Bible Black*, which came out *Braless and Slightly Slack*. There's been a number of suggestions for *Three of a Perfect Pair*. We were thinking of getting tour sponsorship from a fruit and vegetables firm, so we thought of calling it *Tree of a Perfect Pear*.

Uh, great stuff. Looking back on your career, can you identify specific creative high points?

Yes! [*Hearty laughter*] Yes, with relative ease! 1969 was a remarkable year. Incredibly unpleasant and uncomfortable, an awful year on the personal level. On the creative level, it was remarkable for as long as the members of King Crimson had a commitment to the same aim: the group. Then two of the guys fell in love, and that was all over.

After that, it was a question of: Magic has just flown by, how does one find conditions in which magic flies by? I'd experienced it – I knew it was real. So where had it gone, how could one entice it back? That's been the process from then till now.

Can you describe that magic?

It was as if music leaned over and took the band into its confidence, and simply chose for that year to play King Crimson. Without going into more details, it was quite remarkable to be a member of that band at that time. It was not a normal year. You knew something was going on. We had no idea why it was going on or how it was going on. It was, however, going on. Of that there is no doubt. The band had a "good fairy" and nothing we could do could go wrong. But it began to go wrong.

How did you hook up with Brian Eno?

He was a member of Roxy Music. Roxy Music had been taken to E.G. Records by Bryan Ferry at my recommendation when I turned him down for an audition for King Crimson. [*Laughs*] *No Pussyfooting* with

Eno I enjoyed magnificently. In working with Eno, I went and plugged in and played. I didn't have to think about what I was doing. In fact, the two-tape system Eno introduced me to gave me an opportunity to play in a way that I'd been looking for, for a long time: How can I as one single guitar player sound like a string quartet?

You left the music industry for a time after the dissolution of King Crimson in 1974. Eno had left Roxy Music in 1973. Were the two of you feeling similar dissatisfactions around that time?

At that point, Eno was getting heavily stuck into the music industry as I was getting heavily stuck out of it. My return to it was really around the time of [David Bowie's] *Heroes*.

I was in New York and I got a phone call one Saturday night: "Hello, it's Brian. I'm here in Berlin with David. Hold on, I'll hand you over." So Mr. B. came on the line and said, "We tried playing guitars ourselves; it's not working. Do you think you can come in and play some burning rock 'n' roll guitar?" I said, "Well, I haven't really played guitar for three years...but I'll have a go!"

So the following Tuesday I flew over, got off the plane, went to the hotel, threw my cases down, collapsed feebly, and got up to go into the studio too exhausted to think straight. I said, "Would you like to play me what you've been doing?" and they said, "Well, we'll just plug you in!" So they put it up and played it, and I played and just responded to it. The very first time it was "Beauty and the Beast." [*Sings guitar riff*] That was a creative high spot. I had an opportunity to be what I was with a guitar. I was given no ground rules.

How does power work in the current configuration of King Crimson?

I formed the band, but everyone has equal power. In the real world on a day-to-day level, that provides you with problems.

What sorts of problems?

The members of Crimson, by and large, aren't awfully prepared to leave space for other people. When you reach a point where you're not prepared to put up with that anymore, you shout. It may not be a question of anyone in the band being right or wrong but simply that one member has put up with a certain aspect of the other guys quite enough. On *Beat*, we tried to get someone from the outside to organize it: Rhett Davies, the producer. I think it failed, because instead of having at least one of four widely divergent views within the band leading the day, you had one widely divergent view outside the band leading the day. Which is not a judgment on Rhett. I would rather have the wrong judgment of a member of the band than the right judgment of someone outside the band. That has its own validity to me.

How comfortable are you with the current arrangement?

I feel I've created a field in which other people can discover themselves. I'm disappointed that they don't create the room for me to discover myself. That is the dynamic of what happens: I get squeezed out. You have three guys who are very excited about someone providing them with room. And there's me saying, "Great, guys. The three of you are doing wonderful things. Can I come in, please? Is there a space?" So all my best guitar playing is done outside Crimson. I like space – if there's an awful lot going on, I tend not to play.

So where do you get to discover yourself?

In live performance, when the members of the band play as a team. When we write a piece of music together, where everyone involved is simply being themselves and it comes together. For me, that happened more often on *Discipline* than any of the others. "The Sheltering Sky" from *Discipline* wrote itself. We were simply trying to discover who we were for each other. We were in a 14th-century hunting lodge in Dorset and we just played. It was a group composition. It came simply out of the air, while everyone was looking the other way. And it kind of played itself.

Given the upheavals of the early Crimson, does it gratify you that this band seems as if it will meet the three-year commitment it made when it formed in 1981?

In a sense, yes. I could ask you about your marriage: Are there times when you'd rather be single? Crimson made a commitment to stick together despite the easy or the bad times. There is a satisfaction in simply fulfilling a decision.

There's also something possible in continuing relationships which isn't possible in short-term relationships. They have advantages and disadvantages. The disadvantage springs mainly from beginning to believe you know what's going on. How can you find your innocence in the moment? For me, art is the capacity to re-experience one's innocence. So how can I go along and work with the Crimsons as if I'd never worked with them?

Touring took a heavy toll on the early Crimson. Is it any easier now?

I don't like being a member of King Crimson, because it's not at all comfortable, or a nice, easy thing to do, or even professionally a challenge. It is very, very painful, because we're trying to do things "right." So when you turn up to see Crimson at a gig, you can go there relatively confident that the guys are trying.

I say this quite seriously: I wouldn't be a member of King Crimson to earn a living. There's something more there. In '81, when Crimson was out, I felt that it was the best performing live rock band in the world. My feeling is that Crimson is primarily a live band and has not yet found a way of putting it on record.

Where do you get your inspiration?

In '81, something happened which changed my way of working with music. I woke up on a friend's sofa in New York and simply understood something I'd known for a while: music was always present, completely with a life of its own, as a friend. The challenge is not to rush out and look for music, but to be quiet enough to hear the music that's already there.

My approach to being a professional musician changed. Now I work at perfecting the instruments of the professional musician: the disciplines of the hand, the head, and the heart. Which puts one in the position where one is better able to be played by music.

This interview originally appeared in Record, *May 1984.*

Bono

"I often wonder if religion is the enemy of God"

"Ah, I always take you to the most glamorous places," said Bono with a laugh as he hugged me in greeting one afternoon in September 1999. He was being ironic, of course. I'd jetted around the United Kingdom with U2, as I'd covered the group for *Rolling Stone* and other publications. That September, however, we were meeting in a completely nondescript conference room in Washington, D.C., and Bono was about to address a conference on the plight of highly indebted poor countries.

Now, a year and a half later, most people who care are familiar with the extensive, hands-on work Bono has done with the Jubilee 2000 coalition to have the world's richest nations forgive the onerous debts of the most impoverished ones.

Bono got involved partly to complete the work begun by the Band Aid and Live Aid events back in the '80s, partly to find a dignified, compassionate way to mark the new millennium, and partly out of his own spiritual convictions. In many ways, that last motivation intrigued me the most. In his debt-relief efforts, Bono did not travel the typical celebrity route of writing out checks or performing benefit concerts. Instead, he was meeting incessantly with politicians, bureaucrats, and world leaders – often behind the scenes – to lobby for legislation.

It's one thing to confer with Pope John Paul II, former President Clinton, British Prime Minister Tony Blair, or even conservative senators like Jesse Helms and Orrin Hatch. It's quite another to sit for hour after hour with the undersecretary of this-and-that, academic economists, or World Bank functionaries, as Bono did. That's the labor of a true man of faith. "I never thought it would get this unhip," he complained to me at one point.

So when Beliefnet.com approached me about interviewing Bono on his work for debt relief and its relation to his spiritual life, I figured it wouldn't hurt to ask him. After all, religion is hardly an abstract issue for anyone raised in Ireland. Now 40, Bono was born in Dublin, the product of a mixed Catholic-Protestant background. While his lyrics and U2's music have always been suffused with an undeniable spiritual consciousness, Bono and the other band members have stringently resisted being claimed by either religious or political side in Ireland's ongoing "troubles." While informing every aspect of what he does – "God bless" is even his standard telephone sign-off – faith has never been a subject Bono has approached with much ease.

U2 is busy rehearsing for its upcoming world tour, but Bono decided to take a short break – and a genuine leap of faith.

"I've successfully avoided talking about my faith for 20 years," he said after we completed this interview, which he did by phone from Ireland. "But with you, I felt I had to. I said, 'I can't turn this guy down – he's been on every blinkin' boring story!' And I thought, 'It's OK to open up a little bit.' The problem is, when I do these kinds of things, the way it turns out in the tabloid papers here and in England is, 'Bono Pontificates on the Holy Trinity.' And then we're off! At the same time, I can't let them gag me. These are the unformed, unfocused thoughts of a student of these things, not a master."

Fair enough. Ladies and gentlemen, Bono Ungagged.

While the Jubilee 2000 Coalition accomplished a great deal, it failed to achieve its ultimate goal of complete debt forgiveness. The coalition has disbanded, but the work goes on. What is the current initiative, and what is your involvement in it?

This year might turn out to be even more of a millennium year for us than last year. There's a chance that if we focus on the HIV/AIDS crisis, particularly in Africa, that's the shock to the system that might allow for deeper debt relief.

I've had two meetings with Tony Blair in the last few weeks, and he realizes that he is in power at a time of great importance. This is akin to the bubonic plague or Hiroshima or the Holocaust. I think he is going to, along with your new president, work with the industrialized nations and the African leadership to really have a go at this problem. And debt relief will be part of that package.

Do you have the same level of rapport with the Bush administration as you did with Clinton?

Yes. In fact, if you look at the cover of *The New York Times* when debt cancellation went through [Congress], the headline was – and for me it was an amusing triumvirate – "The Pope, U2, and George W. Prevail." We worked very hard to get both Republican and Democratic authorship on that package, and I'm confident the Republican leadership will follow through. In the second debate, [Bush] mentioned debt cancellation as one of the ideas he was excited by.

Because debt relief became a religious issue, you were able to meet with many politicians with whom you probably agree on nothing else. What was that like?

I really have had to swallow my own prejudice at times. Because I was suspicious of the traditional Christian church, I tended to tar them all with the same brush. That was a mistake, because there are righteous people working in a whole rainbow of belief systems – from Hasidic Jews to right-wing Bible Belters to charismatic Catholics.

We had a meeting in the White House, and President Clinton invited Pat Robertson, who I think had referred to him as "a devil" and hadn't visited the White House in eight years. I saw him in the room with Andrew Young, who said, his voice trembling, that this is the most important thing that's come up for him since the civil rights marches in the '60s. Clinton said, "This is a very odd bunch of people. But if you guys could agree to meet a few more times, you could really change the world."

I'm actually starting to like more and more people who have convictions that are unpopular. Now, at what point does an unpopular conviction interfere with your own human rights? Forced female circumcision, for instance. The Catholic Church's stance on contraception. The list goes on. You know, God has some really weird kids, and I find it hard to be in their company most of the time.

When I went to meet the pope, I brought a book of Seamus Heaney's poetry, which he had inscribed for the pontiff. The inscription was a quote from [Heaney's] catechism, from 1947. It said, "Q: Who is my neighbor? A: All of mankind."

Now, for all its failings and its perversions over the last 2,000 years – and as much as every exponent of this faith has attempted to dodge this idea – it is unarguably the central tenet of Christianity: that everybody is equal in God's eyes. So you cannot, as a Christian, walk away from Africa. America will be judged by God if, in its plenty, it crosses the road from 23 million people suffering from HIV, the leprosy of the day. What's up on trial here is Christianity itself. You cannot walk away from this and call yourself a Christian and sit in power. Distance does not decide who is your brother and who is not. The church is going to have to become the conscience of the free market if it's to have any meaning in this world – and stop being its apologist.

During U2's Zooropa *tour, you would often call prominent figures by phone from the stage. In London, you were dressed as the devil character you invented, MacPhisto, and, as you tried to call the Archbishop of Canterbury, MacPhisto remarked that religious leaders were some of his closest friends.*

It's true. I often wonder if religion is the enemy of God. It's almost like religion is what happens when the Spirit has left the building.

God's Spirit moves through us and the world at a pace that can never be constricted by any one religious paradigm. I love that. You know, it says somewhere in the scriptures that the Spirit moves like a wind – no one knows where it's come from or where it's going. The Spirit is described in the Holy Scriptures as much more anarchic than any established religion credits.

For all that, U2 has often been seen as a Christian rock band.

We really fucked that up, though. We really fucked up our corner of the Christian market. Carrying moral baggage is very dangerous for an artist. If you have a duty, it's to be true and not cover up the cracks. I love hymns and gospel music, but the idea of turning your music into a tool for evangelism is missing the point.

Music is the language of the Spirit *anyway*. Its first function is praise to creation – praise to the beauty of the woman lying next to you, or the woman you would *like* to lie next to you. It is a natural effusive energy that you shouldn't put to work. When those people get up at the Grammys and say, "I thank God," I always imagine God going, "Oh, don't – please don't thank me for that one. Please, oh, that's an awful one! Don't thank me for that – that's a piece of shit!"

The most powerful idea that's entered the world in the last few thousand years – the idea of grace – is the reason I would like to be a Christian.

Though, as I said to the Edge one day, I sometimes feel more like a fan, rather than actually in the band. I can't live up to it. But the reason I would like to is the idea of grace. It's really powerful.

You've also been drawn to the spiritual struggles of rockers like Little Richard, Jerry Lee Lewis, and Marvin Gaye.

I was never tormented in the way those early rock 'n' rollers were between gospel and the blues. I always saw them as parts of each other. I like the anger of the blues – I think being angry with God is at least a dialogue. You know, [Robert Johnson's] "Hell Hound on My Trail" – the blues is full of that. And [it runs] right through to Marilyn Manson.

These are big questions. If there is a God, it's serious. And if there isn't a God, it's even more serious. Or is it the other way around? I don't know, but these are the things that, as an artist, are going to cross your mind – as well as "Ode to My New Jaguar." [*Laughs*] The right to be an ass I will hold on to very tightly. I just have to be allowed that.

This interview originally ran on Beliefnet.com, February 2001.

Marilyn Manson

"Christ is the first celebrity"

A few years back, rocker Marilyn Manson gained infamy for ripping up Bibles onstage. Now he says he plans to read the Bible from the stage. A community group called Citizens for Peace and Respect has called for Manson to skip the June 21 Denver stop of the heavy-metal tour Ozzfest. The organization's website says that Manson "promotes hate, violence, death, suicide, drug use, and the attitudes and actions of the Columbine killers."

In response, Manson has promised to "balance my songs with a wholesome Bible reading." The Bible readings, he says, will allow his fans to "examine the virtues of wonderful 'Christian' stories of disease, murder, adultery, suicide, and child sacrifice. Now, that seems like 'entertainment' to me."

So the battle rages on. Perhaps no figure in modern culture is as famous or reviled for his use of religious imagery as Marilyn Manson. In this interview, in which Manson recollects childhood nightmares about the Antichrist and attending services by evangelist Ernest Ainsley, he shows that his dispute with Christianity is as much reaction as provocation.

The same can be said for his views of the media. In the wake of Columbine, Manson was attacked as an indirect cause of the shooting – even though it was later shown that the killers were not Manson fans. At the time, I worked with Manson on a piece he wrote for *Rolling Stone* magazine to defend himself. "A lot of people forget or never realize that I started my band as a criticism of these very issues of despair and hypocrisy," he wrote. He went on to attack the media's ghoulish fascination with the murders: "I was dumbfounded as I watched the media snake right in, not missing a teardrop, interviewing the parents of dead children, televising the funerals. Then came the witch hunt."

Manson isn't naïve about the implications of changing your name from Brian Warner to Marilyn Manson – a conflation of his obsessions with sex, violence, and celebrity – or of making albums titled *Antichrist*

Superstar (1996) or last year's *Holy Wood (In the Shadow of the Valley of Death)*. He's well aware that people might conclude you're out to stir up trouble.

He's also aware that talking about the spiritual premises and implications of his music and his own complex religious upbringing in a setting like Beliefnet.com is to jump into a fiery furnace. What is perhaps most surprising about Manson is how deeply engaged he has been in religious topics, and how genuinely he wants to confront those who are likely to fiercely disagree with him. It's his idea of a good time.

Manson points out that his act only uses the tools made available to him by the media machine. "Marilyn Manson is a criticism of gimmickry," he once explained to me, "while being itself a gimmick."

The Manson critique includes a highly theatrical brand of bone-crunching, guitar-driven rock 'n' roll and lyrics that harshly denounce the crushing effects of conformity. Rather than face life's confusing freedom and difficult choices, Manson says, people disown their humanity to become, as one of his album titles puts it, "mechanical animals."

It is Manson's fascination with violence (which, he points out, we get in a constant stream from many sources) that raises hackles. And it must be said that his message isn't always clear. His songs are laced with nihilism ("All your infants in abortion cribs / I was born into this / Everything turns to shit") and blasphemy ("When I'm God everybody dies").

The persona he assumes – he never breaks character in public – is a distinctly unsettling, sexually indeterminate blend of pancake makeup, bondage gear, lipstick, mascara, and religious imagery. The formula has helped sell nearly 5 million albums.

Though he has flirted with Satanism, his philosophy has far more to do with the radical individualism of Nietzsche or Ayn Rand than devil worship. Manson, a 32-year-old product of Ohio and Florida, is as gripped by religion, as Christ haunted, as anyone I've ever met. Here he explains the origins of that ambivalent attraction.

During my visit to his Hollywood Hills home in 1997, Manson posed next to a gruesome crucifix for part of a filmed interview. Later, seated on his terrace with the grid of lights that is Los Angeles twinkling in the background, he did seem seductively satanic, tempting viewers with all the kingdoms of this world – or, at least, all the potential delights of L.A. "Maybe I should become a Christian and make them all happy," he said. "But if I found Jesus – which, I didn't know he was lost in the first place – I don't think he would be all that different from me."

Manson spoke to me recently about the current state of his soul from his home in the city of the (fallen) angels, Los Angeles.

What was your religious upbringing?

My first memories of religion were being taken to Episcopal church. My father was Catholic, but my mother, I believe, was Episcopal. So I sort of veered off into the watered-down version of Catholicism.

At the same time, I was going to a nondenominational Christian school, where I was taught a very underhanded form of Christianity. For example, my Bible teacher would ask the class, "Is there anyone in the room that's Catholic?" or "Is there anyone that's Jewish?" If there was no response, she would talk about how wrong those other religions interpreted the Bible. So at an early age, Christians already started to appear to me as people who believed that their interpretation of God was the only one that was right.

At least she didn't want to offend anyone...

Then I started to learn about Revelations, and they pumped a lot of fear about the end of the world into us. I used to have nightmares about the Antichrist – what would happen, where it would come from, and who it would be. The Christians also created this myth about the rapture, which, if you look through the Bible, doesn't exist. There is a verse in the Bible that mentions that when Christ returns, he'll come like a thief in the night. So there was a movie they would play for us about the rapture called *Thief in the Night*. It was about how everyone who fell prey to the lure of the Antichrist and got the mark of the beast would be left behind during the rapture. Cars would be abandoned, and people would be starving and killing each other. Everyone else would float up into heaven.

When I turned about 14, I developed a friendship with this guy whose mom was the secretary to Ernest Ainsley, the faith healer, who's very popular in the Midwest. He had a television show, and he was sort of like Liberace mixed with Jerry Falwell – very glitzy, very high tech. He had a gold cathedral, one of the most decadent places I'd seen, until recently when I went to the Vatican – that outdid it! But whenever I spent the weekend with my friend, I would have to go to these Friday-night services that began at midnight.

That sounds wild.

It was odd because you were starting to fall asleep – it's the perfect time to brainwash people. People were tossing money onto the stage and speaking in tongues. It was very terrifying, like a horror show. It may have been what inspired me to become a rock musician!

So that was the point where I started to seek out other interpretations of God. And initially, when you rebel, you go for the obvious choices – heavy metal, Satanism. To me, Satan ultimately represents rebellion. Lucifer was the angel that was kicked out of heaven because he wanted to be God. To me, what greater character to identify with?

So initially I was drawn into the darker side of life. But it's really just human nature. I started to learn that everything that's considered a sin is what makes you a human being. All the seven deadly sins are man's true nature. To be greedy. To be hateful. To have lust. Of course, you have to control them, but if you're made to feel guilty for being human, then you're going to be trapped in a never-ending sin-and-repent cycle that you can't escape from. And you're going to be miserable. Ultimately, you'll be living in your own hell. So there's no need to worry about going to hell, because hell will be on earth.

What are your spiritual beliefs now?

A lot of people like to pass me off as a devil worshipper. That could only be true if I considered myself to be the devil, because I tend to be narcissistic and believe in my own strength and my own identity. I find God to be what exists in what you create. I make music. That's coming in touch with God when I write a story, when I come up with a phrase or paint a picture, because that's about creating. Art gives people a reason to be alive. It gives people something to believe in. I think art is the only thing that's spiritual in the world. And I refuse to be forced to believe in other people's interpretations of God. I don't think anybody should be. There's no one person that can own the copyright to what God means.

When did you begin to encounter resistance because of your beliefs?

Well, resistance always will be the first thing to fuel the fire when you're young. That's how I learned about heavy-metal music. They would have these seminars in Christian school saying, "This is what you're not supposed to listen to." So I immediately went out and bought it.

But when people rail against me for what I do, I absolutely can understand why they would. And I make that a part of my art. My art is not limited to the songs I create but also to the reaction it creates. I like to sit back and look at the whole thing as if it's a tornado that I'm controlling. It's creating chaos. When you create chaos, ideas are turned upside down, and everybody looks at things in a different way.

At the same time, I'm not simply out to shock people. I like to make people think. Since I chose the forum of rock music, people like to pass it off as simple, dumb, and childish, meant to trick teenagers into spending all their money on my records. But that's never why I got into it. I got into it to get laid, basically! No, I got into it to say what was on my mind, and I'm fortunate enough that people are listening. And it amazes me sometimes how many people are listening.

You've always been fascinated by the idea of Jesus as a figure that brings together images of violence, fame, and sexuality.

Absolutely. I've gone to great lengths to express it in my work that Christ is the first celebrity. The crucifix is the most successful piece of merchandise ever created. I think the image of him dying on the cross is very violent. It's very sexual. It's very phallic. And I think it's intended to be all those things. It's intended to make women want to be married to Christ and make men want to be like him. And to cause fear. Some of the scariest buildings I've ever been in are churches. They're beautiful in their ominous architecture. And that image has caused more pain and suffering than a swastika or the hammer and sickle. And those images are taboo, while the crucifix will always be considered holy. But think of how many people died in the name of that image.

You say you recently saw the Vatican. What was that like, and what do you think of the Pope?

It's odd that you ask, because I have the Pope's head, which someone sold me from a wax museum, sitting on the shelf in front of me, staring at me. I don't really have an opinion on the pope. It's strange that so many people look up to him, because if you actually believed Christ's teachings, it would be inappropriate to idolize somebody as much as you do God, and a lot of people look to the pope or the Virgin Mary in a way that's idolatrous. But I don't have a problem with him.

I was kind of overwhelmed by the Vatican. I was overwhelmed by the amount of gold that was used to create the building, while so many people complain about hunger and homelessness and the pain and sufferings of the world. And buildings like that are supposed to be what God intended? It doesn't add up.

Is there a particular religious figure that you most love to hate? Any you admire? You once said to me, "I see someone like Jerry Falwell as the same as Marilyn Manson in some ways. He's stating his opinion, expressing his beliefs, whether he really believes them or not. And it's a form of entertainment, because people pay him for it. Religion to me is entertainment."

I don't really have hatred for any of them. I find amusement in a lot of modern religious figures. And I wouldn't say I have respect for many modern religious figures. But I acknowledge what they're doing. And the ones that do it best I envy, because I see the sheer evil in what they're doing. You have to admire their cunning and their diabolical ways of manipulating the world. It fascinates me, ultimately. I just find myself fascinated with all religious figures throughout history.

This interview originally ran on Beliefnet.com, May 21, 2001.

In Transition

In Transition

I interviewed the artists in this section at moments that marked a significant shift in their lives and careers. The most dramatic was Rufus Wainwright's. His frank chronicle of how using crystal meth had sent him spiraling into what he termed a "gay hell" helped spark a nationwide discussion of the horrific impact of that drug on the gay community. In the case of Trey Anastasio, our conversation took place not long after he had announced that he was leaving Phish, effectively breaking up the band after more than two decades. As he looks back and looks ahead, everything the band meant and all his hopes and fears about heading out on his own come come under scrutiny.

With Eminem, it wasn't so much that he had changed as that perceptions of him were changing. He had just released *The Marshall Mathers LP* to ecstatic reviews, only to suffer the whiplash of an impassioned outcry against the homophobia and misogyny in his lyrics. No one could have foreseen at that point his subsequent fate as a movie star. Other than my Van Morrison interview, our exchange is probably the most tense and uncomfortable in this book.

Eminem

"Clearing the air"

It consisted of 15 minutes on the phone with Eminem, who was just about to go onstage in Boise, Idaho, where he was on tour with Dr. Dre, but in some ways, it was the toughest interview I've ever had to do.

Shortly after the release of Eminem's second album, *The Marshall Mathers LP*, in 2000, Eric Boehlert wrote a column for *Salon*, accusing rock critics of giving the rapper a pass on the misogyny and homophobia in his lyrics. This prompted endless hand-wringing in the very outlets that had wildly praised the album just weeks before. When *Rolling Stone* asked me to write a news story examining the issue, I too jumped into the fray.

Like most alert listeners, I had conflicted feelings about Eminem, which, ultimately, only made him more intriguing to me. I loved his humor, his shifting array of personas, his artistry, and his unflinching willingness to expose himself emotionally. The attitudes his songs express about women and gay people, however, are clearly a problem. I would have loved the opportunity to sit down with him for a lengthy interview that would have explored these issues honestly and in detail. Instead, I got 15 minutes on the phone with an artist who was, understandably, defensive. I'm sure he would deny it, but I could hear a measure of hurt in his voice when he asked me, "It's not about, like, the talent or nothing. It's just about how fucked up the lyrics are?" That emotion quickly solidified into a tough, unyielding posture.

I was partly driven to do this story by a conversation I'd had with a gay friend of mine who, like Boehlert, was incensed that no one in the music community had taken Eminem to task for his lyrics. He spoke powerfully and movingly to me about the issue, so when I was offered a chance to write about it, I felt somehow that I was doing it for him.

A few months later, that friend and I were discussing our favorite albums of the year, and the first one he listed was, *The Marshall Mathers LP*. "You're fucking kidding," I said. "You lectured me for 45 minutes about Eminem's homophobia, how repellent it was, and how he's completely gotten away with it. And now his album is your favorite record of the year?"

"Well nothing else came out that was nearly as interesting," he said, a bit sheepishly. "And, besides, he's really cute."

That conversation, of course, perfectly presaged the startling media transformation of Eminem from public menace to movie-star sex symbol just two years later.

This is about the lyrical content.

This is about the lyrical content? It's not about the lyrics?

It's about the lyrics...

I'm saying, it's not about, like, the *talent* or nothing. It's just about how fucked up the lyrics are?

No.

Because I'm going to be honest with you, I'm just about fed up with talking about my lyrical content, you know what I'm saying? We could talk about it, but, you know, I think I'm on my last leg with this, because, so far, every writer that I've been talking to has given me nothing but, 'So, your lyrical content..." And I haven't heard nothing positive, you know what I'm saying?

The reviews of the album were extremely positive.

When I talk to most journalists, that seems to be what everybody wants to focus on – not the fact that me and Dre are bringing different cultures together, white people and black people, coming to the same shows, and uniting those people. Nobody wants to talk about the positive shit I'm doing. Everybody just wants to talk about the negative. I mean, go ahead, shoot, though, I'm used to it.

You won't be railroaded.

Right. OK.

People say that your lyrics encourage violence against gay people and women.

Whatever. Let them say it. I'm not even trying to defend it. Like I said in one of my songs, "I am whatever you say I am." Whatever you think of me, that's what I am. The truth of the matter is, nobody really knows me. Nobody really knows how I feel, or the real me, besides what I put out there.

I've answered this gay-bashing thing many a time, and if people would listen to the lyrics at the end of the song, I say, "Half the shit I say/I just make it up to make you mad." And you know what? I shouldn't even have to fucking explain myself. I could just say, "faggot, faggot, faggot," and just shut up and leave it at that. But I even go on to justify what the fuck I'm talking about, saying that I'm just saying shit to piss people off. I'm saying it to make people mad. At least I'm taking the dignity to tell people that. And even songs like "Stan," where it's a message to critics, like, "Look, this is what happens if somebody takes my lyrics seriously." "Stan" is about a sick fucking kid who took everything I said literally, and this is the outcome – he crashes his fucking car and he dies. He kills his bitch.

And "Who Knew" takes on similar issues.

Exactly. The things that I said, I never knew that I was going to be selling millions of records. I thought, maybe, thousands of records, not millions. I never thought that in my entire life. I was always an underground artist. I was a battle MC, if anything.

Would you say "nigga" on a record?

Nah, I don't use that. That word is not even in my vocabulary. And the people around me know that, and that's just out of the respect that I do black music. I don't think that you can put race alongside gender, somebody that prefers men, a man preferring a man. A gay person can be of any race, you know what I'm saying? Those are two completely different things. I hear a lot of that stuff, "Well, you say the faggot word, why don't you say the 'n' word?" Those are two completely different things, a whole different ballpark. When you're talking about race, that's a whole different thing. Like I said, I do black music, so out of the respect of that, why would I put that word in my vocabulary?

But there is a lot of violence against gay kids in the real world.

Let me ask you this: Has anybody went out yet and bashed somebody, bashed a gay person when they listened to my record? Has there been a case? OK, then. So what's the point? Everybody knows that half the shit I'm saying is just entertainment. And Dre'll tell you the same thing about his records. And the term "faggot" to me doesn't necessarily mean a gay person. "Faggot" to me, I used that word coming up as a battle MC and that was a way to battle another dude and to take away his dignity, take away his manhood – "You faggot!" That's just a word. It doesn't necessarily mean a gay person.

Everybody uses that fucking word. Everybody uses it. It's just the fact that I'm fucking selling millions of records, so people are coming down on me. Everybody's sitting around in their living room, "Oh, dude, you're a fag. Quit being a fag." And I don't think they're probably talking about a gay person. They're just talking about "fag" as an asshole – "Quit being an asshole. You're being a fag. You're being a dick. You're being a jerk." Whatever.

That may or may not be true, but there is a difference when, as you say, you're speaking to millions of people.

But there's been no case of anybody killing theirself listening to my record – as of yet, knock on wood. There's been no case of any gay bashing going on because of my record. If anything, there's thousands of white kids, millions of white kids and black kids coming to the Chronic tour, throwing their middle fingers up in the air, and all having the common love – and that's hip-hop. They all have a common interest. And I think that, together, between me and Dre, we got the power to change the world. Me and Dre are changing the world right now, as we're on this tour, as we make music together. I feel that we are making racism less and less and less. As far as, like, gay people and stuff, that's their business. I don't care. Truthfully, I don't care. It's not none of my business.

Are you concerned that MTV might back off its support of you if enough pressure is brought to bear on them?

Nah, not at all. And the only reason, the only thing that you could be talking about that I said about fag is in the song "Criminal," when I said that whole little verse or whatever, and then I said, "Relax, guy, I like gay men / Right, Ken? / Give me an amen." So it was even justified then. And I didn't even have to justify it then, but I still did. So the only instance you could be talking about is "Criminal," and the only reason that I said that in the first place is because on my first record when I said the word "faggot," people started blowing it out of proportion. So that's why I made that song "Criminal." And that's why I said, "Hate fags? The answer's yes." Homophobic? Because people were calling me homophobic. That's why I say, "I am whatever you say I am." Whatever you call me, that's what I'm going to be.

But the truth is, people don't know me. The few people that know me, know that I got a good heart. I care for my family. I care about my daughter. I'm loyal to all my friends. But as far as the general public, I don't owe them shit. I don't owe nobody an explanation for a fucking thing. Truthfully. And I still find myself explaining myself, for some reason. Like, I gotta break it down in layman's terms. Like, "Look, listen, OK, the word 'faggot' to me doesn't necessarily mean gay person..."

Until there's a case of a gay bashing while someone was playing a Slim Shady CD, then holler at me. But I think people for the most part – kids, especially, that are listening to my music – get the joke. They can tell when I'm serious and when I'm not. They can tell when I'm being serious, and the entertainment of it. Kids are smarter than we give them credit for.

Well, I know you've got to get onstage. Thanks for taking the time to speak to me about this.

It was good talking to you, man. I like clearing the air about things.

This interview appeared in very different form in Rolling Stone*, August 3, 2000.*

Rufus Wainwright

"Down into the gay hell"

This was one of those compelling stories that just falls in your lap. The publicist at Rufus Wainwright's record company called me one day and explained that Rufus had recently gotten out of rehab and wanted to tell his story. He had a new album coming out, *Want One*, and he didn't want this back story to appear in dribs and drabs. (The album would eventually be released in two parts, *Want One* and *Want Two*.) Once it had appeared fully in print, he could deal with it as he saw fit. He also believed it was a story that needed to be told in case it could help someone. Near as I could tell, however, no one, even the person who called me, knew the details of the story Rufus wanted to tell.

I'd interviewed Rufus a couple of times before, once at a gay-rights rally in Washington, DC, and once for an online site when his second album, *Poses*, came out in 2002. I'd found him funny and candid, and we seemed to get along. I'd enjoyed his debut album, *Rufus Wainwright* (1998), and *Poses*, and I'd also been a fan of his father, Loudon Wainwright III, and his mother, the folksinger Kate McGarrigle. I've had plenty of friends and loved ones who had been in twelve-step programs, and I figured I had been approached about the story because I'm not the sort of writer who would sensationalize it.

Still, it was pretty gripping to meet Rufus one steamy summer afternoon near the Metropolitan Opera House in Lincoln Center, a location he chose because of his love of opera, and listen to him explain for two hours how using crystal meth had nearly destroyed his life. His emotional discussion of his difficult relationship with his father after his parents' divorce was equally unnerving. I'd never done an interview quite like this one, and I haven't since.

I was particularly affected when Rufus described his fear as he talked about his sobriety. "You know, I'm always worried to talk about being sober because it can change at any moment," he said, interrupting another point he was making. "It can change right after this interview."

When he spoke those words, the horror of that scenario flashed through my mind. I shook that thought off and tried to focus.

For his part, Rufus was nervous, which made his typically garrulous speaking style seem even more charged. I realized he also wanted to be close to the Opera House because it helped him feel comfortable. He was wearing a short-sleeved shirt, and he looked healthy and fit. He'd obviously been working out. His wit and humor partly concealed the rawness of what he had to say, much in the way the lushness of his music swathes the serrated edges of the feelings expressed in his songs. As I watched him walk away after we were done, I hoped for the best for him – and for me. Talking with him had reminded me how precarious our hold on our lives can sometimes be.

When the story appeared in *The New York Times*, it got a lot of attention, in part because the *Times* had chosen to use Rufus's quote about descending into a "gay hell" in its headline. As I'm sure everyone knows, writers don't choose headlines, and I felt funny about that one. The lurid excesses Rufus describes in this interview are hardly exclusive to gay people, but some people wrote letters to the *Times* complaining that the headline suggested they were. Still, the number of gay friends who told me that they appreciated my handling of the story – and who confirmed Rufus's characterization of the impact of crystal meth on the gay community – made me feel that his experiences had struck a nerve, and that the headline had strengthened that impact.

Let's just start by talking about Want One.

I expect to make records all my life, and one of the reasons we're outside the Metropolitan Opera – yay! – is that I'd really love to base my career on Verdi, who...each opera he did – I think he wrote his last one in his 80s – just got better and better. It was nothing dramatic, just a steady rise upward.

I was very exhausted after the whole *Poses* experience. I'd made that album and toured behind it, and struck as many poses as I could to keep it going. *Poses* did a little better than the first album, but it was a tough album to tour. I also changed managers twice.

So I got off the road, moved to New York, and got my own apartment for the first time. I'd lived in the Chelsea Hotel before, but I don't really count that as *living* – it was more like, "I used to die in the

Chelsea Hotel." [*Laughs*] So it was going to be the summer of love and joy and fun and craziness. But it just went totally in the other direction. It became belligerent and monotonous and unhappy and exhausting – not at all what I expected. My guts flowed out everywhere. It was like I burst a blood vessel and had to deal with that before I made this record.

What was the nature of the pressure? Was it internal? External?

It was internal and external. For me, it seemed very much in tune with the way the world was going at that point. 9/11 happened and then for about a year, me, as well was many other people, were in shock and just floating around.

Were you in New York on 9/11?

I was. I was getting ready to perform at a John Lennon tribute show, so I was rehearsing. On 9/11, I had to go to the Dakota and rehearse "Across the Universe," and I remember walking across the park, and the park was empty. I walked past the Imagine sign [in Central Park] up to [Yoko's] apartment to rehearse with Sean, and right after that, we all went to Yoko's farm. I was very indebted to her during that period, because she got us all out. More than fear or sadness, I got a feeling of escape when we were driving over the George Washington Bridge. After that, not a lot of feelings were palpable. So those were the exterior causes.

Right after 9/11, I went on tour with Tori Amos for about two months. I remember not too long after the attacks, we were playing down in Florida and there was all this talk about other attacks.

And the anthrax scare was going on.

It was such a mishmash of weirdness. Tori Amos has this rape and incest group, and every night after the show fans who had been raped would come and talk to her. For about the first month, I slammed it – "What is this bullshit?" You know, "She's capitalizing on other people's pain," or marketing it or something. Then about halfway into the tour, I looked at my own life and I was like, "God, I've never had a boyfriend. I seem to really like to get trashed and have sex with people I don't know. And I was raped when I was young." I was about 14. I realized that maybe I'm a victim of this. All of a sudden the tables turned. I never talked to her about it, but that was the beginning of a certain rumbling that not all was well.

Had you suppressed that memory?

No. I felt responsible for it. I was in London and I had picked up this guy myself. I just thought, "It didn't last that long. He robbed me and tried to strangle me, but it wasn't really rape."

During that tour I had a realization that this may be a root of the problems I'd been having. I have been very… I like to say *picky*. But also…let's just say that sometimes it's more just *self-destructive*.

Let's see, "picky" or "self-destructive"?

Whichever. I don't know. It's such a fine line.

Very difficult to discern.

So I had that realization and then I got to New York after the tour and I was ready to make the next record – and, as I said, party my ass off. But it just went the other way. Something grabbed ahold of me. I had been drinking a lot for years, and I was a very fun drunk. I had a good time and I would have loved to end up like Peter O'Toole. But unfortunately, I got into crystal meth. I had done it years before and I knew that this was the dangerous drug for me. This was my drug of choice.

How did it affect you?

I had a few of those gay lost weekends, where everything goes out the window and you want to make pornos and have sex with children. I mean, your mind is completely ravaged. I remember I had this lost weekend in L.A. I had missed a recording session, and then I'd recorded the next day on speed. Then I started to crash and my mother arrived, and we were going to go to Mexico. I was really coming down in Mexico City. I was in this horrible hotel with my mother at my bedside. I was like, "Oh, my God. I cannot believe that I am in this situation." But I got better. Then we had to fly back to LA for the funeral of Lance Loud [the gay icon who came out in 1973 on the TV show "An

American Family"]. I was supposed to sing "Somewhere Over the Rainbow" at the funeral, which was by the pool at the Chateau Marmont.

It was a memorial service?

Yes, and it was pretty amazing. I was friends with him. I really do believe it was at that point…if one is going to speak of higher powers saying, "OK, it's time to put this to rest – this isn't cute anymore" – that happened. That was the end of the fun.

Did anyone know what was going on with you? Your family, or any of your friends?

Nobody of my friends really understood it. I mean, some people did. Certain people, like [transvestite actor] Justin Bond, got really pissed off at me. He was great. Justin was the first to really get mad at me.

How did you deal with that?

I broke down. I felt like I was being scolded by Aunt Jemima or something. He's such a powerful force in the gay world. He was the first to say, "You better watch yourself because you're heading for dangerous territory."

So I was in New York, and one weekend, I decided I was going to clean my apartment. This was a big decision in those days. I said, "Maybe I'll do some coke and clean my apartment." So I did a line of coke and the next thing you know, I'm on the computer looking for sex and drugs. I crossed that line. It wasn't like I went out drinking or anything. I just went from being straight early in the morning to high.

I'm a bit hesitant to talk about all this stuff. I don't know what the impact will be, if any. I only do it in case I can help anybody, and mainly just say that there is no such thing as casual crystal meth use. [*Laughs*]

Anyway, for the next four or five days, I went down into the gay hell – and we're not talking about a bar in the meatpacking district. It was like a world where basically people are going so crazy that they're not making sense anymore. Safe sex is uncool. That's the main thing. I had done this drug a few years ago, and I've seen a marked difference each time. At first, it was definitely safe sex. Then it was kind of like, *oops!* This time, it was like if you were safe you were a nerd. That drug in particular just tunes into the flip side of the gay man.

As opposed to when straight people use it? What's the difference?

For one, I can only talk as a gay man. Years of sexual depravity...not depravity, but of insecurity around sex, and that low-grade discrimination and not being able to feel discriminated against because we're supposed to be so up-and-coming, and that need to belong – speed takes care of all that in one second. It's wildly dangerous. And I do want to say that, even though I'm fine and I made it out of that world – I was one of the nerds who had safe sex, thank God – I'm very mentally fucked up by that experience to this day.

Just in terms of – it was so scary?

No. It *was* scary, but I think perhaps from years – and when I say years, we're talking 2,000 years of treating the gay man's mind as perverted, clandestine, and dirty – when you use speed it reinforces that idea. Or it glamorizes it. I think everybody has a dirty mind. Everybody really does. But certainly when you look at Catholic priests, or how most people think that gay men are child abusers, it's more dangerous. And what's more dangerous is more sexually exciting with drugs. For me, I had some really horrible thoughts that turned me on on that drug, thoughts that are just wrong and that I have to mend. It seems like the more you get into it, the further you get from real love.

And that segues into the album. That line "What has happened to love?" is all about that. That's from the center song ["Go or Go Ahead"], which is about that experience.

Apart from the frightening ideas and the risk of HIV, were you in physical danger?

At one point, I was. It all became very comical, but I was with some ruffians and they were doing the nasty, and I wasn't. I don't want this to come out that I don't like people into leather, but there were some instruments there that let's just say could be used for love or hate. Like, there were a lot of handcuffs. I was like, "I need to get out of here," so I left. Then I realized I had forgotten my wallet there. So I had to come back and search through these dildos and stuff for my wallet. It was funny, and I left and it was fine. For me it wasn't really physical, people hurting me.

Certainly, when I'd done that drug I did a lot of others – a lot of K [ketamine] and Ecstasy. And then I went home and realized the party was over. I thought I was coming down, and I was going to get clean and I was going to stop the war in Iraq and I was going to make my parents love each other – all these wild things which seemed totally normal to me.

Then two days later, I really crashed. I hadn't slept, and I started seeing visions. Then I went blind for an hour. I didn't go totally blind, but what I remember hallucinating was thousands of little boxes of pornography with Jerry Garcia in them! [*Laughs*] And I couldn't speak. And for a moment, I was like, "I'm not going to make it back to the world." But I did.

Were you by yourself through all this?

I had a friend with me, one of my straight boyfriends. And I realized that I needed help, so I went and got it. I went away to Minnesota.

You went to Hazelden?

I went to Hazelden.

Was that a hard decision?

No. It was necessary. Basically what happened is that I had this feeling like I was in a painting. Like New York was a painting, and I was looking at it and I couldn't get in it. It was very sad and tragic. Everything was beautiful and poetic and everybody's lives seemed great, but it all seemed like this weird painting that I couldn't be a part of. It made me wildly depressed and I'd weep. Then I was like, "I have to go somewhere." So I went to Hazelden.

When exactly was this?

It was around nine months ago.

And what was the state of your work at that time?

Well, surprisingly enough, I wrote a lot during this period. I still think that drugs are fabulously inspiring. I'm indebted to them for some of my inspiration, but, you know, you'd kill yourself. And if you're not there, it doesn't matter how inspired you are. That's the problem.

I was very much in tune with the age I am. I'm now 30; I was 29 and a lot of musicians die around that age. So I said, "Fuck art, and took care of myself." And then I got back to New York.

How did you feel?

I definitely felt ready to make the next record. I was vaguely worried about whether it was going to be good enough, but I knew that I had something.

Were you afraid of falling back in with the "wrong crowd"?

I wasn't. What I loved about that whole experience was that I would escape from the crowd I was in. I would appear in front of plebeians, and they would be like, "Oh, my God. You're Rufus Wainwright!" And I would be like, "Yes, I have come down from on high to party with you." There were a lot of *Boogie Nights* moments with me in my bathrobe and 20 naked people playing "Cigarettes and Chocolate Milk." There were a lot of mice in the apartment. It was very weird. It was fun, but you pay a price for that. Every little moment of glistening denial you pay for in full. And I've got a big balance.

You were in rehab for a month?

I was in there for a month.

So you came back and...

I had met [producer] Marius de Vries a few months before going away and we'd immediately connected. He's very good-looking, and he looked great on speed! We recorded a demo for "Oh, What a World," and came up with the idea for Ravel's *Boléro* pretty fast. We were about to make the record, but then I had to go away. He stayed in contact and waited for me to get better.

Before that in terms of my producers –whether it was Pierre Marchand or Jon Brion or courting Daniel Lanois for this album – I was always in a begging position: "Oh, will you please work with me? I know I don't sell as many records as Sarah McLachlan, but I'm talented. I have a certain something..." And they'd be like, "OK, but I usually just make hit records." There was never an ounce of that with Marius. So he got me through and was ready to catch me when I got out.

It's funny, there's this friend of mine, Jack McKeever, who had this very small apartment on the [New York's] Lower East Side, on Clinton Street. He's a wonderful, eccentric man and he decided to build this state-of-the-art studio in his apartment, not knowing what would come of it. As soon as he finished, I got out of rehab and was ready to start the record. So I was like, "Let's start it here."

I'm always worried to talk about being sober because it can change at any moment. It can change right after this interview. But I will say this: The minute I turned inward and started to take care of myself, so many other things slipped into place. The studio was ready, the producer was ready, the songs started coming out. I concentrated on taking care of myself, and the music took care of itself, and it all came very easy. Something was very kind to me.

You're more available to yourself. You're in a better position to marshal whatever resources you have to make something good or resolve whatever issue is confronting you.

And also not to worry so much about if it's going to be the "next big thing," or, "Is this contemporary?" or "Am I cool?" Basically, let it be whatever it is. And that's what happened. I cut 30 songs in six months. Like fully cut – with orchestras or bands or whatever. The record made itself very quickly.

I didn't plan on having a double album. But it happened. I originally wanted to release it as a two-CD set, but the record company had reservations. Then I realized that's a lot to sift through for the average listener. I was talking to Neil Tennant and he thinks albums should be like seven songs. [*Laughs*]

I was listening to Paul Simon's Hearts and Bones *the other day, and it's like 35 minutes.*

There's something in brevity. I decided maybe we'd do it as, like, Part One, Part Two. I've since realized that it's never been done before historically, like Act One and Act Two. No album has ever been released in two parts with the same title, *Want One*, *Want Two*.

How do the two records break down for you?

There were certain songs that really had to be on the first record: "I Don't Know What It Is," "Oh, What a World," "Go or Go Ahead." Then there were other songs that…let's just say, I want to be in Wal-Mart. With the way the industry is right now, you've got to be squeaky clean for at least two seconds. There is some risqué stuff on *Want One*, but I just didn't want any strikes against me. I knew that if people bought Part One at Wal-Mart, they might go down to Itchy Suzy's or wherever and buy Part Two. So that's the main thing.

In terms of your first two records, you've been very well reviewed. You're out there, and you get written about. You're something of a celebrity. But sales-wise, you're not a superstar. Are you OK with that?

We have reached the age where the consumer has to smarten up. People have got to realize that what they spend their money on is what makes the world go round. And I talk about myself – all of us – as consumers. It's really up to the consumer what they want their fate to be.

I mean, I haven't played Europe yet with a band. I've gone over there three times and done solo shows, but I can't afford to fly a band over because the company doesn't see me selling enough records.

I'm one of the people who is most hurt by downloading. On a theoretical level, I have no problem with it. I think that nobody owns music at all. But on the flip side of that…

You want to play Europe with a band.

I want to go to Europe with a band. So it's really up to the consumer. If you want to see me do a big show, and you're a fan, then you should buy my record – or maybe you should buy a couple. Put your money where your mouth is, basically.

Let's discuss some of the specific songs on Want One. *Talk about "Go or Go Ahead."*

That one is specifically about crashing on crystal meth. I wrote that song a while ago, when it was still fun to crash. It harkens into my other problem, which is that I've never really had a boyfriend. I feel like the piano player at the bar, who's always playing while other people are dancing together.

I was laying down the gauntlet at that point: "Love, either you're going to come and conquer me, or I refute you altogether and I only want worldly things" – you know, "vanity fairgrounds" and white limousines – "because you have treated me so badly." So it's a bitter, resentful song.

What do you think this intimacy issue is about?

Well, as I said when we were talking about that tour with Tori Amos, I definitely was affected by that [rape] experience. And there are also a lot of issues with my father – a horrible abandonment problem – which I also sing about on the album. A lot of the reason why I've never been in a relationship is I don't want to be left. I don't even kindle that flame, because I don't want to be abandoned. And then my obsession with my own work is pretty big, too. I mean, I'm pretty in love with myself as well.

And I'm a pretty weird guy. Women find me irresistible – and in a sexual way. It's not like "my fag friend," or a "Will and Grace" thing.

That's interesting. It's like this daisy chain of unsatisfied desire. Straight women like you, and...

I like straight men. And straight men kind of like me in a weird way. They're the ones that I am most compatible with. I don't know if I frighten gay men. I have certainly frightened the gay press. They have not wanted to have anything to do with me for years.

You were on the cover of Out.

I was on the cover of *Out* many years ago as part of something like the 100 most "out" people. I have a bone to pick with the gay press. Maybe that's why they don't like me.

What's the issue?

The issue is that they're stuck with me. They have to realize that I'm the first gay singer who started their career out and who is a bridge to the straight world. It's me or nobody else. Otherwise it's totally cloistered or it's some DJ or maybe Elton John.

I was a little insulted with the last record, that they didn't put me on their covers or do any articles at all. I find that odd. But I think that has a lot to do with the nature of the gay press as well. It's very...*light.*

Before we get back to the album, I wanted to ask you to what extent, if any, was the rock 'n' roll mythology of dying young and leaving a beautiful corpse part of what led to your drug use.

I knew a lot of survivors of that era – Lance Loud, Cherry Vanilla, Robbie Robertson. But no. Probably the one thing that did affect me in terms of that phenomenon was the death of Jeff Buckley.

Affected you emotionally?

Affected me emotionally and personally, because I'd met him a couple of times, and we'd hung out. That whole experience was revelatory because for years I hated his guts.

Why?

Because I was just a bit younger than him and I moved to New York and I gave my tape to Siné like four times and they refused it each time. And he was huge and good-looking, and I just imagined him as this pompous, strong guy. I didn't necessarily want to be him, but my instinctive competitive gene, which is very strong in my family, made him the enemy.

And then about two months before he died, I met him and went out with him. I was struck by this aura of sadness around him – this person was actually very frail. It opened my eyes that you really shouldn't hate anybody. Sure enough, two months later he died. Then I started listening to his music. On *Want Two*, there is a song about him called "Memphis Skyline."

But in terms of like Jimi Hendrix or Janis Joplin, that never appealed to me. I always wanted to live a long time, like Verdi – you know, die at 83, doing my best work. Or like Beethoven, write the last string quartets and then, as he's dying, there was a shot of lightning and he jumped up and tried to conduct it and then he dropped dead.

The whole culture is so totally mitigating against that. There is such an emphasis on youth and so little room for seriousness.

That has to change, only because in these times that we live in – I mean, what are we fighting for? "American Idol"? There's a side of me that does believe that American values are great, or that wants to anyway. The whole war on terrorism is ridiculous, but if it is happening, we have to improve our culture.

So much about American culture sends a message of freedom.

Whenever anybody asks me how I would categorize my music, all I can say is that I would like to be in the canon of the great American songwriters, from Stephen Foster through Bob Dylan – to me! I'm not going to say that other people are bad songwriters. There is a lot of great stuff going on, but unfortunately, there is so much emphasis placed on whether it's "contemporary" or not. Sometimes, I worry about this record. It's not necessarily a contemporary album. I just want it to be good.

As for being contemporary, what are you supposed to do, make a record with Glenn Ballard?

I feel that with *Poses*, I'd hit this line where, it was like, "I think he could jump over. We could get something with beats and rapping in the middle." Like it was edging on, while this record – though I don't think it necessarily destroyed that idea – it is a strong statement. Yes, I love orchestras. Yes, I'm heavily influenced by theater music and opera. And the pop songs I'm going to create are going to be hokey at times, but uplifting. I'm proud of that. But I also think it's going to turn some people off.

Let's get back to Want One. *Tell me about "I Don't Know What It Is."*

I had gone to a party for the Strokes, and there was this mad dash of people running around – publicists, makeup artists, models – and they didn't seem to be going anywhere. That's when the line hit me: "I don't know what it is, but you've got to do it/I don't know where to go, but you've got to be there." As I started writing it, I realized that it wasn't about the Strokes. When I finished that song, I went to rehab.

"Dinner at Eight" is obviously one of the most emotionally charged songs on the album.

I wrote that song a long time ago. I wasn't going to release it at all. I wrote it after my father and I had a really significant argument – we didn't speak for six months afterwards. It all stemmed from a *Rolling Stone* photo shoot. Our wires crossed during that experience.

What happened?

I hadn't had any experience being interviewed, and I had been very flippant about surpassing his career and surpassing him. He'd also been attacked on the other end by interviewers, who asked him, "Did you abandon your children?" So he was raw from that. Then we were doing this photo shoot for *Rolling Stone*, and it was really uncomfortable. But we were pretending to be comfortable. Finally, the photographer was like, "Could you actually touch each other?" Then we touched each other, and that was the photo they used. It's quite a telling photo. My father hates it, but it is telling nonetheless. I was very brazen. It's frightening; I was very puffed up at the time. And then we went out to dinner and had a couple glasses of red wine and I intimated that I had gotten him into *Rolling Stone*. And that was it. We didn't speak for a long time after that.

And I went home and wrote that song. For a long time, I didn't want to release it because I thought it was too mean – a little too close to home. But it stuck with me. And I've since realized that it's kind of a love song. And it's true, with both us being in the same business and having similar experiences, because his father was a writer for *Life* magazine.

Absolutely. I mean, all of this could have been a Loudon Wainwright song.

And him writing about people…

Writing about you.

So we have to face this and deal with it. And subsequently we did. There are always issues that come up – and don't come up. But he is now in a better place, and I'm in a better place. We don't do interviews together, but I love him very much and he's an extremely talented person. And aside from being an artist, he's my father. You always have to respect your father. Well, you don't always have to respect him, but you have to settle things. You have to respect the affect your father has on your life.

That's an interesting way to put it.

A lot of times during my drug phase and my subsequent breakdown, it all came back to my father. Like, before I went away, I either wanted to go to Hazelden or go live with my father. And when I did go to Hazelden, we would be in group therapy and everybody would tell their story and for every man that got up, the minute they would get to their father, that's when the tears came. I think issues with your father have to be dealt with on this earth, whereas issues with your mother, I don't know if they can ever be dealt with on this earth.

My relationship with my father somehow occurred in the world of events. My relationship with my mother was much more primal, internal, and involuntary, like breathing.

There's an event that happens a lot for gay boys and their fathers where...like my father always claims that he knew I was gay when I was very young. When I was four, he claims. My favorite toy was an apron that I called my "put-it-on." Actually, there are great home movies of me running around in my apron and my dad in the back with a scotch, going, "Oh, my God."

This also relates to crystal meth in an odd way. It's connected with abandonment. When a father realizes that his son is gay, a strange detachment happens, which I don't think is done purposely by the father, but mentally it just throws everything upside down. But then at least it's dealt with earlier. They say a lot of gay men actually get closer to their fathers near the end, whereas with their mother it kind of fritzes out at a certain point. Whatever. That's the next record – *Mom.* But I think that song captures a lot of these emotions.

What about "Want," the title song?

I actually wrote it at the institution. The reason I named the album that is it encapsulates what I want. On the last album, "Poses" was the centerpiece, and it's this grand, sweeping epic ballad – and fairly prophetic about somebody's rise and fall. I originally wrote it about someone else, but of course it must have been about me.

I wanted "Want" to be the centerpiece of this album because it isn't the grandest song or the most certain statement. It's much more innocuous and subtle and simple in its structure. That very much reflected the kind of life that I wanted to lead for a while.

Also, desire can take different forms – addiction, need, and want. "Want" is clearly the healthiest of those.

At the point I was writing it, I had been broken down. There's that line, "I really don't want to be John Lennon or Leonard Cohen." Singing "Hallelujah" and "Across the Universe," I'd had glimpses into their worlds and was mesmerized and frightened by that kind of depth. I had wanted that for a long time – to be the great seer of life. But when I got close to it by singing their songs and haunting their haunts, I realized that comes at such a price.

It's important, though, as a songwriter to want to do that. You know, "I want to be the Beatles," or whatever. But as you mature, you realize that that's maybe not the greatest thing to be, or maybe those weren't the happiest people.

And your own self-definition clarifies – you end up wanting to be yourself. What becomes most important is putting forth the fullest, richest expression that you have inside you.

That's all you have to give.

"Beautiful Child" is a strange combination of apocalypse and redemption. Can you describe that song?

That song is pretty crazy. It is apocalyptic. I wrote it a while ago, but then right after 9/11, I was on Yoko's farm, and I was singing it. Everybody's head was so screwed up after that whole event, and I can only say that this is an interior event that happened, I believe. But I did have an apocalyptic vision after singing this song in a field. I saw the heavens open and the moon turn red, and I had this vision of Jesus Christ walking and then Mohammad and then another prophet comes in who has something to do with homosexuality. "The Gay Messiah," which is a song I'm saving for *Want Two*.

This is another big issue. We live in apocalyptic times. Even in terms of what's going on politically right now with gay marriage and gay sex – it's a huge issue, and it has not been dealt with yet.

I don't think I'm the gay messiah, or know whether there is a gay messiah or not. But what I got from this vision is that I'm part of the universe and my music is going to affect change somehow. This is my time. This is the time that everything seems to be settling in both the heavens and the earth for this to happen. So look out!

Finally, how are you feeling?

I'm good. I'm very much at a point in my life where a lot of the wondrous, pink-cloud experience of – I don't want to use the word "recovery" – self-exploratory science has set in and now it's just…I don't know, it's not glamorous like it once was. And I have to realize that.

I'm really humble these days, which I needed to be. And I'm a little worried about what it's going to be like to be out there again performing. I'm just trying to stay humble. I'm trying very much. I'm finding that's the only way to relieve the tension –other than crystal meth.

By "humble" you mean keeping things straightforward, with your feet on the ground, putting one step in front of the other?

Yeah. Keeping it in perspective. And realizing that I'm a blessed individual and I have a great life and I'm very fortunate. And what I do is no more important than what a cleaning lady does – we're all just people. All silly stuff like that.

The other day, I was at this place and I was having a hard time. I wanted to return to my old self, and I picked up this stupid little book which was about puppies – what puppies dream or something. I opened it, and there was this quote that totally saved my life that day. It was by Helen Keller, and it was, "When a door of happiness closes there is another door that opens up. But we spend so much time focusing on that closed door that we forget about the door that's opened up for us." It's very much become about that for me – letting go of the past and embracing the future.

Parts of this interview originally appeared in
The New York Times, *August 31, 2003.*

Trey Anastasio

"It's about doing what you're told to do"

When Trey Anastasio and I met for this conversation on June 20, 2004, Phish had announced its breakup only a few weeks earlier. And just a couple of nights before we sat down to talk, the band had begun its brief farewell tour. I'd interviewed Anastasio three times before, and we'd always found a nice groove together. His strong sense of being part of a musical tradition made him value my experience. I, of course, admired him greatly for what he and Phish had accomplished, both musically and in terms of the powerful community the band had built.

Anastasio was clearly ambivalent about his decision to disband Phish, and I got the impression that he somehow wanted my approval for it. I respected his choice, but didn't see it as the only possible option – which he seemed to need to believe it was. The discussion that arose between us about that issue made this interview special for me. It has the feel of a conversation with something at stake.

✦ ✦ ✦ ✦ ✦

It's not the most promising setting in which to speak to Trey Anastasio, this airless, windowless, entirely antiseptic conference room in the basement of the Trump International Hotel on Central Park West in Manhattan. But it quickly becomes clear that, regardless of the locale, Anastasio brings his own energy and galvanizes the space.

It's Saturday morning, and the guitarist, his hair cut uncharacteristically short, is nondescriptly dressed in jeans and a gray striped shirt. "Ugh," he groans, shortly after taking a seat in a black leather swivel chair at the round table that dominates the small room. "It's such a funny time to be talking about this right now." Of course, "this" is the Phish breakup, which Anastasio had dramatically announced less than a month before at a band meeting at bass player Mike Gordon's house in the group's home state of Vermont. And it's "funny" because, despite the prospect of disbanding, Phish has just released a new album, the intriguingly titled *Undermind*, and is now in the midst of a farewell tour set to culminate in a two-day festival in Vermont in August.

On the two nights before this interview, Phish performed sold-out shows at KeySpan Stadium, the home of the Brooklyn Cyclones, a minor-league baseball team. Ironically, Anastasio had a great time onstage with his buddies. Last night the band even backed fellow retiree Jay-Z on two of the swaggering rapper's signature hits, "99 Questions" and "Big Pimpin'." Twenty-one years of rollicking history die hard.

When Anastasio informed his bandmates that he couldn't stick it out any longer, he began to cry. His feelings seem no more settled now – in fact, they might even be more charged. He is convinced that his musical ambitions have outgrown Phish and that unless he is free of the band and its sprawling organization, their inevitable demands will never permit him to realize the sounds he longs to create or the vision of himself that he is nearly desperate to shape. He has become gripped by the sonic possibilities of orchestras and other large ensembles, some of which he has explored with his 10-piece band, as well as on his recent solo album *Seis de Mayo* and at the Bonnaroo festival last June, where he conducted and arranged his own compositions for the Nashville Chamber Orchestra.

Much of what Phish had become seems genuinely to trouble Anastasio. "Owning a merchandise company," he says, not quite believing the fact as he states it. "I love the people who work on it, but every time I walk in there, I get kind of ill. There's boxes and boxes of posters, and a feeling of the selling of us. I'm not going to be sad when that goes away." On the other hand, he deeply values Phish and the larger community it created. The notion of living without them frightens him at the same time that it exhilarates him.

So for two hours he obsessively explores the many contradictions within those two sets of conflicting emotions. "Music is the language of truth," he says at one point. "It's just too hard to lie to yourself about it." Now almost 40 and standing at a crossroads, Anastasio has set out on a pathless journey to continue to discover that truth and all of its ambiguities.

The Phish breakup came less than a year after the band announced that it was getting back together after a two-year hiatus. What happened?

One of the things I find myself saying to people is, "Is anyone really surprised by this?" I probably had a sense that it couldn't go on years before the hiatus, but there's a lot of pressure in the circle that I live in, where everyone works for Phish.

Here's a real honest moment that happened during the hiatus. I put that solo album out [*Trey Anastasio*, 2002]. Artistically, I felt like it was a great moment. I felt prolific and able to explore music that went in a different direction, with horns and a very different kind of groove. So I went out on the road, and I instantly started having arguments with people in the [Phish] organization. I was being booked into real big places, and I felt like I didn't deserve that yet. But still, there was an expectation that made me feel pressured.

You were being booked into big places to generate enough dough to keep the organization floating?

To a degree. People were just used to it. You know, "It's summer: We're going to Deer Creek." One big argument was the suggestion that I play the Key Arena in Seattle. I said, "There's no way I'm doing that." I had this new band – I couldn't carry that place yet. So we went to the Paramount, and I had a great show. I wanted to play the Fillmore and the Warfield, places like that. But what happened was, let's say we would sell 10,000 tickets in a 20,000-seat venue, that was looked at as a failure.

Meanwhile, I was feeling liberated in a way that I hadn't felt in years, yet it threatened the existence of Phish. I got the sense that there was an incredible inertia. People wanted it to fail – you know, to be bad. Like, "It can't be good; because if it's good, we're doomed!"

The strange thing is that I didn't feel it from the guys in the band or even necessarily from the fans, though there was a little of that. It was more from the organization. I started getting cold sweats when I'd walk into the office. [*Laughs*]

You felt that your new band wasn't being taken seriously?

I remember having a screaming fit backstage the night I played Radio City. I was doing a phone interview and saying things like, "This isn't a side project – it's my *life!*" Which is what art is. The audience expects an artist to be 100-percent present and honest in order to create something that's exciting and worthy of their attention. So you follow your muse. I got that training from being in Phish. Phish was the template for that.

There was an incredible encouragement to be honest and to progress in Phish. Well, it's pretty obvious to anyone who's been around music that if you really follow that path, eventually it's going to lead you into new places. And that started to happen – "I'm going to write some horn sections and some deeper grooves, something new." As soon as I got into one of those new places, I felt excited. But I met with incredible resistance, and I don't know that I was prepared for that. And the pressure from that over the next few years was hard for me to deal with.

So what were you feeling when you announced the end of the hiatus?

Mixed feelings because…I mean, I write a lot of music by nature. I always have. I literally remember writing songs in third grade. It makes me feel at peace. And when I was in Phish, no matter what I wrote, I would give it to Phish. There was stuff that was intended to be big-band charts – Phish would play them.

But around *The Story of the Ghost* [1998], [Phish lyricist] Tom [Marshall] and I had this very prolific period where we did this album called *Trampled by Lambs and Pecked by the Dove* [recorded in 1997 and released in 2000]. I remember starting to work on *Story of the Ghost* with Phish, and that was the first time I got the sense of, "It's hard for us to handle all this material you're bringing in." I understood that, but stuff started to get shelved. *Farmhouse* [2000] was basically everything that didn't make it onto *Story of the Ghost.*

And I had gotten together with [drummer] Russ [Lawton] and Tony [Markellis], the bassist in my solo band, and had this incredible creative outburst. In one day we wrote "First Tube," "Sand," and a lot of other songs – all of which, then, went onto *Farmhouse*, because that had been the history: All things always go to Phish. So that was the beginning of the difficulty, because there's something weird about that. To use "First Tube" as an example – I love playing it with Phish, but it always sounded better to me when I'd play it with my band, because that's Tony's bassline. I took it and gave it to Mike so that Phish could play it, but whenever Tony plays it, it feels right to me.

How did the other members of the band react to this "difficulty"?

Incredibly. And that's part of the real confusion and sadness about Phish going away. The guys were and have been so understanding. There's still this very deep love. It's weird.

But I'm feeling at this point that it's like graduating from high school or something. That might be a comparison that people don't like, but to me, there's no other choice. I tried everything, and this is what has to happen.

Obviously, all the things you're saying are true. There are other projects you want to do, and you have the ability, the resources and the stature to do them. But the one thing that is probably never going to happen for you again is the kind of cultural phenomenon that Phish is. That very rarely happens twice in anybody's life.

I don't think it's improbable – it's *impossible*. I'm never going to get that again. That's what's so scary about this. But, see, I feel that we would just be blowing smoke if we didn't stop. That's a hard pill for people to swallow, but I know it's true, and the other guys do, too.

The day after the hiatus started, I sat down and worked eight hours a day orchestrating "Gayute." That's the first time I had ever stopped working on Phish. *Ever.* When a Phish tour ended, I would sit down and work on Phish. Phish was everything to me up until about Big Cypress [Phish's millennial New Year's Eve celebration in Florida]. And then I just couldn't maintain it anymore. I was trying, but, just naturally, I found myself doing stuff outside of Phish. As soon as that started, it was less than it had been, and the right thing to do is leave it. It's going to end sometime, right?

Well, maybe, maybe not. I mean, some bands break up, others go on. It has ended, but it didn't have to end. You ended it.

What you just said points to why it upsets me to be looked at as the guy who took Phish away. Part of what made Phish what it was, from my standpoint, was 100-percent focus. People say, "I remember going to see Phish in 1994, and it was one song after another for 90 straight minutes, and there were the big balls," and this, that, and the other thing. Well, you know how much work it takes to make that kind of stuff happen? There's an element of smoke and mirrors to the notion that we just get up there and do that.

In 1994, every night I would rush back to the hotel and work for six hours on the next night's set – literally. I'd go through a whole pad of paper working on the song list. I had checklists of things like, "I want a piano solo every four songs." I would work on the way the keys changed. When one song ended, I'd do a whole-step rise to the next song to keep the excitement going – "I need a song in E-flat after the one in D." That was the way it was.

So, yes, of course, it could go on. But I couldn't maintain that. And once I stopped doing that, what people saw, maybe in like '99, was a sloppier Phish. And I can't live with that. It made me feel like this thing that I cherished was being disrespected.

Plus my musical tastes have changed. There's other things I want to do, and I can't fight that anymore. I tried for about five years and it was becoming unhealthy.

I feel like…it's scary being controversial.

You're being honest.

I was scared to say these things. I was just feeling tired from the whole thing. What happened was it started being, "Well, how many shows are you willing to do?" And it was less and less. We had three nights at Madison Square Garden booked for Halloween. We're giving them up. That's hard for me to do. I'm not sure I'll ever play there again, and I love playing the Garden. The energy – it's like being fed from a giant hose! And Halloween at the Garden? Come on. There was a time when I would be counting the days till those shows – the hours, the minutes, pacing in circles waiting to get onstage. So things have changed.

When the hiatus ended, you mentioned that drugs had become part of the problem with Phish. Was that one way of dealing with the tensions?

There are no drugs around now, but there were for a while. There was always pot and stuff – I mean, we always partied a bit. But all of a sudden, everybody was a wreck. I think that was an attempt to generate energy in a false way. It didn't look to me to be about partying and getting high. It was more about maintaining.

"If your thing is gone, and you wanna ride on..."

Exactly. But here's the clincher, because I was curious about how the hell did this start happening? Why are people suddenly taking all these drugs? For the summer [2003] Phish tour, I said, "I'm going to do less drugs and alcohol than I've ever done." I did no caffeine, no alcohol, no socializing. An hour or two of Ashtanga yoga every day. I had a veggie juicer backstage, I was meditating before I went onstage. And when I looked at the IT Festival video recently, which was the last show of that tour, I thought everybody looked really tired. Now, I'd never been in such good shape in my life and the music is great, but there's something in our eyes that looks tired, compared to Big Cypress.

Someday the truth about Big Cypress will come out – we were partying in the hot dog with the walls up! It was unbelievable. And yet, when I look at our eyes in that show, they're just glistening with joy and energy. I mean, I get *chills* when I see Big Cypress. So my realization at that point was, it's not drugs. That was like a painkiller Band-Aid.

What's painful, the real knife twist, is now that we've made this announcement, the tiredness is gone. So we're out there killing. But it's because it's finite. Last night we came offstage and we were laughing, because we really were cooking. It was *explosive* – "Oh, this is what we were looking for!" And Page said, "It wouldn't have happened if we didn't know that it was limited." If it was going to just roll on forever, we couldn't have dug that deep. Does that sound crazy?

It sort of sounds like having sex with your ex-wife. Doesn't it make you...

...think why did we do this?

Exactly. Like, "That was spectacular. So why am I leaving again?"

I know that's going to happen. People's reactions are funny too, depending on who you talk to. When you talk to [veteran concert promoter] Ron Delesner–who I love, he's one of the last old-school guys – he's like, "Ah, yeah, you'll be back when you need the money. I've seen it a million times. Like the Eagles – when hell freezes over."

Maybe this is just a young, naïve person speaking, but I don't think we're going to do that. I really don't. The other thing is, I'm not the kind of person who does that. When I've broken up with girlfriends in the past, that's it – never again. Before I got married, I was in a long relationship. We broke up, I walked out the door, threw my shit in the car, and I've never spoken to her again. I don't like to look back.

And I *hate* bands that do it. I'm going to offend people here, but every time it happens, it makes me want to vomit. So unless we changed our name to Phowl and wrote all new material, to go backwards would be…like, I wish Jane's Addiction hadn't done it. Why'd they do that?

There's all kinds of reasons why people do it.

People get broke.

Or they forget. I mean, look at Simon and Garfunkel.

Why are they doing it? Because Paul Simon needs the money?

I think that after a certain point, the question, "Why should I do that?" becomes, "Why am I not doing it?" Like 10 years from now, after you've done your orchestral projects and other things, you might find yourself saying, "Now, why don't I want to play with those guys again?"

I'll tell you why. And let me say this while I'm young and brash – even though I'm somewhere in the middle of being young and old, I can't figure it out. In *Guitar World*, is 40 old?

Anyway, I'll tell you why: Because it always *sucks*. Always. Guaranteed. It wouldn't be the same. Our fans, everybody would come out, and they'd all live lies. I would be much happier to step aside and let some young person come in and take that energy and run with it.

When I was walking offstage Friday night in Brooklyn, [tour manager] Brad [Sands] said to me, "That was like a Tyson fight!" It was just an explosion of energy. And that's the way people are going to remember Phish. I'm not going to be able to do that when I'm 50, and I don't want to come back and have it be a half-assed version.

The only possible way it could ever work would be if it were completely reinvented. And that's the problem. We talked about that before the hiatus, and it didn't happen – because it *can't*. You can't go onstage without a hundred people screaming for "Fluffhead." I wrote "Fluffhead" when I was 19. There's an inherent energy to be pulled backwards. So, if that energy is saying, "Go backwards!" and my heart is saying, "Go forward!" it starts to be a problem.

So if we came back…we *can't* come back. We can't. The scary part is, if we do end up broke and homeless, and they're offering us huge money. [*Pauses*] But the Police didn't come back!

That's true. There are bands that didn't come back.

The Clash didn't come back. They're cool!

But it looked like they might come back before Joe Strummer died.

Oh, God. Try to imagine that. They're not young and angry anymore. Does anyone want to see that? It would be a nightmare.

Well…

You don't want to see the Clash again, do you?

Um...

Do you? You kind of do! But do you want to see them do "London Calling"?

Of course. What would you want them to do? But Strummer's dead, so that's not a good example. You can call it nostalgia, but if you go see the Rolling Stones, they're still great. Bruce Springsteen getting back with the E Street Band is another example. In a culture in which things so often seem disposable, that was a statement that things can last. It was also a statement about community.

But is it art? Look at the great artists. Every fucking one of them. Picasso. Miles Davis. Michelangelo. Mozart. These people did not look back. Ever. They were movin', movin', movin'. But I see what you're saying. The endurance of a relationship is valuable and exciting.

But I'm just going to throw this out there: The Stones are great – it doesn't move me. I've seen them, and I don't care anymore. Personally, Mick Jagger is not my role model for what I want to be. He looks to me like a guy clinging to his youth, and I am *not* going to do that. I won't say that about Keith Richards though – he's still the coolest guy on the planet!

Look, I saw the Stones at the Tower Theater in Philadelphia a couple of years ago, and they burned the place down. Jagger was playing harmonica, banging a tambourine, singing his ass off – he was soaked in sweat. They played like they had everything to prove. And, as for performing the same songs, a song means something different when you perform it at 40 – let alone 60 – than it did when you were 20. Certain songs – and maybe "Fluffhead" is one – are not going to survive that. But if you go hear Tony Bennett, he's still got his voice and he's still reading those songs. There's something moving about that.

Maybe it's just an aspect of my personality that I feel like there's something else out there. Maybe the reason I feel no one should be surprised about Phish is because anyone who saw the way Phish progressed would know. There's 350 songs or whatever in 21 years, and everything kept changing, changing, changing. That's what people *liked* about Phish.

You've talked about this from an artistic standpoint, but is it difficult for you personally to leave Phish behind?

I think I'm going to have to face some deep demons when this thing actually stops. I'm nervous about it.

Why?

Because I like to be in the center of that kind of energy. When you take that away, and I have to wake up the next morning and find something to do, I'll probably go nuts. I may just lose it.

But how could this be bad? The word *risk* has been floating around the Phish camp forever. We've talked and talked about it. So, isn't this risk?

You can see risk as its own reward, but the whole point is that it's a risk. Inherent in the idea of risk is the possibility of failure, mistakes, misdirections.

That's why I'm nervous. I'm going to have to confront the possibility of not being accepted, of taking my risk and having everybody not like it.

But that's what the hiatus taught me, because that happened, and I didn't fucking care. I realized that it doesn't make any difference – I *have* to do it. It's bigger than me. Not following your heart or your muse causes a deep degradation of your soul. And that's what was happening the last five years. I felt a sagging in the heart.

So what kind of music do you see yourself making?

My set at Bonnaroo is reminiscent of where I'd like to go. There was an orchestral set with a 40-piece orchestra. Then I had all my musicians play with the orchestra. And then I did my rocking set after that with the horn section. Somewhere in there, I feel a combination coming where it would all come together.

Even the other guys in the band understand that. Fish was at Bonnaroo, and he was in tears when I came off the stage. He said, "I've always known you were going to do this." So it's a good feeling. And I can't live without it. It's like I can't die and not hear this music that I'm imagining.

When you look back, how do you see your development as a musician and composer?

It's funny, I don't think I was interested in improvisation when Phish started. When you listen to the first Phish album, the music's *all* composed. All of it. There's like eight big pieces.

This whole "jam band" thing? We weren't a jam band in the beginning. We were a progressive rock band. I listened to PFM and Brian Eno – those were my high school heroes. My friends and I used to smoke pot and listen to *Another Green World*, or put the headphones on and listen to *The Lamb Lies Down* on Broadway and do bong hits.

Peter Gabriel is a hero of mine – and he's another guy who quit his band! [*Laughs*] I don't know if people know that "Salisbury Hill" is about the day he quit Genesis – "My heart goin' boom boom boom," and all that? It's interesting when you hear it from that perspective.

The other night I watched some of the Phish show from the audio truck in 5.1 sound, and it was almost like standing onstage. The guitar lines you were playing sounded to me almost like the cadences of speech, like the way people talk, or the way you talk.

Right.

And I was watching you as you were playing. With so many musicians, their physical gestures mimic the sounds they're making. But you were leaning forward very intently and looking out, as if you were listening for something. And it seemed like your playing was an attempt to articulate whatever it was you were hearing. Does that make any sense to you?

It does. I have to be careful about...I don't want it to sound ridiculous, but I definitely feel like I'm listening to something. [*Laughs*] I have this feeling that there's a pattern that exists. I really do believe this. I mean, I *know* it. Even right now if you listen, right in this room I can hear about a thousand layers of rhythm: the air conditioner, the air, the sound in my head. There's tones. It's all there, and it's just the sound of life. And if you listen to it and play it, people respond.

The way you learn that is to watch people while you're playing. You start realizing that they hear it, too. They don't know it, but when you play it, people respond – "Oh, I know that!" – because they're hearing the same thing. And when I'm playing onstage, I find myself looking out, not usually into people's faces, but over their heads and up. And the endless possibilities, the depth of it all, occasionally will come to you.

Even sometimes when I'm listening to music in the car, this thing happens to me – I wonder if it happens to other people – where you're driving and when something good happens on the stereo, all of a sudden you become aware of the mountains in the distance. Everything just opens up. I think that's because the musician hit on something real, and anytime something real happens it resonates with the basic pattern of life. You suddenly become aware of, "Oh, my God, there's all these mountains and sunshine and clouds!"

When you experience that live, you want to go there more, and you start to find little doorways into it. And basically the doorway is listening. People don't really listen that much. Just *listen*. You want to learn how to play guitar? Sit in a room and listen and write down 20 things that you hear, and then try to play them. You have to get your own blocks out of the way to access that – all the fears and brick walls that you've put up through your life: "Oh, I'm not good at this," or "I'm supposed to play this riff," or "This is what I was told is good." You've got to drop all that somehow. And it takes a long time.

Was there a moment when you felt you had really discovered your own voice as a player, where you felt like, "I'm able to play all the things I'm hearing"?

I think it's happening now. Maybe that's part of this process. Maybe as you push further and further into your own voice, it gets harder to coexist as a group. The group mind, while it can be glorious, can also have a watering-down effect.

But, see, I don't think there *is* really an individual voice. I don't. I think there's one big voice, but there's individual ways to access it. There *can't* be an individual voice, because we're not individuals. And yet we are. We're all individuals, but we're all connected to one bigger thing. So in that moment onstage, where I'm playing something that sounds like an individual voice, it's a voice that's telling of something beyond me. So if it looks like I'm listening, I am. I'm trying to.

Sometimes it's too much. It freaks me out. That's a problem with playing improvised music, like with Phish – it's so right that it has a tendency to wreck your regular life, because you can't communicate normally. When it goes well on stage, everybody talks at the right time. So if I go out to a bar sometimes after a show, I go insane because nobody's listening to each other, and it's this cacophony of wrongness!

That's hysterically funny.

Onstage, it's peaceful, despite the loudness. Maybe that's why people are mad that we're taking Phish away. Maybe other people feel that too. That it's peaceful.

Well, it's hard to find those doorways in. People will miss that.

I will too. Like I said, I might go insane. But I'll probably just wake up and start writing something new.

Maybe it comes down to this: Whether you stay in something or leave it, it's about doing what you need to do.

Exactly. It's about doing what you're *told* to do – from the inside. That's what it is.

This interview originally appeared in Guitar World, *October 2004.*

Retrospectives

Retrospectives

It's no surprise that artists agree to do interviews these days primarily to promote their current projects. Sometimes, however, occasions arise – typically anniversaries or other celebrations – when they'll talk about things from a broader perspective. Doing interviews like that is enjoyable because you're freed from having to talk about a work that may not be that great. Retrospective conversations tend by their very nature to hit the high points, the most compelling moments in an artist's career, and the passage of time often allows subjects to speak more candidly then they can when they're still in the heat of the battle.

The interviews in this section are all retrospectives of that kind, and they seem to be characterized by thoughtfulness and consideration. The time that has passed since some of them were done lends them an unsettling feeling of déjà vu from time to time – as when Don Henley alludes to the first American invasion of Iraq or Jackson Browne talks about CIA activity in Latin America. Consequently, as I reread the interviews in this section, I found myself not only reflecting on the events these artists were discussing, but the time, now past, at which we spoke – and the times we live in now.

Jackson Browne on Music and Politics

"You respond with your heart"

This interview with Jackson Browne ran in the 20th-anniversary issue of *Rolling Stone* (as did the George Harrison interview and the first Paul McCartney included in this book). At the point at which I spoke to Browne, the idea for the issue was to have each artist speak about a specific topic, in this case the relationship between music and politics. That idea eventually got dropped for the issue as a whole, but this interview still retains that focus.

This was the first major story I did on Browne, though many more would follow. We spoke sitting on the grass in the park that runs along the beach in Santa Monica. I would learn over the years that Browne preferred to do interviews outdoors, a charming reflection, it seemed to me, of his California upbringing.

A few years after this interview, I was working on another story about Browne when he called me because he was in New York and it was urgent that we speak – he had some very important things that he needed to discuss with me. That was fine with me. Where? He wanted to meet that afternoon in Central Park, but since it was a Sunday and he's pretty recognizable, I thought we'd be disturbed. I suggested that, given the seemingly pressing nature of whatever was on his mind, maybe we should meet at my office since no one was likely to be around on the weekend and it would be quiet.

I could hear the disappointment in his silence. "What's the matter?" I asked. "Well," he said, a little sheepishly. "I also wanted to get some sun." You can take the boy out of the California, but…

With your last album, Lives in the Balance*, you made a transition from writing about personal matters of the heart to taking on political subjects like Central America. One of the main charges against people like you getting involved in politics is, "Why should we let this entertainer tell us how we're supposed to run our government?" How do you respond to such charges?*

Well, here's the difference. I write my material; Reagan doesn't. He reads his. That's also true of newscasters. I never really considered myself an entertainer.

What's happening now is that people are finding their political feet in every walk of life. Ideas that might have been attributed to radical people in the '60s are now held by people of every walk of life: the idea of disarmament, the idea of nonintervention, issues about peace and the environment. People who don't think "entertainers" should have a voice in politics would just as soon leave war to the generals and politics to the "professional" politicians. To me, that's the opposite of a democracy. A democracy implies that we have the participation of everybody on every level. I'm very pleased that on *Lives in the Balance* I was able to articulate ideas that I've held for a long time. You have to remind people: "Look, this is the United States, remember? The thing we're fighting for? The freedom we're tying to preserve? I'm exercising it."

Despite your distrust of "professional politicians," you did some fund-raising concerts for candidates in the mid '70s.

That was something that happened, I guess, in '76. Historically, it's worth noting that that was the first time they had put all these limitations on campaign contributions. So you could get a lot of money calling every person who bought a ticket a "contributor." There was suddenly this loophole. Everybody loved that, politicians especially: "Ha! That's how we'll get the money!" And I did have some experiences with them that I didn't really care for. After about two of those – one for a candidate here in California and one for Jerry Brown – I decided not to do that anymore. I didn't really like the prospect of being linked to a particular person's ability to carry out his promises.

The biggest problem I have with electoral politics is that the whole premise is faulty. The idea that you're going to hire someone to take care of things for you – ideally, it would be great. Everybody researches the issues and goes with the person who's going to carry out the policies as the voters think they should be carried out. Instead, politicians sell themselves in a cosmetic way, and people vote for them without finding out what they really represent or how they're going to pull these things off. And then they forget about it until the next time the elections come up.

Having made an album as political as Lives in the Balance, *do you find yourself thinking differently about your earlier, more personal songs?*

Some of my early songs reflect a less specific version of what I'm talking about now. "Before the Deluge" could be taken to be about the nuclear-power issue. "For Everyman" is about a sort of vague and optimistic belief in humanity.

It seems a clear statement against individualism.

And the idea that it's "you against the world." No matter where you go, you still have to contend with other people. On my last tour, that song and a song like "For America" went very well together. There are some songs I don't care to sing anymore, but that's probably because I'm not 18 anymore.

Do you believe that political songwriters have to be political all the time?

No, I can't think of one who is. Most people write a political song because of an issue or because the subject has touched them in some way. If they become known as political songwriters, it's really a way of categorizing them. Steven Van Zandt, you could call him a political songwriter. Actually, until his album *Voice of America*, I never would have thought of putting out an album of all political songs. Because people have the vague feeling that politics is all about bullshit and deception, I always felt a little bit like apologizing for anything that dealt with political subjects. You know: "I'm sorry I have to mention this, but not everything is as it should be."

Somebody like Steven is all the more brilliant because a person who makes rock 'n' roll the way he does and wears leopard pants, snakeskin boots, skull earrings, and wears his telecaster somewhere between his ass and his knees – for him to be singing the word *justice* is very powerful.

Do you feel that political consciousness among rock performers is increasing?

A lot has changed in the last couple of years because of the acceleration of events: Band Aid, Live Aid, "We Are the World," Farm Aid, "Sun City." There's an acceleration of events on the general topic of peace and the well-being of the planet – ending with the concerts for Amnesty International – where you actually have a chance to get in touch with the discrepancies that exist in our worldview.

People are fond of pointing out that there was a lot of activism in the '60s and then the '70s were sort of dormant. Now in the '80s, there seems to be a lot of concern again. Maybe things work in cycles. But I would say that there is a progression. Within a year or two of an event that centered on extreme hunger and starvation in Africa, you were also having events with many of the same artists discussing human rights. It's possible to really begin connecting these issues. The issues of hunger and peace are related – specifically by the arms race and by the fact that our world's resources are going into technologies that can't be used, while people go hungry.

You said that beliefs that were held by a radical fringe in the '60s are now widely shared. Given the general move to the right in this country, aren't those views really more marginal than ever?

It would have been inconceivable 20 years ago that even radical people would understand – to the degree to which everybody understands now – what the CIA has been up to. There were very few people who understood what happened in Central America. I think these subjects are more out in the open now. But it's not as if radical people are going to save the world. It's not as if I expect there to be a revolution in the United States.

Did you ever think that was going to happen?

In the late '60s, I thought there was going to be a real breakdown in the fabric of society. Those people who were continually given the short end and being continually oppressed were going to begin to tear it down. I felt the whole thing was very shaky.

In the '60s, there were the Watts riots and a lot of demonstrations against the Vietnam War. There was this all-encompassing feeling that something really huge was wrong that people couldn't see. I think that much is, of course, still true.

At one point, I became a little ashamed of myself for writing the song "Before the Deluge," in which I project a huge cataclysm. I felt, "How wrong to idly project such a catastrophic event, to dabble in your imagination with the idea of so many people being wiped out and dying." But it doesn't keep me from singing the song – I think it was on a lot of people's minds.

When you write a song about a political subject or play a benefit, what do you see as the effect

Well, it's always something specific. It's like I have to do something, right? And if it's, say, going to Central America, I felt like I had to try to put into perspective something that was really unclear.

There's nothing about the other struggles in pop music that appeals to me. I don't dress very well, and I'm not very young anymore. I don't play guitar a lot. Really, I'm a songwriter, and these are the subjects that came out. "Soldier of Plenty," I remember writing the first verse and going to sleep and the next morning looking at this thing: "God is great, God is good / He guards your neighborhood." I thought, "What are you talking about? Can you really be singing a song about this?" I didn't know what the song was about until it was written.

So when you ask, "What do you think you're going to accomplish with one of these songs?" the answer is I don't really know. But I know that in going to Central America, I was really moved to want to do something. I thought it would be worth anything to get a point across, perhaps to let people know that the issue is not whether or not one of the poorest countries in the world is a threat to our security but whether or not they have the right to the same opportunities we have.

How did your visits to Central America affect your songwriting?

I had already started "For America" and "Lives in the Balance" before I went to Central America. When I went down there, I met some Nicaraguans. Everywhere you go, if you're a musician, you're handed a guitar, you're asked to sing. I think of those purest of motivations I had when I was 14 or 15, the idea of playing the guitar and singing about something and moving people, expressing something inside me. Those are, I imagine, the reasons people become singers there, too. I realized that their songs were about everything from love to the reconstruction of their society. I thought it would be too hard to talk about those things in a song.

And it isn't easy. There are all these songs that we don't think of as political that comment on things that are political. Like I would never have known that the song "Shout" was about cruise missiles, but I would imagine that Tears for Fears' fans knew. If the band did any interviews, they would have occasion to know. Look at Ry Cooder's song "Borderline." It's a beautiful, human song about people who come here expecting something, and Cooder's certainly not known as a political songwriter. But there's his song, and it has political implications.

Are there other political songs or songwriters you admire?

I think Rubén Blades is really incredible. He talks about subjects that have political implications, and he speaks about it completely from a human point of view. He portrays the life of a policeman – maybe a member of a death squad – waking up and talking to his wife and kissing his kids goodbye as he leaves to go arrest someone. Songs like that are very provocative. A song like "Russians" by Sting goes really far to raise questions. Questions like whether or not the Russians love their children. I mean, it's an *annoying* question. Of *course*, they love their children. No one said they *don't* love their children. But the more you think about it, we *act* as if they don't.

What was the first political music you remember hearing?

The first music that I heard that I really went crazy for was Bob Dylan's. Songs like "Talkin' World War III Blues" or "The Lonesome Death of Hattie Carroll" and "Blowin' in the Wind." Those songs were political, and it was a time when the civil rights movement was in full sail. It was 1963–1964 – I come from that period of time; the early '60s was when I started playing the guitar. Of course, I heard Woody Guthrie and Pete Seeger, too, and the Staples, Sonny Terry and Brownie McGhee. A lot of blues artists. But Bob Dylan, Bob Dylan, Bob Dylan.

Has any of Dylan's more recent stuff disturbed you?

He's always been a preacher. That's something I didn't know then. I mean, he's been a political singer. He's been a nihilist. He's been a foggy voice in a completely wasted scape.

Bob Dylan is always incredible. It used to be that I would get *the* Bob Dylan album, and I would breathe it for six months or a year or until he put out the next one. Around the time I started making my own music, I stopped following him that closely. If, when I die, they open my brain and do a cross section, like the rings of a tree or something, they will find several years in there where there's nothing but Bob Dylan.

I don't need for Bob Dylan to become one thing or another. What he is, is a constant – a constant mystery, always a surprise.

You've been engaged in political activity for about 15 years now. What is it that makes you believe it's worth continuing?

What do I think the impact has been? I made an album and for almost the first time went around and did as much press as I could do. I wound up doing hundreds and hundreds of interviews on political subjects in a lot of rock publications and a lot of dailies, a lot of TV video shows or TV news programs. And that has an effect.

What is that effect?

If I were a person interested in these subjects and feeling that "My God, doesn't anybody care what's going on?" and I heard a song like "Lives in the Balance" coming over the radio, I'd be happy to hear it. I'd welcome it. I think a song can have a connecting effect. The effect is that it produces a dialogue. And there's not a lot of political dialogue on rock stations or on MTV.

Do you think that because early in your career you established yourself as a songwriter who took people's inner lives seriously, people are more willing to trust you now that you're doing political songs?

I think that people come and go. There are undoubtedly people who haven't really listened to my music since they were in school or something. Or if they hear it now, they hear it on the radio. That's about people's lives changing. But what happened with me is that I changed in terms of what I wanted to talk about. I have less of a capacity to talk about internal things.

As a result of my getting older, the world has become more interesting to me. There are a lot of great things at stake. I take things personally. People always used to ask me, "Do you think you got involved in this nuclear-power issue because you have kids?" I don't think that's true at all, because the people who design these plants have kids. People who profit on nuclear weapons have children. I don't think it's a matter of that. In the course of events, a situation becomes very critical, and you do whatever you can. You respond with your heart, you respond with as much of your ability as you have to effect a change.

What do you think prevents more people from becoming politically involved?

I think the real thing people are scared of is that their lives will change in such a way that they won't be fun anymore: "I'm going to become completely immersed in this, and I won't be able to talk about anything else. I won't be able to go enjoy myself or have a vacation and go where I want to go. I won't be able to ski." You want to keep your sense of humor. I mean, it's possible to enjoy life and to want social justice. It's important; as a matter of fact, it's your *duty* to have fun, to enjoy life and maintain a robust attitude toward it. But it does seem like an interruption to many people who don't really think about it. Sooner or later the big interruption comes, where it's your own life that's interrupted by very real events – whether it's war or whether it's the shutdown of a factory.

What do you think about the criticism that political artists or political people in general are compensating for an inability to deal with their own personal lives?

You mean that it's some kind of an escape, a retreat into a valiant cause as opposed to dealing with the humdrum of the everyday? [*Laughs*] That could be a big pitfall. I don't think it's the case with me. I'm very committed to working out my relationship with my girlfriend and the people I'm close to in my life, my kids.

Actually, I think it's a broader question than you asked: whether there isn't something reassuring about looking into the world and finding injustice and pitting yourself against it. Particularly where there are benefits and people do things for free, out of the goodness of their hearts and as volunteers – it's very fertile ground for malcontents. Sometimes people are just going to be *impossible.*

Do you mean the artists themselves or the political organization involved?

Well, artists are impossible anyway. But with rally stuff or movement work, there's always somebody with a complaint, and you wonder if that person isn't complaining about, say, nuclear power because he's just a complainer. There's a lot of people in the peace movement who could not agree if their lives depended on it, and what they're suggesting is that lives *do* depend on it.

For instance, this one huge peace rally in 1982 – Peace Sunday. The group that held the permit for the park said, "If you don't use our slogans and let us define the name of the event and what will be draped across the front, then we won't give you the permit and there won't *be* any rally."

It was a matter of some fairly radical people having a problem with being seen in agreement with some fairly moderate people. No one could agree, and the permit did lapse. In the end, the city officials got together and said, "*Please*, can we give you a permit for the park, instead of your doing this thing in the street?" Even then, there were problems. They didn't want Joan Baez to sing, and they didn't want Bruce Springsteen to sing. Evidently, it was just about somebody having their control circumvented. I didn't know a thing about it, but I brought them on, and everybody got to hear Joan Baez and Bruce Springsteen. But you get the feeling sometimes that the movement is full of people that are just malcontents.

Do you see Live Aid and events like that as being the fruit of, say, the MUSE [Musicians United for Safe Energy] concerts, which you helped organize in the late '70s?

Not really. Every decade has its events, and this one has had several so far. MUSE was kind of an experiment. One of the things that really didn't work was that when you shed a lot of media attention on something for a brief period of time, when it goes away people think that the problem has gone away. Also, it was measured in terms of whether it reached its stated goals. Because we didn't make $3 million – we only made a million and a half, and some of that was spent on a movie – it was portrayed as being unsuccessful. What happened before *No Nukes* was Bangladesh. Before that, you had Woodstock. And Woodstock was a political event, if you realize that we were at war in Vietnam and this was half a million people coming together to express an ideal of peace.

Were the '60s an especially complex time for you?

When people talk about the '60s – it's impossible to talk about the '60s – it means so many things, so many things were going on. It's all subjective. For instance, I had heard about Charles Manson. And this guy, Mike Deasey, had been out there once trying to record Charles Manson and all those people. He suggested that there was a lot of tribal unity there, but very sexually free. For someone who was – I think I was 19 at the time – I thought, "Yeah, let's go out there." It sounded *great* to me. Then Terry Melcher said, "Well, no, actually, you better not, because it's a little strange, it's a little odd." And Mike Deasey – who was a guitar player and a really nice guy – said, "Don't mess with it." When I say it sounded great, I mean in the depths of my ignorance it sounded great.

What about the utopian aspect of '60s politics? Have you dismissed the idea that it's possible to create a society that works on the basis of completely alternative values?

No, but you have to get it for everybody. The thing is, it's possible to ignore all the injustice in the world and immerse oneself in one's own development. That's sort of utopian. I think that many people decided you have to take care of yourself in order to be able to help anybody anyway, so they began finding ways to coexist with the way things are. People put out food products that are healthy, and they imagine, "Gee, if everybody ate this stuff, everything would be great!" But not everyone can afford it.

What are your spiritual beliefs? Are you religious?

I think that without justice, you have a hard time leading any kind of a spiritual life. And I think recognizing other people's dilemmas is more important than reaching some sort of a pure spiritual state. My favorite slogan is, "If you want peace, fight for justice."

I kind of accept the idea of reincarnation. Only because it's inconceivable to me that we only get to be here once. It almost doesn't matter what you believe about what happens after death. I think the best values you can have are worthwhile regardless of whether they get you to heaven or not. Truth is its own reward, and justice is needed here on earth during our lives.

Are you afraid your activism will make people perceive you as a cause monger?

I worry about it. And you should do everything you can to guard against being perceived that way. But in the end, what people think about you is their business. I don't believe you can control how people feel about you; it's too much work. You have to take the trouble to try not to be misunderstood. Other than that, I think that how people see that has as much to do with how they are as the way I am. Most people encourage me. It's just natural to want to give something back to people if you feel grateful that you're in a position to communicate.

Where do you see the relationship of music and politics going?

I think that rock 'n' roll is one of the main communications mediums. It's one that people really care about and are attuned to a lot more than to the 6 o'clock news. Fundamentally, people are smart. They know that there's a lot more to the news than what this smiling idiot on the TV is telling them. So rock 'n' roll is a much more viable way of communicating concerns and needs.

I really think people are going to wake up, because in the last seven years there's been a real experiment in going the wrong way. People invested in an incredibly nostalgic view of this country. It's an exciting time, because people in every part of the spectrum of rock music are finding a way to attune themselves to the changes that are going on. It's not only very invigorating, but things are connecting.

This interview was published in Rolling Stone, *November 5, 1987.*

The Eagles on the '70s

"We were young and the world lay stretched out before us"

"I don't know why fortune smiles on some / And lets the rest go free," sings Don Henley on "The Sad Café," the concluding song on the Eagles' last studio album, *The Long Run*. Those lines capture eloquently the degree to which the Eagles had come to see the superstardom they enjoyed in the '70s as a kind of curse that generated dissension among the band's members, critical controversy, creative paralysis, and a nearly metaphysical discomfort with the hedonistic delights – however fully indulged – that success brought in its wake.

Things started out innocently enough. When the Eagles were formed in Los Angeles in 1971, the group – guitarists Glen Frey and Bernie Leadon, bassist Randy Meisner, and drummer Don Henley – set out on an exuberant exploration of the country-rock synthesis that had been a hallmark of earlier California bands like the Byrds and the Flying Burrito Brothers. The Eagles' first three albums – *Eagles* (1972), which yielded the hits "Take It Easy," "Witchy Woman," and "Peaceful Easy Feeling"; *Desperado* (1973); and, as guitarist Don Felder was joining the band, *On the Border* (1975) – were distinguished by catchy melodies, reassuring harmonies, and a fascination with outlaw imagery.

On *One of These Nights* (1975), the Eagles began to examine the dark side of the California dream, a concern that grew into an obsession on *Hotel California* (1976), the band's greatest album. Novelist Joseph Conrad used the term "fascination of the abomination" to describe the hypnotic power that self-destruction can exert on the soul, and that phrase well suits *Hotel California*'s depiction of a gorgeous paradise – the geographical end point of American aspiration – transformed into a kind of sunny hell of unsatisfying pleasure.

With *Hotel California*'s massive success, Henley and Frey clearly emerged as the main voices of the Eagles, not only because their song-writing and singing had come to define the band's vision, but because – with the departure of Leadon and Meisner and the addition of guitarist

Joe Walsh and bassist Timothy B. Schmit – they were the last remaining members of the original lineup. Battles over the direction of the group, anxiety over crafting a worthy follow-up to *Hotel California*, legal struggles with the band's management, and a growing perception by critics of California rockers as spoiled, narcissistic sybarites created an environment in which three years passed before the release of *The Long Run*, a process that left the group exhausted and disaffected. When Frey announced in 1981 that he had begun work on a solo album, the Eagles' breakup became official.

On a bright day this past August, Henley and Frey met at Henley's home in Beverly Hills to do their first interview together since the Eagles' split. Fresh from the extensive tour that followed the release of *The End of the Innocence*, Henley seemed relaxed and happy. Frey appeared comfortable as well, despite a solo career that stalled in the late '80s. Frey's image – and that of the Eagles – had also not been well served by his recent "Hard Rock/Rock Hard" ads for Jack LaLanne, which implied that his years as a '70s rocker consisted of little more than pointless excess.

But if the past was the subject of the day, the future loomed as well, in the form of a projected Eagles reunion. Henley and Frey are starting to write songs together, and other former members of the group are being recruited for a possible album and tour next year.

Already the backlash has begun. "Don Henley must die," psycho-punk Mojo Nixon screams on his new album. "Don't let him get back together with Glenn Frey." So history is once again repeating itself, but this time around, Henley and Frey seem to have the equanimity to enjoy themselves more naturally and, at least in the short term, to settle in for the long run.

Do you think of the '70s as a distinct era, or does it blur around the edges?

GF: Well, it can sort of be defined by the life of our band, because the band started in the fall of '71 and broke up probably sometime in 1980, so we were working together for the whole decade.

DH: The decade has some definite parameters for me because I came out to L.A. in the summer of 1970 from Texas. And then the band. I think of the *Desperado* period, which was '73, and then '75, which was

One of These Nights. I think '75 was around the point when the '70s changed – '74, '75, '76.

GF: We changed, too.

DH: Yeah. And then late '76 started another period – the *Hotel California* period. That's when disco and punk were starting to come in, and I guess that was the beginning of the '80s.

What do you mean, that's when the '70s started to change and you changed? What were those changes?

GF: We got a little more serious; maybe we became more politically active. You know, something happened around the time of the bicentennial. We got *Hotel California* out by Thanksgiving 1976 – we wanted badly to have an album out in that year.

I remember interviews in which you'd say that the record was about more than California. It was really about America.

DH: America, in general, California being the microcosm. That didn't seem to take. I mean, it just went in one ear and out the other.

GF: There was a time, somewhere in 1976, when I thought things were going to get better. We had gotten rid of Nixon. We had a Democrat in the White House. Jimmy Carter and the boys were going to have barbecue on the hill.

The president was quoting Bob Dylan.

DH: It seemed like the '60s were back for a second.

GF: And then Khomeini…

DH: And the helicopter mechanics. Events conspired against ol' Jimmy.

Let's go back a bit. The two of you come from very different parts of the country. What brought you to California?

GF: Well, I grew up in Detroit, so I never really had any desire to go east. Being from the Great Lakes and watching the sun set in the west, that's where I wanted to go. I played in one of the only bands in Detroit that did surfer music!

What was your sense about it when you got here? Did it meet your expectations?

GF: Oh, I think I was a little bit intimidated, a little awed. But you get over that. I came here once and went back to Michigan and *really* decided I hated Michigan. Then I figured I better just go and try to make something out of my life in California.

What were your first impressions when you got here, Don?

DH: Kind of *gaw-lee!* I mean, I used to read a lot of the fan magazines, the music magazines of that day, and everything musically that excited me seemed to be emanating from here. It was all happening here. There were the Byrds; Crosby, Stills, Nash & Young; Linda Ronstadt and Joni Mitchell, Steppenwolf and Spirit. The thing that definitely pushed me in this direction was that Kenny Rogers had discovered my little group [Shiloh] in Texas, and he lived here. He was the only person we knew here, and we didn't know *anybody* in New York. So he was instrumental in our decision to come out this way, with the promise of an album, a record deal.

We came here the first time, I believe it was February 1970. We came out to cut a single, not really to move here. I remember driving into town; we came up on the Hollywood Freeway. It was a nice, clear February night, one of those nights when the town looks really pretty. I had never seen the Capitol Records Tower – I was freaking out. It was like there was this big metal and concrete symbol of the recording industry. I had so many Capitol records when I was a kid – 45s, you know, when they had that purple label with the Capitol dome. I believe the writing was in silver. It was a manifestation of all my childhood records. I was awestruck. I had never seen any terrain like this. Where I come from there are rolling, gentle hills but no vistas like this. Of course, I had never seen a grid of lights like that in my life. It just went on forever.

What about when you got the Eagles together? What were your ambitions?

GF: I think we had a lot of optimism. You don't know any better than to think that you can do really well. I mean, every time you put together a band, you think, "This is going to be the one."

DH: The best band in the world – until you really get to know everybody. We were young, and the times were exciting, and the world lay stretched out before us. The beginning is when it's great. Money and girls were the two big motivations – that's what it was for everybody. Then you become a serious artist and set out to change the world.

GF: There was a time during 1976, 1977, where the record business went crazy. That was when *Hotel California* came out, and *Saturday Night Fever* and also *Rumours* by Fleetwood Mac, and…

DH: *Frampton Comes Alive!* – for a minute.

GF: That was the music business at its decadent zenith. I remember Don had a birthday in Cincinnati, and they flew in cases of Chateau Lafite Rothschild. I remember that the wine was the best and the drugs were good and the women were beautiful and, man, we seemed to have an endless amount of energy. *Endless* stores of energy. Hangovers were conquered with Bloody Marys and aspirin, you know what I mean? There were no two-day purges or hiding in your bed. It seemed that you bounced back, you were resilient.

DH: There was much merrymaking. Those kinds of record sales were unprecedented. I guess everybody thought it was going to continue like that. Lots of money was spent on parties and champagne and limos and drugs. And then, of course, the bottom fell out.

GF: I know we were pissed off, but the music business seemed a little friendlier to me.

DH: It was friendlier to the young man or woman starting out. It wasn't quite the claw-your-way-into-the-business that it is now. It was much more organic, as was the world. The whole country-rock movement – I hate that label, but for lack of a better term – was even connected to environmentalism, because it was a music that had grown in part out of country music. It was very much connected to the earth, and everybody was wearing earthy clothes and celebrating the outdoors.

The very term "country rock" suggests a rural origin.

DH: It was a very natural time. And it all made sense with the music. Then in the late '70s, there was a backlash against that. Music started to become very urban oriented, a reflection of the concrete and steel and the pace. So we didn't, to paraphrase Joni Mitchell, get back to the garden. If we did, we didn't stay there. The country, the natural sound that is connected with nature, has gone out of music pretty much. I lament that loss, that contact we had with nature.

GF: When the '70s started, music wasn't giving much hope. There was almost no way that musically the '70s was going to be on a par with the '60s. The only people that even got remotely close were Crosby, Stills, Nash & Young, but all their problems – they sort of blew it. But they had that myth going for a while. Looking back on things, the music of the '70s doesn't sound that fucking bad to me at all. You can name the great albums of the '70s. I don't know if you can name the great albums of the '80s, but if you do, how great are they compared with *Layla*?

What other records do you think really stand out?

GF: I might forget some things, but I'm thinking of a string of Elton John hits. We had the Spinners, we had the Philadelphia Sound – I liked those records. It's kind of funny even to have resented disco compared with where that kind of music has gone. Some of the older disco songs, shit, if it's Harold Melvin and the Blue Notes, those are pretty good fucking records. Some of the Donna Summer records I like better than the things that I've heard recently. There's a lot more craft and a lot less programming, that's for sure.

DH: Some great R&B records were being made in the early '70s – that wasn't only in the '60s.

How do you feel about your own stuff?

DH: I pretty much like the same things and hate the same things now that I did then. I mean, we knew when we were making those albums that some of the songs weren't very good. We were trying to run a democracy, and there wasn't a hell of a lot we could do about it. We just had to swallow it, just to keep the group happy and together. As time progressed, there would be another album, Glenn and I would put up more of a fight to try to get the quality of each song to rise. But, I mean, shit – we were what? Twenty-five, twenty-six, twenty-seven years old? We weren't exactly mature. We were growing up in public, you know?

I look back at some of the lyrical content and cringe sometimes, but we were just as mature as anybody else that age, I guess.

A few moments ago you both were describing what a great time you were having as the '70s kicked into high gear. But as the decade went on, your records got darker and darker. Why was that?

DH: I think we knew intuitively that it would pass. We could sense the future. It was kind of idyllic. It was very exciting. It was a time of discovery. And people were just friendlier in general. But I think intuitively we were aware of the end of the boom. Not exclusively for ourselves, but the nation.

Was there a sense that the tensions within the band or that the tensions between the two of you were getting channeled into your work?

DH: We did use the tension a lot to be creative. We would divide up into factions. It was me and him against them, in general, and we would use that. We were very much for quality music and growth and mature subject matter. At the same time, we wanted to be successful. We wanted to get a big audience. We felt that was the whole purpose of being in the record business in the first place. There were some people in the band who didn't, for one reason or another. Guilt. And I understand that, you know. But the tension took its toll after a while. It finally got the better of us.

GF: The band just got bigger and bigger, and it became unmanageable. I think the underbelly of success is the burden of having to follow things up. We started to run out of gas. Don sort of blew his literary nut on *Hotel California*. I mean, we covered it, from love to sex to drugs to the future of the planet to…

DH: Religion.

GF: We weren't thinking about selling 15 million records at the time. It's one thing if you have a couple of hit singles and get a gold record. That's different from selling 15 million albums. There's only a few artists who have had the education of having to continue working on stuff after some sort of blockbuster success. So it wore on us. We spent a lot more time in the studio toward the end of the decade, and we got a lot more critical of our own work, because we wanted it to be better than the last thing we did. We probably should have just given up and written a couple more love songs and put out *The Long Run* a couple of years earlier. Now I realize that.

DH: So much momentum built up that instead of controlling the momentum, we started getting pushed along by it. Instead of having maybe six months or a year after *Hotel California* to sit back and take a deep breath and assess the situation and figure out what direction we should go in, we plunged into another album. The beast wanted to be fed. We tried to feed it, and we were pretty much paralyzed. Like Glenn said, I didn't have much left to say at that point. I don't think any of us did. We were pretty tired.

Obviously the two of you went through a real bad patch. Do you have any regrets?

GF: So much time has passed now that I'm not even mad at the guys I was *really* mad at. We just sort of drifted. The Eagles were like an ongoing nightmare for us toward the end.

DH: It was also responsible for the failure of several relationships with the opposite sex.

GF: Yeah, we weren't doing really well with that.

You once called your relationship with Don "my longest successful romance."

GF: Well, here we are. We're still laughing.

DH: Yeah, the women came and…it was funny, he and I would live together for a while and write a certain body of material. And then one of us would get a girlfriend, and the other guy would move out. And that guy would break up with his girlfriend and be ready to move back in, and then the other guy would have a girlfriend. But the music always came first. We wanted it that way. I mean, it would have been nice – we wanted to have relationships with girls and have the band, too. But it just didn't seem possible. We were wedded to the muse or that vision – whatever it was and however murky it might have been.

Do you feel optimistic about working together again?

GF: Well, we're going to see. It will be interesting. There's certainly a lot to write about.

DH: I think we've matured a great deal. We have a better perspective on the world and our place in it. I mean, I want to stress that we had a *real good time*. We're pointing out the low points, but we had a great fucking time.

Your interviews about the Eagles always seem to emphasize the downside of things. But on a day-to-day basis it had to have been fairly enjoyable.

DH: Shit, yeah! I mean we were living…this was the dream that we all had. This is why we came to California. It just got bigger than we ever expected it to. It kind of scared us, I guess.

GF: We tried to maintain that underdog frame of mind.

DH: But it was hard to be an underdog when you're selling 12 million records. [*Laughs*]

GF: Led Zeppelin might argue with us, but I think we might have thrown the greatest traveling party of the '70s. It was called the Third Encore. Almost every night when we were on the road, we would throw this fabulous mixer. We'd hand out 3E buttons, and we'd invite all the key radio people and as many beautiful girls as we'd meet from the airport to the hotel and whatever. We had our own sound system and we played Motown and blues records and had this terrific party every night.

How were you able to get up the next day?

GF: You go to bed at four or five and you get up at noon or 1 o'clock. If you're playing multiple nights, you don't travel, and you don't sound-check. The Eagles – we didn't really have to sound-check very much.

Who did you see as your competition in those days?

DH: Fleetwood Mac was the competition, but it was a friendly competition.

GF: I thought about competition more in the earlier days. You know, once you become successful, you realize that you're competing with yourself. Somebody else making a good record can't keep you off the charts. We used to have these T-shirts that said, "SONG POWER," because we felt that was what we had going for us. There was, even in the early '70s, too much emphasis on packaging. There was already dry ice and smoke bombs. I looked at Jethro Tull and some of those bands as the people we were competing against.

Bands that were about spectacle?

DH: Yeah, we were deliberately minimalist, to a fault probably. We were accused by one critic of loitering onstage – which pissed us off then. Now we can laugh about it. That's what's great about being 40 – that shit's funny now.

Did you feel at any point like your identity was wrapped up in being one of the Eagles?

DH: I still think of myself, in some part of my mind, as being that. There is still in most cities, no matter how popular I am as an individual artist, a bunch of guys in the audience who at some point will start going, "Ea-*gles*, Ea-*gles*, Ea-*gles*." Some nights I get pissed off and say, "We'll get to that in a minute, but right now I'm up here. It's my name that's on the ticket." But it's certainly something we're both proud of. We accomplished a lot. We were also a socially responsible band. We did our part to give something back to the community and charities of various kinds.

GF: We didn't get to do quite enough, I think.

DH: No, we didn't, again because there was a lot of disagreement.

GF: This is something that disappointed Don and me toward the end of the '70s. A couple of things happened. First of all we did a bunch of benefits.

DH: We got some flak for that. We learned at the very end of our career that it's not really a good idea to do benefit concerts for individual politicians. For causes, yes. But for individual politicians it's not really a good idea – for us or for them. I mean, we've had various drug busts, and politics is so ruthless now that the opponent can always drag that kind of stuff up. And it's not good for us, either, because you have to maintain that outsider thing to some extent.

How did your political sensibility develop?

GF: Linda [Ronstadt] started going out with Jerry Brown. [*Laughs*]

DH: The first things we did were for the various American Indian tribes around California. It started out as an environmentalist-nature thing. We used to go camp out in the desert and do peyote rituals. The photo of us on our first album is one when we were ripped on peyote. So I think it started out with Indian folklore and myths, which is where the name for the band came from.

GF: And then the antinuclear movement started.

DH: Jackson Browne was influential on us in that respect.

Do you feel that politically the '70s suffered a hangover from the failed ideals of the '60s?

DH: Yeah, I'm still writing about it. The dream was unfulfilled. In the late '70s, greed reared its ugly head. We turned from a society that was concerned with our brother and our fellow man into a society that was very self-centered, self-concerned, about money and power. That took us into the '80s, but it really started at the end of the '70s. I guess it was a result of a disillusionment that the '60s didn't quite pan out. For all the publicity about the baby-boom generation and how we were going to change the world, we weren't in control. The same people who had always been in control were *still* in control. While we were out taking drugs and preaching flower power and having rock concerts and love-ins, people were running the country.

It sometimes seems that the Eagles are on the radio now as much as in the '70s. How does it feel to be driving in your car and hear your songs?

GF: It seems like all of our best songs have risen to the top – they're the ones that get played over and over again. You know, you get these printouts of your publishing, all the songs you've written, and of the Eagles songs, there are about eight or ten that just consistently do big numbers – and they also happen to be the ones I like. It just reminds you that maybe you are good at what you do and that what you did when you were young is still good now. That makes me feel good.

DH: I feel good about it, too. It depends on the mood I'm in. Some days "Hotel California" will come on the radio and I'll turn it up and listen to it. Some days I'll just turn it off or punch another station.

You also are in the relatively rare position of having lent an expression to the language: "Life in the fast lane."

DH: Yeah, I wish we had a nickel for every fucking time somebody's used that.

GF: We do! [*Laughs*]

The Eagles had a hard time with the critics – a situation you didn't help by denouncing the New York Dolls from the stage in New York. Do you remember that incident?

GF: God only knows what me, a microphone and a big PA could have done on any night. You know, it's hard to… We were…

DH: …angry young men, using that anger to propel ourselves forward. It's not something we were really angry about. It's not like we lost sleep about the New York Dolls.

GF: No, I think critics in New York were the real burr under our saddle. We became the symbol for that laidback, rich, and don't-give-a-shit California lifestyle, you know what I mean? "These guys aren't struggling artists. Are you kidding?" Even when you're first coming out, they think you jump in your convertible and go to the beach, and then, when the sun's going down, you go to the club. We just had a problem with the New York critics. The New York Dolls were their flavor of the month, so that was probably why that came out.

DH: The New York Dolls, where are they now? All these so-called seminal groups, I don't get it. I don't understand what the big hoopla was about. We would just do things to irritate once in a while. But the resentment of us was part of a larger resentment – there always was a cultural rivalry between New York and L.A. New York has a certain amount of chauvinism about itself, and we fed the fires by talking back.

Instead of ignoring it, we always had some rebuttal, which in retrospect was probably not a good idea. And then communications broke down completely. There was Irving Azoff's famous statement: "He is an Eagle and as such does not talk to the press."

GF: That's when they started treating us nicer.

You spoke earlier about being educated by your success. What are the lessons of that education?

GF: That you have to strive for perfection, but in rock 'n' roll, you have to settle for excellence. We tried for three and a half years on *The Long Run* to make every note perfect, and we couldn't. Rock 'n' roll is not supposed to be perfect. I mean, we would overdub for days on guitar parts and things, when…

DH: In retrospect, that's kind of silly. We spent too much time working on the album, when all one need do was listen to early Stones records to realize that all this striving for perfection is totally unnecessary. That's one thing. You learn a lot about human nature. We have more of a sense now of our place. I'm able to relax and enjoy it a lot more now and not take everything quite so seriously. Every time something bad happens, if you get a bad review or you have a bad performance, it's not the end of the world. Life goes on. You get perspective.

That's the part of rock 'n' roll that is not talked about much. We get to travel a lot. You see a crowd of 10,000, 20,000, 30,000 people every night. You read local newspapers, and you really get an overview of what's going on in this country. Sometimes it's heartening, and a lot of times it's frightening. You see the problems are widespread, and they're pretty much the same everywhere. If you spend any time touring the rest of the world, you can get a whole perspective of the globe and where this country stands in it. I mean, we've got a lot of work to do here. The underlying problem is greed and self-centeredness and the lack of a sense of community. Not enough people give a shit – that worries me.

What do you feel is the Eagles' legacy?

GF: It's hard for me to say. We've left this collection of records, this body of work. In the end, I think our work mirrored the times and that's what remains. That's what people will probably enjoy. For some people it will be nostalgia, and for other people it's like archaeology, like me listening to records from the '40s. That's not nostalgic for me, because I was never there. We are fortunate enough to be one of the bricks in the building.

DH: I'm delighted that we have a history. We made all those albums and we stayed together that long, which was a long time for a rock 'n' roll group, even amid all the turmoil.

It changed my whole life, didn't it? It's what I always wanted to do. I went to college for four years and studied, but I never had any intention of doing anything except this. It just worked out from certain twists of fate or something. I used to wonder about all that stuff – why me? Why not somebody else? But we did work hard and we were very determined.

Do you ever feel your past as an Eagle is a burden?

GF: I think if you had asked Don and me that question two or three years after the band broke up, we'd have thought about it a lot more than we do now. We're lucky enough to have gone on and done a few other things, so it's just part of us now. I don't see it as a problem. It was a problem maybe when I was 32 and making my first solo record. I've enjoyed the last 10 years as much as I enjoyed the '70s.

What's your sense about the future?

GF: I just decided to be open to the possibilities. I think anything is possible in the '90s. Some things seem possible that wouldn't have seemed possible a few years ago, related to maybe working with some of the guys again. Those possibilities are starting to show up.

DH: Glenn and I were of like mind about several things, and now that we're older and more mature, we can apply what we've learned. If we do have another go-around, I think we can do a lot of positive things – for the environment, for the homeless, for any number of elements of society that need help where the government may have abandoned them. I mean, rock 'n' roll now for me is not necessarily an end in itself. It's a means to some other end, to trying to improve the world and the community. Rock 'n' roll has always been that from the standpoint of rebellion, but I'd like to build upon that and make it a little more adult. Let's face it, there's not going to be anarchy in this country, or even in the

U.K. So let's get with the program and start effecting some real change and get something done, besides just yelling and screaming about it.

From an artistic standpoint, you've been able to say what you want to say in your solo work and still reach a very sizable audience. Why do you want to work with the Eagles again?

DH: It won't change what I write about. It will increase the audience, which is the good part. I would get a lot more ears turned toward what I have to say. I'll probably write exactly what I would have written anyway.

People long for the past, because it's so much safer than the future. The future is so uncertain, but the past is very concrete. We're living in very uncertain times. Even with the end of the cold war, there are other considerations now: the economy, global warming, ozone depletion, widespread pollution of all kinds. And now this war in the Middle East has just flared up. There's a comfort people take in going back – I don't know if it's healthy or not. It's like people want to take the '70s and pole-vault them over the '80s and put them in front of them in the '90s.

There are also a lot of young people who weren't there the first time around.

DH: Yeah, they're at my concerts. It's odd. I could understand it in terms of the Beatles or somebody like that: "I missed the '60s – I want to know what it's all about." But the '70s? I guess I'm too close to it. But, you know, music is not in great shape right now, as far as I'm concerned. Music is not very musical anymore. People don't even have to be musicians anymore. They don't have to be able to sing anymore. They can borrow other materials and just do what they want over it. I just got a tape from some local record company. They used part of one of our songs from the '70s and just rapped over it. I resent that – go make up your own fucking music. They don't even have to make up their own grooves anymore. Man, I think that's bad for art, bad for music.

And as for the Eagles reunion?

DH: I've had 10 good years of a solo career. I'm satisfied and happy I have proven my point. And I'm happy to go back and have a little camaraderie and share some of the decisions. It gets to be a burden sometimes. It gets kind of lonesome. But I'm ready. My skin's a lot thicker now. I mean, even this Mojo Nixon thing doesn't particularly bother me. It must mean I'm famous; I guess I've made it. And I will die, Mojo – just not on your schedule.

This article appeared in Rolling Stone, *September 20, 1990.*

Nile Rodgers on Disco

"That colorful circus, that menagerie of weird players"

As the year 2000 was approaching, *Entertainment Weekly* put together a list of popular music's 100 most significant moments, one of which was the 1979 release of the Sugarhill Gang's "Rapper's Delight," the single that brought hip-hop to the masses. That song's irresistible raps are propelled, of course, by the equally irresistible beat of Chic's "Good Times," a Number One hit that same year.

Since I was assigned to write the entry for "Rapper's Delight," I took the opportunity to arrange a phone interview with Chic's guitarist, Nile Rodgers, who wrote and produced "Good Times" with the band's bassist, Bernard Edwards. In addition to his stylish, groundbreaking work with Chic, Rodgers co-wrote Sister Sledge's "We Are Family" with Edwards, and produced David Bowie's "Let's Dance" and Madonna's "Like a Virgin," among many other landmark recordings of the late '70s and '80s.

I'd seen Rodgers interviewed in a VH1 series about the '70s that I had also worked on, and was struck by the fresh, insightful, and very funny things he had to say.

When I spoke to Rodgers, he did not disappoint. Our 30-minute conversation was a classic example of a dilemma that music journalists often face – if they're lucky. Here I was, with a terrific interview with a smart, articulate, innovative artist, and I was going to be able to use exactly one quote from him in the 200-word piece I was writing about "Rapper's Delight." When I thought about assembling this book, being able to give Rodgers the space he deserved was a primary motivation.

While doing an interview by phone is never ideal, this one proves that, with the right subject, you can still communicate deeply. "I know I'm long-winded and opinionated," Rodgers told me, almost apologetically, when we were done. But more than opinions, he had great ideas, and for that reason, I was happy to stay on the phone as long as he wanted to talk. He was both provocative and entertaining.

I loved Rodgers' idealistic vision of disco – a genre and scene often stupidly dismissed by critics – and his fabulously democratic interpretation of the door policy at Studio 54. I was also moved by the vulnerability of his response to the Disco Sucks movement – in particular, the Disco Demolition night organized by a local radio station at Chicago's Comiskey Park on July 12, 1979. Disco records were gleefully destroyed that night, signaling the death of a utopian dream for Rodgers, as well as the reassertion of some of the darker forces forever lurking in the shadows of American culture.

At what point did you begin to sense that there was a phenomenon known as disco?

I was a nightclub person at the time, and any cultural community has its own labels for things. We didn't look at this big phenomenon that the media called disco as our world. Our world was what we called clubbing – "nightclubbing," like Grace Jones would say. That's what we were doing.

Even though disco music was part of the club scene, there was a real difference to us. Traditionally what we considered disco music was when there was an artist, but someone else produced the music and did these tracks that had a certain kind of style to them – you know, that had the high hat going psst psst psst psst, and a lot of the singers went [*sings falsetto*], "*Doo doo doo/Doot doot doodle doo doo.*"

It was bizarre to us because we didn't know if it was called disco because of the music or because of the environment. But that scene became a great opportunity for someone like me – mainly a band musician – to have a commercial platform, a pop base, and still do good music. It was fantastic. A lot of R&B bands jumped on the disco bandwagon, and certainly Chic did that.

Chic songs became anthems of the scene, anthems of the moment. It's as if that whole culture became a subject for the music.

Absolutely. It was the most hedonistic time that I had ever experienced. Obviously, I wasn't around during the Roaring '20s, but that's what it felt like to me. In most of the songs that we wrote, we were actually taking lyrics and concepts from the Roaring '20s. It was like when

Prohibition was lifted, and the whole country went nuts. That's what the '70s felt like to me.

I'm a product of the '60s; I'm sort of like a hippie kid. The '60s were really introspective, because of the drug scene and the politics. So it almost seemed like in the '70s, everyone said, "Well, forget fighting everyone else's battles. Now I'm just gonna bask in the sense of a job well done." In the '60s, we felt like we put an end to the war. We felt like we abolished racism, or certainly started off on a new road. Women were asking for equality; gay people were saying, "Give us our rights." So during the '70s, we said, "OK, great, we did all of this cool stuff. Now – let's party!"

I used to be in the Black Panthers and a lot of my friends were killed and went to jail. So when the '70s came around, it was almost like...

"Burn, baby, burn/Disco inferno..."

Exactly! [*Laughs*] I gotta tell you, man, when that song came out I used to think to myself, "Are we in a clever music-writing phase or what?" Only a few years before that, if you said, "Burn, baby, burn," the whole world was terrified. Like, three years before, if a black person had come out with a record that went, "Burn, baby, burn," the right-wingers, the Ku Klux Klan and the John Birch Society would say, "Goddamn, we gotta go get dem niggers!" [*Much laughter*] Now, you go "Burn, baby, burn," and you just put the word disco after it, and...

People are out on the dance floor, throwing their hands in the air.

I actually thought the disco scene felt more liberating than the hippie movement. With the hippie movement we always felt different. We even used to call ourselves "freaks." When we walked down the street, straight people would look at us and go, "Hey, look at that guy with the green hair!" You almost wanted that reaction. But the interesting thing about disco is that everybody wanted to be like us. It was weird. But in a way, disco was the beginning of the lowering of the bar.

You mean musically?

Yeah, because disco was the beginning of producers controlling the music. That's why I say the Village People are disco. Earth Wind & Fire is not disco, even though they had records that were played in discos. Kool & the Gang is not disco. Chic is not disco. But Ecstasy, Passion & Pain are disco. Donna Summer is disco. Those are people where someone comes up with a concept and you then look for the person that fulfills it. Producers realized that, "Wait a minute. I can create artists, because I got the formula. I know what works."

Now a lot of people criticize me and say, "But, Nile, you're one of the people that started doing that." And I say, "But that's not necessarily true, because in fact, what we did was we gave the sound to artists." For the most part, I worked with people who made me better. I did Bowie, Madonna, Mick Jagger, Sister Sledge, Diana Ross. For the most part, I don't take a person who can't sing and then make 'em sound good. I mean, I've done a few of those [*laughs*], I have to be honest. Not a lot of 'em. Basically someone writes you a big check, and you go, "No problem. I'll make them a star." We knew we had that power, but we tried to not dole it out so much. [*Laughs*]

Let's talk specifically about "Good Times." That song transcended a variety of genres and is still out there. Talk about how you came up with it.

What happened was, I was hanging out with John Deacon, the bass player from Queen, one night, and we were talking about things that you talk about in discos at five o'clock in the morning. Then somehow I went home. I couldn't sleep because in the hedonistic '70s, all we did was party 24 hours a day. Sleep was really low on the priority scale. So in the middle of the night, I came up with this groove. I thought, "Damn, this is happenin'!"

Were you in a studio or in your apartment?

I was in my apartment. But we were writing a Chic record at the time, so we had the studio booked. The way that we did Chic records is [bassist] Bernard [Edwards] and I would come up with little thumbnails of grooves. Then we'd put them together and work out the arrangements in the studio. No rehearsing or anything. Most of the time when we got to the studio, the other person had not heard the idea yet.

So I came in with this idea, and Bernard was late. I was so excited that I started playing it with Tony Thompson, the drummer. We were grooving, and just with guitar and drums it sounded like a hit! Bernard walks in and he hears Tony and I jamming – I can picture this whole thing in my mind while I'm talking to you – and right away his artistic ears just go, Bang!

So he picked up his bass, and he started playing. We all used to record basically in the same room, and Tony played drums so loud that Bernard couldn't hear me. So I just started screaming to him, "Walk! Walk!" Bernard used to love walking on the bass. He had been wanting to walk in a song ever since we had been together, and this was the right time. So he went, "Yeah!" and [*hums the bassline to "Good Times"*]. He looked at me and said, "Like that?" And I said, "Bingo!" I screamed to the engineer – Bob Clearmountain, "Make it red!" which means put it in record, and we knocked it out in one take.

What about the words?

The thing is, you gotta remember we already had a bunch of hits by the time we did "Good Times," so when we wrote that song we were trying to encapsulate the whole decade, the whole disco thing. We looked back at the Roaring '20s, at the beginning of the talkie films, because so much of Chic was based on that stuff. If you look at the album cover that that track comes from, *Risque*, we built a set that looked like an Agatha Christie murder mystery, where Bernard is playing the master of the house and we have the French maid and I'm the detective. So we were really acting out that whole fantasy.

We took an Al Jolson song called "A Quarter to Nine" that went [*sings*], "The stars are gonna twinkle and shine/This evening, about a quarter to nine." Then we listened to another song, the Prohibition song, "Happy days are here again/The skies above are clear again." So we went, check this out: "Happy days/Are here again/The time is right for making friends/Let's get together/About a quarter to ten…" We were being clever. It wasn't plagiarism now – it's not "a quarter to nine," it's "a quarter to ten."

Of course, then, those lyrics, which were a hybrid of postmodernism, wind up becoming the song that becomes the big hip-hop record, where somebody else takes our music now and says we're going to do that to you! You take Al Jolson and Irving Berlin and retool their stuff, then the Sugarhill Gang takes our thing and retools it to come up with "Rapper's Delight." It was sort of an ironic justice.

How did you feel when "Rapper's Delight" came out? Were you surprised?

There were two reactions. One night, I went to this little club, a predominantly black club called Leviticus that I used to go to all the time. All the DJs and bartenders were my friends, and in those days DJs would rap over records. They would go to the breaks – the break in a record was the most important part. That's how Chic became Chic. Our very first song had a break on it, and no one had heard that before. When we did "Dance, Dance, Dance (Yowsah, Yowsah, Yowsah)," the record breaks down and goes [*sings*], "Dance, dance, dance, dance." It was all about the break.

So when a record would come to the break, the DJs at the clubs would start rapping over it. I was loosely listening to "Good Times," which was playing in the background, and then, when it came to the break, the DJ kicked in "Rapper's Delight." I wasn't really paying attention to it. You gotta remember, we were huge then, so me going in a club and hearing my song was totally normal. I'm talking to the bartender, and he's all excited because he's the one who brought the record. He's asking me how do I like it? I'm thinking it's the DJ rapping over the record, so I'm going, "Man, that guy is unbelievable. He's the best I've ever heard. He's got three different voices," because I couldn't see the DJ booth from the bar.

Then the guy laughed and said, "Yeah, I bought it at a record store in Harlem this morning." I said, "What do you mean you bought it this morning? Bought what?! You bought 'Good Times'?" He said "No, it's a record called 'Rapper's Delight.' " I went over to the DJ booth, and they showed it to me. It had the Sugarhill label. We played it and I said, "Wait a minute – that's my song! As clever as it is, that's copyright infringement!" [*Laughs*] I said, "Bro, if I could do that shit, why don't I just go get an Elvis record and we could go [*hums "Good Times" bassline and sings "Blue Suede Shoes"*]." So we contacted them, and we basically settled out of court.

So there were two reactions. One was, I thought it was the greatest thing I'd ever heard when I thought the guys were there doing it live. And then my second reaction was, "Damn, you can't take my record!"

That says so much about the transition from the '70s into the '80s. How did that moment strike you?

Well, here's the thing that really hurts a person like me, and when I say "hurt," I mean it in a very spiritual way, down to the core. I came from the '60s – really political, peace and love, the world is free for everybody and should be a beautiful, wonderful, rainbow place. That's where I come from.

When the '70s went down, I still had that mentality. So when the '70s ended with that whole Disco Sucks thing, I swear to God it felt to me like Nazi Germany. If you look at that image that they were showing on the news – people at a baseball stadium breaking records – and you go to Germany and you see these bonfires with books, it looked scary to me.

I really believe the DJs that did that were just having a joke. But what happened is that these guys were joking, and the people who spiritually fit the mold of hating showed up.

Exactly. You have to be careful with stuff like that. I don't have to tell you – race can never be discounted as a factor in America.

It felt so racist, because we had had a whole decade of equality on many different levels, especially in music. And what was the backlash against? Was it really against the music? Or was it against the people dominating the music? People used to say to Bernard and me all the time, "You guys are paying the rent here." Our records were bigger than the Rolling Stones, bigger than everybody. So it felt to us like the old boys' network was taking the power back.

Think about this: In my group of friends, every night we just went to the best club. For eight months, the best club would be a transvestite club because they got the best DJs, the best music, the best people, the best everything. It's the place to be. Then it would change to an all-black club: Best music, best crowd, best drugs, best girls. Then it would change to a Latin club. It just kept changing. The club people went wherever the hot club was – it didn't make any difference. Everybody felt the same.

All my friends felt totally comfortable no matter how outrageous the scene was. That's why Studio 54 worked. It took the whole movement and said, "Wow, let's put this in one building." And they used to keep it balanced. They'd say, "If there's too many straight people, it doesn't work. If there's too many gay people, it doesn't work. If there's too many black people, it doesn't work." They just kept it that colorful circus, that menagerie of weird players that were part of that scene.

To people sitting on the fringe, this brought up all their fears: "What's going on? The faggots are normal now? The transvestites are normal now? The niggers are normal now? And I can't even get *in there?* They're cooler than me? Fuck that!" It was like, "Where's Kansas? Where's Foghat? Where's our good old rock 'n' roll?" Those dudes couldn't get into Studio 54.

There was a humongous backlash. After that, once you were associated with disco, it was the end of your life. It was like your head was chopped off. So Chic took the positive and the negative from disco. We took all the heavy record sales, but when the backlash came, the ax fell on our heads, too.

One quote from this interview appeared in Entertainment Weekly, *May 28, 1999.*

Jeff Tweedy Remembers Uncle Tupelo

"We wanted to write the things we belived in"

This talk with Jeff Tweedy of Wilco is another example of how speaking over the telephone doesn't necessarily lessen the intimacy or quality of an interview. As the Sony / Legacy label prepared to reissue all four albums by the pioneering alt-country band Uncle Tupelo – the band in which Tweedy got his start – I was asked to write the liner notes for a single-disc Uncle Tupelo compilation, *89/93: An Anthology*, which would introduce the reissue series.

Tweedy, Jay Farrar, and Mike Heidorn formed Uncle Tupelo in Belleville, Illinois, and the band released its first album, *No Depression*, in 1990. The combination of heartland desperation, punk intensity and hard-core country authenticity on that album and its follow-up, *Still Feel Gone* (1991), struck a chord with fans searching for music that was not mired in '60s classic rock and that was not panderingly commercial, cartoonishly "rebellious," or pointlessly nihilistic. A third album, *March 16–20, 1992*, which was produced by Peter Buck of R.E.M., found the group performing acoustically and serving an aesthetic challenge to its grunge-obsessed contemporaries. That album attempted nothing short of an update of roots country and folk for contemporary listeners. *Anodyne*, which turned out to be the band's final album, was recorded live in the studio with no overdubs for Warner Bros., and the move to a major label helped split the band up.

As the two singers and songwriters in Uncle Tupelo, Tweedy and Farrar were the band's twin poles. They were often compared to John Lennon and Paul McCartney, and their silent falling out proved the fissure that ultimately cracked the band apart. Tweedy formed Wilco; Farrar called his new band Son Volt. In this conversation, which took place right at the start of 2002, Tweedy reminisces about what excited him about Uncle Tupelo when the band first took shape, and how he felt when the final deal went down.

You, Jay Farrar, and Mike Heidorn hooked up around the time you were starting high school. What was your sense about them when you were kids?

It was freshman year. In the preceding couple of years before high school I'd been getting into punk rock. It felt like a very uncommon thing, almost like a secret.

How did you find out about it?

I started buying records when I was really little, and I also started buying *Rolling Stone* and *Creem* when I could find them. So I read about punk, and then found a few of the records that somehow slipped through the cracks and ended up at the Target near our house. Not long after that, a punk-rock record store actually opened up in Belleville, a store that was handling a lot of stuff I'd never seen before. That had a big impact as well.

Who would be the audience for that store? Most stores like that would only open in college towns or cities.

I don't think the store was interested in profit. I think it was a trust-fund kid, a guy who was into punk rock and opened up a tiny store next to a dog-grooming place. It was a block from my house. I hung out there as much as possible and bought records with quarters. It was called the Record Works.

I don't think I noticed Jay until we shared an English class in freshman year. You were supposed to interview and write about the person next to you. I didn't interview Jay – we didn't get each other as partners. But you were supposed to read your essay out loud to the class, and the person who interviewed me said, "Jeff's favorite band is the Ramones." And the person who interviewed Jay said his favorite band was the Sex Pistols, or something like that. After that class, it was pretty much imperative that we talk to each other. I found out that he was in a band with his brothers, just a good garage band doing a lot of Ramones songs. I was basically learning how to play guitar at the time, and we were thrown together by circumstance. We were the only people we knew that liked punk rock.

And then you played together?

After I followed him and his brothers around for a while, playing grade-school dances and basically getting booed by 10-year-olds, I lugged their gear and I eventually weaseled my way into the band. I was playing second or third guitar on songs that probably only ever had one guitar in the original arrangements. But after a while, I think I really wore thin with Jay's brothers and I don't know if I'm the reason for it, but they just stopped playing. They would turn my amp down most of the time when we played. It would be a battle to keep my amp, like, *on*...

Because?

I guess I was just very, uh, *enthusiastic*. [*Laughs*] But not very good.

Was Mike in the band at this point?

Mike wasn't the drummer in that band with Jay's brothers. Mike's sister was dating Jay's brother, so Mike would get thrown with us a lot of times. If we needed somebody to buy us alcohol or drive us somewhere, we'd go with Jay's brother and Mike's sister. Somehow we would end up feeling like we were being forced to hang out with Mike. [*Laughs*] To be honest we were a little ambivalent toward Mike because we thought he was really nervous. He was so hyperactive he made us nervous. But he did have a set of drums. He was playing standing up.

Like Slim Jim Phantom or Dave Clark.

Yeah. I guess we decided that we were going to start a "psychedelic" band. That's what we kept calling it. [*Laughs*] We were drawing on, like, Chocolate Watchband, the Sonics, the Pretty Things, stuff like that. Punk rock had led us to the original punk rock, or what was being called that by Pebbles compilations. We just decided we wanted to be a garage band, but psychedelic music is what we called it.

Your gigs were pretty successful with this group.

Yeah. We would rent this place in Millstadt and basically because there were only one or two cops in the entire town, it was easy to buy a bunch of kegs and have everybody from all the local high schools come and drink. Having the party was more important to most people than seeing us play. But we were there.

You were charging admission, right? And making a fair amount of dough.

We were making a lot of money. We would make enough to divide it up, and almost every time we did, Jay or I would end up with a new Vox teardrop guitar. It was all going toward stupid '60s gear.

What did it feel like the first time you got onstage?

It's hard to remember. Like I said, I was really enthusiastic. I just think of myself as being completely oblivious – just raw energy, really excited by it.

Things reached a point where you got interested in writing your own songs. How did that come about?

Jay's brother was singing with us and, if I'm remembering it right, he was getting ready to go into the Army. So he was bowing out. We had already tried to write some songs in the style that would fit in with our repertoire. And it was daunting. At that point, we got pretty frustrated with being that type of band. A lot of bands were happening then like the Chesterfield Kings and the Unclaimed, garage bands that were doing it all the way, with the outfits and the haircuts. We knew we would never be able to accomplish that [*laughs*] – it looked like a lot of work. So we decided we'd try to write our own songs and, by that point, somehow we had developed a taste for country and folk music. I don't think there was a conscious decision to be any kind of band at that point. It's just that's the kind of songs we started writing. That was the music that was the most exciting to us.

Where had you heard that stuff?

Personally, I had heard it at family gatherings, having uncles and cousins that played guitar. In that part of the country, it's around you a lot. Johnny Cash records – you get issued them at the chamber of commerce or something. That was while I was growing up, and I probably rejected it for a long time, dismissed it as old people's music. But through punk rock and garage bands, through being music fans and broadening our sense of what could communicate raw energy, it came down to the essence of songwriting and conveying emotion. We were also attracted to the darkness of that music. I remember having the revelation at some point that that music was scarier than Henry Rollins could ever be in a million years.

Were you conscious of how distinct this was from what might be on commercial radio or MTV, or from what the kids at school liked?

By that time, having found a small enough group of people that liked punk rock and would make the pilgrimage to St. Louis once a month to buy records, we were pretty defined by hating everything else [*laughs*] – hating the radio, not really caring, not wanting to be that at all, and in a lot of ways, dismissing some great music. Once that identity was formed though, we were more interested in fitting in with Hüsker Dü and Dinosaur Jr.

The first two Uncle Tupelo records established the band, and Belleville became, for the people who responded to you, almost like Springsteen's Asbury Park, a place that was both itself and a kind of metaphor. Did that surprise you? Did you have a sense of what you were drawing on in your work? When people started rendering back a vision of the place you were from, could you recognize it?

For a long time, we were just playing in St. Louis, if that, or practicing in Belleville. We were writing songs and intuitively focused our attention on the only things we knew. We were really earnest young men. We wanted to write things we believed in, that applied to our lives, and as small as Belleville was or as small as we felt our universe was, that was what was available to us. Predominantly, the first two records have all those songs about our area, and a lot of them were written before we had toured very much. Shortly after that, when we started playing outside the region, it did start to become an obvious distortion, just the way people perceived it. It's hard for me to say, because it's such an obvious distortion now.

What do you mean?

Just that I know people picture us growing up in some Brixton squalor. The image that's been presented to me is very different from what it was. I remember coming home one time and a police officer who lived across the street from me had just seen our first national press in *Rolling Stone* and we were talking about how horrible Belleville was. He came over and said, "Jeff, you had a good time growing up. We played ball! You were on the baseball team." And he was right. It wasn't that bad. It's, like, accentuate the negative. At the time, we commented to ourselves that Belleville wasn't so bad – it's just as bad as everywhere else we had been and everywhere else we were going.

At what point did you feel that what you were doing was distinctive and good? When did "Let's try to write some songs" become "This has its own integrity"?

When we first started playing in St. Louis, it was exciting that we didn't see a lot of bands on the landscape that sounded like we did. I don't know if we ever internalized that what we were doing was anything that different in the grand scheme of things. We had an innate sense that what we were doing was right, but we didn't have any grandeur to it.

What would you say the spirit of the band was at that point?

We were doing what we had always wanted to do, from going to see bands pile out of vans into tiny clubs in St. Louis and set up and play for 20 people. There was a romance to that for us, whether we admitted it or not. It was definitely exciting to be at that level. The way I feel right now, Uncle Tupelo very much appreciated every step. Every step was definitely a shock. When we got our first gig in St. Louis, it was a shock. When we did our first tour it was a shock. When we signed a record deal – no matter how bad it was [*laughs*] – it was a shock.

What made you choose Peter Buck to produce the March 16–20, 1992 *album?*

After we finished *Still Feel Gone*, we really wanted to try and play some acoustic music, just do some folk songs. At this point, we were becoming more interested in folk than country. We were finding field recordings at the library – Jay spent time doing that – buying obscure Folkways records, and becoming more and more drawn to boiling things down to the essence. Country music was one step and folk music was another step in that these people just had a microphone shoved in their face and they had no idea of its implications. We were just trying to get to something, some pure elemental music. But our goals were modest. We booked this time with Peter Buck because he had expressed interest in recording the second record, and we'd kind of turned him down. This was our way of saying, "Let's go check it out."

Why didn't you want to work with him the first time around?

I think we were afraid to mess up the formula, because we thought we'd had a smashing success with the first record. [*Laughs*] So we went to Georgia with the idea, "If we get two songs, it'll be a single. If we get six songs, it'll be an EP. And who knows? Maybe we'll get a record." There wasn't much more thought put into it than that. We rehearsed three or four times before we went down and compiled notes on what songs we knew, as far as the covers we were doing, and outlined what new songs we had that would fit in to playing them acoustically.

Around this time Mike was making his exit. How were you feeling about that?

I was sad about it, but at the same time by this point we weren't afraid of Mike anymore. [*Laughs*] We were very close, and Mike was a necessary foil or link between Jay and I. We could communicate through Mike.

How would that work?

Mike would take everything with a lot of humor, so any intensity that would swell up between Jay and I would be diffused with some comment from Mike that brought things back into perspective as to how ridiculous we were being. Or on a one-on-one level explaining something to Mike or talking about something with him. Just looking back I think this is how it worked.

So it wasn't like, "I'll tell Mike and he'll tell Jay..."

Right. The dynamic was there, and that's how it evolved. I didn't perceive Mike's leaving as being a threat, because I wasn't aware of it at the time.

Had something changed? I'm assuming that early on your relationship with Jay was more direct.

I probably started out being very much in awe of Jay – that he could play guitar and sing and do things that I really wanted to do. Then over time I worked really hard to get better because I was putting my stuff next to Jay's. I wouldn't have sung if it wasn't for Jay because he encouraged me to sing. I guess you could call it encouragement – just refusing to sing my songs. [*Laughs*] Regardless, it ended up being encouragement. Definitely at some point I didn't think of it any different than we were equals. We were both writing songs and contributing to this band that we'd grown up with. I know that I definitely got more confident over time. And that probably just changed the dynamic enough for it to be different.

What did Buck do as a producer? How do you feel the album came out?

That's the record I'm most happy with. I think Peter basically encouraged us to stick to our vision of what we had set out to do. He didn't try to interfere much, and he has a really good ear for when things are done. He maybe stopped us sooner than we would've stopped on some things, and coaxed us to go a little further on others. But in general it was pretty transparent. He sat and read the newspaper and did the things that stereotypical non-engineering producers do. [*Laughs*] But he created an environment, which is what I think the best producers do, an environment for us to play how we wanted to play and have it sound really good when we came in and listened to it.

As things moved along from there, major labels started to get interested and eventually you made a deal with Warner Bros. Did you feel good about that?

After making the two loud records that were reflective of how we played live and had all this bombast to them – when we finished *March* and it came out, it felt very much like the boldest thing we'd ever done. That's probably the only time I felt that what we were doing was really against the grain of what was happening.

That was our big concern. The big question to the labels we were talking to at the time was, "Would you have allowed us to make this record?" Somehow, somebody convinced us they would have. [*Laughs*] And to give them their due, they did allow *Anodyne* to happen. That was the appeal at the time – to make non-major-label-sounding records and see how much we could get away with. We did *Anodyne* without any overdubs – just went and did this weird live country record.

In a lot of ways, Anodyne *sounds like an unspoken conversation between you and Jay, with Jay expressing his dissatisfaction in songs like "Slate" and "Chicamauga." Were you struck by what he had to say on that record?*

That didn't really come to me. I was oblivious, really having a great time. I felt I was getting better at writing songs, and I felt the band was getting better and that we were being truer to what we wanted to do, truer to the kind of music that we professed to like. It felt like it was growing. So I was kind of oblivious to it.

In a lot of ways, I looked at Jay's lyrics as being a continuation of some of the heavy dark things he had written about in the past. I never perceived them as being directed at me. If I ever went back and listened to that record as a conversation, I would think it was one person seriously trying to tell another one that their relationship's over, while that person is very much preoccupied with playing a video game. [*Laughs*]

During that time, there was a show in London that you had talked about doing acoustically and ended up doing electrically. It turned out to be a disappointment. What is your memory of that?

I definitely had frustrations because sometimes I felt like Jay was uncomfortable with our successes.

Why?

I don't really know. Maybe it wasn't something he believed in. Maybe it was just him needing to feel invigorated. I'm sure he had his reasons. I've done a lot of analysis over the years, but it really just ended up being just the way it was. I was frustrated with the situation where we were playing music from our current record and had gone to the trouble of bringing acoustic guitars, and then we ended up playing a show that was really heavy on what we used to do. We weren't moving forward anymore. Maybe we were just moving at different speeds.

Was there tension because Warner Bros. wanted to release one of your songs, "The Long Cut," as the first single from Anodyne*?*

Honestly, I very much wanted to believe that everything we had ever professed to be about – or maybe I felt like we were about – would take care of those situations without talking about it. If anything, it created anxiety in me that Warner Bros. would single me out over Jay, because that just added to the tension. I would have been happy – and I sincerely believe this – to be a part of that band forever, on a 50-percent basis. You only had to come up with six songs a year. It was ideal for somebody who is prone to laziness. [*Laughs*] We could hide in each other's successes and failures - it wasn't entirely on either one's shoulders. I was very comfortable with that. Little things that would shake that up – like having a single picked over one of Jay's songs – were disturbing to me, probably more than they were to Jay.

Did you think it was going to get to the point that Jay would leave?

It did feel like it was final, and I was pretty devastated by it for a while. And when I say "a while," it was probably a shockingly short time, because like I said, I was having such a good time. At this point [drummer] Ken [Coomer] was in the band, and [bassist] John [Stirratt]. I was playing with new people – I'd never played with anyone other than Jay and Mike in my entire life. From my perspective, too many great things were happening to let anything get in its way. I don't know why, but at some point I naïvely accepted it. It was a challenge to see – since I wrote songs – to see if I could write 12.

A mythology has grown up about what Uncle Tupelo was, what it meant, how it affected people, its significance. Having lived it, how do you feel in relationship to that?

I'm the most uncomfortable talking about that because I don't feel like I completely understand it. As much as I believe that what we did was honest and sincere, I have a lot of trouble imagining what people hear in it now – other than its just being something of interest to me because it's like looking through a photo album and reflecting. I don't know what it is about the music that would appeal to people over time. But I'm also so appreciative of it. I'm amazed that I got to be in a band that would generate the kind of cult following that a lot of the bands that I've loved in my life have had. And maybe that's part of what inhibits my accepting it.

I recently interviewed Paul McCartney and he was talking about how weird he felt after John Lennon died, how John got elevated to this stature where people would say, "John was the Mozart, Paul was the Salieri." People have made comparisons like that about Uncle Tupelo as well – "Jay is the dark, serious one, and Jeff is the pop guy." How have you handled that over the years?

I've come to terms with it. Enough time has gone by where I don't feel like I'm in competition with Jay. We've both established ourselves as what we are, and probably what we were to the band. Jay has an unwavering idea about music and he's very comfortable refining that and moving around within that framework. I've always needed to have some kind of musical catalyst to get things to come out of me emotionally, like trying to do things I wasn't sure I was able to do. In the context of Uncle Tupelo, I wasn't sure that I could even play guitar, so my sense of satisfaction definitely comes from exploring, and Jay's comes from embracing what he's good at.

Do you listen to his stuff?

I don't really listen to it a whole lot. I haven't sat down and scrutinized any of his records. They all sound like Jay to me, which is an accomplishment. Over time it hasn't changed that much and there's a set of values that I have that doesn't really apply to Jay. I can't really evaluate his records the same way I scrutinize my own.

I certainly appreciate that more over time than I maybe did initially after Uncle Tupelo broke up. I understand the impulse of people drawing lines and trying to qualify who was responsible for what, and at some point when a band breaks up I think there's a scurrying around to claim some of that responsibility: "I was the one responsible for this…" But it's all so internal. People want to be recognized, that's just the way people are. Nobody likes being dismissed. It's probably been a good thing for me to be dismissed because it's ended up being a catalyst for me. People have diminished my role in Uncle Tupelo, and I've been able to accept that as a challenge.

If you could pick a couple of tunes from Uncle Tupelo that mean the most to you, which would you choose?

Unfortunately, one of them's not on this record, but "Sandusky" is probably the track I'm most proud of. It's an instrumental, it was a real collaboration and it just kind of came out of us in the studio, real improvised natural music, very simple. I think it's beautiful. I also don't feel I was that much a part of it, because it just happened, and maybe that makes it easier to listen to it. That's the one that sticks out in my mind the most. I also think of the *March* record.

I'm sorry. It's really hard for me to pick tracks out. The last two records, mostly. I would say the takes on *Anodyne* – a lot of them still kind of make me smile. "New Madrid," I've never heard it that way since.

Anything we haven't touched on that you would like to talk about?

Oh, I don't know. It's something I haven't thought about very much in a long time.

There does seem to be a lot of enthusiasm for the compilation.

I'm actually excited about it. It's like getting to make a record without doing anything. [*Laughs*] And I'm curious if it'll find new people. So we'll see.

Parts of this interview, which took place on January 3, 2002, appeared in the liner notes to the Uncle Tupelo collection 89/93: An Anthology, *which came out on March 19, 2002.*

Pete Townshend on a Year in the Life

"All those things are about turmoil really"

In 1993, Pete Townshend brought *The Who's Tommy* to Broadway and found a third new career for himself – after rock star and book editor – as a musical playwright. But the production's five Tony Awards – including one for Townshend for Best Original Score – are only the beginning of the story. The overwhelming success of *Tommy* has encouraged Townshend to plan other adaptations of his recorded work and to make the theater his primary artistic outlet.

Bold new directions don't present themselves so easily when you're 48, but Townshend has never been comfortable within the framework of the narrowest definitions of rock 'n' roll. The solo album he released in 1993, *Psychoderelict*, was characteristically ambitious in both its conception and its stage presentation. The saga of an aging rocker battling failure, substance abuse and his own persistent hopes for creative rebirth, *Psychoderelict* has sold fewer copies than any other album in Townshend's career. But onstage, where Townshend performed the album's songs as theater pieces featuring actors as well as a crack band, *Psychoderelict* came to full dramatic life. In those shows, Townshend also played Who songs and material from his earlier solo albums to tumultuous response.

So Pete Townshend is, undeniably, one of the big stories of 1993. But he has never been interesting exclusively for his own work. Ever since the Who emerged in 1965, he has consistently delivered some of the sharpest, most articulate commentary on the vagaries of the musical and cultural scene. Who better to offer perspective on the past year than this man – who is as honest as he is outspoken, as insightful as he is passionate?

What music caught your attention this year?

There are a couple of bands I liked. I thought Onyx was really good. I liked the Spin Doctors album, even though it's fairly middle-of-the-road. I didn't like the U2 album *Zooropa*, which surprised me because it got such spectacular reviews – I couldn't work out what the fuss was about. Rickie Lee Jones sent me her new CD, and that's a masterpiece – she's operating at genius level. Rykodisc released a Richard Thompson collection that is wonderful. I played Lenny Kravitz's record a lot – it's great. Nils Lofgren's record, which was released early this year, is a fucking shit-kicking guitar record, really wonderful. He's got a great, great sound.

What did you like about Onyx?

They're dealing with the gang issue, so in a way they're not so much a band as a manifestation of something that's actually going on, on the street. The fact that they're doing it so openly allows you, as an outsider, to understand why kids in gangs are angry, why they're frustrated. I felt more clued in after listening to that record – which I don't get very much from the guitar bands, because I don't feel they're saying anything new.

You seem more open to rap than many of your contemporaries. What do you think bothers them about it?

A number of different things. Rap introduced a new rhythm, a steep jazzy shuffle, a real extreme swing, which I don't think people who have been brought up with backbeat rock 'n' roll can get with. It's an offensive rhythm, it's too fast. Strangely enough, if you skipped a generation and stuck it on the back of big-band dance music, you'd have a much closer relationship. It's more that kind of rhythm.

The other thing is the repetitive nature of sampling, scratching, those kinds of things. They're meant to be irritating – like the electric guitar was meant to be irritating. The electric guitar as I developed it with Jim Marshall was a weapon. I'd go in and say, "Jim, I've got these American amplifiers, I love the sound, but they're not fucking loud enough. What can you do?" And he had this technician, this little guy with glasses, who'd come in and [*peering, nodding sagely*] say, "How much louder?" I'd say, "I want it 50 times louder. This guitar is a fucking machine gun. I want it to be so loud that nobody can hear themselves think."

What's happening with rap is that we're seeing another moment of discontinuum – if that's a word – a radical change. I can understand why some people are confounded or intimidated by it, because that's what it's meant to do. It's meant to be in your face, like the Who were. If I was young now, I would probably listen to as much rap as I would guitar music.

What was your problem with Zooropa*?*

I've not really jacked into U2 since they became big and famous. I listened to *The Joshua Tree* once, and I thought it was an impressive record, but I didn't want to go back to it. It seems to me that what they're about now is impressing. Around the time of *Joshua Tree*, I thought, "This is a band who are going for the Biggest Band in Rock 'n' Roll mantle – and let them have it." I've been there, it's a crock of shit – and I feel it might be undermining their potential artistry. I don't want to shoot them down just because they're up there. Quite the contrary. I am friendly with them all, so I suppose I want to like their music. But I find myself not sufficiently engaged by them as a band.

It's difficult as an artist to criticize any other artist; what you're supposed to do is rave or keep your mouth shut. I remember being torn to pieces by Lou Reed fans because I didn't like *New York* enough.

Speaking of Lou Reed, the Velvet Underground reunited this year. Did they mean anything to you the first time around?

You know, it's interesting. When I look at interviews with young musicians, they often do a fly-past of their big influences. And it seems as though David Bowie, the Velvet Underground, and Jimi Hendrix have been a kind of engine for every young musician since the dawn of time. I was obviously deeply affected as an established musician by Hendrix, but I never got with the David Bowie/Velvet Underground thing. It's never touched me.

You have to remember that we were happening coincidentally with the Velvet Underground. Our first trips to New York were when Andy Warhol and the whole Max's Kansas City thing were happening. I remember drinking with John Cale a dozen times. So I felt close to what they were doing, but what seemed far more significant would be the success of, say, the Doors, which just seemed to be meteoric and sudden and absurdly huge. Jim Morrison's Christ picture was all over fucking New York.

I remember seeing the Who open for the Doors at the Singer Bowl in New York, in 1968.

That's right. And he was already fucked up.

It did seem like the beginning of the end.

I remember giving him a lecture.

What did you tell him?

I said, "How do you feel?" and he said, "I feel fucking terrible, I'm really hung over." He was holding a beer. I said, "Maybe you shouldn't be drinking. You're just going to make yourself feel worse." And he said, "It's the only way I can get through this shit." I said, "Well, you can always just stop. You don't have to destroy yourself. It's like any other job, you can stop when you want to fucking stop." I wish I'd taken my own advice [*laughs*], because it took me a long, long time to stop with the Who. But he just seemed to be heading for a train wreck. There's an element of that with Eddie Vedder as well – you know, being an unwilling star. But I think Eddie's better supported; there's great people around him.

There was a lot of talk this year about the new generation gap. Do you buy it?

I do think there is a Gen-X thing going on, but what appears to be a rebellion is actually a kind of psychosis. [*Laughs*] I read an article in *Mondo 2000* about the problem of marketing to people under 25 these days. It was so funny. They said it's very unpredictable. What seems to happen is that a kid reads an advert – say, buy the new Pearl Jam record – then reads somebody else's advert that says buy the new Janet Jackson record, then reads another advert for, say, the Spin Doctors. He decides he wants to buy the Spin Doctors and then goes and buys Janet Jackson.

They said that kids switch at the last minute so that they don't get tricked into buying something that they want, because they think they want it only because somebody else wants them to want it.

That's truly brilliant.

Also, there's a certain ridiculousness about our own generation, which they can perceive. We said certain things were going to happen, and they didn't happen. We devoted our whole lives to changing certain things that we manifestly failed to change – you know, failed on such a grand scale that you almost wonder whether anybody was really trying. I was thinking the other day that Abbie [Hoffman] at Woodstock really was correctly despairing. He was fucking right. All those people at Woodstock saying, "A new dawn has come," and [Detroit activist] John Sinclair was in jail for a joint because the FBI didn't think that he was the right kind of political animal. And the FBI's lawyer and I would be sitting on the Concorde together.

What about concerts you've seen this year? You saw Clapton early in the year, didn't you?

That was a really important concert for me. In February, he did the Royal Albert Hall thing he does every year. This year, he just played blues. It was like a history of the blues through the eyes of Eric Clapton. It was a blinding concert. Toward the end, the show got hotter and hotter, and out came the electric guitar. And Eric played a fantastic blues solo on "Bottle of Red Wine." You sometimes forget – because Eric is such a tasteful player – how fucking fast he can play, without any double-stopping or string pulling or any fancy techniques. Really exemplary virtuoso guitar playing.

And you saw Madonna last night.

It was one of the most exciting events I've been to. It reminded me of *The Wall*, that spectacular, momentous buildup. The music was great, the dancing was great. It's like a Broadway show, a real revue.

You made your move to Broadway this year with Tommy. *Were you nervous about that?*

Yeah. I was very worried that if Broadway failed, it would halt *Tommy* as a property for probably another 10, 15 years. And that would have been a shame, because my instincts told me this is the right time. One of the things that was very disturbing is that I knew that if it was successful, it would change my life. I was excited that if the show did well, it could feed my future creative life, but I was also frightened that maybe I should be retiring, you know? Maybe I should just be taking the money I already have and slowing down, getting out of show business. I was worried that I would get drawn into a kind of ecstasy from the success of the show. It wasn't that I didn't want the show to be a success, but I would argue with [director] Des [McAnuff]. He'd say, "Don't worry, it's going to be really successful." And I'd say, "But Des, that's what I'm worried about." As ever, my instincts were right. The thing I had to worry about is not that the show was going to flop but that it would be too much of a success. It could destroy me.

How has it affected you?

I'm OK with it, but it's made New York a completely different place for me. When I come to New York now, I have a family. I can go to my little yellow theater, and there are people there that love me. I have investors lining up to invest in any crazy idea I come up with. So I'm pulled to New York – and pulled out of a rather unsatisfactory life at home, where for 25 years I've been married to somebody who doesn't like show business very much. It's quite a good thing that my wife doesn't like show business, but it does make it difficult. I've got a young son, and I don't like to be away from him, but I feel dragged into the excitement and vigor of New York.

Do you feel you're perceived in a different way there now?

I don't think the Who were perceived to be hugely successful until the very end, when strangely enough, they were in decline. But if you have a hit show, it shows up in Variety, and people can see what's happening. You know, the Tony is the first artistic award I've ever had. I've only ever had performance-related awards before, you know, special services to the music industry, that type of thing. I've never won a

Grammy or anything for my creative work. At this time in my life, it's like getting a knighthood.

When I left the Who, I went directly into my publishing job at Faber and Faber, because I was really worried about my hearing. I was worried that if my hearing continued to deteriorate at the rate it had in the previous five years – which it hasn't, it's stopped deteriorating –I would be deaf by now. I had two specialists tell me that I would be deaf by the time I was 40. And I mean completely deaf, beyond help with a hearing aid or anything. In fact, nothing like that has happened. The tinnitus that I got in those years has also stopped. It's still there, but I'm not bothered by it. Anyway, I went to work at Faber, and I began dealing with words and ideas, but I missed music.

What's great about theater is that it brings music and writing together. And the fact that the show has been honored by the public, by the establishment, and by quite a few critics – although I know you didn't honor it – it's made me feel like the two or three things that I can do have come together in a good way for me. I do see myself as a dramatist now, as pretentious as it sounds. I think that anything I do as a songwriter or a composer is going to be linked in some way to live storytelling.

Since you mentioned my review of Tommy, *surely you know that I had no problem with the original music – I loved the album, and I saw the Who perform it a number of times. I just felt the ending – with its emphasis on family and "normality" – compromised the much more mysterious, more unstable ending of the album.*

I absolutely accept that. When we decided to go the way we did, we knew there would be difficulties. Interestingly, as a result of your piece and a couple of others, I went to Des and said, "What we've really got to do is fix this word normality." I used it rather clumsily, and to be pedantic about it, what I actually meant was that he was healthy. There's a couple of places where I used it as a kind of lazy rhyme against reality.

What about the "family values" aspect of the ending?

I'm in a failing family, so you might regard some of the things I'm saying as hypocritical. I don't see myself as a good father or even a decent man. When I talk about the importance of family, I'm just saying, "I wish I could do that." I remember when I was a kid, my father was a musician, and my mother was a singer, and they had a crazy life. Two fiery people who split up when I was very young, and I was dumped with my grandmother for two years. I was very lonely, never heard from my father at all. My mother used to come down on the weekend for an hour to see me, dressed incredibly seductively. She was beautiful, and I just longed to be with her. I just wanted to be with my fabulous, exciting, brilliant, beautiful parents. Instead, I was with this bitter, crotchety, clinically insane grandmother.

My father eventually got back together with my mother – a rather faithless woman who was having affairs behind his back – for my sake. She'd found a lover who was going to take her to an oil country, and my father didn't want me to go, so he took her back. My mother's side of the story is that she took him back, you know, for my sake. We've had both sides of it.

Both agree, of course, that whatever they did, it was for your sake.

What actually happened was that they got back together and had another couple of kids, and my life was fairly normal from then on. It really was normal. I had come from hell. I was with my grandmother, who used to make me sit like this [*sits absolutely still*]. If I moved my foot, she'd say, "Stop fidgeting." It was a fucking nightmare. My father used to send me five shillings a week, a fabulous amount of money in those days. And I would go to the shop with my grandmother and buy myself a toy, and she would take the toy and put it in a cupboard. Then when my mother came to see me, my grandmother would make me get all the toys out as though I'd been playing with them. Then when my mother had gone, I'd have to put them all away again. She was a complete head case.

When I got older, the first guitar I smashed was because of her. My father was going to buy me a guitar for my 11-year-old Christmas, and he would have bought me a fabulous instrument. But what fucking happened is that she bought it! She bought me a guitar like you see on the wall of a Spanish restaurant, a phony guitar. I was excited for a while, standing in front of the mirror, but I realized very quickly that I was never going to be able to play anything on it. My father said, "Well, let's see what happens." So I struggled with this fucking instrument for two years, and finally my father let me buy a decent guitar for three quid. I also got myself a little amplifier and went electric. One day my grandmother ran into the room and said, "Turn that fucking row down!" I did a Keith Moon, long before I'd ever met Keith Moon. "You think that's a fucking row? Listen to this!" And I got my guitar and smashed it over the amplifier. John Entwistle was in the room with me.

I realized what I'd done was – well, for one, I'd smashed a "perfectly good guitar," as John Hiatt says –symbolically smashed the guitar my grandmother had given me and exorcised the whole thing. From that moment on, I found I could actually forgive her.

You also released Psychoderelict *and toured this year.*

Going on the road with my album, deciding that it would be my last album – I don't know if it will be or not – and deciding that I would do some shows was partly to see whether I could still do it. But I also felt I had to prove to myself that having a show on Broadway didn't mean that I wasn't still a rock star. All those things are about turmoil really. The beginning of the year, I was very happy. I was meeting wonderful new people, making regular trips to New York. But toward May, June, I started to get uneasy, and I'm still in that place. I'm still not sure how I'm going to do the things I want to do without traveling an enormous amount – which is again something my wife and I find difficult. So there's a kind of feeling of dread that runs through me – my oldest daughter, my younger daughter, and all my friends, including my wife – that we're heading for difficult times, because of the career I want, which is a show-business career. And show business is destructive. It's both disturbing and incredibly exciting.

There is this feeling about people my age in the vanguard of the aging rockers, you know, the people who sneered at the old and celebrated the blindness and stolidity of the young James Dean ideal, that I'm doing something a bit different. I'm not bashing the door down to get back into stadiums. I'm not trying to come up with another hit to knock Madonna or Paula Abdul off the charts.

I'm interested in where I stand in the group that includes people like Mick Jagger and Keith Richards, Paul McCartney, possibly David Bowie – people of our age who are at the point where they actually have to face the fact: Are we going to change or not? Do rock stars of our generation deny themselves the right to go and make millions of dollars in Las Vegas? Are we allowed to do that? I think at the moment, we're not.

Right.

If Roger Daltrey went to Las Vegas, there'd be problems. But it's difficult, because the fact of the matter is that Roger could put together a revue based on the Who's music, get into Las Vegas, and make a million dollars a week. I found a way to continue my career without going to Las Vegas. I'm just using Las Vegas as a metaphor – I mean, a Who reunion tour would be the same thing.

Well, what do you think about what some of your contemporaries have done? I mean, what's your sense about the Stones? Did you hear Jagger's record this year?

I loved it. It seemed to be a very dignified record. It started to look like he was going to have a hit, but then he went into the studio to write more Stones tunes. They're my favorite band, so whatever they do, I'm a fan. I occasionally take the mickey out of Mick, but nobody takes the mickey out of Keith Richards and gets away with it. And I love Charlie – he's one of the great, great drummers. Eric Clapton said to me: "You know, it's so great that the Stones went out on the road with *Steel Wheels*, because Charlie has never been better. He's playing the shit out of the band."

What's next for you?

Well, I'm going back to London to mount *Iron Man.* That starts rehearsal today. Try and work out what I'm going to do about my life, you know, as a family man. Looking forward to mounting *Tommy* in the U.K. – with great trepidation. We've just kicked off the *Tommy* tour in the U.S. I've got another very good idea, I think, about how to rescue *Quadrophenia* – if it had female voices, I think it would have *West Side Story*–type potential. I might try and develop *Psychoderelict* as a piece for the theater, make it longer. I cut it really aggressively for the record. So I've got a few things happening, but all works in progress.

Next year is also the Who's so-called 30th anniversary. How can you have a 30th anniversary of a broken marriage? I just don't buy it. But I love those guys, and I'm not going to be hard-hearted about it. I won't tour. But mind you, I said that in '89, and they said, "But, Pete, you'll make $70 million." I said, "I'll tour." So I don't want to be too obdurate. We'll see what happens.

This article appeared in Rolling Stone, *December 23, 1993*

Michael Stipe on Not Looking Back

"I've always referred to the Beatles as elevator music"

Michael Stipe, 34, sits at a huge conference table in a meeting room at the Four Seasons Hotel, an expansive New York City vista visible outside the window. Wearing clunky black glasses that simultaneously make him appear comical and serious, Stipe looks like French playwright Jean Genet reincarnated as the chairman of a multinational corporation. It's suitable somehow.

Surrounding Stipe is an array of bottles of water, tumblers, cups and pots of coffee, and a healthy sampling of semi-homeopathic elixirs. R.E.M. threw a party the previous night after the MTV Music Video Awards ceremony, which the group attended. Though in casual conversation, none of the band's members could recall exactly which four awards R.E.M. had won, the foursome were nonetheless happy to celebrate. The bash lasted well into the morning, and Stipe – not to mention your intrepid reporter – is hung over.

Still, there's no denying that the singer has rebounded strongly. It's early afternoon, but Stipe, up and working since midmorning, has been doing interviews to promote the new R.E.M. album, *Monster*. Now he's ready to switch gears for an hour to discuss the changing face of the rock 'n' roll scene.

R.E.M. are pivotal figures in the music's history, a crucial link between the underground pioneers of the '60s and '70s and the current crop of innovators rechanneling the mainstream. "We're the acceptable edge of the unacceptable stuff," R.E.M. guitarist Peter Buck once said about the band, but these days the definition of what's acceptable is rapidly broadening – and R.E.M. are an important reason why.

Michael Stipe reflects on those matters and, hangover remedies near at hand, speaks of what's past, passing, and to come.

Do you have any particular generational identification?

No. I did not feel at all like a yuppie, although I realize that R.E.M. was kind of the soundtrack to that. We were on the edge of the yuppies, maybe, the ones who wanted to be hip or whatever, but who at the same time were doing the total '80s thing. I really never grasped that concept. I felt a real division.

Was there a point at which you became consciously aware of the difference between you and elements of your audience?

At one point, I just became acutely aware that people my age or a few years older did not have the same values or priorities that I have – at all. Not to say that mine were that well defined, but theirs seemed *very* well defined – but not by them, by someone else. They were just kind of going with it. Of course, they looked at me as if I were a scarecrow – unless I was onstage, in which case I was entertaining. But on the street it was like, "Get out of my fucking face. Get off our sidewalk."

Do you feel like there's a generational schism now?

I think there definitely is. Kurt Cobain's death really drew a line between those who got it and those who didn't. Just culturally speaking, removing ourselves from all the personal stuff, an event like that really fucking drew the line.

But even young people aren't unified in what they think of Cobain's death.

There is a lot of contempt. Go on the Internet and there are as many jokes about Kurt's death as there are people affected by it.

Last night, this guy sitting behind me screamed out during the Cobain memorial, "He was a junkie."

"And you're an asshole." But mythologizing Kurt is really something that he would abhor. It's something I abhor. But everything that we're talking about really happened. As a person, as an artist, it's not fair to… You have to put him up pretty high to say that his death had that effect. But it really did.

Would you be willing or interested to offer a definition of alternative?

Neither willing nor interested. [*Laughs*] I mean, with songs being co-opted by AT&T and Pizza Hut within three weeks of hitting radio, the turnaround is so quick that there probably really is no alternative. What is alternative is probably something that's very slippery and not really covered in the media. I'm not sure we're even aware of it.

Isn't it possible that "alternative" is less a style of music than a way of going about things?

Yeah, I'd go for that. It's more an attitude. The term has been so co-opted by the music and entertainment industry that it doesn't mean anything anymore. It's just another way of labeling a group of musicians, filmmakers, or what have you. Now, we have alternative models. What the fuck? It means nothing.

There's an older generation of artists that you've talked about a lot – the Velvet Underground, Patti Smith, Iggy Pop. What qualities of theirs inspired you?

Passion. They had their thing, and for whatever reason, they were secure enough in it that they just went forward, damn the consequences. By not listening to whatever the word of the day was, or the sound of the day, these people forged their own paths and became, for that reason, incredible influences. Maybe in the case of the Velvets, 10 years later or 15 years later, not even in their own time.

Speaking of following your own path, R.E.M. has never really conformed to expectations, whether mainstream or underground. For example, while many people associate progressive music with noise and abrasiveness, R.E.M. has never been afraid of beauty and subtlety.

I had a conversation with Tori Amos where she was talking about vulnerability in music. There are artists who leave themselves vulnerable, and that might mean not being afraid of something that's beautiful. The Velvet Underground – some of those unbelievably delicate nursery-rhyme songs, with little tiny voices and a viola playing, or a simple piano figure in amongst all the white noise stuff; there's something about not being afraid of being vulnerable that really sets those people apart.

Beauty can be very challenging, as well. It can really be challenging. It's so much easier to write about angst and anger and fear and darkness and fucked-up feelings than to write about incredible, intense happiness. Happiness just sounds dorky. We've all experienced it, but it's much harder in a pop song to pull that off. It's much easier to pull off the darker stuff.

Along similar lines it seems that as a singer you've been attracted to ballads, another not very fashionable taste.

I like power ballads. "Love Hurts" by Nazareth – that was deeply influential. "Sweet Emotion."

I also remember your performing "Moon River" in concert, and even Lou Gramm's "Midnight Blue," I think while it was still on the charts.

That's a great song.

What attracts you to stuff like that?

Honestly? A clever chord progression. I can hear the melody of a song I don't know in an elevator and I'll hum it all day. That's what the attraction is. It usually has very little to do with the words.

What impressed me, though, was that anybody would expect R.E.M. to treat a song like that ironically, but your version seemed...

Really genuine. Yeah. It wasn't ironic, and it wasn't comic. [*Pause*] Do you know why I love "Moon River" so much? Did I ever tell you this? You know the line, "my huckleberry friend"? I always thought it was Huckleberry Hound, which was one of my favorite cartoons when I was a kid. [*Laughs*]

Perfect. I always thought it was because of some profound Southern connection. Moving right along, have you ever thought that rock 'n' roll was dead?

I believed it when I read it a few times, and I thought, "Uh-oh, better find a new job." But it was bullshit. Here comes some great new band, and it's just as alive for me as it ever has been. It doesn't have to be *Never Mind the Bollocks*, it can be one song on the radio. It could be a video.

Did any of the '60s icons like the Beatles or the Rolling Stones mean anything to you when you were growing up?

[*Shakes his head no*] I've always referred to the Beatles as elevator music, because that's exactly what they were. "Michelle" in German is the one Beatles song that meant something to me, because I was in Germany when I was seven years old and heard it on the radio and thought it was really pretty. I mean, I didn't know they were the Beatles. I've never sat down and listened to a Beatles record from beginning to end. Those guys just didn't mean a fucking thing to me.

It was exciting last night to see the Rolling Stones, because I know that I will never go see them in concert; I have no desire to watch them perform a two-hour show. But to see the truncated, commercial version of it last night was exciting: I watched Mick Jagger perform – that was kind of cool. But they don't mean a fucking thing to me either. The Monkees and the Banana Splits meant a lot more to me – and whoever did "Yummy, Yummy, Yummy." I mean, that was the stuff I really knew and loved. "Honey," all the Glen Campbell stuff.

Was there any particular transformative moment in your life, as far as music is concerned?

I remember as a teenager knowing that the 1970s were the dullest, most ridiculous time, that culturally it was just like…it was *bankrupt*. There was nothing there, nothing at all. I think that's what punk rock came out of, and why to me at the age of 15 when I discovered it, it was like, "Holy fucking god, this is *unbelievable*. Nobody knows about this, and here it is."

You were in St. Louis?

I was in St. Louis, yeah. Somebody left a *Creem* magazine under his chair in study hall, and I picked it up and started reading it. I'd never really paid much attention to music magazines or music. I liked "Benny and the Jets," and "Rock On" by David Essex, and "Crocodile Rock," and…what else? There *was* nothing else. I picked up this issue of

Creem, and there was this article by Lisa Robinson about the New York scene. It had a photograph of Patti Smith – she looked like a vampire – and talked about Tom Verlaine and the Ramones. Lisa was comparing punk rock to an old static-y black-and-white television set, and popular music as being lurid color, well-formed, glossy. The little static-y black-and-white TV was absolutely…it was my heart and soul, and I knew it. It was like, "Wow…fuck. Fucking wow! This is amazing." At that point, I started getting *Rock Scene* magazine and *Creem*. Then later, *New York Rocker*, *Trouser Press*, and *The Village Voice*. That was when I went, "Something's going on here." It made me want to get on a bus and go to New York.

What did you do instead?

I stayed where I was. But I went to this fucked-up hardware store, and they had this discount music section with all these eight-tracks that were marked down that nobody wanted. It was covered with a plastic tarp because the roof leaked, so you had to go under the plastic to get to the stuff. I bought both New York Dolls' albums for 99 cents on eight-track and the Velvets' *Live '69*. I bought *Radio Ethiopia* on eight-track.

That's just incredible.

That was where it was at. When I read about those New York bands, they talked about the Stooges and the Velvets. And they talked about the Doors – Patti Smith went on and on about Jim Morrison, although I never really had much interest in him for some reason. I think the Lizard King thing was just kind of like, "What?" [*Laughs*] I didn't really get that. But I read Arthur Rimbaud's entire collected works before I knew his name was not pronounced Rim-bawd, because Patti Smith said he was a huge influence on her. I was 16 years old. It was pretty wild shit. But that's not to say I stopped wearing bell-bottoms, because I didn't. That took another three years. [*Laughs*]

One last thing: You once wrote a line in "Little America": "I can't see myself at 30." Is there a point at which…

It's funny, but I can't remember if it was "can't" or "can." I need to listen to the song and try to figure it out.

I think it was "can't."

I know what I meant by the song, "I don't buy a lacquered 30." Yeah, and here I am at 34. I don't feel very lacquered. I don't feel like a bug stuck in amber, which is cool. I don't feel 34. I mean, my friends range from 15-year-olds to 55-year-olds. It's weird. It's all attitude, isn't it? Kinship and attitude. I don't really feel like I'm any particular age at all.

I'm going to be 40 in six years. It used to be, like, "Oh my god, 40." But 40 doesn't seem that weird to me. It seems weird, maybe, to think of being 40 and doing what I'm doing now. But I'm sure I'll be doing some version of it – I hope, gracefully – as a 40-year-old.

A shorter version of this interview appeared in Rolling Stone, *November 17, 1994*

Styles of Masculine Will

Styles of Masculine Will

The three interviews in this section, which were all done within a two-year period for *Rolling Stone*, represent a certain personal high point for me. Having the opportunity to interview three men in three different areas of the arts for whom I had so much respect, and then to get the space to really do those interviews justice, was a privilege I'll never forget. I tried to take even further advantage of it by running much longer versions of the Martin Scorsese and Don DeLillo interviews in the academic journal *South Atlantic Quarterly*. Slightly edited versions of those longer interviews appear here.

The Keith Richards interview was a thrill because it's so rare to speak with someone of his stature who is willing to speak so bluntly. His manager, Jane Rose, told me that when I left the room as we were all getting ready to leave, Keith turned to her and said, "You're going to kill me." Indeed, his psychologically incisive remarks about Mick Jagger made headlines around the world, prompting Jagger to respond that he had no interest in commenting on "Keith's problems." Keith's evisceration of the Billboard Top 10 at that time is pretty hilarious as well. Among its other impacts, this story prompted the manufacturers of Rebel Yell to call me to ask where they could send Keith a case of their fine product, which, as I mention in the introduction to the piece, he was drinking throughout the interview. I wish I'd mentioned that, anticipating Busta Rhymes by nearly 15 years, I was drinking Courvoisier.

I borrowed the title for this section from Susan Sontag's *Styles of Radical Will* for no more elaborate reason than I've always liked it. The range of her intellectual curiosity and her eagerness to obliterate distinctions between high and low art seem appropriate to reference in a section that groups a literary novelist, a filmmaker, and a rock star. Given her recent death, this title also stands as a small tribute to her inspiring achievement.

As for the idea of "masculine will," it seems to me that – with the notable exception of hip-hop, of course – there's been a kind of embarrassment about masculinity in the arts for the past two decades or so, and a consequent flight from it. The work of these men stands as a rebuke to that.

To varying degrees in each instance, what I see in these artists is a fascination with the deep conflict between personal will and the civilizing demands of community; an unflinching attitude toward violence; a rigorous lack of sentimentality, as distinguished from raw, genuine emotion; an uncompromising intellectual force; an attraction to demanding social codes, and a dignified acceptance of the price inevitably exacted by conviction. Although they've found other, more suitable homes in this book, it certainly would have been possible to include Johnny Cash, Al Pacino, and Bruce Springsteen in here.

One final note: When reading my exchange with Keith Richards about Bruce Springsteen accompanying Patti Scialfa to one of Keith's recording sessions, it's useful to remember that, though they're now models of enlightened domesticity, Patti and Bruce began seeing each other while Bruce was still married to Julianne Phillips. That transgression is the source of Keith's chiding humor.

Keith Richards

"I'll be totally honest: I love Mick"

A drink in one hand and a cigarette in the other, Keith Richards dances around the New York office of his personal manager, Jane Rose, as *Talk Is Cheap* – his first solo album after a quarter century with the Rolling Stones – blasts out of the stereo. Beyond enjoying the grooves, Keith is also attending to business: he's checking out slides, trying to choose cover art for the record. "Just put it in a brown paper bag," he says jokingly at one point to Steve Jordan, with whom he wrote and produced the album. "I don't give a shit about the goddamn cover."

The emphasis on content is characteristic – and it extends to Richards's collaborators. When Jordan, a hot New York sessionman who used to be the house drummer for "Late Night With David Letterman," is complimented on the album, he simply says, "It's a real record. We weren't trying to do anything hip." Along with guitarist Waddy Wachtel, keyboardist Ivan Neville, and bassist Charley Drayton, Jordan is a member of the core band that plays on *Talk Is Cheap* and will tour with Richards after its release. "In 10 days," Richards says, "if you give me the right guys, I'll give you a band that sounds as if they've been together for two or three years. I'll make them sound like a *band*. Mainly because *I* need it, and that communicates itself."

Talk Is Cheap serves up a rich sampling of Richards's musical roots – from the Cajun flavor of "Locked Away" to the funk of "Big Enough," from the Memphis soul of "Make No Mistake" to the rockabilly of "I Could Have Stood You Up." And of course, "Take It So Hard," "How I Wish," and "Whip It Up" rock with a force reminiscent of his classic work with the Stones.

Another track, however, "You Don't Move Me," evokes the Stones not only in its slashing guitar sound but in its subject, Mick Jagger. The song vents the anger and bitterness Richards felt when Jagger decided to pursue his own solo career in 1986 rather than tour with the Stones after they released *Dirty Work*. Accusing Jagger of greed and selfishness, the song also chides the singer for the commercial failure of his two solo records, *She's the Boss* and *Primitive Cool*: "Now you want to throw the dice / You already crapped out twice."

Later in the week, Richards turns up for his interview at Rose's office sporting red-tinted shades, gray corduroy slacks, a white jacket and the same T-shirt he wore four days earlier, which bears the legend OBERGRUPPENFUEHRER ("major general of the troops"). After fixing himself a Rebel Yell and ginger ale and lighting a Marlboro, he drapes his jacket on the back of one of the chrome-and-leather chairs in the office's conference room and goes to work.

Like everyone in New York this August, Richards complains about the wilting heat, but he seems in an upbeat mood. After the interview he will race down to Madison Square Garden to catch INXS and Ziggy Marley. Now 44, Richards describes himself as a family man. In addition to two teenage children from his stormy relationship with Anita Pallenberg, he has two little girls from his marriage to New York model Patti Hansen. He looks weathered but fit, the leathery skin on his arms hugging his well-developed biceps.

Pleased and relieved to have completed *Talk Is Cheap*, Richards nonetheless remembers the frustrations that led him to make the record after years of saying that he had no desire to compete with the Rolling Stones. When he speaks about Jagger – and what he sees as Jagger's betrayal of the Stones – his hurt pride is evident. As he speaks, affection blends with resentment, and a need for reconciliation battles with an equally strong desire to be proven *right* about the integrity of the Stones. Richards's manner at such moments recalls nothing more than one of those exhausting conversations with friends whose lovers have left.

"It's a struggle between love and hate," Richards sings on *Talk Is Cheap*. Amid such ravaging emotional ambivalence, the Stones are talking about regrouping next year for an album and a tour. "Mick's and my battles are fascinating," Richards says. "When you've known somebody that long, there's so much water under the bridge that it's almost impossible to talk about." And then, for three hours, he talks.

After 25 years with the Stones, how does it feel to have completed your first solo record?

It sort of goes like this [*sweeps his hand across his brow*]: *Ph-e-e-e-w*. It's kind of strange, because it was never in the cards for me. It was not something I wanted to do. Also, in the back of my mind, doing a solo record meant a slight sense of failure. The only reason I would do a solo album was because I couldn't keep the Stones together.

As far back as 1971, you said that you didn't ever want to be in a situation where you had to decide whether to keep a song for yourself or give it to the Stones.

Yeah, there's all those things. To put yourself into a split situation, to have to decide – it's hard. Fortunately or unfortunately since the Stones have taken this break or whatever – you know, *weren't working* – I didn't have to worry about that particular problem.

You see, *Dirty Work* I built pretty much on the same idea as *Some Girls*, in that it was made with the absolute idea that it would go on the road. So when we finished the record and then…the *powers that be* – let's put it like that [*laughs*] – decided suddenly they *ain't* gonna go on the road behind it, the team was left in the lurch. Because if you didn't follow it up with some roadwork, you'd only done 50 percent of the job.

Do you feel that Dirty Work *didn't do well because the Stones didn't support it with a tour?*

Well, there was no promotion behind it. As it came out, everyone sort of said "Well, they've broken up," or "They're not gonna work." So you got a lot of negativity behind it.

It seemed like it was released into a storm of chaos.

It was – mainly, I think, to do with the fact that Stu [Ian Stewart, the pianist with the early Stones and the band's longtime road manager] died at that point. The glue fell out of the whole setup. There's not a lot of people who realize quite what a tower of strength he was and how important he was within the band.

The first rehearsal that was ever called for this band that turned out to be the Rolling Stones, at the top of this pub in Soho, in London, I arrived, and the only guy there is Stu. He was already at the piano, waiting for the rest of this collection of weirdos to arrive. On the surface of it, he was very different from us. He was working – he was a civil servant. The rest of us were, like, just a bunch of layabouts.

Stu was somebody that couldn't tell a lie. I think one of the first things he said to me was "Oh, so you're the Chuck Berry expert, are you?" At the time, Chuck Berry wasn't in Stu's bag of tricks. His thing was Lionel Hampton and Leroy Carr and Big Joe Williams – you know, swing, boogie freaks. And so Chuck Berry to him was frivolous rock 'n' roll, until I got him to listen to the records and he heard Johnnie Johnson [Berry's longtime pianist]. In fact, one of the last things Stu said to me before he died was, "Never forget, Keith, Johnnie Johnson is alive and playing in St. Louis." And the funny thing is within a few months I'd found Johnnie, and he's even on this record.

So Stu's death was part of the problem. Then what happened? Was it that Mick didn't want to tour?

In all honesty, it was Mick decided that he could do…I don't know whether "he could do better" is the best phrase, but he felt, actually, that the Rolling Stones were like a millstone around his neck. Which is *ludicrous* – and I told him so.

He said that to you?

Yeah. Yeah. He said, "I don't need this bunch of old farts." Little do you know, Sunny Jim.

I spoke to him about it the other week, because now he wants to put the Stones back together – because there's nowhere else to go. And I don't want to knock the cat. Mick's and my battles are not exactly as perceived through the press or other people. They're far more convoluted, because we've known each other for most of our lives – since we were four or five. So they involve a lot more subtleties and ins and outs than can possibly be explained. But I think that there is on Mick's part a little bit of a Peter Pan complex.

It's a hard job, being the frontman. To do it, you've got to think in a way that you're semidivine. But if it goes a little too far, that feeling, you think you don't need anybody, and Mick kind of lost touch with the fact of how important the Stones were for him. He thought that he could just hire another Rolling Stones, and that way he could control the situation more, rather than battling with me.

My point around *Dirty Work* was this was the time when the Stones could do something. They could mature and grow this music up and prove that you could take it further. That you don't have to go back and play Peter Pan and try and compete with Prince and Michael Jackson or Wham! and Duran Duran. But it's all a matter of self-perception. Mick perceived himself as still having to prove it on that level. To me, 25 years of integrity went down the *drain* with what he did.

How would you explain that?

Mick is more involved with what's happening at this moment – and fashion. I'm trying to grow the thing up, and I'm saying we don't need the lemon-yellow tights and the cherry picker and the spectacle to make a good Rolling Stones show. There's a more mature way of doing it. And two or three years ago, Mick couldn't see a way clear to do anything different. So therefore he had to go backwards and compare himself with who's hitting the Top 10 at that moment.

The last Stones show I saw was at the Fox Theatre, in Atlanta, in 1981, and it was just the band, without the gimmicks.

To me, the interesting thing about Mick is that he could work this *table* better than anybody in the world. And the bigger the stages got, it was a feeling that he had to use every inch of space on that stage. He would say that you've got to get to as much of the audience as you can when you're playing stadiums. But the bigger the stage, the more stagy it got. Mick didn't appreciate that he had a band that he could rely upon, come hell or high water. I guess he took it for granted eventually and thought that he could hire that. And you can't hire that kind of thing.

At one point, you seemed to feel that Walter Yetnikoff, the president of CBS Records, had encouraged Mick to go solo, that he believed that Mick was the Stones.

At the beginning, yes. But it's understandable that somebody just walking in on the Rolling Stones…it's an obvious thought. Mick is going to be talking to them. He's the frontman. *Since* then, Walter has certainly changed his mind. [*Laughs*] They thought that, oh, if you've got it together with Mick, then you've got the Stones, because the next person to talk to is myself. And I've been a junkie, unreliable – in business people's minds, I'm the dodgy artistic freak. I'm not the one that's going to be up in your office talking business at 10 in the morning. So it's an understandable attitude to take. But it certainly didn't help keeping the Stones together at the time.

Didn't Yetnikoff hook you back up with Sarah Dash, who sings with you on the album?

She's a friend of Walter's. She happened to be popping by to see him at the time, and I said, "Oh, Sarah, I haven't seen you in donkeys' years." When I first met Sarah, she was 15 or 16. She'd just started working with Patti LaBelle and the Blue Bells. This was in '65. She had a chaperone with her – nobody could get near her. They used to call her Inch, I think, Sarah. She's still a dinky little thing, but what a girl, what a voice.

So by going to see Walter, I found the chick I wanted to sing on the album. The only other girl singing on it is the now infamous Patti Scialfa.

Springsteen has managed to tarnish his reputation.

Yeah, it was kind of surprising. In fact, the last overdub that Patti did for this record, she walks in with this guy. "Hi, Patti, how're you doin'?" We're talking. The guy is standing in the doorway, and I turn around, and suddenly I realize it's *Bruce*. [*Laughs*] Oh, oh, *naughty, naughty, naughty*.

Had you met him before?

I've met Bruce two or three times. We've had several good chats, usually at some release party or premiere, and we just end up in the corner talking. He's a sweet guy, a nice guy.

Mind you, I think four-hour shows really are *way* over the top. To me, a great rock 'n' roll act does 20 minutes. [*Laughs*] I remember the Paramount, where you got the Impressions, Jackie Wilson, Joe Tex, and everybody does just their absolute supreme *best shot*! A lot of the shows you get these days are very self-indulgent. I don't think anybody can be enthralling for four hours onstage playing rock 'n' roll.

You've been recording on your own for years. Had you built up a big backlog of songs?

Not really. All of the songs on this album were written last year. There's also a whole backlog of songs with the Stones that I didn't touch. I wanted it to be completely separate. Of course, certain ways of doing things hung over. For the Stones, I would write for what Mick could sing, what I thought was the best thing that Mick could handle.

On this album, the songs are not *that* much different in structure or in content, even. I managed to do some of the things that with the Stones I'd say, "Nah, can't do that. Too complicated." I realized this writing with Steve Jordan. That was the other great thing: that I found somebody else to work with. To me, teamwork is important. The enthusiasm from the other guys is incredibly important, and these guys gave it to me all the way. They would never let me indulge myself. For instance, with the Stones, if I'm writing something and they're hitting it in the studio and I'd break down because I'm not quite sure how the bridge would go or something, I'd stop playing, and everybody'd stop playing, go off for a drink, and a phone call, and, an hour later, come back and try it again. With this lot, if I stopped, they'd just carry on. They'd look at me: "Pick it *up*, pick it *up*, man!" "Why, you goddamn nigger! *Nobody's* kicked me up the ass like that." At the same time, I enjoyed it, because they were right. I would just pick it up again and get back in there.

Did you find yourself getting uptight about not wanting a song to sound like a Stones song?

No, I didn't. It was the other way. My idea was if I allowed myself to think, "I can't do it like that, because it would be just the way I'd do it with the Stones," that would be phony.

My main hang-up, first off, was, "Who the hell am I gonna play with if it ain't Charlie Watts?" If I'm gonna work on my own after 20-odd years of working with this great drummer, who's going to have, without looking at each other, the same feel, the same contact? The beauty of Steve and myself finding each other at that particular time was that it was a very natural changeover, since Steve and Charlie know each other and respect each other's work very much.

Where are Charlie, Bill Wyman, and Ron Wood on all of this? Are you in touch with them?

Well, yeah. In fact, in the last month or so, I've been in touch with them. Mick suddenly called up, and the rest of them: "Let's put the Stones back together." I'm thinking, "*Just* as I'm in the middle of an album. Now what are you trying to do, screw me up? Just *now* you want to talk about putting it back together?" But we talked about it. I went to London, and we had a meeting. I think you'll find a new album and a tour next year from the Stones.

Will you be touring with your band?

With this lot, yeah, sure. I need to get on the road, and the only way you're gonna get on the road is to make a record. Since '86, I've slowly been putting the team together. This basic band: Drayton, Steve, Ivan Neville, Waddy.

I don't want to do a big deal, you know, big stadiums and all that. I want to play some good rooms – theaters. We're just starting to talk about it. Basically I just want to do some class joints, some nice 3,000, 4,000 seaters.

It's startling to hear "Big Enough," which has such a James Brown feel, as the first track on the album. Was that the first tune you recorded?

It's not exactly the first thing, but it was fairly early on. It was just Steve and myself, just drums and guitar. It was incredibly long, almost a jam. But the groove on it was just so strong and, as you say, the James Brown feel of it was so evident that what happened was, during last winter, James played the Apollo. Steve and I went up there, and we saw Maceo [Parker, James Brown's saxman], and we looked at each other and went, "Dig it. Maceo." So we got in touch with Maceo to give it that horn thing.

The bass end was another problem, because we cut it with just guitar and drums, we had the drums tuned very low down. There was an awful lot of bass on the drums. And every time we tried to put a bass on it, it would just get in the way. So we thought about it, and once again, Steve, who's got a great ear [*snaps his fingers*]: "Ah, it's got to be Bootsy" – who used to play with James. So Bootsy [Collins] drove from

Ohio – because he doesn't fly – for one evening and heard it, grinned, and did it. So that's how James Brown the track was – it ended up with James's guys on there!

On the other end of the spectrum from "Big Enough," you have "I Could Have Stood You Up."

To me, that was "a little stroll through the rock 'n' roll alley." I actually started to cut these tracks a year ago, just about today, at about this *time* [*laughs*] – that's why I'm looking at my watch – up in Montreal. We got about seven tracks in ten days, so I felt already, "This thing's going well, this band is cooking."

Who was up there with you?

Charley Drayton, Steve, Ivan, Waddy, and myself. Since we'd worked with Johnnie Johnson on the Chuck Berry thing, I really wanted to work with him. My next thought was, "I don't know if I've got anything in that vein for this album." So Steve and I worked on it a bit, and I came up with that one thing. We wanted to do some sessions with Johnnie, so we got it together, and Johnnie – who happens to *love* me, for some reason…

Well, your analysis of Chuck Berry's music in Hail! Hail! Rock 'n' Roll, *where you point out that it was all based on Johnnie Johnson's piano chords, might have something to do with it.*

I would have never thought about it, except I went through that process and saw it. The guy's 68, 69 years old, and he probably plays more regularly than just about anybody on this planet. He has five or six gigs a week in St. Louis. He's one of the hidden masters of American music to me. Also, given the fact that Stu had said what he said [*folds his hands in prayer*].

"I Could Have Stood You Up" is also a reunion of Stones alumni: Mick Taylor, Bobby Keys, Chuck Leavell. Had you played with Mick since he left the Stones?

When he played the Lone Star last year, I popped up for a number or two. I hadn't seen him for quite a few years. It's sort of a mystery to me – and it's also a mystery to Mick Taylor – as to why he left the Stones. [*Laughs*] I said, "Why did you *leave* like that?" And he said, "I ask myself that all the time. I don't know why I did that."

But being in the Stones is a weird thing, I guess for Mick, you've been in the Stones for five or six years, and you think you can expand. He wanted to play drums. He wanted to produce and write. Right or wrong – because Mick Taylor is just a brilliant guitar player. That's what he is. But from the inside, you think, "I've done this. I've got this now. Now I can go out on my own. I'm a bit bored with this."

And Mick Jagger made the same decision – and the same mistake. Whether it's a mistake or not, it didn't work out the way he thought it was going to work out. Maybe it's got something to do with the name Mick. [*Laughs*]

It seems that the Stones developed a very unsentimental attitude over the years about people who were sucked into their vortex and sometimes did great things, but sometimes also damaged themselves.

It made them – and maybe even for the better – come face to face eventually with themselves. Maybe sometimes in the worst possible way. Maybe that ultimately is one of the most important things about the Stones – that, for some unknown reason, they strike at a person at a point and in a position that they don't even know exists.

There was always a sense about the Stones and about your own life, certainly, that this is nothing other than what it looks to be.

It's certainly for real. The other thing about my life and the Stones' life is that there was nothing phony about it. If anybody was going to take knocks, we were going to, along with everybody else. It isn't that we were sitting up on some comfortable faraway paradise and putting out this stuff and saying, "Well, fuck yourselves up." We got beat up more than anybody.

I've always just tried to avoid doing anything that would make me cringe. Anything I do, I like to be able to live with. No matter how on the surface – you know, "What a bum, what a junkie" – at least it's real. And I can live with it. If I fuck up, the whole *world* fucks up with me! [*Laughs*]

You once said that you never wanted anyone to feel that there was anything they could find out by going through your garbage can that they couldn't find out by just asking you.

There's always this thing in show business: you have an "image," and you play it to the hilt, but you're not really like that "*in my private life*," et cetera. In other words, it's an *act*. And maybe for them that's OK. But for myself, what I do, I'm too intense about it.

I mean, I'm a family man. I have little two-year-old and three-year-old girls that beat me up. I'm not the guys I see on MTV, who obviously think they *are* me. There are so many people who think that's all there is to it. It's not *that* easy to be Keith Richards. But it's not *so hard*, either. The main thing is to know yourself.

I was forced into the position of honesty because they *went* through my garbage can and it was all over the front pages – to the point where people think that I'm far more Errol Flynn or notorious than I actually am. But I know what people think: "We'll give them that Keith Richards *look*." With my friends, the "Keith Richards look" is, like, a great *laugh*. And it's got nothing to do with the moody bit – it's just the way I look if I don't smile. And this [*points to his skull ring*] is to remind me that we're all the same under the skin. The skull – it has nothing to do with bravado and surface bullshit.

To me, the main thing about living on this planet is to know who the hell you are and to be real about it. That's the reason I'm still alive. The chart I was Number One on longest was the Next One to Kick the Bucket. I headed *that* chart longer than I ever did Records! [*Laughs*] Because whatever it was I did, no matter how stupid or flamboyant or irresponsible it may have seemed from the outside – and I can understand it appearing like that – it's always been very important to know what I'm made of and what I'm capable of doing. And making sure that nobody else suffered in the process. And if they did, it would only be from a misconception of *themselves*, not of me.

Obviously, a whole mythology has been built up around you. You must walk into situations all the time where people expect you to be "Keith Richards." How does that affect you?

I try and disillusion them, because I don't have an "act." It's impossible for me. It's very embarrassing.

Charlie Watts, in fact, is a far more honest man than I am – to himself, to everybody. He never even wanted to be a pop star. It still makes him cringe. But because he liked the music – and loved playing with me and with Mick and knew that it was a great band – he's willing to go along with it. Chicks screaming at Charlie Watts – to him, it's ludicrous. He wanted to be Max Roach or Philly Joe Jones – his idea of himself is that. And to have to live with being some teen pop idol for Charlie is very difficult, because he's not like that at all.

They're such a weird collection of guys – the most unlikely collection of people to be a good rock 'n' roll band. Hell, half of them hate the idea of being a rock 'n' roll star in the first place. It's already embarrassing to them; they want to be serious *artists*. And when you're living and working with people like that, it's very difficult, if you're phony or if you go… That's what happened to Brian [Jones]. He really got off on the trip of being a pop star. And it killed him. Suddenly, from being very serious about what he wanted to do, he was willing to take the cheap trip. And it's a very short trip.

Has Mick heard "You Don't Move Me"?

Yeah, he's heard it. I played the whole album to him – what? – last week, two weeks ago.

Here in New York?

Yeah. He talked all the way through it. [*Laughs*] But I went to the john and took a pee, and as I was coming out, I saw him dancing in the front room. So then I went back to the john and slammed the door loud and walked out again, he's sitting back like this [*sits straight in his chair and folds his hands in his lap*]. I don't know what he really thinks about it, because it's all tied up with what happened with his solo stuff.

What he put out, to me, is exactly the reason, as we were talking about before, why we didn't go on the road behind *Dirty Work*. He wanted to compete on a different level. The sad thing about it was that I felt it was totally unnecessary in that he had no grasp of the idea of the integrity of the Stones.

What does it make you feel like since Mick didn't want to tour behind Dirty Work *but now he's done a tour of Japan and he's going to do a tour of Australia?*

Great. Go to Australia in their midwinter. Go on. I've got other things to do. Go there. Go there with your jerk-off band.

He knows how I feel about it. Whether he'll ever admit it to himself, I don't know. I'll be totally honest: I *love* Mick. Most of my efforts with Mick go to trying to open his eyes: "You don't need to do this. You have no problem. All you've got to do is just grow up with it." And that's what he should be doing.

I mean, 99 percent of the male population of the Western world – and beyond – would give a *limb* to live the life of Riley, to live the life of Jagger. To be *Mick Jagger*. And he's not happy being Mick Jagger. He's not living a happy life. That's unacceptable. I've *got* to make him happy! [*Laughs*] I've failed if I can't eventually get my mate to feel good about himself, even though he's very autocratic and he can be a real asshole. But who can't be an asshole at times?

The siege mentality kind of worries me about Mick. Nobody can get in there, even me, who's known him longer than anybody. What bothers me sometimes about him is not being able to get through to him. He's got his own vision about himself, which is not actually who he is. So he has to play a game; he has to act. He's not about to give you *anything*. He's not about to give *anything* away. He'll be flip.

And I don't mind him reading this shit, because this is part of my attempt to help him along. It's a very sad thing to me to have a friend that…especially when he's in such a privileged position and should be able to live one of the best lives ever. Everybody, as I say, would give limbs to be Mick Jagger, to be able to live like that. And not to be *happy*? What's so *hard* about being Mick Jagger? What's so tough? It's like Bob Dylan's phrase once: "What's so hard about being one of the Beatles?" Although, you could say that about *Bob*, too. Now I'm *really* gonna get shit, man! [*Laughs*] This exaggerated sense of who you are and what you should do and worrying about it so much – why don't you just get on with it and stop trying to figure all the angles? That, to me, is a waste of time.

Now you're in the situation where your own solo record is coming out. Do you feel any sense of competition with Mick?

Obviously, the situation is there for it to be perceived that way. No, I don't feel any sense of competition with Mick. Whether Mick feels a sense of competition *with me* – that's another question. Why we didn't go on the road behind *Dirty Work* – that might be an answer to that.

You mean he felt that it was more your record or...

...or who runs the deal. I think to Mick that's more important than it is to me. I tip my hat to Mick a lot. I admire the guy enormously. In the '70s, when I was on dope and I would do nothing but put the songs together, turn up, and not deal with any of the business of the Stones, Mick took all of that work and weight on his shoulders and did it *all* and covered my ass. And I've always admired him very much for that. He did exactly what a friend should do.

When I cleaned up and *Emotional Rescue* time came around – "*Hey*, I'm back, I'm clean, I'm ready; I'm back to help and take some of the weight off your shoulders" – immediately I got a sense of resentment. Whereas I felt that he would be happy to unburden himself of some of that shit, he felt that I was horning in and trying to take control. And that's when I first sensed the feeling of discontent, shall we say. It wasn't intended like that from my point of view, but that's when I first got a feeling that he got so used to running the show that there was no way he was going to give it up. That, to him, it was a power struggle.

To turn away from the Stones for a moment, what do you make of the state of rock today? Some have said this is the worst period in the history of rock 'n' roll.

My cheap answer to that would be "Yeah, wait until *my* record comes out!" [*Laughs*]

I wanted to run the Top 10 singles by you and get your impression of them.

All right, run 'em down.

Number One is "Roll With It," by Steve Winwood.

Steve is great, but the record, *eh*. He's not pushing anything further. I mean, he's a great musician, but he doesn't seem to me to have a driving desire to really do anything. If he bothers to work, it's fantastic. I think he's one of the best English musicians that we have.

At the same time, my problem with Stevie – he's gonna fuckin' hate me forever for saying this – is that he's kind of faceless. What's Number Two, George Michael?

Number Two is "Hands to Heaven," by Breathe.

Never heard it. Don't know nothing about it.

Number Three is "Make Me Lose Control," by Eric Carmen. He had a hit recently from the Dirty Dancing *soundtrack.*

A nice PR job.

Number Four is "Sign Your Name," by Terence Trent D'Arby.

He's more interested in Terence Trent D'Arby than he is in anything else, as far as I'm concerned. Hey, a nice-looking boy, but hung up on himself. A great voice, but that's not enough.

"1-2-3," by Gloria Estefan and Miami Sound Machine.

A Holiday Inn band, a club band that made it. Very nice. Love the girl. Like *Dirty Dancing*: just to watch, yeah. But it palled really quickly.

"I Don't Wanna Go On With You Like That," by Elton John.

Reg, give me a Rubens, and I'll say something nice. Reg Dwight. Lovely bloke, but posing.

"I Don't Wanna Live Without Your Love," by Chicago.

Chicago? I haven't heard it. Chicago to me was always…I mean, you'll get a lot of put-downs this way, guy! [*Laughs*] You've got to forgive me. I haven't heard that particular record, but I would think "contrived."

"Monkey," by George Michael.

Shave and go home. He's a wimp in disguise.

"Hold Onto the Night," by Richard Marx.

I don't know the particular record, but I have a feeling – why do I say this? – *maybe* there's something interesting in there?

And Number 10 is "Just Got Paid," by Johnny Kemp.

I wish *I* just got paid! Who the *hell* Johnny Kemp is I don't know.

I also wanted to ask you about the current superstars.

U2, I like. I like Bono very much. When I worked with him, I'd never heard him. I found the guy very interesting and very open. Then, afterwards, I started listening to them. It's human music; it's not push-button music.

I'm especially disappointed with you black guys, just pushing buttons and shit. They are, to me, really fucking up. With the drum machines and the engineers that have never – you set up a drum kit and say you're gonna use a live drummer and they go, "What? How do we record a thing like that?" Music's got to do with people, not pushing buttons. It's kind of weird that George Michael is Number One on the black charts. Because, *'ey, 'ey*, what happened to Little Milton? What happened to the soul?

You mentioned Bruce Springsteen earlier. What about his music?

Bruce? That's a tough one, because I like the *guy*. But the music…I don't know. I'm the toughest taskmaster of all time. I'm going to annoy a lot of people. Bruce? To me, it's pretentious.

What's pretentious about it?

I love his attitude. I love what he *wants* to do. I just think he's gone about it the wrong way. These are just my opinions, and OK, I'll annoy the lot of you. Bruce? Too contrived for me. Too overblown.

I know you haven't liked Prince in the past. Has your opinion of him changed?

Prince, I admire his energy, but he's riding on a wave. To me, Prince is like the Monkees. I don't see anything of any depth in there. He's very clever at manipulating the music business and the entertainment business. He's more into that than making music. I don't see much substance in anything he does. Too much appealing to…a Pee-wee Herman trip. And I like Pee-wee Herman better than Prince. He's appealing to the same audience. To me, it's kid stuff.

What do you think about Guns n' Roses?

Not much. I admire the fact that they've made it despite certain resistance from the radio biz. I admire their guts. But too much posing. Their look, it's like there's one out of this band – one looks like Jimmy, one looks like Ronnie. Too much copycat, too much posing for me. I haven't listened to a whole album to be able to talk about the music.

I'm a very hard taskmaster. I know that everybody's gonna say, "Oh, he's putting everybody down."

Well, tell me what you like.

I don't like much. And I don't want any of these guys to feel like, "Oh, he's an old fart, blah-blah-blah. But we're up there, blah-blah-blah." I'm not interested in that. My main thing is, What are you trying to do, just be famous? Or have you got something to say? And if you do, are you forgoing it in order just to be famous?

I've always liked AC/DC, all right? I like U2; I really do. I think Bono, especially, has something special. INXS, I'm quite interested in. I like Tracy Chapman. Ziggy Marley, I find very interesting because he's not just "the son of." He's avoided being, I hate to say this, Julian. He's taken from his father and built on it, but he's not just "the son of Bob Marley." He's got his own things to say, and he's serious about it.

I wanted to ask you about Chuck Berry. If you take 45 Chuck Berry songs, 15 of them will be among the greatest rock songs ever written and 30 will be the most clichéd formulas.

And two or three of them just *trite*. The saddest thing about Chuck Berry is that his biggest-selling record is "My Ding-a-Ling." But that's what he deserves, because of his attitude toward what he does. He hasn't sussed out his own worth. He has no *idea* of his impact on popular music. Chuck just wants the bread. And there's nothing *wrong* with that, because it's the only way a guy from his era, from where he came from, could get out.

And also getting ripped off in the past, that's what he learns. But he's carried it around for 30 years.

He's a loner. That's why I could work with Chuck Berry, because he's very much like Mick. It's a siege mentality: "*Nobody's* going to get into *me*." And "If I give a thing away, I'm a weakling." The truth is the more you give, the stronger you are. The more of a man you are. Who are you scared of? What's so scary that you've got to lock yourself up?

In that scene in the movie where you turn around and give him this look, it seems like you're going to have a fight or something.

A shoot-out? Yeah. Yeah. Yeah. That's pretty true. Yeah, just about. Most of the band, the guys behind me are going, "Keith in this situation is gonna pull out the blade and just slit the motherfucker's throat." I'm biting bullets, because I'm trying to show the band that, to get this gig together, I am gonna take some shit that I wouldn't take from *anybody*. I'm *not* gonna let Chuck get to me that much. Whereas anybody else, it would be toilet time.

You say the Stones may be getting back together. Given all that's happened, couldn't that be seen as just a case of knowing that this is an opportunity to make $40 million and...

A hundred. [*Laughs*]

Well, what do you say to that?

What can I say about it? However much you make, the same percentage goes toward keeping it together. The overhead's tremendous. The amount of money – I find it as mind boggling as anybody out there on the street. You say, "Yeah, he's a fucking multimillionaire, and blah-

blah-blah." The one thing you find out when you make a lot of money – and it always sounds *trite* when you say it, but it isn't – is that it's not the important thing. It doesn't add one iota to your happiness in life. It just means you have different problems to deal with. And it brings its own problems, like "Who are you going to put on retainer?"

It's much better to be rich than poor, but not for the reasons that you would automatically think. I grew up with no bread at all. I was talking to Steve Jordan and Charley Drayton – black cats, you know, fairly well-off middle-class cats. I grew up poorer than they did. We just about made the rent. The luxuries were very, very few. I know what it's like down there. There wasn't a lot of chances for someone, the way I grew up. My dad worked his butt off just to keep the rent paid and food for the family. People are more important than anything else. Rock 'n' roll, anything else, people are more important.

I know you and your father were reconciled a few years ago. Are you still on good terms?

Oh, yeah. Dominoes every Friday night. In fact, I'm late for the game right now!

Does he live in New York?

He lives about 45 minutes out of town. Oh yeah, now that we're together, we're very tight.

You described yourself earlier as a "family man." What about your marriage and your kids? Obviously your wife, Patti Hansen, has her own business to do, and you have what you do.

Patti's a mother now. She doesn't do much. She does one job, two jobs a year. This is my second time around with families. I have a son – Marlon's 19. Angela's 16, and she's just left school.

I have this new family. I live in a house-load of women, which sometimes can drive me totally 'round the bend, which is why I need to work and get on the road. I love 'em all, but it's weird to be living with a load of chicks – it doesn't matter what age they are. For a guy, the only guy in the house, you gotta call up another cat and say, "Hey, come over, or I'll just drop over there!"

And my old lady knows this, bless her heart. That's why I married her, because I'll only get married once. But Patti and I, we have a good thing going, and it's just kept going. I'm a lucky guy.

With you and Patti, is it the sort of arrangement where somebody is taking care of the kids all the time?

No, I hate that. I'd never have that. It's only Patti and me and the kids. There's other people who clean up the house, but it's not like there's a nanny and she brings the kids down once a day to play with for teatime and then fuck off. No way. You live all together.

Sometimes I wake up in the middle of the night, and there's both my kids in the bed. They've managed to find their way, and we're all in the same bed together. [*Laughs*] You get more out of it like that, and so do the kids. Family is a special thing. You can't really talk about it, except to say that if you get a chance at it, try it out, because it's one of the most special things that you'll ever get on the face of this earth. It gives you that final missing link of what life's about. While they're looking upon you as the most wonderful person in the world because you're "Daddy," they do more for you than you do for them.

How is your health?

You tell me.

You look good. You sound great.

I've lived my life in my own way, and I'm here today because I have taken the trouble to find out who I am.

The problem, however, is people who think they can live like Keith Richards.

That's what I mean. The biggest mistake in the world is to think that you have to emulate somebody else. That is fatal. It's got nothing to do with me. If people want to be like Keith Richards, then they better have the same physical makeup. I come from a very sturdy stock – otherwise I wouldn't be here.

At this point, to what degree is your identity tied into being a Rolling Stone?

Well, I've always been one, from the start of…if you want to call it my professional career. And I never wanted to be anything else. For the last couple of years, I've had to deal with *not* being one. At first it broke my heart.

What I've learned from not being a Rolling Stone for two years probably will help me be – if the Stones come back together, which they will – will *help* me be…what can I say, "a better Rolling Stone"? [*Laughs*] Or make the Rolling Stones better.

I have a little more confidence in myself, by myself. I found that I can, if I have to, live without the Rolling Stones. And that my only job isn't desperately trying to keep a band together that maybe needed a break.

The last question I want to ask you is about legacy. All the bluesmen you admire – there's a legacy of theirs that you've carried on. Do you have a vision of how you'd like yourself, the Stones, your music, to move forward?

Well, then we get back to the break around *Dirty Work*. My vision of the Rolling Stones was that this was the *perfect* point and opportunity, at our state and our age, to carry on and mature and prove it. I played with Muddy Waters six months before he died, and the cat was just as vital as he was in his youth. And he did it until the day he died. To me, that is the important thing. I mean, what am I gonna do now, go for job retraining and learn to be a welder? I'll do this until I drop. I'm committed to it and that's it.

I want to try and make this thing grow up. Elvis couldn't do it. A lot of them didn't do it. It's important to prove that this isn't just teenage kids' shit and you should feel embarrassed when you're over 40 and still doing it. That's not necessary. This is a job. It's a man's job, and it's a lifelong job. And if there's a sucker to ever prove it, I hope to be the sucker.

This interview appeared in Rolling Stone, *October 6, 1988.*

Don DeLillo

"I have an idea of what it's like to be an outsider in this society"

It began like this: In May 1988, a friend in the publicity department at Viking called and said that Don DeLillo's new novel, *Libra*, about the assassination of President Kennedy, would be published soon, and that, uncharacteristically, DeLillo might be willing to do some interviews. Because DeLillo had written a piece about the assassination for *Rolling Stone* in 1983, my friend thought *Rolling Stone* was one magazine DeLillo might talk to.

I was delighted. I asked him to send along the galleys for the novel, and said I'd bring it up with the magazine's executive editor. The galleys arrived with a note that read, in part, "As I told you over the phone, DeLillo has been very reluctant to give interviews in the past. But with the right person, and with the proper format (one restricting itself mostly to the book itself, and to the life and times of Lee Harvey Oswald), DeLillo might be agreeable. A few biographical details won't hurt, but he's wary of the full treatment."

Everyone at *Rolling Stone* went wild over the book. I wrote my friend that we were willing to do the interview on more or less whatever terms DeLillo stated. He passed our request along to DeLillo. DeLillo turned us down.

I talked to my friend. Would it help if I wrote a letter directly to DeLillo – that is, addressed to DeLillo by name, delivered to my friend to pass along to DeLillo – telling him what the interview would be like and explaining a little bit about myself? It might.

I spent a couple of hours writing the letter. It included earnest sentences like, "In addition to being a senior writer at *Rolling Stone*, I hold a Ph.D. in contemporary fiction from Indiana University, and I'm very familiar with all your novels." It also included a paragraph summary of how I thought *Libra* related to his earlier books, which, with true journalistic economy, I later plumbed for the introduction I wrote for the interview when it eventually ran in *Rolling Stone*.

As I wrote the letter, I was both haunted and inhibited by the references to journalists in DeLillo's books. It was hard, at least in my own mind, not to sound like one of his characters. I consciously used the term "full-length interview" in the letter, rather than the first term that came to mind – "major piece" – because of a specific passage in which the filmmaker in *The Names* speaks about writers: "You know how I am about privacy. I'd hate to think you came here to do a story on me. A major piece, as they say. Full of insights. The man and his work… The filmmaker on location. The filmmaker in seclusion. Major pieces. They're always major pieces."

Writing for *Rolling Stone* presented complexities along that line as well. The magazine that gives DeLillo's novel *Running Dog* its title bears some resemblance to *Rolling Stone*. And, as someone who writes primarily about rock 'n' roll, I've always loved the passage in *Great Jones Street*, in which a television reporter from ABC shows up at the apartment of Bucky Wunderlick, rock star in self-exile, to ask for an interview:

"Who are you?"

"ABC," he said.

"Forget it."

"Nothing big or elaborate. An abbreviated interview. Your televised comments on topics of interest. Won't take ten minutes. We're all set up downstairs. Ten minutes. You've got my word, Bucky. The word of a personal admirer."

"Positively never."

"I haven't done this kind of massive research since I've been in the glamour end of the business," the reporter pleads – a plea ("I'm very familiar with all your novels") that touches the heart of an ex-academic now at play in the fields of popular culture.

Anyway, I gave the letter to my friend and went on vacation. It was late June by this time. When I returned around July 4, there was a message on my answering machine from my friend. "Don liked your letter," he declared. (Student eternal, I confess to thrilling at the words.) Don – suddenly, now, he was Don – was more interested in doing the interview; he would call me – himself! – to discuss it further.

One afternoon a few days later, the phone rang at work: "This is Don DeLillo." The questions were simple and friendly: "How do you go about doing one of these things?" (We meet someplace quiet and talk for about two hours with a tape recorder running.) "Do you do much editing?" (Yes, for reasons of space and because a lively spoken conversation does not necessarily translate directly into a lively printed interview. [For the record, all material of interest that was edited out of the interview as it appeared in *Rolling Stone* for reasons of space has been restored for this version.]) "Where do you want to do this?" (Wherever you like that's quiet.) We arranged to meet at his house a few weeks later.

The train ride from midtown Manhattan to the picture-book Westchester suburb where DeLillo lives offers a capsule view of virtually the entire spectrum of American life. After leaving Grand Central Station, the train comes up from underground at 96th Street on Manhattan's East Side, rolls serenely through Harlem, then crosses the Harlem River, and enters the devastated landscape of the South Bronx. The journey continues through the North Bronx, the working-class neighborhood where DeLillo, whose parents were Italian immigrants, grew up and attended college at Fordham University. Finally, the train passes into Westchester's leafy environs.

At DeLillo's station, the author and his wife, Barbara Bennett, were waiting. The sun was blazing. A crushing August heat. Like the train trip, which links the quotidian splendor and the nightmarish underside of the American dream, the brutal weather seemed appropriate. "This is the last comfortable moment you'll have for a while," DeLillo said with a smile as he got in the car. "The car is air-conditioned, but the house isn't." Bennett, who was driving, jokingly suggested that we do the interview in the car or perhaps at a local bar. When I told the couple about the hard time I had recently interviewing a musician who was frustratingly inarticulate and far more adept at talking around questions than answering them, DeLillo turned around and assured me, "I plan to be exactly that way myself."

One of the major voices in American fiction for nearly two decades, DeLillo, now 51, said he rarely grants interviews because he lacks "the necessary self-importance." "I'm just not a public man," he said. "I'd rather write my books in private and then send them out into the world to discover their own public life."

"*Libra* is easier to talk about than my previous books," he continued. "The obvious reason is it's grounded in reality and there are real people to discuss. Even someone who hasn't read the book can respond at least in a limited way to any discussion of people like Lee Oswald or Jack Ruby. It is firmer material. I'm always reluctant to get into abstract discussions, which I admit my earlier novels tended to lean toward. I wrote them, but I don't necessarily enjoy talking about them."

Still, *Libra* – DeLillo's ninth novel – is more of a culmination than a departure. DeLillo's first novel, *Americana* (1971), ends in Dealey Plaza, in Dallas, the site of the Kennedy assassination, and references to the slaying turn up in several of his other books. The piece DeLillo wrote for *Rolling Stone* in 1983, "American Blood," effectively serves as a précis for *Libra*.

Moreover, rather than advancing yet another "theory" of the assassination, *Libra* simply carries forward the themes of violence and conspiracy that have come to define DeLillo's fiction. "This is a work of the imagination," he writes in the author's note that concludes the book. "While drawing from the historical record, I've made no attempt to furnish factual answers to any questions raised by the assassination." Instead, he hopes the novel will provide "a way of thinking about the assassination without being constrained by half-facts or overwhelmed by possibilities, by the tide of speculation that widens with the years."

In *Libra*, DeLillo describes the murder of the president as "the seven seconds that broke the back of the American century." But this cataclysm differs only in scale from the killings that shatter complacent, enclosed lives in *Players* (1977), *Running Dog* (1978), and *The Names* (1982). Similarly, the college football player who is the main character in *End Zone* (1972) and the rock-star hero of *Great Jones Street* (1973) both achieve an alienation that rivals the emotional state DeLillo sees in Lee Harvey Oswald. Apocalyptic events profound in their impact and uncertain in their ultimate meaning shadow *Ratner's Star* (1976) and *White Noise* (1985), just as the assassination does the world of *Libra* – and our world, a quarter of a century after it occurred.

The interview took place in DeLillo's backyard; afterward, we went off to a diner on the town square – a village center DeLillo approvingly described as "like something out of the '50s" – for a late lunch of burgers, fries, and Cokes. In his yard, DeLillo sat on a lawn chair and sipped iced tea. Fortunately, the yard was shady, and the sky clouded over a bit. Even so, the heat, the humidity, the lush green of the grounds and the eerie din of cicadas gave the scene an almost tropical feel. DeLillo – wiry and intense, wearing jeans and a plaid shirt open at the collar, speaking with deliberate slowness in a gripping monotone – seemed the image of a modern-day Kurtz, a literary explorer of the heart of darkness comfortably at home in the suburbs of America.

The Kennedy assassination seems perfectly in line with the concerns of your fiction. Do you feel you could have invented it if it hadn't happened?

Maybe it invented me. When it happened, I was not a fully formed writer; I had only published some short stories in small quarterlies. As I was working on *Libra*, it occurred to me that a lot of tendencies in my first eight novels seemed to be collecting around the dark center of the assassination. So it's possible I wouldn't have become the kind of writer I am if it weren't for the assassination.

What kind of impact did the assassination have on you?

It had a strong impact, as it obviously did for everyone. As the years have flowed away from that point, I think we've all come to feel that what's been missing over these past 25 years is a sense of a manageable reality. Much of that feeling can be traced to that one moment in Dallas. We seem much more aware of elements like randomness and ambiguity and chaos since then.

A character in the novel describes the assassination as "an aberration in the heartland of the real." We still haven't reached any consensus on the specifics of the crime: the number of gunmen, the number of shots, the location of the shots, the number of wounds in the president's body – the list goes on and on. Beyond this confusion of data, people have developed a sense that history has been secretly manipulated. Documents lost and destroyed. Official records sealed for 50 or 75 years. A number of suggestive murders and suicides involving people who were connected to the events of November 22. So from the initial impact of the visceral shock, I think we've developed a much more deeply unsettled feeling about our grip on reality.

You have been interested for a long time in the media, which certainly played a major role in the national experience of the assassination. Television had just made its impact on politics in the 1960 election, and then for the week following the murder, it seemed that everyone was watching television, seeing Jack Ruby's murder of Lee Harvey Oswald and then Kennedy's funeral. It's as if the power of the media in our culture hadn't been fully felt until that point.

It's strange that the power of television was utilized to its fullest, perhaps for the first time, as it pertained to a violent event. Not only a violent, but, of course, an extraordinarily significant event. This has become part of our consciousness. We've developed almost a sense of performance as it applies to televised events. And some of the people who are essential to such events – particularly violent events and particularly people like Arthur Bremer and John Hinckley – are simply carrying their performing selves out of the wings and into the theater. Such young men have a sense of the way in which their acts will be perceived by the rest of us, even as they commit the acts. So there is a deeply self-referential element in our lives that wasn't there before.

The inevitable question: Where were you when John Kennedy was shot?

I was eating lunch with two friends in a restaurant on the west side of Manhattan and actually heard about the shooting at a bank a little later. I overheard a bank teller telling a customer that the president had been shot in Dallas. And my first curious reaction was, "I didn't even know he was in Dallas." Obviously it was totally beside the point. But the small surprise then, of course, yielded to the enormous shock of what these words meant. I didn't watch very much television that weekend. I didn't watch much of the funeral. I have a kind of natural antipathy to formal events of that kind. But certainly a sense of death seemed to permeate everything for the next four or five days.

You refer to the assassination at various points in novels prior to Libra, *and of course you wrote an essay about the assassination for* Rolling Stone *in 1983. What finally made you feel that you had to pursue it as the subject of a novel?*

I didn't start thinking about it as a major subject until the early part of this decade. When I did the 1983 piece in *Rolling Stone*, I began to realize how enormously wide-reaching the material was and how much more deeply I would have to search before I could begin to do justice to it. Because I'm a novelist, I defined "justice" in terms of a much more full-bodied work than the nonfiction piece I had done, and so I began to think seriously about a novel.

Possibly a motivating element was the fact that Oswald and I lived within six or seven blocks of each other in the Bronx. I didn't know this until I did the research for the *Rolling Stone* piece. He and his mother, Marguerite, traveled to New York in '52 or early '53, because her oldest son was stationed at Ellis Island with the Coast Guard. They got in the car and drove all the way to New York and eventually settled in the Bronx. Oswald lived very near the Bronx Zoo. I guess he was 13 and I was 16 at the time. I suppose this gave me a personal nudge toward the material.

Turning it into fiction brought a number of issues to the surface. If I make an extended argument in the book, it's not that the assassination necessarily happened this way. The argument is that this is an interesting way to write fiction about a significant event that happens to have these general contours and these agreed-upon characters. It's my feeling that readers will accept or reject my own variations on the story based on whether these things work as fiction, not whether they coincide with the reader's own theories or the reader's own memories. So this is the path I had to drive through common memory and common history to fiction.

Did it seem odd that some reviews evaluated your theory of the assassination almost as if it were fact and not fiction?

Inevitably, some people reviewed the assassination itself, instead of a piece of work that is obviously fiction. My own feeling at the very beginning was that I had to do justice to historical likelihood. In other words, I chose what I consider the most obvious possibility: that the assassination was the work of anti-Castro elements. I could perhaps have written the same book with a completely different assassination scenario. I wanted to be obvious in this case because I didn't want novelistic invention to become the heart of the book. I wanted a clear historical center on which I could work my fictional variations.

Apart from the personal reason you mentioned, why did you choose to tell the story from Oswald's point of view?

I have an idea of what it's like to be an outsider in this society. Oswald was clearly an outsider, although he fought against his exclusion. I had a very haunting sense of what kind of life he led and what kind of person he was. I experienced it when I saw the places where he lived in New Orleans and in Dallas and in Fort Worth. I had a very clear sense of a man living on the margins of society. He was the kind of person we think we know until we delve more deeply. Who would have expected someone like that to defect to the Soviet Union? He started reading socialist writing when he was 15; then, as soon as he became old enough, he joined the Marines. This element of self-contradiction seemed to exemplify his life. There seemed to be a pattern of self-argument.

When he returned from the Soviet Union, he devised a list of answers to possible questions he'd be asked by the authorities upon disembarking. One set of answers could be characterized as the replies of a simple tourist who just happened to have spent two-and-a-half years at the heart of the Soviet Union and is delighted to be returning to his home country. The other set of answers was full of defiance and anger at the inequities of life in capitalist society. It carried a strong sense of his refusal to explain why he left this country to settle in Russia. These mutually hostile elements seemed always to be part of Oswald's life, and, I think, separate him slightly from the general run of malcontents and disaffected people.

It's almost as if Oswald embodied a postmodern notion of character in which the self isn't fixed and you assume or discard traits as the mood strikes you.

Someone who knew Oswald referred to him as an actor in real life, so there is a sense in which he was watching himself perform. I tried to insert this element into *Libra* on a number of occasions.

I think Oswald anticipates men like Hinckley and Bremer. His attempt to kill General Edwin Walker was a strictly political act: Walker was a right-wing figure, and Oswald was, of course, pro-Castro. But Oswald's attempt on Kennedy was more complicated. I think it was based on elements outside politics and, as someone in the novel says, outside history – things like dreams and coincidences and even the movement or the configuration of the stars, which is one reason the book is called *Libra*. The rage and frustration he had felt for 24 years, plus the enormous coincidence that the motorcade would be passing the building where he worked – these are the things that combined to drive Oswald toward attempting to kill the president. So in this second murder attempt, he presages the acts of all of the subsequent disaffected young men who seem to approach their assassination attempts out of a backdrop of dreams and personal fantasy much more than politics.

You quote Oswald's statement about wanting to be a fiction writer, and you describe him as having lived a life in small rooms, which is a phrase similar to ones you've used to describe your life as a writer. Do you see Oswald as an author of some kind?

Well, he did make that statement in his application for the Albert Schweitzer College. He did say he wanted to be a writer. He wanted to write "short stories on contemporary American life" – and this, of course, is a striking remark coming from someone like him. There's no evidence that he ever wrote any fiction; none apparently survived if he did. But the recurring motif in the book of men in small rooms refers to Oswald much more as an outsider than as a writer. I think he had a strong identification with people like Trotsky and Castro, who spent long periods in prison. I think he felt that with enough perseverance and enough determination these men would survive their incarcerations and eventually be swept by history right out of the room, and out of the self. To merge with history is to escape the self. I think Oswald knew this. He said as much in a letter to his brother – it is the epigraph [to *Libra*]: "Happiness is taking part in the struggle, where there is no borderline between one's own personal world, and the world in general."

We can take Oswald's life as the attempt to find that place. But he never could. He never lost sight of the borderline. He never was able to merge with the world in general or with history in particular. His life in small rooms is the antithesis of the life America seems to promise its citizens: the life of consumer fulfillment. And it's interesting that a man like Oswald would return to this country from Russia with a woman who, of course and understandably, was completely amazed by this world of American consumer promise. It must have caused an enormous tension in his life – her desire to become more fully a part of this paradise she'd been hearing about all her life and his ambivalent feelings about being a husband who provides for his family and at the same time being a leftist who finds an element of distaste in consumer fulfillment. In one of his apartments in Dallas, he actually worked in a room almost the size of a closet. This seemed almost the kind of negative culmination of a certain stream that was running through my own work of men finding themselves alone in small rooms. And here is a man, and not even a man I invented, a real man who finds himself in a closet-sized room planning the murder of General Walker.

You read the Warren Commission Report and traveled quite a bit. Did you do other research for Libra*?*

I looked at films and listened to tapes. Hearing Oswald's voice and his mother's voice was extremely interesting. Particularly interesting was a tape of an appearance Oswald made on the radio in New Orleans in the summer of 1963. He sounds like a socialist candidate for office. He was extremely articulate and extremely clever in escaping difficult questions. Listening to this man and then reading the things he had earlier written in his so-called historic diary, which is enormously chaotic and almost childlike, again seemed to point to a man who was a living self-contradiction. Nothing I had earlier known about Oswald led me to think that he could sound so intelligent and articulate as he did on this radio program.

The movie I looked at is a compilation of amateur footage taken that day in Dallas, and it covers a period from the time the president's plane landed in Dallas until the assassination itself. It's extremely crude footage, but all the more powerful because of it. I suppose the most powerful moment is also the most ambiguous. We see the shot that kills the president, but it seems to be surrounded in chaos and in shadow and in blurs. The strongest feeling I took away from that moment is the feeling that the shot came from the front and not from the rear. If that's true, there had to be more than one assassin. In fact, it's hard to escape that feeling. The other strange moment, I suppose, is when dozens and dozens of people are seen shortly after the shooting running up a set of stairs that proceeds right toward the grassy knoll and toward the stockade fence that separated Dealey Plaza from a parking lot. I hadn't read in any earlier accounts that there had been such an exodus from the scene, and seeing it was shocking because it seemed to indicate that people were running in the direction they thought the shots had come from, not just four or five people, but possibly as many as fifty. And it's just another of those mysteries that hovers over the single moment of death.

At one point you describe the Warren Commission Report, which is 26 volumes long, as the novel that James Joyce might have written if he had moved to Iowa City and lived to be a hundred.

I asked myself what Joyce could possibly do after *Finnegans Wake*, and this was the answer. It's an amazing document. The first 15 volumes are devoted to testimony and the last 11 volumes to exhibits, and together we have a masterwork of trivia ranging from Jack Ruby's mother's dental records to photographs of knotted string. What was valuable to me specifically was the testimony of dozens and dozens of people who talk not only about their connection to the assassination itself but about their jobs, their marriages, their children. This testimony provided an extraordinary window on life in the '50s and '60s and, beyond that, gave me a sense of people's speech patterns, whether they were private detectives from New Orleans or railroad workers from Fort Worth. I'm sure that without those 26 volumes I would have written a very different novel and probably a much less interesting one.

How long did it take to write Libra*?*

A little over three years. The only time I had to do this much research was in writing *Ratner's Star*. But I found doing this novel much more invigorating, because the reading I had to do dealt with real people and not with science and mathematics and astronomy and so on. And for the same reason, I'm sure the experience of writing this novel will stay with me much longer. I'm certain I'll never quite get rid of these characters and this story. They'll always be part of my life.

What was your writing regimen once you started working on the book?

Well, this book is unusual in my own experience because I worked two sessions a day at the typewriter, and this is the first time I've ever done that for an extended period. I worked in the morning, roughly from nine to one, and then again in early evening for about an hour and a half.

I couldn't do all the research, all the reading, in one extended stretch and then begin to write the novel, because there was simply too much reading to do. So I had to space it chronologically. This meant that often I worked much of the day at the typewriter and then spent the night or part of the night trying to catch up. One week I'd be exploring the Bay of Pigs, the next week the Italian mafia, and the next week the Yuri Nosenko affair, and the next week the U-2 incident. So I felt that I had to write nearly twice as much in a given day just to keep up.

Given the complexity of the subject, was there any point that constituted a breakthrough for you?

Once I found Oswald's voice – and by voice I mean not just the way he spoke to people but his inner structure, his consciousness, the sound of his thinking – I began to feel that I was nearly home free. It's interesting that once you find the right rhythm for your sentences, you may be well on your way to finding the character himself. And once I came upon a kind of abrupt, broken rhythm both in dialogue and in narration, I felt this was the prose counterpart to not only Oswald's inner life but Jack Ruby's as well. And other characters too. So the prose itself began to suggest not the path the novel would take but the deepest motivation of the characters who originated this prose in a sense.

The title Libra *seems to reflect the concern in your novels with the occult and superstitions of various kinds. What fascinates you about those nonrational systems?*

My work has always been informed by mystery; the final answer, if there is one at all, is outside the book. My books are open-ended. I would say that mystery in general rather than the occult is something that weaves in and out of my work. I can't tell you where it came from or what it leads to. Possibly it is the natural product of a Catholic upbringing.

Libra was Oswald's sign, and because Libra refers to the scales, it seemed appropriate to a man who harbored contradictions and who could tilt either way.

Did you consider other titles?

The first title I considered was the one I used for the *Rolling Stone* piece, "American Blood." As the months passed, the only other title that interested me as I went along was *Texas School Book*, which seemed to have a sort of double resonance. It was, of course, the Texas School Book Depository where Oswald worked, and the notion of schoolbooks seemed relevant to his life and his struggle. But finally, when I hit upon this notion of coincidence and dream and intuition and the possible impact of astrology on the way men act, I thought that Libra, being Oswald's sign, would be the one title that summarized what's inside the book.

Did you select the photo of Oswald that's on the cover?

I asked Viking to consider using it, yes. It seems that picture would be one of the central artifacts of Oswald's life. He is holding a rifle, carrying a revolver at his hip and holding in his free hand copies of *The Militant* and *The Worker*, two left-wing journals he regularly read. He's dressed in black. He's almost the poor man's James Dean in that picture, and there's definitely an idea of the performing self. He told his wife that he wanted her to take this picture so that their daughter may one day know what kind of person her father was.

In the author's note at the end of Libra, *you say the novel might serve as a kind of refuge for readers. There is an implication that searching for a "solution" to the mysteries of the assassination, as the CIA historian Nicholas Branch does in the book, leads inevitably to a mental and spiritual dead end. What does fiction offer people that history denies them?*

Branch feels overwhelmed by the massive data he has to deal with. He feels the path is changing as he writes. He despairs of being able to complete a coherent account of this extraordinarily complex event. I think the fiction writer tries to redeem this despair. Stories can be a consolation – at least in theory. The novelist can try to leap across the barrier of fact, and the reader is willing to take that leap with him as long as there's a kind of redemptive truth waiting on the other side, a sense that we've arrived at a resolution.

I think fiction rescues history from its confusions. It can do this in the somewhat superficial way of filling in blank spaces. But it also can operate in a deeper way: providing the balance and rhythm we don't experience in our daily lives, in our real lives. So the novel which is within history can also operate outside it: correcting, clearing up, and – perhaps most important of all – finding rhythms and symmetries that we simply don't encounter elsewhere. If *Ratner's Star* is, in part, a way to embody what it is all about – that is, if it's a book of harmonies and symmetries, because mathematics is a search for a sense of order in our lives – then *Libra* is, in a curious way, related to *Ratner's Star*, because it attempts to provide a hint of order in the midst of all the randomness.

From a certain vantage point, your books can almost be taken as a systematic look at various aspects of American life: the Kennedy assassination; rock music in Great Jones Street*; science and mathematics in* Ratner's Star*; football in* End Zone. *Do you proceed in that methodical a fashion?*

No, not at all. That notion breaks down rather easily if you analyze it. *Americana* is not about any one area of our experience. *End Zone* wasn't about football. It's a fairly elusive novel. It seems to me to be about extreme places and extreme states of mind, more than anything else. Certainly, there is very little about rock music in *Great Jones Street*, although the hero is a musician. The interesting thing about that particular character is that he seems to be at a crossroad between murder and suicide. For me, that defines the period between 1965 and 1975, and I thought it was best exemplified in a rock-music star. *Ratner's Star* is not about mathematics as such. I've never attempted to embark on a systematic exploration of American experience. I take the ideas as they come.

On the other hand, some specific American realities have a draw for you.

Certainly, there are themes that recur. Perhaps a sense of secret patterns in our lives. A sense of ambiguity. The violence of contemporary life is a motif. I see contemporary violence as a kind of sardonic response to the promise of consumer fulfillment in America. Again, we come back to these men in small rooms who can't get out and who have to organize their desperation and their loneliness, who have to give it a destiny and who often end up doing this through violent means. I see this desperation against the backdrop of brightly colored packages and products and consumer happiness and every promise that American life makes day by day and minute by minute everywhere we go.

In The Names, *which is principally set in Greece, you speak about the way Americans abroad especially seem to feel the imminence of violence.*

I do believe that Americans living abroad feel a self-consciousness that they don't feel when they are at home. They become students of themselves. They see themselves as the people around them see them, as Americans with a capital A. Because being American is a sensitive thing in so many parts of the world, the American response to violence and terror in places like the Middle East and Greece is often a response tinged with inevitability, almost with apology. We're just waiting for it to happen to us. It becomes part of a sophisticated form of humor that people exchange almost as a matter of course. The humor of political dread.

Humor plays an important role in your novels. Do you see it as providing relief from the grimness of some of your subjects?

The humor isn't intended to counteract the fear. It's almost part of it. We ourselves may almost instantaneously use humor to offset a particular moment of discomfort or fear, but this reflex is so deeply woven into the original fear that they almost become the same thing.

Your first novel, Americana, *was published when you were about 35, which is rather late. Did you think of yourself as a writer before that?*

Americana took a long time to write because I had to keep interrupting it to earn a living, which I was doing at that time by writing freelance, mostly advertising material. It also took a long time because I didn't know what I was doing. I was about two years into the novel when I realized I was a writer – not because I thought the novel would even be published, but because sentence by sentence and paragraph by paragraph I was beginning to see that I had abilities I hadn't demonstrated in earlier work, that is, in short stories I'd written when I was younger. I had a feeling that I could not solve the structural problems in *Americana*, but it didn't disturb me. Once I realized that I was good enough to be a professional writer, I simply kept going in the somewhat blind belief that nature would eventually take its course.

I started work on *End Zone* just weeks after I finished *Americana*. The long-drawn-out, somewhat aimless experience of writing *Americana* was immediately replaced by a quick burst of carefully directed activity. I did *End Zone* in about one-fourth the time it had taken me to write *Americana*.

At what point were you able to earn your living as a fiction writer?

Starting with *End Zone*, I stopped doing every other kind of writing.

Movies frequently come up in your work. When did they become significant for you?

I began to understand the force that movies could have emotionally and intellectually in what I consider the great era of the European films: Godard, Antonioni, Fellini, Bergman. And American directors as well – Kubrick and Howard Hawks and others.

What did you find inspirational about those directors?

Well, they seem to fracture reality. They find mystery in commonplace moments. They find humor in even the gravest political acts. They seem to find an art and a seriousness which I think was completely unexpected and which had once been the province of literature alone. So that a popular art was suddenly seen as a serious art. And this was interesting and inspiring.

Both The Names *and* Ratner's Star *are pretty exacting texts. Is the difficulty of those books part of a commitment you feel you need to demand from readers?*

From this perspective, I can see that the reader would have to earn his way into *Ratner's Star*, but this was not something I'd been trying to do. I did not have a clear sense of how difficult this book might turn out to be. I just followed my idea chapter by chapter and character by character. It seems to me that *Ratner's Star* is a book which is almost all structure. The structure of the book is the book. The characters are intentionally flattened and cartoon-like. I was trying to build a novel which was not only about mathematics to some extent but which itself would become a piece of mathematics. It would be a book which embodied pattern and order and harmony, which is one of the traditional goals of pure mathematics.

In *The Names*, I spent a lot of time searching for the kind of sun-cut precision I found in Greek light and in the Greek landscape. I wanted a prose which would have the clarity and the accuracy which the natural environment at its best in that part of the world seems to inspire in our own senses. There were periods in Greece when I tasted and saw and heard with much more sharpness and clarity than I'd ever done before or since. And I wanted to discover a sentence, a way of writing sentences that would be the prose counterpart to that clarity – that sensuous clarity of the Aegean experience. Those were my conscious goals in those two books.

It's rather uncommon for contemporary writers not to give readings or teach. Why don't you do those things?

Well, the simplest answer is the true one: I never liked school. Why go back now? I simply never wanted to teach. I never felt I had anything worth saying to students. I felt that whatever value my work has is something of a mystery to me. Although I could discuss with limited success what devices I've used to build certain structures in my books, I wouldn't know how to help other writers fulfill their own visions. And besides I'm lazy.

Do you have a sense, because of the extreme issues raised in your work, that one part of your readership is drawn from the fringes of American society?

Yeah, one segment of my readership is marginal, but beyond that, I find it hard to analyze the mail I get and make any conclusions as to what kind of readers I have. Certainly, *White Noise* found a lot of women readers, and I don't think too many women had been reading my books before that. So I really can't generalize. In the past, I got a lot of letters from people who seemed slightly unbalanced. This hasn't been happening for the past three or four years. It seems that the '80s have been somewhat more sane than the '70s, based on my own limited experience of measuring letters from readers.

In The Names *and some of your other books, language itself seems to be one of your subjects. That self-referential quality parallels a lot of theoretical work being done in philosophy and literary criticism these days. Do you read much writing of that kind?*

No, I don't. It is just my sense that we live in a kind of circular or near-circular system and that there are an increasing number of rings which keep intersecting at some point, whether you're using a plastic card to draw money out of your account at an automatic teller machine or thinking about the movement of planetary bodies. I mean, these systems all seem to interact to me. But I view all this in the most general terms, and I have no idea what kind of scientific studies are taking place. The secrets within systems, I suppose, are things that have informed my work. But they're almost secrets of consciousness, or ways in which consciousness is replicated in the natural world.

There also seems to be a fascination with euphemism and jargon in your books; for example, the poisonous cloud of gas that creates an environmental disaster in White Noise *is repeatedly referred to as the "airborne toxic event."*

It's a language that almost holds off reality while at the same time trying to fit it into a formal pattern. The interesting thing about jargon is that if it lives long enough, it stops being jargon and becomes part of natural speech, and we all find ourselves using it. We might all be disposed to use phrases like "time frame," which, when it was first used during the Watergate investigation, had an almost evil aura to it, because it was uttered by men we had learned to distrust so deeply.

I don't think of language in a theoretical way. I approach it at street level. That is, I listen carefully to the way people speak. I find that the closer a writer comes to portraying actual speech, the more stylized it seems on the page, so that the reader may well conclude that this is a formal experiment in dialogue instead of a simple transcription, which it actually is. When I started writing *Players*, my idea was to fill the novel with the kind of intimate, casual, off-the-cuff speech between close friends or husbands and wives. This was the whole point of the book as far as I was concerned. But somehow, I got sidetracked almost immediately and found myself describing a murder on the floor of the stock exchange, and of course from that point the book took a completely different direction. Nevertheless, in *Players*, there is still a sense of speech as it actually falls from the lips of people. And I did that again in *Libra*. In this case, I wasn't translating spoken speech as much as the printed speech of people who testified before the Warren Commission. Marguerite Oswald has an extremely unique way of speaking, and I didn't have to invent this at all. I simply had to read it and then remake it, rehear it for the purposes of the particular passage I was writing.

Often your characters are criticized for being unrealistic – children who speak like adults or, as in Ratner's Star, *characters whose consciousnesses seem at points to blur one into the other. How do you view your characters?*

Probably *Libra* is the exception to my work in that I tried a little harder to connect motivation with action. This is because there is an official record – if not of motivation, at least of action on the part of so many characters in the book. So it had to make a certain amount of sense, and what sense was missing I tried to supply. For example, why did Oswald shoot President Kennedy? I don't think anyone knows, but in the book, I've attempted to fill in that gap, although not at all in a specific way.

There's no short answer to the question. You either find yourself entering a character's life and consciousness or you don't, and in much modern fiction I don't think you are required to, either as a writer or a reader. Many modern characters have a flattened existence – purposely – and many modern characters exist precisely nowhere. There isn't a strong sense of place in much modern writing. Again, this is where I differ from what we could call the mainstream. I do feel a need and a drive to paint a kind of thick surface around my characters. I think all my novels have a strong sense of place.

But in contemporary writing in general, there's a strong sense that the world of Beckett and Kafka has redescended on contemporary America, because characters seem to live in a theoretical environment rather than a real one. I haven't felt that I'm part of that. I've always had a grounding in the real world, whatever esoteric flights I might indulge in from time to time.

There seems to be a fondness in your writing, particularly in White Noise, *for what might be described as the trappings of suburban middle-class existence, to the point where one of the characters describes the supermarket as a sacred place.*

I would call it a sense of the importance of daily life and of ordinary moments. In *White Noise*, in particular, I tried to find a kind of radiance in dailiness. Sometimes this radiance can be almost frightening. Other times it can be almost holy or sacred. Is it really there? Well, yes. You know, I don't believe as Murray Jay Siskind does in *White Noise* that the supermarket is a form of Tibetan lamasery. But there is something there that we tend to miss.

Imagine someone from the third world who has never set foot in a place like that suddenly transported to an A&P in Chagrin Falls, Ohio. Wouldn't he be elated or frightened? Wouldn't he sense that something transcending is about to happen to him in the midst of all this brightness? So that's something that has been in the background of my work: a sense of something extraordinary hovering just beyond our touch and just beyond our vision.

Hitler and the Holocaust have repeatedly been addressed in your books. In Running Dog, *a pornographic movie allegedly filmed in Hitler's bunker determines a good deal of the novel's plot. In* White Noise, *university professor Jack Gladney attempts to calm his obsessive fear of death through his work in the Department of Hitler Studies.*

In his case, Gladney finds a perverse form of protection. The damage caused by Hitler was so enormous that Gladney feels he can disappear inside it and that his own puny dread will be overwhelmed by the vastness, the monstrosity of Hitler himself. He feels that Hitler is not only bigger than life, as we say of many famous figures, but bigger than death. Our sense of fear – we avoid it because we feel it so deeply, so there is an intense conflict at work. I brought this conflict to the surface in the shape of Jack Gladney.

I think it is something we all feel, something we almost never talk about, something that is *almost* there. I tried to relate it in *White Noise* to this other sense of transcendence that lies just beyond our touch. This extraordinary wonder of things is somehow related to the extraordinary dread, to the death fear we try to keep beneath the surface of our perceptions.

What was the idea in Running Dog *of locating the pornographic movie in Hitler's bunker?*

Well, this made it an object of ultimate desirability and ultimate dread, simply because it connected to Hitler. When the Hitler diaries "surfaced," in quotes, in the early '80s, there was even a more berserk reaction to them than there was to this film in *Running Dog*. If anything, I was slightly innocent about my sense of what would happen if such an object emerged. What I was really getting at in *Running Dog* was a sense of the terrible acquisitiveness in which we live, coupled with a final indifference to the object. After all the mad attempts to acquire the thing, everyone suddenly decides that, well, maybe we really don't care about this so much anyway. This was something I felt characterized our lives at the time the book was written, in the mid to late '70s. I think this was part of American consciousness then.

What about the fascination with children in your books?

Well, I think we feel, perhaps superstitiously, that children have a more direct route to the kind of natural truth that eludes us as adults. In *The Names*, the father is transported by what he sees as a kind of deeper truth underlying the language his son uses in writing his stories. He sees misspellings and misused words as reflecting a kind of reality that he as an adult couldn't possibly grasp. And he relates this to the practice of speaking in tongues, which itself is what we might call an alternate reality. It's a fabricated language which seems to have a certain pattern to it. It isn't just gibberish. It isn't language, but it isn't gibberish either. And I think this is the way Axton felt about his own son's writing. And I think this is the way we feel about children in general. There is something they know but can't tell us. Or there is something they remember which we've forgotten.

Glossolalia or speaking in tongues could be viewed as a higher form of infantile babbling. It's babbling which seems to mean something, and this is intriguing.

Ratner's Star, *which has a child as its central character, seems to juxtapose the intense rationality of science with a variety of mystical experiences, like speaking in tongues.*

Well, *Ratner's Star* is almost a study of opposites, yes. Only because I think anyone who studies the history of mathematics finds that the link between the strictest scientific logic and other mysticism seems to exist. This is something any true scientist might tend to deny, but so many mathematicians, in earlier centuries anyway, were mystical about numbers, about the movements of heavenly bodies and so forth, while at the same time being accomplished scientists. And this strange connection of opposites found its way into *Ratner's Star*. Modern physicists seem to be moving toward nearly mystical explanations of the ways in which elements in the subatomic world and in the galaxy operate. There seems to be something happening.

You've been denounced as a member of the paranoid left. Do you have a sense of your books as political?

No, I don't. Politics plays a part in some of my books, but this is usually because the characters are political. I don't have a political theory or doctrine that I'm espousing. *Libra* obviously is saturated with politics, of necessity. Certainly the left-wing theories of Oswald do not coincide with my own. I don't have a program. I follow characters where they take me and I don't know what I can say beyond that.

How do you assess your own works? Are there specific ones that you feel are your best or your favorites?

My feeling is that the novels I've written in the 1980s – *The Names*, *White Noise*, and *Libra* – are stronger books than the six novels I published in the '70s. This may be what every writer feels about more recent works. But I think the three novels I've written in this decade were more deeply motivated and required a stronger sense of commitment than some of the books I wrote earlier, like *Running Dog* and possibly *Great Jones Street*, which I set out to write because I had become anxious about the amount of time that had passed since I finished my previous book and I wanted to get back to work. I think one of the things I've learned through experience is that it isn't enough to want to get back to work. The other thing I've learned is that no amount of experience can prevent you from making a major mistake. I think it can help you avoid smaller mistakes. But the potential for a completely misconceived book still exists.

There's something of an apocalyptic feel about your books, an intimation that our world is moving toward greater randomness and dissolution, or maybe even cataclysm. Do you see this process as irreversible?

It could change tomorrow. This is the shape my books take because this is the reality I see. This reality has become part of all our lives over the past 25 years. I don't know how we can deny it.

I don't think *Libra* is a paranoid book at all. I think it's a clear-sighted, reasonable piece of work that takes into account the enormous paranoia which has ensued from the assassination. I can say the same thing about some of my other books. They're *about* movements or feelings in the air and in the culture around us, without necessarily being *part* of the particular movement. I mean, what I sense is suspicion and distrust and fear, and so, of course, these things inform my books. It's my idea of myself as a writer – perhaps mistaken – that I enter these worlds as a completely rational person who is simply taking what he senses all around him and using it as material.

You've spoken of the redemptive quality of fiction. Do you see your books as offering an alternative to the dark reality you detect?

Well, strictly in theory, art is one of the consolation prizes we receive for having lived in a difficult and sometimes chaotic world. We seek pattern in art that eludes us in natural experience. This isn't to say that art has to be comforting; obviously, it can be deeply disturbing. But nothing in *Libra* can begin to approach the level of disquiet and dread characterized by the assassination itself.

A shorter version of this interview appeared in Rolling Stone, *November 17, 1988, and a longer version appeared in* South Atlantic Quarterly *89 (1990).*

Martin Scorsese

"The ring becomes an allegory of whatever you do in life"

When I grew up in Greenwich Village in the '50s and early '60s, the neighborhood was not the bohemian theme park that it is today. Of course, there was a strong, long-standing, and genuine bohemian presence – the writers, painters, poets, beats, and political progressives who constituted the reverse image of the mainstream '50s of conformity and McCarthyism. There was also a significant, though subterranean, gay presence, one that would explode onto the surface in the late '60s after a riot at a bar on Christopher Street called the Stonewall.

But the Village that I grew up in was an Italian neighborhood, a place where you were defined by what parish you lived in, where everybody went to church on Sundays and the kids went to Catholic schools, where the streets were lined with fruit and vegetable stands, and where everybody knew that if your apartment was robbed, if your purse was stolen, if anything went wrong, you didn't call the police, you went to the mob. The mob guys hung out in bakeries, in barbershops, in the storefronts with blackened windows they called social clubs. These guys hated problems in the neighborhood that were not specifically connected to their own activities – such problems only served to confuse things, antagonize the bought police, and create more problems. They would listen to you and, in order to enforce the notion that only certain types of crimes were permitted in this neighborhood, they often would help you.

The instinctive clannishness of the immigrant community, the code of silence that ruled all mob-related activities, and the simple fact that in this country, then or now, the lives and needs of working-class, ethnic people – too isolated, untrusting, and proud to make demands of the government, too unpolished and prole for the right wing, too independent and unfashionable for the left – don't matter much, created the sense that, in terms of the larger world around us, we didn't exist. In the eyes of others, we were invisible.

This was especially true for the children and grandchildren of the Italians who came here from the old country. The old-timers – the "greaseballs," the ones who, as we used to say, still seemed as if they "just got off the boat" – simply recreated, to as great a degree as possible, the lives they had lived in Italy. But we, their offspring, grew up with television and the New World imperative to invent a "better" life. We were taught not to speak Italian, to obey the authorities, to do well in school. We were the hyphenates: Italian-Americans. My father, not a man especially known for his restraint, would stop a roomful of conversation dead if he happened to overhear someone call me Tony. "His name is Anthony," he would announce absolutely. "Tony is a hoodlum's name."

But in our rage, we became hoodlums anyway. No one – at least no one we knew, least of all our parents and grandparents – had the slightest idea how anything really worked, how we were really supposed to create our New World lives. The old country receded, but America – the land where Americans lived – seemed no less foreign than it ever had. Our grade schools – Our Lady of Pompeii, in my case – were jails of discipline, repression, and superstition. We lived nowhere but the streets, but we owned the streets. We'd get high, occasionally steal, indulge in exultant vandalism, but our primary rush was violence.

Essentially, the subjects of our violence were people who lived in the American culture from which we felt excluded. Given where we lived, we engaged in some perfunctory gay-bashing, though the gay men fought back – the spark that would eventually kindle the Stonewall? – which greatly discouraged and frightened us. The main problem with gay-bashing, however, was that, despite how it shored up our sexual identities, it didn't provide much of a kick. In some deep way, we understood that the gays, after all, were ultimately as excluded as we were. What could it mean, therefore, to victimize them?

Our enemies, then, in this class war became people whom we called "tourists," a category that applied to anyone who walked the streets of our neighborhood and who was white, middle- or upper-class, and seemed to have more opportunities than we did. They were people we envied and, while we affected a streetwise condescension toward them, we in fact hated them. While it often seemed emotionally useful to have women watch us intimidate and assault their escorts, we never attacked women. Too easy, and sex wasn't the point. Nor did we rob anyone. That seemed petty, beneath us. It wasn't about money.

It was about exerting control over our streets, violence for the sheer, ecstatic fun of it, for the explosion of release. It was wilding. If we were aimless, if we had no idea where we were going, we would make it dangerous to go where we were. If we were invisible, we would enforce our presence, make ourselves matter.

Long after I had left that world behind – the police were becoming too intolerant of our mayhem; I had too many troubling memories of people we'd hurt – and consciously determined, as a friend put it, "that it was upward-mobility time," I saw *Mean Streets* by Martin Scorsese. Scorsese had grown up nearby, in Little Italy, the neighborhood next door. The kids from that neighborhood were at least as bad as we were, but we regarded them as hicks, sort of the way northern Italians to this day regard Sicilians, or urban Italians regard their rural compatriots. Even so, *Mean Streets* was the first time I had seen the world I had known growing up represented in a work of art. I was so astounded that virtually every other aspect of the movie was lost on me. Here was someone who clearly shared all the contradictory feelings of coming from a place that continued to mean so much, even while, for hundreds of reasons, it had to be judged and rejected. Rejected, but acknowledged. Acknowledged, and perhaps even honored.

From that point on, the films of Martin Scorsese haunted me. For me, watching *Mean Streets* (1973), *Raging Bull* (1980), or *GoodFellas* (1990) is like looking through an album of photographs from my youth, like disappearing into a world of my past – a world that still, in many ways, for better or worse, often seems more substantial than the worlds I move in now. I was thinking about all this when I went to interview Martin Scorsese in the fall of 1990, shortly before *GoodFellas* opened.

✦ ✦ ✦ ✦ ✦

Martin Scorsese's apartment sits 75 floors above midtown Manhattan and offers an imperial view that encompasses Central Park and the Upper East Side and extends out toward the borough of Queens, where Scorsese was born in 1942. The calming grays and blacks and whites of the living room's decor combine with the apartment's Olympian height – so high as to eliminate almost all street noise – to make New York City seem a distant abstraction, a silent movie playing in Martin Scorsese's picture window. *Mean Streets* it's not.

For *Mean Streets*, you would have to go to the roof and look the other way, behind you, down toward Little Italy, the Italian ghetto on the Lower East Side where Scorsese came of age in the '50s and '60s. Scorsese returned to that neighborhood – or at least to a virtually identical neighborhood in the East New York section of Brooklyn – with *GoodFellas*, which is based on Nicholas Pileggi's book *Wiseguy* about the middle-level Irish-Sicilian mobster Henry Hill and his 25-year career in the criminal underworld.

The movie reunited Scorsese with his homeboy, Robert De Niro, for the first time since *The King of Comedy*, in 1982, and assembles a veritable who's who of superb Italian-American film stars, including Ray Liotta, Joe Pesci, Lorraine Bracco, and Paul Sorvino. Scorsese himself wrote the screenplay with Pileggi. Grisly, funny, violent, and riddled with moral questions posed by matters of loyalty, betrayal, and personal honor, *GoodFellas* also returned Scorsese to the themes that pump at the heart of some of his most urgent films, most notably *Mean Streets* (1973), *Taxi Driver* (1975), and *Raging Bull* (1980).

Though the usually dapper Scorsese is casually dressed in jeans and a faded blue shirt, he is anything but relaxed for the interview. He didn't realize the interview would involve so much time – at least two hours. What about the other things he'd arranged to do? His two daughters, Catherine and Domenica, would soon be coming by the apartment (he had recently separated from his fourth wife, Barbara De Fina). He needs to make some phone calls, change some things around, work some things out. After we start to talk, he moves back and forth between a chair that serves as something of a command center – located, as it is, next to a phone and a movie projector and opposite a wall with a pull-down screen on it – and a place closer to me on the white couch.

Scorsese speaks in the style of a born-and-bred New Yorker. He formulates his thoughts out loud, as if they were terrifically important but continually in flux, in need of constant refinement. Asked a question, he starts talking immediately, stops abruptly, starts and stops again and again until he finds his groove. He gestures for punctuation and emphasis, fires off staccato bursts of insight when he's on a roll, laughs wildly at his own improbable characterizations and verbal excesses. At times, the sheer nervous energy of his intellect propels him out of his seat, and he speaks while standing at his full height – he's quite short – for a minute or two. He walks over to a cabinet several times for nasal and throat sprays to ease the effects of the asthma that has afflicted him since childhood. He alternately concentrates on me with a ferocious intensity and seems to forget I'm there at all.

A filmmaker in a kind of tumultuous internal exile, Scorsese sits edgily poised in splendid isolation over the city that remains one of his most fertile obsessions – and looks to the future with hope and apprehension.

I want to start with GoodFellas. *Obviously you have returned to some familiar terrain. What brought you to that specific project?*

I read a review of *Wiseguy* back when I was directing *The Color of Money* in Chicago, and it said something about this character, Henry Hill, having access to many different levels of organized crime because he was somewhat of an outsider. He looked a little nicer. He was able to be a better front man and speak a little better. I thought that was interesting. You could move in and get a cross section of the layers of organized crime – from his point of view of course.

It's a version.

It's his perception of the truth. Where if somebody gets shot in a room and there's five people who witnessed it, you'll probably have five different stories as to how it happened. So I got the book and I started reading it and I was fascinated by the narrative ability of it, the narrative approach.

Henry has a real voice.

He's got a wonderful voice and he has a wonderful way of expressing the lifestyle. He reminds me of a lot of the people that I grew up around. It had a great sense of humor, too. So I said, "This will make a wonderful film." I figured to do it as if it was one long trailer, where you just propel the action and you get an exhilaration, a rush of the lifestyle.

That acceleration at the end of the film is amazing. When Henry is driving around like a madman, blasted on cocaine, trying to deal for guns and drugs while the police helicopter is following him, and, through it all, he keeps calling home to make sure his brother is stirring the sauce properly for dinner that night.

Yeah. The sauce is as important as the helicopter. That's a whole comment about drugs, too. When I read about that last day in the book, I said I'd like to just take that and make it the climax of the film. Actually, the real climax is him and Jimmy in the diner. A very quiet moment.

When you talk about the world you grew up in, as it happens, it is virtually the same world I grew up in. I went to Our Lady of Pompeii in Greenwich Village.

Great!

On Bleecker Street.

It was the West Side, though. You were on the West Side. That's a funny thing, on the East Side, we didn't have the influx of other cultures, that very important bohemian culture.

My family was Italian and working class – I wasn't part of that. I grew up in a world as enclosed as the one that you describe. But there was always this sense that there was something else. I mean, when I was a kid, the Village Voice *office was around the corner. So when it got to the point where like, as kids, everybody was getting in trouble with the police, I had a very clear vision that there was some way out.*

That there was another world. We didn't know that.

It's a very clear distinction. The bohemian world of the Village was like another world, even though you only lived a few blocks from the Village.

I never went to the Village until I enrolled at NYU in 1960. I grew up on the East Side. From 1950 to 1960, for 10 years, I never ventured past Houston Street, past Broadway and Houston. My father took me on a bus when I was five years old or something. I remember Washington Square. I was on a double-decker bus. And I remember a friend of mine,

I was about nine years old, his mother took us to the Village on a little tour to see the little houses and flowers. It was like a wonderland, because they had flowers. It was a very different culture.

I was used to wonderful stuff, too, on Elizabeth Street, which was five grocery stores, three butcher shops all on one block. Two barbershops. And it was barrels of olives – which was great. Growing up down there was like being in a Sicilian village culture. It was great. But you come from there so you know. It's complicated to explain to people who didn't grow up in it.

It is. When I'm trying to tell people about it, I refer to your movies. I don't know any other representations of it.

A good friend I grew up with just sent me a letter. He just saw *GoodFellas* and he said he had just spent a sleepless night remembering what a great and incredible escape we both made from that area, from that whole lifestyle.

I first saw Mean Streets *after I had left New York to go to graduate school in Indiana. I had never been west of New Jersey, and I saw* Mean Streets...

In Indiana!

And it was like, "Wow, somebody got it. There it is."

That's the whole story of *Mean Streets*. I mean, I put it on the screen. It took me years to get it going – I never thought the film would be released. I just wanted to make an anthropological study; it was about myself and my friends. And I figured even if it was on a shelf, some years later people would take it and say that's what Italian-Americans were like on the everyday scale – not the Godfather, not big bosses, but the everyday level. This is what they really talked like and looked like and what they did in the early '70s and late '60s. Early '60s even. This was the lifestyle.

Why was it important to do that? To document that?

Oh, you know – myself. Why does anybody do anything? You think you're important so you do a film about yourself. Or if you're a writer, you write a novel about yourself or about your own experiences. I guess it's the old coming-of-age story.

Actually, there were two of them for me: *Who's That Knocking on My Door?* and *Mean Streets. Who's That Knocking* I never got right, except for the emotional aspects of it – I got that.

I watched it recently and was struck by how strong it was. How do you feel about it at this point?

I dislike it. Only because it took me three years to make. And we'd make the film and we'd work on a weekend and then for three weeks we wouldn't shoot and then we'd work another weekend. So it wasn't really a professional film to make. It took three years to make. The first year, '65, I cast it. We did all the scenes with the young boys and we had a young lady playing the part of the girl. But later on we came up to about an hour and ten minutes and there was no confrontation. The young girl was always seen in flashbacks and asides. It was all between the boys. So you never understood what was happening between the Harvey Keitel character and the girl. The conflict was, of course, being in love with a girl who is an outsider, loving her so much that you respect her and you won't make love to her. Then he finds out she's not a virgin and he can't accept that. It's that whole Italian-American way of thinking.

Finally, we got it released by '69, when we were able to put a nude scene in it. In 1968, we shot a nude scene. In '68, there was a new tolerance about nude scenes. Very old, wonderful actors and actresses were playing scenes in the nude – it was very embarrassing. We had to get a nude scene. We shot it in Holland, because I was up in Amsterdam doing some commercials for a friend. We flew Harvey over and we got the young ladies there and we did this nude scene. I kind of smuggled it back into the country in my raincoat, put it in the middle of the film, and then the film was released. But it was still a rough sketch to me. It's the old story: if I knew then what I know now, it would be different.

One of the most interesting parts of the movie is the sexual fantasy sequence while the Doors's "The End" is playing.

Well, that was the scene done in Amsterdam. That was fun.

The Oedipal drama in the song underscores the Oedipal struggle of the Keitel character. Using that song also captures the way that you were profoundly affected by what was going on culturally in the '60s. But for the characters in your movies, the '60s don't seem to exist. Their world is...

Medieval! Medieval. Well, that's the thing. When I was about to release the film, we were having a problem getting a distributor and my agents at William Morris said to me, "Marty, what do you expect? You have a film here in which the guy loves a young woman so much that he respects her and he won't make love to her. Here we are in the age of the sexual revolution, and you're making a movie about repression! Total sexual repression. Who's going to see it? Nobody."

Yeah, that was my life. When I went to Woodstock in '69, it was the first time I started wearing jeans – afterwards. I took cufflinks; I lost one of the cufflinks. Certainly it was having come from that neighborhood and living there completely closed in, like in a ghetto area, not really leaving till the early '60s to go to the West Side. So I had one foot in the university and the other foot in *Mean Streets*. I became aware of other people in the world and other lifestyles, other views, political and otherwise, much later. But I was quite closed off. It was like somebody coming out of the Middle Ages going to a university.

In a documentary that was done about you, you said that you would see certain things when you were young and you would say, "Why don't you ever see this in a movie?" I was wondering about what it was you were seeing, or what you felt was missing then in the movies?

It is the way people behaved. I'd be sitting and watching something on television. My uncles would be in the room. My mother would be there. One of my uncles would say, "That wouldn't happen that way. What would really happen is such and such. He would do this and she would leave him and the guy would kill the other guy." They would work up their own versions of the film noir that we were watching, and they were actually much better. And it had to do with what was based in reality. What would really happen.

That's an interesting aspect about your movies. Obviously you're completely soaked in film history and you've seen a million movies. But your movies never become just movies about movies. There's never anything cute or clever about them. Even when Henry in GoodFellas *says, when the police are coming for him, that things don't happen the way they do "in the movies," it doesn't seem contrived. Of course, you got that from the book.*

I was going to take that out, but I left it in because I felt it had more of an honesty to it. I always find that sort of thing too cute or too self-conscious – though I don't mind being self-conscious at all. I like Joseph Losey's films. You see the camera moving, it's very self-conscious. But it took me years to understand the precision of it and the beauty of that. And I don't mind the self-conscious aspect. What I do mind is pretending that you're not watching a movie. That's absurd. You are watching a movie and it is a movie.

But Henry did say, "They don't come to you like you usually see in movies." So he's not talking about this movie. He's talking about other movies that you see. And I was even thinking of saying, "I know you're watching this as a movie now." I was even thinking of putting that in. Then I said, no, it gets too – what's the word for that? – maybe academic to get into that. There's a falseness about that that I wanted to avoid.

That approach to things relates well to the subterranean world you deal with in GoodFellas *and some of your other movies. You depict a real world of consequences, in which people don't get a lot of chances to make mistakes. There is a clear sense that if you step out of line, if you do the wrong thing, you're going to pay for it.*

That's very important. These guys are in business to make money, not to kill people, not to create mayhem. They really want to make money. If you make a big mistake, you bring down heat on them, you bring attention to them, you cause strife between two crime families, somebody has to be eliminated. It's very simple. Those are the rules. You can't make that many big mistakes. You don't rise in the hierarchy if you do. It's very much like a Hollywood situation where how many pictures could you make that cost $40 million that lose every dime? You can't. It's purely common sense. And so they work out their own little elaborate set of rules and codes.

It's also a means of working out a certain version of the American dream. Henry says he'd rather be a wise guy than be the president of the United States.

It's better, because you can do anything you want. And you can take anything you want, because, like Henry says, if they complain, you hit them. It's very simple. And this is the great country for it, because the opportunity here is endless.

However, I always quote Joe Pesci, who pointed out that wise guys have a life cycle – or an enjoyment cycle – of maybe eight or nine years, ten years the most, before they either get killed or go to jail and start that long process of going in and out like a revolving door. I try to give an impression of that in the film when Henry gets to jail and says, "Paulie was there because he was serving time for contempt. Jimmy was in another place. Johnny Dio was there." This is like home for them. Then the life begins to wear you down. The first few years are the exuberance of youth. They have a great time – until they start to pay for it. Tommy [DeVito, played by Pesci] starts doing things, just unnecessary outbursts. Look why Jimmy [Conway, played by De Niro] goes to jail – because he beats up some guy down in Florida. It's a long story in the book; in the film, it's totally unimportant as to why they're even there. We did it so quickly to show you how, just as fast as it happened, that's as fast as he could go to jail for something he forgot he did.

Tommy and Jimmy in GoodFellas *are, like Travis Bickle in* Taxi Driver *(1976) and Jake La Motta in* Raging Bull, *walking powder kegs. What interests you about characters like that?*

There are a thousand answers to that. It's interesting. It's good drama. And you see part of yourself in that. I like to chart a character like that, see how far they go before they self-destruct. How it starts to turn against them after a while – whether it's shooting people in the street or arguing in the home, in the kitchen and the bedroom. How soon the breaking point comes when everything just explodes and they're left alone.

You once said that the La Motta character in Raging Bull *never really has to face himself until he's alone in his prison cell, hitting his head against the wall.*

Totally. That's the one he's been paranoid about all along. I mean, it gets to be so crazy. If his brother, and if Tommy Como, and if Salvie and if Vicky did everything he thought they did, he can do one of two things: kill them all or let it go. If you let it go, it's not the end of the world. But, no, no, he's got to battle it out in the ring. He's got to battle it out at home. He's got to battle it everywhere until finally he's got to deal with that point where everybody else has disappeared from him and he's dealing with himself. He didn't let it go. Ultimately it's *you.*

Is that the source of all that violence, of all that paranoia and anger?

Oh, I think it comes from yourself. Obviously, it comes from Jake. It comes from your feelings about yourself. And it comes from what you do for a living. In his case, he goes out in the morning and he beats up people. And then they beat him up and then he comes home. It's horrible. It's life on its most primitive level.

But that doesn't account for the sexual paranoia.

Well, yeah. I don't know if it does. But I am not a psychiatrist. It just comes from the fact that the guy is in the ring and you feel a certain way about yourself. When you're punching it out, you feel a certain way about yourself. You could take anyone, you see; the ring becomes an allegory of whatever you do in life. You make movies, you're in the ring each time. Writing music – if you perform it, you're in the ring. Or people just living daily life, when they go to their work – they're in the ring. And it's how you feel about yourself that colors your feelings about everything else around you. If you don't feel good about yourself, it takes in everything that you're doing – the way your work is, the people who supposedly love you, your performance of lovemaking – everything. You begin to chip away at yourself and you become like a raw wound. And if a man spits across the street, you say he spat at you. And then you're finished. Because then nobody can make a move. You'll think: "Why did you look at me that way?" Who's going to be with you? Who can stay with you?

At the end of GoodFellas, *you leave Henry in a more problematic spot than the book itself does. Is there any reason for that?*

It's not about Henry, really; it's about the lifestyle. Henry's the one who gives us the in; he opens the door for us, but basically, it's about all these people. He's just left out in God knows where, annoyed because he's not a wise guy anymore. I was more interested in the irony of that. There wasn't a last paragraph in the book saying, "Now I know what I did. I was a bad guy, and I'm really sorry for it" – none of that. Just, "Gee, I can't get the right food here." It's right in line with when he says as a kid, "I didn't have to wait in line for bread at the bakery." It's the American way – getting treated special. It's really a film about that. It's a film about getting to a position where you don't have to wait in line to get served in a store.

A significant issue in the arts in recent years – particularly in your case, with The Last Temptation of Christ *(1998) and* Taxi Driver *– has been various attempts at censorship. What are your feelings about that?*

Obviously, I'm for freedom of expression. I was very glad that *The Last Temptation of Christ* was able to be made by an American company, that I didn't have to go to Europe or to some other country to get the money for it. That's what this country is about, to be able to do something you believe in. I'm for freedom of expression, but in each generation, there are threats to it, and you have to keep battling and fighting. I'm concerned about the educational system because it seems to be at a low level at this point in our history, and a lot of kids are not learning about this, are not learning that they have to fight for this freedom in this country. I don't necessarily mean going to the Mideast. I'm talking about fighting for it at home, fighting for it in your school, fighting for it in your church. Because they have a low level of education, many people are not going to know that. They're going to take it for granted and it's going to become worse and worse of a problem, and there's going to be fewer people to make sure that we secure these rights, to take the right stand.

That's all I'm concerned about. I don't like a lot of the stuff I see – it's offensive to me. But that's what it's about. You have to let it go. As far as my way of dealing with subject matter, I can't let anybody tell me, "Don't do that, it will offend people."

On one level, when I'm dealing with a Hollywood film, I have to do a certain kind of subject matter that will make a certain amount of money. If I decide to make less money, I can take a risk on subject matter. So the only criterion on the films I'm willing to take risks on is that it be honest about your own feelings and truthful to what you know to be the reality around you or the reality of the human condition of the characters. If you don't believe in it, why are you making it? You're going to offend people to make some money? What for? It doesn't mean anything. The money doesn't mean anything. All that matters is the work, just what's up on the screen. So that's it. I'm not like some great person who's out there undaunted, fighting off all these people. I didn't think any of this stuff would really cause trouble – let alone *Taxi Driver*. *The Last Temptation*, I knew there would be some problems, but that's a special area for me. I demand that I get to speak out the way I feel about it, even within the Catholic Church. Some of my close friends are priests and we talk about it. I just heard from one today, and they support me.

But you must think about the potential impact of your movies. I remember your saying that you were shocked when audiences responded in an almost vigilante fashion to the end of Taxi Driver.

To *The Wild Bunch*, too, they reacted that way. I was kind of shocked.

It would suggest there's some kind of fissure between your moral and spiritual concerns and how the films are perceived.

No, I went to see the film that night and they were reacting very strongly to the shoot-out sequence in *Taxi Driver*. And I was disturbed by that. It wasn't done with that intent. You can't stop people from taking it that way. What can you do? And you can't stop people from getting an exhilaration from violence, because that's human, very much the same way as you get an exhilaration from the violence in *The Wild Bunch*. But the exhilaration of the violence at the end of *The Wild Bunch* and the violence that's in *Taxi Driver* – because it's shot a certain way, and I know how it's shot, because I shot it and designed it – is also in the creation of that scene in the editing, in the camera moves, in the use of music and the use of sound effects, and in the movement within the frame of the characters. So it's like…art – good art, bad art, or indifferent – whatever the hell you want to say it is, it's still art. And that's where the exhilaration comes in. The shoot-out at the end of *The*

Wild Bunch is still one of the great exhilarating sequences in all movies, and it's also one of the great dance sequences in the movies. It's ballet.

Now *Taxi Driver* may be something else entirely, I don't know. The intent was not necessarily the reception I saw. I know it can't be the reaction of most of the people who have seen the picture. I was in China in '84 and a young man from Mongolia talked to me at length about *Taxi Driver*, about the loneliness. That's why the film seems to be something that people keep watching over and over. It's not the shoot-'em-out at the end.

Living in New York, obviously violence is around you all the time.

Oh, come on. I just took a cab on 57th Street, we're about to make a turn on Eighth Avenue, and three Puerto Rican guys are beating each other up over the cab. *Over* it – from my side, onto the hood, onto the other side. Now, this is just normal, to the point where the cabbie and myself don't say anything. He just makes his right turn and we move on.

But complaints about violence in your films don't bother you?

It's never stopped me. If I'm making a more commercial venture like *The Color of Money*, it's something else. It becomes a different kind of movie and I think you can see the difference. My new film will be something else. It's a more mainstream commercial film for Universal Pictures.

What are you doing?

It's a remake of *Cape Fear*, the 1962 film directed be J. Lee Thompson, with Robert Mitchum and Gregory Peck. Bob De Niro wants to do it. It's more of a commercial venture. You have a certain kind of responsibility to the audience on a picture like that because, number one, you have certain expectations from the thriller genre. You work within that framework and it's like a chess game. You see if you can really be expressive within it. I don't know if you can, because I always have that problem: loving the old films, I don't know if I can make them. You become more revisionist. *New York, New York* was obviously revisionist. But *The Color of Money* I went half and half, and it should have been one way.

New York, New York *pitted its period style against completely unnerving contemporary emotions in the plot.*

That was conscious. That was a love of the old stylization, a love of those films, but then showing what it really is like as close as possible in the foreground. That's what they call revisionism and that's why the picture – besides being too damn long, it's sprawling – didn't catch on.

Are there any new directions in which you'd like to move your work?

I have a lot of things in mind and I want to be able to branch out and go into other areas, different types of films, maybe some genre films. But there's no doubt, even if I find something that's dealing with New York society in the 18th century, I usually am attracted to characters that have similar attributes to characters in my other films. So I guess I keep going in the same direction. I'm fascinated by history and by anthropology. I'm fascinated by the idea of people in history, and history having been shown to us in such a way that people always come off as fake – not fake, but one-dimensional. And I'm interested in exploring what they felt and making them three-dimensional. To show that they're very similar to us. So just because the society around them and the world around them are very different, it doesn't mean that they didn't have the same feelings and the same desires, the same goals and the same things that haunt us in modern society. And in going into the past, maybe we can feel something about ourselves in the process.

It seems like that was a lot of the impetus behind The Last Temptation of Christ, *too, a desire to portray Christ in more three-dimensional terms.*

No doubt. To make him more like a person who would be in this room, who you could talk to.

There's a genuine concern with spiritual issues in your movies, at the same time there is also a brutal physicality. How do you square that?

It's just the struggle, that's all. The struggle to stay alive and to even want to stay alive. Just this corporal thing we're encased in and the limitations of it and how your spirit tries to spring out of it, fly away from it. And you can't. People say you can do it through poetry, you can do it through the work you do, and things like that. Thought. But you still feel imprisoned. So the body is what you deal with, and it's a struggle to keep that body alive.

You spend a great deal of time thinking about the world that you grew up in. But you are no longer part of that world. Does that create any complexities for you?

Oh, because you left it behind doesn't mean that you don't have it. It's what you come from. You have an affinity to it and very often you have a love of it, too. I can't exist there now. I don't belong there anymore. But I can damn well try to make sure that when I use it in a film like *GoodFellas*, I make it as truthful as possible. What's wrong with that? It's part of your life, and if you try to deny that, what good is it? A lot of what I learned about life came from there. So you go back and you keep unraveling it. For some people, it was the family; for other people it's the state. I don't know. Me, it was the subculture.

What things do you learn there?

People are usually the product of where they come from, whether you come from a small farm in Iowa and you had your best friend next door and you went swimming in the old swimming hole. In other words – whether you had an idyllic American childhood or you were a child in Russia or you were a child on the Lower East Side – the bonds you made, the codes that were there, all have a certain influence on you later on in your life. You can reject them. You can say, "OK, those codes don't exist for me anymore," but the reasons for those codes are very strong. The most important reason is survival. It's very simple. Food, safety, survival. It comes down to that. That struggle of the human form, the corporal, the flesh, to survive – anything to survive. And you learn in each society, it's done a different way. And all these rules are set up and you learn them and they never really leave you. It's what everybody learns when you're all kids in the street or in the park. Those things you carry with you the rest of your life.

And then, of course, it causes problems because your response to certain stimuli at that time was one way, and when you get the same sort of stimuli now, you've got to be very careful you don't respond in the street fashion. Because they're different people. They don't really mean it. It's very funny because it's like I've seen people do things to other people that I said, "My God, if a guy did that, if that woman did that to me or a friend of mine back in 1960 or in that neighborhood, they wouldn't be *alive*." And you have to realize it's a different world. You just learn how to get in and out of the moral inlets of this new world, whatever the hell it is. I don't know what it is. Basically, I'm here, in this building. I stay here. Here in this chair. That's it. I answer the phone. They let me out to make a movie. People come over to eat. I mean, I just do my work and see some very close friends. That's all. So that's what it comes down to. So in a funny way all the trauma of trying to find the new ways to react to the same stimuli in these new societies, it's kind of past me.

If you go to a cocktail party, someone comes over to you…and some strange *insult* occurs. You know, "How *dare you!*" In the old days, in those neighborhoods, certain people, if you stepped on the guy's *shoe*, you could die, let alone come over and *insult* him. He'd kill you. It's so funny. Oh you'd be surprised how the insults come – it's just wonderful what they do. And people wonder why you don't want to talk to anybody. But it's fascinating. One person in a university, in the academic world, was introduced to me. We were having a few drinks after the David Lean American Film Institute dinner, and the woman said, "I must say I'm an admirer of *some* of your films, because, after all, I am a woman." Who needs it? Look, I make a certain type of film and that does bring out certain things in certain people. What can I say? So you try to avoid it.

Don't you have a sense of losing touch with things?

No. You come from a certain time and place. I can't turn and say, "Well, gee, I'll only listen to rap music now." I can't. I still listen to older rock 'n' roll; I listen to the music that I like. You come from a certain time and place and you can't… Maybe there are some people who can – a painter or a novelist, let's say, or some filmmakers – who can keep up with the times and move along with what audiences expect today. I just think we are of a time, and the generations that come after us, we'll either still speak to them or we won't. We'll maybe miss two or three generations, and then a third or fourth generation will pick up what we did and it will mean something to them. But, I mean, you take a look at when you had the French New Wave and the Italian New Wave in the early '60s, with the jump cuts and the freeze frames, the destruction of the narrative form. You had a lot of Hollywood directors trying similar things, and it didn't work. And the guys whose work stayed strong are the ones who were not swayed by what was fashionable, who stayed true to themselves. And it's hard because they got rejected. Billy Wilder – everything from the mid '60s on was rejected. Especially, I think, one of his greatest pictures: *The Private Life of Sherlock Holmes*. There were a lot of others who tried these flashy techniques and now you look at their films and they don't come out of an honesty, they don't come out of a truthfulness. And I don't say they were phonies. But they were saying, "Hey, that's a new way of doing it, let's try that." But if you can't tell the story that way, tell it the way you know how to.

What do you think is the flash stuff now?

I think the formula – what do they call them? – high-concept pictures, probably. A high-concept picture has a basic theme. You can say it in one sentence: "A fish out of water." But high-concept pictures have been around for a long time under different guises. In some cases, they were very beautifully made vehicle films for certain kinds of stars. Bette Davis. Clint Eastwood. If you went to see a person, you knew what kind of film you were going to see. OK, there were a lot of films that were like that, but they had a little more style to them, they had better actors in them, they were better written. But now the more money that's spent on a film, the bigger the audience has to be. Which means it's got to make more money. So you've got to cut it down to the best common denominator that you can get – and probably the lowest – so that it reaches more people.

A lot of it is the flash kind of cutting that goes on. The man who broke that into films originally was Richard Lester with *A Hard Day's Night*. You really saw the influence of television commercials on the film, and it worked. And now, the influence of MTV, let's say, over the past eight years on movies, maybe the audience attention span is a bit of a problem now. Things have to move faster. And you feel that. But you can be true to yourself. You can really do it in this business, but it has to be for a price. Everything's for a price.

Your movies have been pioneering in their use of music, but now with MTV, everybody's using music.

Well, I think they're using it cheaply, unimaginatively. They're using it basically to say, "OK, it's 1956." They're using it to tell you which period you're in.

In your movies, the relation between the song and the scene takes on so many aspects. I was thinking about the scene in GoodFellas *where that corpse is rolling around in the garbage and the coda from "Layla" is playing.*

That was shot to "Layla," you know. We played a playback on the set. All the murders were played back on the set to "Layla," because it's a tragedy. A lot of those people, they didn't really deserve to die. It's like the unveiling, it's like a parade, it's like a revue, in a way, of the unfolding tragedy. It has a majesty to it, even though they're common people. You may say "common crooks," I still find that they're people. And the tragedy is in the music. The music made me feel a certain way and gave a certain sadness to it and a certain sympathy.

One term you've used to describe the making of Raging Bull *is "kamikaze filmmaking." What did you mean by that?*

That I threw everything I knew into it, and if it meant the end of my career, then it would have to be the end of my career.

Did you honestly feel that?

Absolutely, yeah. I don't know exactly why, but I did. I just felt it would probably be the end of it, but I might as well throw it all in and see what happened.

But why, because it might prove too much for people to take?

Well, I was making a certain kind of film. Films at that time...don't forget, it was the beginning of the Reagan era. Sylvester Stallone had created his own new mythology and people were more into that. And *Raging Bull* comes out. Who's going to see it? Who cares about this guy? Nobody – that's what I thought. And maybe some people would say, "Well, you were right, because nobody saw it." The film came out a week before *Heaven's Gate* and the whole studio went under. It only made a certain amount of money. The whole mood of the country was different. Big money was being made with pictures like *Rocky* and eventually the Spielberg-Lucas films. I mean, *New York, New York* was a total flop, and it opened the same week as *Star Wars*. We're all close friends, George and Spielberg and myself. At that time they were the mythmakers and to a certain extent continue to be. So at that time, I knew which way the wind was blowing and it certainly wasn't in my direction. Therefore, I just did the best I could with *Raging Bull*, because I had nothing and everything to lose. I knew that I'd probably get movies to make in Europe or something. But I'm an American. I have to make movies about this country. So what do you do? You just say it's the end of your career, but you don't know any other way to do it, and you do it that way. That's what I meant by kamikaze. It takes a certain kind of passion to do that. *Taxi Driver* had a kind of kamikaze effect too. Passionate. That's another movie I didn't expect anybody to see. It was done out of real love for the subject matter and for the characters. Or, I should say, out of empathy with the characters in it.

When you talk about Cape Fear, *it seems that you want to make a genre film on your own terms without subverting the genre.*

Subverting the genre, I think, would be a problem. Hopefully, I will try to blend the genre, in a sense, with my expression of it, with the elements that I'm interested in, and see if it doesn't derail it too much. If it enhances it, and I get the best of both, that would be great. I don't know if I can. I still wouldn't be interested in doing – as much as I *adore* them – the old musicals. I have no words for some of them, they are so beautiful. I still want to do something with a musical where it's got an edge to it. But I would be able to, this time, get a clearer idea of how to approach it.

What's the difference now?

New York, New York, we made it up as we went along. We had a pretty good script by Earl Mac Rausch and we didn't pay any attention to it. The two methods of filmmaking – the improvisatory style and the old studio style, where you have to build sets – didn't blend. You're wasting money that way, because the set was built and you would improvise yourself into another scene. And then you'd have to *reimprovise* yourself *back* into that set. It was crazy. I think we got some real good stuff out of it – and some real truth about that world and relationships between creative people. But I think it could have been more concise, maybe shorter. Maybe there was too much music. The repetition of scenes between the couple was really more like *life*, where a scene repeats itself and repeats itself and repeats itself until finally…

…it becomes tension-producing watching it. It's very unsettling.

And that's the idea. The way, if you're in a relationship with someone and you've talked it out and talked it out and talked it out and you can't sit, you can't go in the same room! Maybe in that case, it's successful – but I don't know if it's entertainment. I can guarantee you, you're not going to have the head of a studio say, "Marty, let's make a picture where the people get so tense – and it's a musical, OK? And people come out thinking about their own lives, oh my God, and their four marriages, and they get upset – and we'll give you $50 million to make it!" No! They're not going to do it.

That's like when you told a studio head who asked you why you wanted to make The Last Temptation of Christ *that you wanted to understand Jesus better.*

I said that to Barry Diller, and he didn't expect that, Barry. He kind of smiled. He didn't really expect that. It was really funny. It's true, though. And I had to learn that that picture had to be made for much less money. You're that interested in something personal – "We'd like to see what happens with it, but here's only seven million. You can do it at seven, not at twenty-four."

You've said over and over that you don't see yourself as especially literary. But on the other hand you'll talk about The Gambler *as a model for* Life Lessons, *your contribution to* New York Stories, *and, of course,* The Last Temptation of Christ *was based on the Kazantzakis book. Why do you downplay that aspect of your work and your thinking?*

I'm still cowed a little by the tyranny of art with a capital A. And there has always been the tyranny of the word over the image: anything that's written has got to be better. Most people feel it's more genuine if you express yourself in words than in pictures. And I think that's a problem in our society. And, I've said it many times in interviews, I come from a home where the only things that were read were the *Daily News* and the *Daily Mirror*. Those were the two newspapers, and I brought the first book in. And there were discussions about whether or not I should bring the book in the house, too.

What do you mean?

They were worried.

That you would become...

God knows.

I mean my parents didn't graduate from high school either, but...

They didn't graduate from grammar school, my parents.

My parents were obsessed with education and with my going to school.

Oh, no. Mine wanted me to continue because they understood one thing: you go to school, you make a little more money. It's as simple as that. But what I was doing then was out of the question. First, I was going to be a priest and that was one thing. They could take that. To a certain *extent*, they could take that. But when I started to have books come in the house and go to New York University, which was a secular situation, not a parochial, not a church-oriented place. It was in the '60s, you know? They're not educated people. They said the college is too liberal. It's communist. That sort of thing.

Were they paying for you to go there?

My father paid, yeah. They both worked in the garment district. They paid. So having difficulty reading. I'm not a fast reader, although I'm forcing myself to read as much as possible now. I'm sort of catching up on books that I should have read 20 years ago, forcing myself to read a lot. And usually in certain areas, like ancient history or historical novels, good ones, strong ones. And trying to get to read faster that way.

There are certain kinds of films that are more literary-based. Joseph Mankiewicz's pictures are on a more verbal level – and I love them. *All About Eve*, *Letter to Three Wives*, *Barefoot Contessa*. They had a sense of dignity because of their literary background.

I could talk about this for ages. The literary will always have the upper hand here.

Even though it's become such a visual culture?

Oh, God, yes. I mean look at the things taken seriously. The greatest casualty in terms of being honored is Alfred Hitchcock. And his movies are purely visual. He was never given an Academy Award. He got the Life Achievement award, but was never singled out for best director. *Rebecca*, I think, won the best picture of the year, but I don't think he won director. Because, again, they said, "Well, he's got clever scriptwriters and he does clever things with the camera."

Which of your movies means the most to you?

Well, *Mean Streets* is always a favorite because of the music and because it was the story of myself and my friends. It was the movie that I made that people originally took notice of. But I could never watch the whole thing. I've watched scenes of it. It's too personal. I like certain elements of *Raging Bull*. I like the starkness of it – and the wild fight scenes. The subjective fight scenes, as if you were in the ring yourself, being hit in the ear. Frank Warner's sound effects are just so wonderful. I like the look of a lot of it. And I love Bob and Joe Pesci and Cathy Moriarty and Frank Vincent. I love the performances. Nick Colasanto. It was just wonderful.

Taxi Driver*?*

No.

No?

I like Bob in it. Oh, I like everybody in it. Cybill Shepherd was wonderful there. Jodie Foster. But *Taxi Driver* is really Paul Schrader's. We interpreted it. Paul Schrader gave the script to me because he saw *Mean Streets* and liked Bob in it and liked me as a director. And we had the same kinds of feelings about Travis, the way he was written, the way Paul had it. It was as if we all felt the same thing. It was like a little club between the three of us. Paul Schrader and myself had a certain affinity, and we still do, about religion and life, death and guilt and sex. But the original concept is all his. Now you know another guy can come along and ruin it. I'm not being falsely modest. But you've got to understand that the original idea came from him. And that's something that I think over the years, when they say, "Martin Scorsese's *Taxi Driver*," that's something that can be very painful to Paul. It's really his.

Raging Bull is something else altogether. It came from Bob, and Paul helped us with it and then we worked it out again. We rewrote it, Bob and I, and the same thing with *The Last Temptation of Christ*. Paul worked on it and then I rewrote it myself with Jay Cocks. But the two that I feel most nostalgic for are *Mean Streets* and *Raging Bull*.

What about some of the other movies that people don't necessarily put in the first rank of your films?

Well, on one level, they were all hard work, learning experiences. In conjunction with, let's say, Ellen Burstyn in *Alice Doesn't Live Here Anymore*, I needed to do something that was a major studio film that was for a certain amount of money and to prove that I can direct women. It was as simple as that. *After Hours* was trying to learn, after *The Last Temptation of Christ* was pulled away, how to make a film quicker. And *The Color of Money* was trying to do a real Hollywood picture, with movie stars like Paul Newman and Tom Cruise. But each one was a lesson, like going to school. And *Cape Fear* to a certain extent will be that way too. Although in *Cape Fear* – the key there is I got Bob De Niro. And that's like… it's fun. It becomes something else.

How would you describe your working relationship with De Niro?

We're interested in similar traits of people. Like I said, we felt that we understood certain things about Travis. And it's very rare when three people, the actor, the director, and the writer all feel the same way about it.

What did you understand?

You feel you understand the rage; you understand that you have certain feelings yourself. You're not afraid to say to each other, to the people who are seeing the movie, that those are aspects of ourselves. Many people have it under control. This character doesn't. He starts to act out his fantasies. Living in this city, at a certain point, you may want to kill somebody. You don't do it. This guy does it. It's simple. He crosses over. But we understand those implications. OK, we're talking violence there. But also the pain of romantic rejection. It doesn't mean that you're always rejected. It means that a couple of times when it happens you feel a certain way and you carry that with you for the rest of your life. And you can pull from it, you know?

Bob is not a guy who knows movies the way I know movies. He can't sit with me and Schrader and talk about *Out of the Past*, Jacques Tourneur's film noir. He doesn't know it. And yet that makes it purer because he's just relating to what's there. It's better.

King of Comedy and *Raging Bull* really stem from Bob. *Last Temptation* from me. *Taxi Driver* from Paul. *Mean Streets* came from me. It all kind of shifts and slips and slides around, and we always find ourselves coming around. The roulette wheel keeps moving and we stop and look at each other, and we're all in the same place: "Oh, it's you again." It's that kind of thing, where you seem to grow together rather than apart. It's good because there's a trust. And it isn't true where you say, "Oh, it's telepathy." Yes, to a certain extent there is telepathy involved, but not entirely. Once we're in the groove we very rarely have disparate points of view.

The two of you have created characters that have really entered the culture. How many times have you seen somebody imitate De Niro's scenes from Raging Bull *or the mirror scene in* Taxi Driver*?*

We improvised the mirror scene. That's true. I did improvise him talking in the mirror: "Are you talking to me?" It was in the script that he was looking at himself in the mirror, doing this thing with the guns, and I told Bob, "He's got to say something. He's got to talk to himself." We didn't know what. We just started playing with it, and that's what came out.

You've become synonymous with the notion of a director with integrity. It seems, on the one hand, it must be tremendously gratifying. On the other hand, it seems like maybe it can potentially be paralyzing.

No, I feel really good about it. I do feel gratified that people feel that the work is – I don't know what words you want to use – personal or uncompromising. No matter what happens, though, there are compromises. You can say, "Yes, I'm going to make *The Last Temptation of Christ* and give me $7 million and I can do it." But it's compromised at seven million. I would have liked certain angles. I would have liked extra days for shooting. But OK, that's artistic compromise, and what the film has to say is not compromised. One has to realize it's scary, because you have to keep a balance. You want to get films made that express what you have to say. You try to do that, but it's a very delicate balance.

I'd also like the chance to do exactly what I'm doing now with *Cape Fear*, for example: try to do a great thriller and to give the audience what they expect from a thriller, but also to have those elements which make my pictures somewhat different. I will try. I'm in this period now where I want to start exploring different areas, and you've got to make use of each film you make. You've got to learn from it and you have to utilize it to get your own pictures made – the difficult ones, I should say, because they're all, in a way, your own pictures. And no matter what happens, the really hard ones, you're only going to get a certain amount of money for them anyway. So you've also got to think of making money for yourself for the lean years, when you have pictures you're only getting paid a certain amount to make. There are so many different variations. It's playing a game, a line that you're walking, taking everybody very seriously – the studios and what they need, what you need. And, see, every now and then you can come together. Like in *GoodFellas* we all came together. So that was the best of both worlds: $26 million to make a personal movie. That's very interesting. The rest, no, there's no guarantee of anything. Each picture you make you try to learn from, and you try to cover your tracks. Every movie wastes money to a certain extent, but you don't do it to the point where…

…you create problems for yourself.

…where you create real problems. But it's not that rational. It's not, "My God how rational he sounds" – God forbid if I do – it's really a matter of being careful and smart. The artists coming out of America in film come from Hollywood. And I'm proud to be associated with Hollywood because of that. I lived in Hollywood more than ten years. Even then, they thought I was still living in New York.

I live in New York. My parents are here, my kids are here. But I'm still a Hollywood director, and I'm always proud to be considered that by the rest of the world. To show that America, every now and then, will give me something to do, or give something to other guys – Stanley Kubrick, David Lynch – who do very personal pictures. There's so much fun involved sometimes that it's enjoyable. But it's dangerous.

A shorter version of this interview originally appeared in Rolling Stone, *November 1, 1990. A longer version then ran in the* South Atlantic Quarterly *91 (1992).*

Index

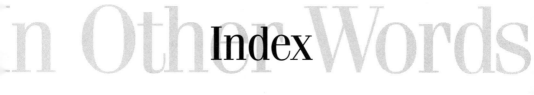